MANDAR JAMSANDEKAR is a Director at Precision Technical Analysis Pvt Ltd, a pioneering company in the field of technical analysis in India. In the last two decades, Precision Technicals has trained more than 40,000 people in the use of technical analysis for trading and investing.

Mandar is also owner of Precision Broking and creator of two of India's best technical analysis strategy software for investment and trading — PROFISION and PROFISION Pro — and also the creator of Running Price and Stagnant Price logic.

A SEBI registered Research Analyst, he regularly appears on business television channels, including ET NOW and BTVi. He also writes for newspapers.

A TEDx speaker and a passionate trainer, Mandar's mission in mentoring his clients is to make their stock market venture successful.

To stay updated on his latest research, you can log on to www.precisiontechnicals.com or join his YouTube Channel — Precision Technicals. You can also connect with him on his Twitter handle — @mandarj2002.

Mandar is also the author of the bestselling book *How to Make Money in Day Trading*, also published by Vision Books.

~

Also by
Mandar Jamsandekar

~

How to Make Money in Day Trading:
Trade on An Invitation

~

TRADING AND TECHNICAL ANALYSIS COURSE

HOW TO TRADE SAFELY AND PROFITABLY

Mandar Jamsandekar

Author of the Bestseller
HOW TO MAKE MONEY IN DAY TRADING

www.visionbooksindia.com

www.visionbooksindia.com

Disclaimer

The author and the publisher disclaim all legal or other responsibilities for any losses which investors may suffer by investing or trading using the methods described in this book. Readers are advised to seek professional guidance before making any specific investments. This book is meant purely for the purpose of investor and trader education.

A Vision Books Original

First Published 2018
Reprinted 2019 (Twice), 2020, 2021

ISBN 10: 81-7094-987-4
ISBN 13: 978-81-7094-987-9

Published by
Vision Books Pvt. Ltd.
(Incorporating Orient Paperbacks and CARING imprints)
24 Feroze Gandhi Road, Lajpat Nagar 3
New Delhi 110024, India.
Phone: (+91-11) 2984 0821 / 22
e-mail: visionbooks@gmail.com

Printed at
Anand Sons
C-88, Ganesh Nagar, Pandav Nagar Complex
Delhi 110 092, India.

Contents

Part II

~

Technical Trading Course

Preface

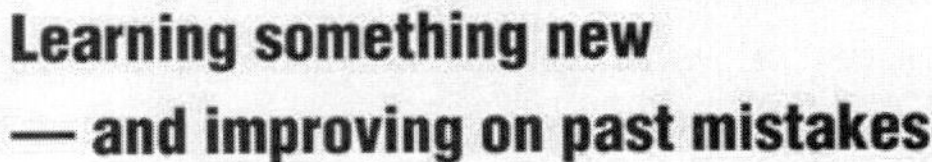

There is no age bar, nor any specific qualification needed to succeed in the stock markets.

A step a day can take us miles in our quest of achieving success.

Take that first step today towards improving your such trading and analysis skills.

Many centuries ago in the ancient Indian epic, The *Mahabharata*, there was a mighty warrior by the name Arjuna who was on the verge of a war with his uncles and cousins. Before the war could start he got into a confused state of mind. He lost his confidence at the thought of killing his own relatives and loved ones. He wondered what good a victory would be with his hands coloured by the blood of his own people.

This was the occasion when his friend, philosopher and guide Lord Krishna gave Arjuna wisdom by providing answers to his questions. Lord Krishna also highlighted to Arjuna that all wars have first to be won in the mind before they can be won in real life.

Before you start reading this book always remember that I want you to be the Arjuna of the Indian stock markets.

Just as knowledge shared in the *Bhagavad Gita* is available for all, the knowledge of technical analysis is also not limited to a select few. You, too, can become a good technical analyst and chart yourself to prosperity.

This book will always serve as a guide by your side in your venture in the stock markets.

I'm happy to be your mentor!

Wishing you success!

List of Abbreviations

DII	Domestic Institutional Investor.
DJIA	Dow Jones Industrial Average.
DJTA	Dow Jones Transportation Average.
EMA	Exponentional Moving Average.
F&O	Futures and Options.
FII	Foreign Institutional Investor.
HB	Higher Bottom.
HNI	High Net Worth Individual.
HT	Higher Top.
IPO	Initial Public Offer.
MA	Moving Average.
MACD	Moving Average Convergence Divergence.
NYSE	New York Stock Exchange.
OHLC	Open, High, Low and Close.
P/E Ratio	Price / Earnings Ratio.
RBI	Reserve Bank of India.
RSI	Relative Strength Index.
SEBI	Securities and Exchange Board of India Ltd.
SMA	Simple Moving Average.
USFDA	United States Food and Drug Administration.
WMA	Weighted Moving Average.

Part I

~

Trading and Technical Analysis

Chapter 1

~

Introduction

IN MY TWENTY-PLUS YEARS IN THE STOCK MARKETS I have been learning every day. The desire to learn led me to a lot of books, articles, websites and magazines, which helped me learn a great deal. At all time, I kept in mind the words of my guru — "Read everything but do not follow anything blindly; take only what you want."

I improvised on my guru's advice and decided to measure everything in terms of its advantage and disadvantage. This has helped me greatly in my stock market career since 1995. In the initial ten years, I would study from eight in the morning till eleven at night. Nothing in life comes free. If you want to learn, you have to work hard, spend money, put in hours of practice, have a good mentor to guide you — and the world will then be yours. Having read the "10,000-Hour Rule" in Malcom Gladwell's book *Outlier,* I believe that I have actually experienced this happening in my life.

I have always wanted to give back to society what I learnt in life after a lot of hard work. Thus, I want to share my market learning in a way which would help future generations understand technical analysis and apply it to trade in a better way. I want to make certain improvisations in the learning process in the form of better quality content, which means good charts, good explanations, a clear understanding of the psychology underlying price behaviour, and the resultant charts, price formations and, most important of all, the reasoning behind every trading decision using technical analysis. This book is my contribution to technical trading and training which I hope will enhance interest among enthusiastic investors and traders for generations to come. It is my way of giving back to the society.

~

The idea of writing this book came from the feedback I regularly receive while conducting my technical analysis workshops across the country. A common feedback has been, "I was under the impression that I knew technical analysis but this workshop has given me plenty of new things to learn. I wish I had attended your training session a few years back."

Many stock brokers have been complimentary about the insights they received in my workshop sessions. They said that they would have been far more successful in the profession had they undertaken the training ten years earlier.

A software professional once told me that while he had learnt technical analysis and its tools online but it was the workshop which finally gave him the confidence to pursue a career as an investor and a trader.

In one of the workshops I was discussing the importance of managing risk. Among the participants in the batch was a doctor who could not control his emotion and stood up to share his experience. Being a doctor, he said, he knew that prevention was better than cure but when it came to his investments, he had lacked the courage to implement risk management. The explanations that I had given, and the practical way we had analysed stocks with focus on "AIM" — "A" for trade Analysis, "I" for trade Implementation and "M" for trade Monitoring — was a eureka moment for him. Had he implemented AIM earlier, he said, he would have saved a lot of money.

The feedback over the years, coming from people varying in age from 17 to 75 years, working in different professions, and having different levels of expertise has been revealing.

It reinforced for me the importance of right knowledge which can enable people to improve and gain confidence in their stock picking skills, and thereby generate trading profits. Such feedback keeps me going, and the fact that I have been able to touch people's lives through stock market training has given me a sense of fulfilment and immense satisfaction. Now I want to share this knowledge with an even larger number of people. The vision is to take technical analysis to every household in India.

My training journey has taken me to many cities in India and I have learnt from my participants as much as they have learnt from me. I have written this book with the objective that the reader gets the same expertise as those who attend my seminars on trading and technical analysis.

~

There is a general perception that technical analysis is complex and difficult to understand. Many people therefore don't even look at it.

Through this book I have tried to make technical analysis as easy to understand as possible. Most of the concepts and theories that I have covered will enable the reader to select a stock, build a trading strategy, calculate a price target, place a stop loss and set a time target.

Most importantly, it is my hope that after reading this book you would gain expertise in technical analysis and be able to independently interpret the charts and trade successfully.

Even if a small fraction of the market participants read this book and start using technical analysis for trading or investing, I would feel that I have contributed in some small measure in growing the awareness about technical analysis in India, and that would be my biggest satisfaction.

~

This book discusses safe and simple trading strategies using technical analysis, along with the underlying logic of each, so that they can be easily understood and used with confidence by individual traders and investors. Throughout the book we discuss selected parameters of technical analysis which help us in analysing stocks, indices, commodities, currency, and any other market which has good trading volumes, namely liquidity, with the help of charts.

This book offers you many unique takeaways:

1. It is a practical technical trading course in the form of a book.
2. Every strategy and theory contained in this book is explained along with its underlying logic and psychology.
3. It shows you how to read the fundamentals underlying technical charts.
4. It reveals the following two brand new and copyrighted price patterns which I've developed:
   - Listing breakout pattern; and
   - Trend change breakout pattern.
5. It provides learning with the help of good quality charts.
6. It provides an understanding of the 3 Ws, namely What, Works, When.
7. It provides a safe and systematic approach which largely eliminates the ever prevalent fear and greed factors which cost investors and traders heavy financial losses and at times also emotional setbacks.
8. Finally, this book gives you a complete perspective on how to "AIM" for profits:
   - A = **A**nalysis for generating a buy or a sell view on a stock with risk management, and with tentative price and time targets.
   - I = **I**mplementation of the analysis, including care to be taken while getting into a trade.
   - M = **M**onitoring the trade. Knowledge about monitoring your trade will help you stay in it with confidence. It will help you implement risk management in the right way. It will also provide you solutions related to the most common questions which people face, namely when to book profits.

The AIM framework has evolved over twenty years of analysing stocks technically.

The fear gets taken care of by "A", namely analysis, which tells you about the risk involved in that trade even before you enter it. "M", i.e. monitoring helps you to exit the trade when the trend changes, thus taking care of the greed factor.

Some Common Myths Clarified

Myth No. 1: All I Need to be Successful in the Stock Market is Money

"All I need to trade in the stock market is money. With that I can start trading and make a fast buck. Minimum time, maximum gain. Why invest for long if I can make money in a day?"

Such thinking is scary. It is also very common.

In my twenty-plus years of experience in the stock markets I have come across a large number of people who hold this wrong belief. They enter the stock market with a view that having some money is more than enough to grow rich. They try their hand at day trading and investing, and indiscriminately follow all possible ideas which come to them from friends, the Internet, television, etc.

In all cases, the end result is the same.

Some stocks work, some fail. Yet this wrong belief ensures that their hopes keep rising. Trading positions get mutated into investments as they become loss-making propositions. Equally, investment trades are squared off when they show signs of making money.

Without the right knowledge, exposure and experience one makes all sorts of mistakes, constantly experimenting with various ideas in an effort to make some money. Finally, hope comes to an end either due to self realization or when family members or friends get involved to rectify the mistakes committed. Those who go through this experience give the market a bad name. They narrate their bad experiences to others without acknowledging their own mistakes.

This myth can only be removed by acquiring investment knowledge. That will help you select the right stocks to trade and also help you pick them at the right price, and by applying appropriate risk management techniques. As you read this book, you will learn how to do so and also begin to enjoy the experience.

Myth No. 2: I Know Technical Analysis

Nowadays investors and traders have easy access to online trading. With a stricter regulatory framework than used to be the case, India has witnessed an increase in online transactions by individuals using trading terminals on their computers or from their mobiles. These terminals also provide them access to charts and various other technical parameters. In technical analysis, the parameters remain the same — it could be a candlestick, a moving average, or any other indicator — whether seen on a trading terminal, a mobile application or a technical analysis software. Merely having access to these parameters, however, does not mean that you have the knowledge required to profitably deploy your hard earned money and to ensure that it grows.

An apt example would be the game of cricket. Indians love this sport. In India, the game is played everywhere — in cricket stadia, in public grounds, on the roads, in parking lots, in alleys, etc. Even the God of Cricket Sachin Tendulkar started out playing in an alley, but he did not play serious cricket in alleys or on roads. He played serious cricket professionally, in proper cricket grounds and stadia. Though the game remains the same, and the equipment that the game is played with remains the same — the bat and the ball — but the quality of the game played in proper grounds is different from that seen on roads and alleys. No doubt, we have seen cricket legends start from the roads and alleys but they need to move on to proper stadia and cricket grounds, and play with proper equipment, in order to become legends. Had they not been serious about becoming great cricketers, they would have continued playing on the roads and alleys.

Your hard earned money is involved when it comes to the stock market and therefore you need to handle it seriously. Simply having access to candlesticks, moving averages or other indicators does not make you a technical analyst. Such access is just about 20% of what's required for success in the stock markets.

It is up to you to decide whether you want to be a legend of the streets and alleys or want to do professional justice to your hard earned money. The choice is yours, you must make it wisely.

Can serious professions be learnt and mastered on the Internet? Can you become a doctor, an engineer, or a cricketer merely by acquiring knowledge from the Internet? If the answer is no, then do you think learning technical analysis and trading are possible by relying solely on the Internet?

Read this book carefully, understand the strategies it contains, and the underlying logic guiding the strategies, the reasons for what is right and what is not, and you will realize that mere access to a chart does not give you the ability to properly understand what it is telling you, nor the confidence to take appropriate trading decisions. So, please read this book till the last word to understand and imbibe the knowledge it contains. I would also suggest that you keep a highlighter or a pen by your side in order to prepare your own notes for future reference.

This book, and my practical technical analysis workshop, can give you a eureka moment of your life.

Myth No. 3: Complicated Means Intelligent!

In my years of market training I have come across two sets of people — those who want to stay with just a single parameter, say, for example, a moving average, or a particular indicator, or some single tool. The other set of people like to complicate their analysis with multiple parameters, changing them all the time. At times, these changes are based on the experience of a few trades. I believe both these approaches are wrong. Complicating your analysis is pointless because finally it only leaves you confused, while sticking to just a single parameter may not work well in all market conditions.

People who are victims of this myth often overlook the fundamental fact that it's the price which moves an indicator, and not *vice versa*.

Talk to a thousand traders and you will get a thousand ideas. People make some calculations, generate buy and sell signals, use technology and, hey presto, they become algo traders!

Please do not run after such illusions and such people. If you do, time will show you that it was a wrong thing to have done. These are things which will make you go off-track and lose your focus.

In life, simple things work best most of the time. We tend to complicate matters only when we are unable to understand or do something in a simple way. The irony is that people have a wrong belief that complicated means intelligent. The truth is that businesses and individuals who made it big in life did so because they kept things simple.

Myth No. 4: I Have Analysed the Stock, Therefore It Has to Work!

In the stock market you can analyse a stock endlessly but you cannot make the stock price move the way you want it to. This is something which you need to keep in mind at all times. The fact that you have analysed a stock does not mean that the trade that you enter into will therefore necessarily be profitable. On day one, namely the day when you enter the trade, the chances of the stock moving in your favour, or the stop loss getting triggered, are equal (50:50). Since the price may not move as per our wish, therefore we use the stop loss to control our risk.

I have seen people puzzled at the first mention of a stop loss. They ask, "Why a stop loss if you know that the stock is going to go up, and you want us to buy it. Is it not a 'sure-shot' stock pick?"

You need to understand that there is no such thing as a sure-shot pick, whether in life or in the markets. If you believe that you want only sure-shot stock picks, then you are not made for the stock market. Somebody who cannot implement a stop loss should not be investing or trading in the market. This may sound a bit harsh but it will save you from losing your shirt. This is applicable to any type of market analysis that you may follow — fundamental or technical.

Analysis is no magic. Rather, it is a science and an art which you need to have a passion for. That a trade will work out well simply because you've analysed it is a risky myth. Beware of it.

You should understand that in the stock market every method works well sometimes and fails at other times. As an investor or trader, your focus should be more on making your method work most of the time. There would always be failures but if you are aware of what works when, and what fails when, it will help you generate better results.

The key is to understand that all your trades cannot be winners. This is so for the simple reason that while you can analyse and predict to the best of your abilities, you cannot make the price move as per your expectations.

Myth No. 5: Buy Low, Sell High

This is actually not a myth because this is a strategy which we all want to implement. When you buy low and sell high it means you buy something at, say, 100 and sell at 120, thus making a profit of 20. So this is a good strategy. Human nature and emotions, however, are such that they may not allow you to follow this strategy. Over the years I have in fact seen people do just the opposite — they run away from the market when stocks and indices are falling, and flock to the market in huge numbers when prices are making highs. This is something which I have seen happen again and again over the years, and that's why I call it a myth.

If you ask somebody whether buying low and selling high is a good strategy, the answer would be an immediate, "Yes, it is a correct strategy." But if you ask them to invest when the market or the index is falling, they would be reluctant to do so.

If this is the case, then should this not be considered a myth?

When the index is falling, people are scared. They fear that the price might fall even further, and they would make losses if they buy. Therefore, though they believe in buying low and selling high, they may not actually do so in real life.

Thoughts and actions can be aligned only when you have clear knowledge, and only when you know what is right and what is not. So, this myth too can be overcome with knowledge.

Myth No. 6: It's Good to Follow Celebrity Experts

I have seen traders and investors follow celebrity experts, the ones who have a habit of commenting or giving advice on anything and everything that happens. You will find their presence on social media, like Facebook, Twitter, blogs, message boards of business websites, etc. Please understand that such people are a risk to your money. You won't realize this till you experience it. But why go through such an experience?

To be a winner in the stock markets, humility is very important.

Celebrities have a habit of believing that they know everything and can even read somebody's mind and therefore start commenting on all matters. Never follow such people in the stock market. They will take you off the track. This is an important reason why serious investors and traders should stay away from social media. On social media, often a man logs in using a woman's name — and *vice versa!* Real people show their real identity but 90% of the social media is built with fake identities, and rude, uncivil comments on anything that comes up.

Stock market investing is serious business. If you are serious about trading and investing, and want to profit from it, you need to stay away from loudmouths.

I am puzzled why such people who seem to know everything never become advisors. Be that as it may, this is nothing but immaturity. The bottom line is that a serious a investor or trader who makes money would rarely want others to know too much about his thinking. He considers his stock market venture as a business and a serious investor or trader considers himself to be a businessman who is here to stay for a long time. No businessman will freely discuss his business plans with all and sundry, will he?

Always remember that the markets demand humility.

Talk to any mature market person. Somebody who has seen bull markets as well as bear markets come and go, and the advice you will get would be no different.

While buying clothes you can have an approach of "*Jo dikhta hai wo biktaa hai* (What is displayed is what sells)." But you should not have this approach when it comes to the stock market. A related point is that when everybody starts talking about a particular stock, or about a rally in a particular stock, you will often find that the rally gets arrested, or the stock stops moving. Stocks which are not discussed on television channels or in the social media display the best of moves. The moment the name of a stock starts surfacing prominently in the media, you should be alert that the move may soon end!

Once you become aware of these common myths, you can save yourself from getting entangled in any of them.

Stock Market Home Truths

This book covers a set of tools which have been crafted and seasoned over the last twenty-year period, over bull, bear, as well as dull markets. The following are the important home truths which you should always keep in mind:

- Stock market investing and trading involves risk.
- Historically, it has been proven that equity investments perform well over a longer period of time.
- Having a positive attitude is very important to survive and flourish in the financial markets.
- To be successful in the market, implement Mandar's 80:20 Investment Rule: Success is due only 20% due to strategy and 80% due to discipline.
- The world's best investors and traders also face loss-making trades. One important quality which separates them from others is their ability to accept their mistakes. When a stock does not work in their favour and makes a loss, they exit the trade fast and wait for another opportunity. They understand and accept that profit and loss are an ongoing process in the financial markets. They do not jump to any conclusion about a system or a strategy based on a week's or a month's experience. They understand that one has to go through good as well as bad patches in the markets. Sailing through the storm with conviction about your strategy, and implementing correct risk management are what help you win.
- Managing risk is very important. That is what will help you survive and flourish in the stock market for a long period of time.
- Often we equate the complicated with intelligence but I believe that we get into complications when we cannot do things in a simple way. Therefore, keep things simple.
- Amateurs search for some golden key which will help them open this money box called stock market. You need to know that there is no such magic. Instead, the golden key is using market analysis for taking informed decisions, along with proper risk management.

- Right knowledge is vital for you to manage your hard-earned money.
- Investing *via* the mutual funds route is also a good option to grow your wealth.

~

Test Your Learning

Questions

1. Right knowledge is more important than trading capital. (True / False?)
2. Does a complicated strategy mean successful strategy. (True / False?)

Answers

1. True
2. False

AS YOU READ THIS BOOK, HIGHLIGHT THE MAIN POINTS FOR LATER REFERENCE. YOU WILL ALSO COME ACROSS POINTS WHICH ARE REPEATED MULTIPLE TIMES IN THE BOOK. SUCH REPETITION IS DELIBERATE SO THAT IMPORTANT LESSONS GET REGISTERED IN YOUR MIND. ALSO, PREPARE NOTES TO CREATE YOUR OWN PERSONAL GUIDE ON TECHNICAL ANALYSIS WHICH WILL HELP YOU WHEN YOU TRADE.

Chapter 2

~

Risk and Time Relationship

INVESTING AND TRADING IN THE FINANCIAL MARKETS involves risk. The reason people take this risk is because they are attracted to the high returns that their investments can generate.

Equally, most people want to make a lot of money in a very short period of time. If this happens for you, well and good; but what if it does not? That is why it is important for you to also think about the risk side of this business.

When you are analysing stocks, you will find that some stocks have the potential to move quickly while others are likely to make a move over a longer period. A proper analysis can give you a tentative time frame for the target move to be achieved. This time frame can be

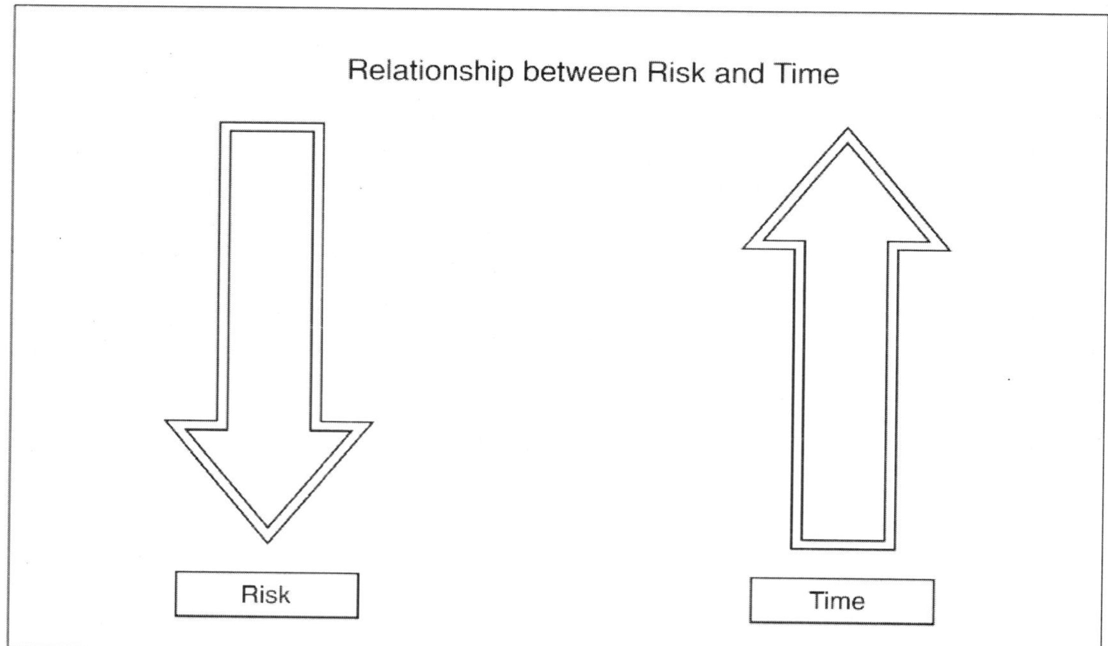

Figure 2.1: **Risk reduces over a longer time horizon trade**

~

anything from a day to a year, or even more. Given an option, most investors and traders get attracted to stocks with shorter time targets. This point leads to something which is very important for you to understand: there is a direct relationship between risk and time.

This relationship can easily be understood from Figure 2.1 and Figure 2.2.

As the time duration of a trade reduces, the risk increases; as the time duration of the trade increases, the risk reduces.

This relationship has nothing to do with any analysis that you may have done. **Irrespective of the analysis, stocks picked with a short term view will always carry higher risk as compared to a trade with a slightly longer time frame.**

When you consider your trading profile, this aspect of risk and time framework is an important factor which you need to take into consideration.

The irony is that if a hundred people were asked whether they would like to make money in the long term or do so quickly, more than 80% would pick the short term. The maximum number would want to trade short term — but with low or no risk at all! That, of course, is a fairy tale scenario.

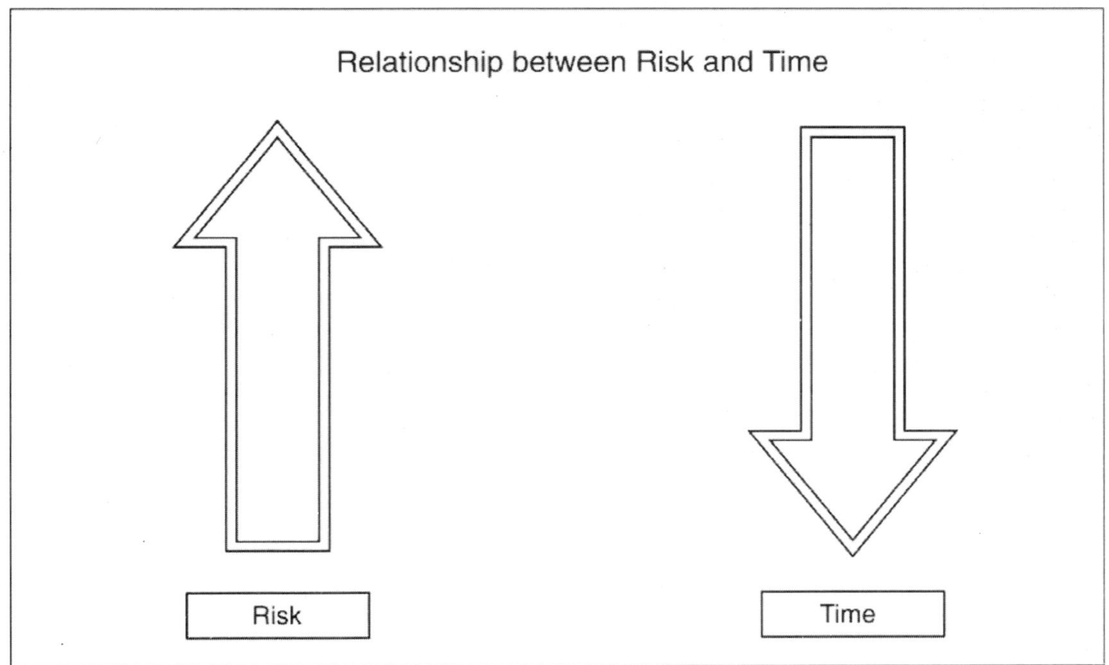

Figure 2.2: **Risk increases with a smaller time horizon trade**

~

Quiz: Risk and Time Relationship

Questions

1. Investing and trading in equity, commodity, and currency markets do not involve high risk. (True / False?)
2. Risk increases as the time duration of the trade shortens. (True / False?)
3. Risk reduces as the time duration of the trade increases. (True / False?)
4. Focusing on reducing risk is more important than focusing on returns. (True / False?)
5. Attracted by the prospects of high returns, most investors and traders overlook the risk involved. (True / False?)
6. The aspect of risk and time frame is not an important factor in selecting your profile. (True / False?)

Answers

1. False	2. True	3. True
4. True	5. True	6. False

RISK REDUCES WITH AN INCREASE IN THE TIME DURATION OF A TRADE AND INCREASES IF THE TIME DURATION OF A TRADE IS SHORTER.

Chapter 3

~

Know Your Trading Profile

First Know Yourself, Then Enter the Market

YOU NEED TO HAVE CLARITY ABOUT WHICH TRADING PROFILE SUITS YOU before you get into the choppy waters of the stock markets. History shows that people come to the market with an idea of making a fast buck. Day trading, therefore, attracts them — just like a moth is attracted to light. Once mistakes pile up, the novice shifts from being a day trader to a positional trader — and if the stock price moves opposite to his or her expectation, then is born an accidental long term investor! This happens out of the fear of making a loss, and not as a result of knowledge or understanding of the benefits of being an investor. There are plenty of examples where a person started out with a lot of energy as a day trader but loss-making positions made him shift his outlook from day trading to investment. And, then, the individual gets stuck in the stock concerned. Many a time this kind of an experience inhibits the person from investing in the stock market ever again.

So before you start analysing or executing stock market trades, you need to know who you are, namely whether you are:

1. An intraday trader;
2. A swing trader / positional trader / short term investor; or
3. An investor.

You have to be clear which of the above profiles you are comfortable with. It is possible that you may even fit in multiple profiles. That's fine, so long as you have clarity. If you have the maturity to stick to the stock selection as well as entry and exit based on a particular profile, then you can adopt multiple profiles too. One important aspect to take care of when adopting multiple profiles is never to change your profile mid-trade just because a particular trade is not working in your favour.

To decide which profile suits you best, use the following criteria:

1. Knowledge level;
2. Funds;
3. Risk appetite;
4. Returns expected; and
5. Time available for tracking your investment or trade.

Knowledge required for each of the profiles is different, so are the associated risks, return, funds and time. You can decide your comfort level and compatibility with a particular profile based on these criteria.

New market participants often under the impression that money is lying about everywhere in the markets and can be made by doing just about anything. So, at times, they think of making a fast buck, at other times they adopt a longer time horizon like investors do and, at times, they carry their positions for a few days. In other words, they change their strategy every now and then. Also, they like to hear only favourable news and opinion, and talk only to people who think alike. They ignore reality and live on hope. All this is nothing but a recipe for a sad ending.

You can make use of Table 3.1 to decide the profile which fits you best. This table displays a comparative assessment of the three profiles to help you decide which suits you.

Another important consideration while picking a profile is the taxation aspect. At the time of writing, in India, currently, tax on long term capital gains made from equity investments held for more than one year is lower than that on profits from swing and intraday trades.

So, before you go any further, pick the profile that fits you best. And for your future reference, record in writing your reasons for selecting the particular profile(s).

Table 3.1

Profile Characteristics of Day Trader, Positional Trader and Investor

Profile	*Knowledge Needed*	*Trading Capital*	*Risk*	*Returns*	*Time Requirement*
Intraday Trader	Yes	Low	High	Low	High. Monitoring during market hours.
Swing / Positional Trader or Short Term Investor	Yes	Medium	Moderate	Moderate	Medium. Monitoring required once at the end of the day.
Investor	Yes	High	Low	High	Lower. Monitoring once in a week.

~

Quiz: Trading Profile

Questions

1. Before you enter the market, it's important to be clear about your profile from among intraday trader, positional trader or investor. (True / False?)
2. What are the criteria which help you decide your profile?
3. The intraday trader's profile carries higher risk as compared to the investor's profile. (True / False?)
4. The Investor profile carries lower risk in comparison to that of the intraday trader. (True / False?)

Answers

1. True
2. Knowledge, Funds, Risk, Returns, Time
3. True
4. True

FIRST, GET CLARITY ON WHO YOU ARE. THEN STAY WITH YOUR SELECTED PROFILE. DON'T SUDDENLY CHANGE YOUR PROFILE JUST BECAUSE A TRADE HAS MOVED AGAINST YOUR EXPECTATION.

Chapter 4

~

Importance of Controlling Emotions

IN FINANCIAL MARKETS YOU WILL BE FLOODED with information from various sources, including television channels, magazines, research reports, the Internet, brokers, relatives and your own friends. The authenticity of the information, and the way markets digest such information is something which will always remain a puzzle. In particular, you would come across lots of information on television and the Internet on a wide range of topics and markets. You should not block any information from flowing to you but you need to learn how to process it properly and then decide whether a particular bit of information is useful to you or not. This gains high importance in today's digital world where people often "show off" their knowledge by forwarding something which they have received without giving a thought to its authenticity.

For example, let's assume that the market is expecting an interest rate cut from RBI. Let's further assume that the central bank duly obliges — and yet the markets fall instead of rising. For a common investor, a rate cut is a positive event and a buy signal, but the market savvy may feel that the markets had already gone up enough on the expectation of such an interest rate cut and, now, because the outcome is as per expectations, they start booking profit!

Some years ago a tsunami hit the shores of Tamil Nadu. It was a sudden, unexpected event, and the markets initially tanked in panic. The ignorant took the tsunami to be a negative development and sold off. Knowledgeable investors, on the other hand, felt that the widespread destruction would create opportunities for the city to rebuild. It meant that a lot of cement and steel would be required for redevelopment, and thus the markets started moving up again from the very next day.

When former RBI governor Raghuram Rajan once said in London that the world was heading for a 1930-like depression, it created headline news. It would be natural for a long term investor reading such a headline to panic. Anyone would be nervous upon hearing something like this from an eminent economist such as Raghuram Rajan. At such times, however, another behaviour comes into play. People often don't read the complete transcript; they tend to create a view based merely on the headline. Thus, sentiment gets manipulated by sensational headlines. Had you read the transcript fully, Rajan had only suggested that the whole world needed to come together in creating rules and regulations for the international banking system. Countries cannot have different rules, he had said, and if they did, then one fine day we could head towards a 1930-like depression. Had you read the whole transcript, you would not have panicked. The problem is that most people tend to read only the headlines and react accordingly.

What I wish to highlight is that emotions play an important role in the stock market. Fear and greed are the dominant factors which influence our decision making abilities. You must not allow people, media, the Internet, etc. to work on your emotions. To remain cool, you need to be able to independently assess what is relevant and what is not.

~

Let's consider an example. In June 2015, Mastek announced a demerger of its business. Due to this announcement, the price of Mastek share fell overnight from approximately ₹450 to ₹144. The business press ran screaming headlines such as, "Mastek crashes by 66%." If you were holding this stock in your portfolio, and were not aware of the demerger, then you too would have been apprehensive upon reading something like this on a business website. Some investors may even have sold the stock due to the fear of a further fall. In real terms, however, because of the demerger somebody who held 100 shares of Mastek at ₹450 was eligible to get 100 shares of Mastek which traded on the exchange at ₹144, plus 100 shares of Majesco which was to be listed on the exchange at the approximate price of ₹300. So, in a way, there was no change in the monetary value of your portfolio. Somebody who did not realize this may have exited the stock in panic after reading the headline.

~

You will also often come across business television shows where two or more analysts are discussing a stock. One is extremely positive, while the other is extremely negative. Both have their own reasons for their views. To add to the confusion, you will have the anchor suggesting that now it is up to the viewer to decide what is right and what is not!

When Nifty falls from, say, 8,900 to 8,100, you will hear talk of 7,600, 7,200, and even 6,500 levels. And when the Nifty moves up from, say, 7,950 to 8,300 you will hear figures and statements such as, "8,900," "Market will hit a new top," etc.

When the markets are falling, business channels will call for discussions only analysts with bearish views, and when the markets are making new highs, they invite only those investors and analysts who typically have a bullish view. You need to be aware that every day you will come across an example which will tend to make you question your opinion; and have an emotional impact on your judgment.

If you don't want this to happen to you, you should know everything about your trade — good, bad and ugly, everything. You need to know why you entered it, the possible returns that can be generated the risk involved in it — and only if that is acceptable should you even be in the trade.

Most importantly, you need to keep yourself grounded at all times. Do not focus on the anticipated profit in a trade. Be humble, think about the risk when you want to enter a trade, and enter it only if you consider the risk acceptable. This will allow you to stay cool and calm during the trade. Correct analysis and correct trade entry lead to profits; therefore, as the stock moves as per your analysis, profits will automatically follow. Do not have a mindset of generating unimaginable returns. Also, do not have unrealistic expectations from the stock market.

Process all the information flowing to you independently, and only then decide which trade to take and which opportunity to ignore.

The AIM strategy discussed in this book will help you keep a check on the destabilising emotions of fear and greed.

~

Quiz: Emotions

Questions

1. Fear and greed are major factors which influence decision making abilities in the market. (True / False?)
2. What kind of an impact do the emotions of fear and greed have on an investor or a trader? (Negative / Positive?)
3. The emotions of fear or greed can't be controlled. (True / False?)

Answers

1. True 2. Negative 3. False

OVERCOMING EMOTIONS COMPLETELY MAY NOT BE POSSIBLE, BUT YOU CAN CONTROL THEM BY ACQUIRING INVESTING AND TRADING KNOWLEDGE THAT HELPS YOU TAKE WELL CONSIDERED DECISIONS.

Chapter 5

~

Types of Market Analyses

THERE ARE TWO MAIN TYPES OF ANALYSES which are widely used in the financial markets:

1. Fundamental analysis; and
2. Technical analysis.

Fundamental analysis analyses business numbers while technical analysis analyses price movements. Both can even go hand in hand, since technical analysis also helps you gauge the fundamentals of a company by looking at its stock price movements.

In a way the two types of analyses are linked to each other. The only problem is that investors generally do not use them in combination. Typically, either one or the other of the analysis is followed, as per the situation or individual preference.

Often, people start off an investment with the help of technical analysis, complete with a stop loss and target price, but if the price starts moving against expectations and triggers the stop loss, they tend to justify holding onto the stock by advancing fundamental reasoning.

This is nothing but clinging to forlorn hope that one day the stock will rally. This is a wrong strategy and people who follow this are later stuck with non-performing stocks for years.

Fundamental Analysis

Fundamental analysis is generally used for judging the valuation of a business. The methodology involves studying the economy, the business sector in which the company operates, the company's management, and its financial performance. Based on such factors, investors try to judge whether the company's revenues and profits are growing, whether it would be able to repay its debts, and also assess if the management is cooking its account books, which is not such an uncommon occurrence.

There are two ways an investor can analyse the fundamentals of a company — one is by looking at its past performance in order to project its future prospects, and the second is by talking to the company management about its plans and then making a judgment about its future performance.

The first option can be used by any investor but the second one is a bit difficult as company managements may not want to talk to anybody and everybody who calls or shows up.

The limitation in the first option is that there are many examples of supposedly good companies, such as Satyam Computer, cooking their books for years on end, and that too when international auditing firms were their official auditors. This makes it a bit difficult for investors to have faith at face value.

Notwithstanding that, you can generate amazing results if fundamental analysis is used in combination with technical analysis. This combination will almost surely help in reducing your risk.

Some important factors to look for in fundamental analysis are:

1. Business sector the company operates in;
2. Company's management;
3. Profit / loss for the last five years;
4. EPS;
5. P/E ratio;
6. Book value;
7. Dividend track record;
8. Bonus track record;
9. Cash reserves;
10. Assets;
11. Debt;
12. Location; and
13. How — and how much — does government policy impact the company.

There can be many other parameters as well which a fundamental analyst may use to improve his analysis.

Analysts make a judgment about the stock price of a company after analysing all these factors. Usually, such analysts are employed by large brokers and financial institutions and their views are more appropriate for long term investments. With a bullish view on the future valuations of a company, they either advise a buy signal or start buying the stock in their portfolio. With a poor valuation forecast, they put out a sell on the stock, suggesting that existing investors should sell the company's stock.

Technical Analysis

In this book, our focus is technical analysis; its practical use in trading and investing, and things which work and things which do not. **The objective of this book is not only to make you a successful chartist but also a successful investor and trader.**

Accordingly, we will be discussing only those technical topics and parameters which can be both actually implemented and which work in practice. Technical analysis is a vast field and in the last one hundred years there have emerged numerous theories related to this topic. Every individual who has put in days and nights into charts has contributed to its growing knowledge base. Now, if you were to decide to follow all the theories, the only end result would be confusion. Therefore we need to follow a select set of tools, indicators and parameters which can help us in different market phases. Most important of all, we need to know when to be actively trading in the market and when to take a holiday from charts. This book explains all these points in detail, and with examples.

Finally, successful traders tend to have some points in common:

1. They are able to control their emotions of fear and greed.
2. They know that not all their trades will be winners. They have the maturity to understand that winning and losing trades are an ongoing feature. What matters is that, eventually, the profits from winning trades should be more than the losses from losing trades.
3. They have a strategy ready before they start trading — and they have the discipline to follow their predefined strategy.

~

Quiz: Market Analysis

Questions

1. Fundamental analysis is the study of the business of a company through its balance sheet. (True / False?)
2. Technical analysis is the study of share price movements. (True / False?)
3. Fundamental analysis and technical analysis go hand in hand. (True / False?)
4. All trades have to be winning trades. (True / False?)
5. Fundamental analysis never fails. (True / False?)

Answers

1. True	2. True	3. True
4. False	5. False	

FUNDAMENTAL ANALYSIS WILL HELP YOU UNDERSTAND THE VALUATION OF A BUSINESS. TECHNICAL ANALYSIS WILL HELP YOU DECIDE THE BEST ENTRY AND EXIT POINTS INTO A STOCK.

Chapter 6

~

Introduction to Technical Analysis

TECHNICAL ANALYSIS IS THE STUDY OF PRICES USING CHARTS. Is it possible to read prices without the help of a chart? If so, that could perhaps save you money in subscribing to a charting software. When you touch somebody who has fever, you come to know that there is something wrong because you can feel the abnormal heat. You would, however, not be able to gauge the exact temperature merely by touch. Charting without a software is also the same. A technical analyst without a charting software is like the captain of an Airbus A380 airliner who does not have an altitude meter, or like a doctor without the required medical equipment, or an engineer without his tools!

Technical analysis is a complicated sounding term for a basic approach to investing. This is one reason why so many stock market enthusiasts shy away from this field. As we progress you will understand that not only is technical analysis simple, but it is also useful for your investments.

It is much like swimming. Till the time you learn how to swim you are scared of getting into the water. As you learn how to swim, however, you start enjoying it. Then you want to be in the water all the time. The same applies here; the moment you learn technical analysis, you want to look for trading opportunities on charts. You will start spending your time researching charts, analysing them, trying to identify trading opportunities. With the help of charts, the indispensable trader's tool, you can identify the risk involved, the likely returns, and also the time period for which you would have to remain invested in a stock. As you learn more and more, you will start loving the charts and they, in turn, will start talking to you.

Does charting eliminate all the mistakes in investing and trading? Will it prevent you from getting into loss making trades?

No, but it would surely reduce them.

Just as being a good driver does not guarantee that you will never scratch or damage your car, the same applies to charting. You can analyse a stock but you can't make it move as per your wish. That's not possible because numerous factors are involved in price moves. But by having knowledge of charting and implementing proper trading rules, you can improve your strike rate and your performance. You will also be able to effectively manage the risk involved in a trade.

Technical analysis does not seek to determine the intrinsic value of a company. Rather, it seeks to decipher the demand and supply forces acting on its stock price. The demand and supply forces can be due to a variety of reasons, one of which could be the fundamental developments taking place in a company. Other factors could be government policies, news, new orders, introduction of new products, etc.

Technical analysis is a study for predicting probable future price moves based on past price movements. It is predicated on the promise that prices would usually react in the same way in the future as they did in the past. So, for example, if a stock had faced resistance going above a certain price level in the past, then the stock price would not be able to break past that level easily even in the future. If the price does break through the level, it would suggest that there is something extraordinarily positive happening in the company which the investment community is taking on board by going past the earlier resistance level on the charts.

In the chart in Figure 6.1, for example, you will see Nifty facing resistance at approx 6,350, a level at which it earlier faced resistance in 2008, then in 2010, and again in 2013 when Nifty reached that level for the third time.

After making a top in 2008, the index witnessed a sharp sell-off. Again, in 2010, when the price reached that same level, people remembered the way the index had reacted from this level in the past. They remembered that Nifty had witnessed a sharp fall from this level in 2008 and so they had to wrestle with the possibility of a sell-off happening again. Therefore, as the Nifty came closer to the earlier top, investors and traders started squaring off their long

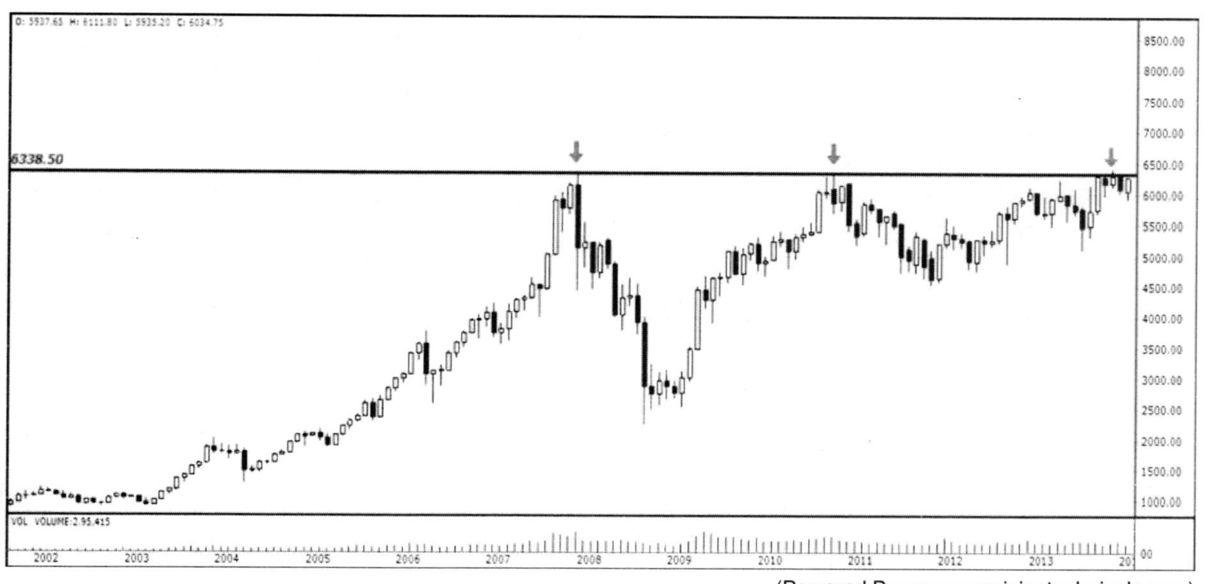

(Powered By: www.precisiontechnicals.com)

Figure 6.1: **Monthly chart of Nifty displays a triple top resistance — in 2008, 2010 and 2013 — highlighted by the down arrows.**

~

positions, i.e. started selling. Those who did not have a position saw this as an opportunity to go short. Both the squaring-off of long positions, and fresh shorts, automatically applied brakes to the up move in the index. The same phenomenon was repeated when the Nifty again reached that same level in 2013.

~

Quiz: Technical Analysis

Questions

1. Technical analysis is a study of prices using charts. (True / False?)
2. It is possible to analyse price without a chart. (True / False?)
3. Technical analysis works on the underlying demand and supply. (True / False?)
4. Technical analysis is a study for predicting future price movements based on past price movements. (True / False?)

Answers

1. True
2. False
3. True
4. True

PRICE MOVES ARE GOVERNED BY DEMAND AND SUPPLY. TECHNICAL ANALYSIS HELPS IN READING THIS EQUATION ON THE PRICE CHARTS.

Chapter 7

~

Share Prices and Chart Time Periods

PRICE IS A CONSENSUS BETWEEN A BUYER AND A SELLER. This means that a price is formed when both a buyer and a seller are ready to buy and sell at that level. If the buyer wants to buy at ₹100 but the seller wants to sell at ₹101, then a trade does not take place — and neither is a price generated. Therefore when a price is generated, it captures the thinking of both the buyer and the seller involved in the trade.

The most important point to grasp here is that a price is created due to the existence of contradictory views in the market. The creation of a price has various reasons to it. Thus, the price is created not only because of sentiment but also due to people who study a stock, based on which they then trade it. So, price can be created by people with knowledge of technicals, fundamentals, as well as other factors, like rumours, tips, gut feelings, astrology and lot many other things which drive a person to trade in the market. **Irrespective of the reasons, a price is a fact because it is something that has already happened.** A price is created when a person has already traded, which also means that he is liable, or responsible, for its profits and losses depending on the outcome of the trade. If an investor has sold some stock, then he is responsible to deliver those shares and if he has bought some then he has to pay for the delivery taken. A price once formed is, therefore, a fact which contains in itself various ideas with which people came to the market and entered a trade. Therefore, it is important for us to be able to read the significance of price. By doing so, we are able to understand the way the buyers and sellers have positioned themselves. Thus, understanding the price — price action as it's often called — is nothing but understanding the way the forces of demand and supply are acting.

Remember, also, that all the other parameters, in technical analysis such as indicators and oscillators which are used for analysing whether the price will go up or down are derived from price alone. If we understand the language of the price, then we have won the battle of understanding demand and supply which govern the stock markets.

Price Fields

The four important fields in the price are:

1. Open = O
2. High = H
3. Low = L
4. Close = C.

For different period charts, the periodicity is the only thing that changes while the four price fields remain the same. Together, these price fields are often referred to as OHLC.

The charts that market participants analyse could be for different time periods. Intraday traders may want to look at the 1-minute (1-min) chart, 3-minute (3-min) chart, 5-minute (5-min) chart, 15-minute (15-min) chart or a 30-minute (30-min) chart, whereas investors would want to look at daily, weekly and monthly charts.

The OHLC fields remain the same for all the different time period charts.

Thus, for example, for a 1-minute chart:

1. Open will be the opening price for that particular 1-minute period.
2. High will be the highest level the price has reached during that 1-minute period.
3. Low will be the lowest level the price has reached during that 1-minute period.
4. Close will be the closing price for that 1-minute period.

The same logic will be applicable for all the different time periods.

For example in case of a daily time period chart:

5. Open will be the opening price for the day.
6. High will be the highest level the price has reached during that day.
7. Low will be the lowest level the price has reached during that day.
8. Close will be the closing price for that day.

Utility of Price Fields

OHLC levels play a very crucial role when it comes to analysing price movements. These price fields can provide you the following information:

- They tell you the way buyers and sellers have positioned themselves.
- They help you in understanding the demand and supply situation.
- They tell you the strength of a stock price move.
- They indicate the intensity of trading activity in the stock.
- They help in identifying turning or reversal points for the price.

Selecting the Right Time Period Chart for Your Profile

Should an investor get worried about the fate of his investment if the stock falls sharply during a day? No. Should an intraday trader look at the monthly chart when making his trade decisions? No.

Technical analysts and traders must understand the relationship between their profile and the appropriate time period of chart they should be looking at.

A short term chart will show the emotions of the demand and supply situation prevailing in the short term. This is useful for a short term trader. On the other hand, an investor with a 1-year or longer view, needs to analyse long term charts.

Selecting the right time period chart for analysis is therefore very important. Table 7.1 summarises the relationship between your profile and the different time period charts.

Table 7.1

Appropriate Charts for Different Types of Traders and Investors

	Profile	*Chart Time Period*
1	Day Trader	5-minute chart
2	Short Term Investor, Positional Trader	Daily chart
3	Investor 6-month view	Weekly chart
4	Investor 1-Year and more	Monthly chart

~

Quiz: Price Fields

Questions

1. The price is a consensus between a buyer and a seller. (True / False?)
2. Price is created due to contradictory views. (True / False?)
3. Price discounts everything. (True / False?)
4. Which are the four important price fields?
5. An Intraday trader should take decisions analysing a monthly chart. (True / False?)
6. Investment decisions should be taken after analysing a monthly chart. (True / False?)

Answers

1. True	2. True	3. True
4. Open, High, Low, Close	5. False	6. True

SELECTING THE APPROPRIATE TIME PERIOD CHART TO ANALYSE WILL HELP IN PICKING OPPORTUNITIES WHICH SUIT YOUR PROFILE.

Chapter 8

~

Types of Price Charts

TECHNICAL ANALYSIS IS A STUDY OF PRICE MOVEMENTS with the help of charts as the tool. Prices have a habit of repeating their previous history. Price charts help in interpreting price movements which, in turn, depict the sentiments of traders and investors. When used properly, charts can provide you a great deal of information about stock price movements:

- Based on your strategy, charts can tell you when to buy or sell a stock.
- Charts help you prepare a proper risk management strategy for your trades.
- Charts give you an idea of the risk and the returns involved in a particular trade.
- Charts help you determine important support and resistance levels.
- Charts help in identifying trends.
- You have a better chance of success when you execute trades near support or resistance levels. Thus, even in the case of a failure, charts help in minimizing the risk involved.
- When analysed on a chart, price movements also tell you about the angle, or steepness, of the trend which further determines whether the price rise or fall will sustain.
- Reading price data also helps in identifying and separating genuine and false moves.
- Most important of all, when you have clarity as to what is happening to the price on the chart, you automatically tend to be in control of your emotions which have a major impact on your decision making ability.

The commonly used types of charts are:

1. Line chart;
2. Bar chart; and
3. Candlestick chart.

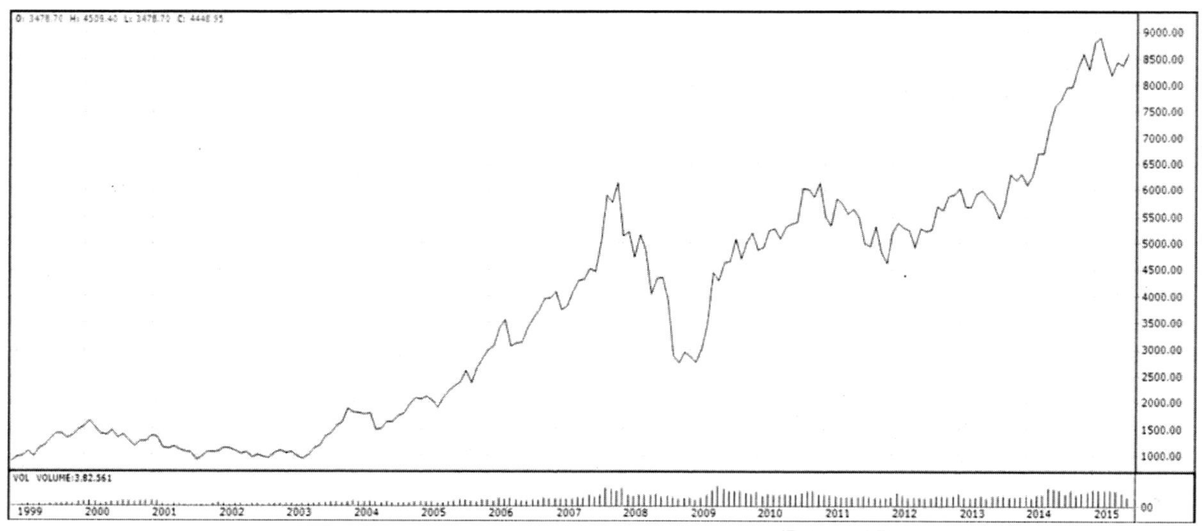

(Powered By: www.precisiontechnicals.com)

Figure 8.1: **Monthly line chart of Nifty**

~

Line Chart

This type of chart is plotted using only one price field, usually the closing price. When we use only one price field for each period, the outcome is automatically a line. This can be seen in the chart in Figure 8.1.

In the case of a line chart, while we can judge the overall price trend but it is difficult to judge the way buyers and sellers positioned themselves within each period of time. Thus, for example, a line chart won't show the intraday price movements, and so on. This limitation arises because of only one price field having been used.

Advantages

1. Line charts are used for identifying trends over longer time periods.
2. Line charts also help to identify the support and resistance levels when the other types of charts do not show us a clear picture.

Disadvantage

The way traders or investors have positioned themselves during a particular period — whether long or short — cannot be identified by looking at a line chart.

The way to overcome the limitation of this type of a chart is to use all the four price fields which then gives us a more clear picture. When we use all the price fields — open, high, low and close — we come to know how the traders and investors have reacted at a particular price. This gives us a lot of information about the sentiment of the market participants and therefore the possible direction in which the price will move next.

The inclusion of all the four price fields can be achieved by using either a bar chart or a candlestick chart.

Bar Chart

In a bar chart, all the four price fields are displayed. These price fields, namely the open, high, low and close are shown in the form of bars.

Let's understand the structure of these bars.

In Figure 8.2, you can see a bar with the four price fields displayed on it.

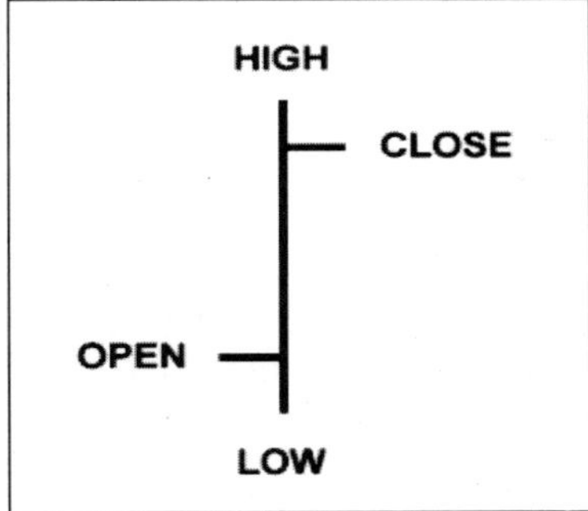

Figure 8.2: **Single bullish bar**

~

To plot a bar we need to first draw a line joining the high and the low, and then draw a horizontal line on the left which denotes the open, and one on the right which denotes the close.

So when we look at a bar like the one plotted in Figure 8.2, it tells us that the price closed at a higher level than the level at which it opened, signifying that it was a bullish day.

Advantages

The bars reveal bullish and bearish periods. A bar can also tell us the level of bullishness judged by the distance between the open and the close.

The logic is simple: prices go up because of buying and they fall because of selling. When we look at the four price fields using this logic, they tell us whether the period concerned was bullish or bearish, mildly bullish or mildly bearish, or whether it was a period of indecision.

The bar plotted in Figure 8.3 tells us that the closing price for that period was lower than the opening price. This reveals that this period witnessed net selling, due to which the price closed at a lower level as compared to its open.

Thus, during this period the bears, or the sellers, were more active than the buyers, i.e. the bulls.

This is how bar charts help us in identifying the bullish and bearish sentiments in price.

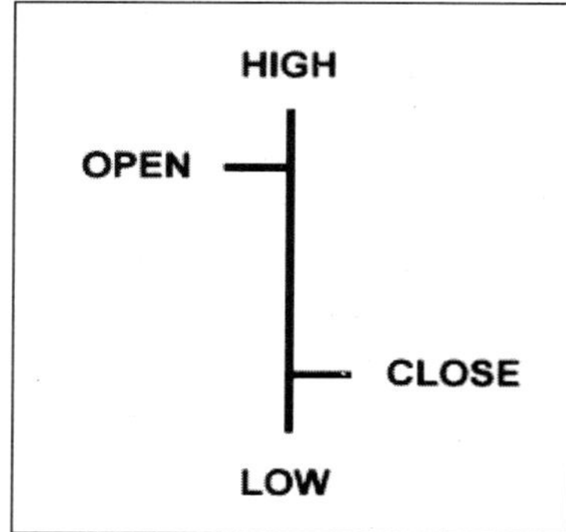

Figure 8.3: **Single bearish bar**

Disadvantages

The problem with bar charts is that when you are looking at an overall chart, namely a chart with many bars, it becomes a bit difficult to immediately and easily identify which bars are bullish and which are bearish.

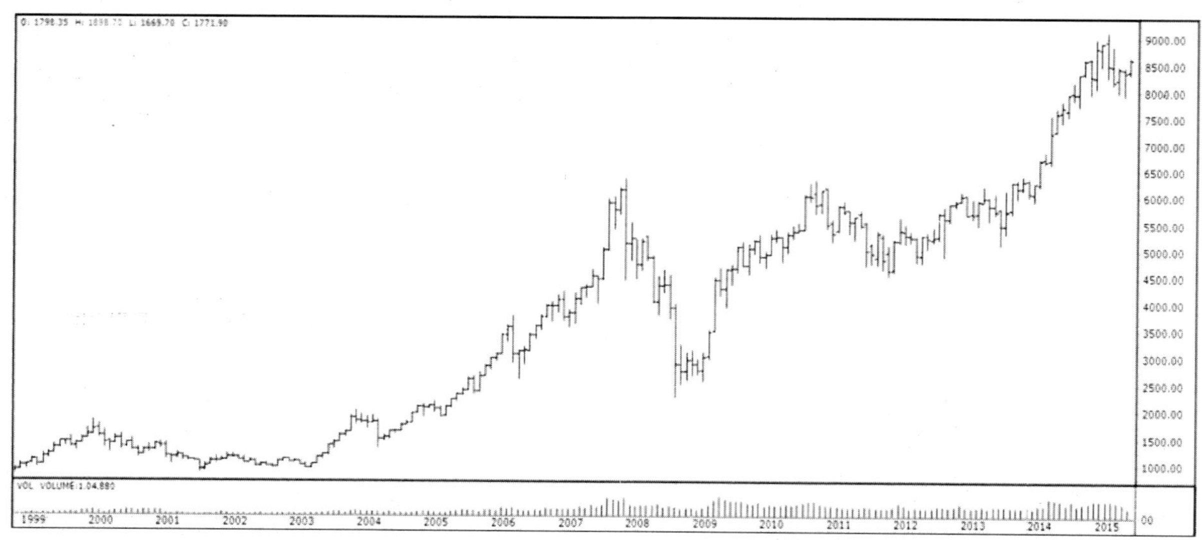

(Powered By: www.precisiontechnicals.com)

Figure 8.4: **Monthly bar chart of Nifty**

Technical analysis is all about reading the price, and if you can't easily and quickly read the price, or if a chart creates confusion, or is not able to give you an immediate visual interpretation, then it is not worth using.

Let us see this with an example.

Consider the chart in Figure 8.4. If asked to identify whether a particular period is bullish or bearish, would you be able to do so by looking at the chart in Figure 8.4? Yes, you could, but it may take some time to do so because you would have to carefully compare the open price and the close price, namely check whether the left hand side horizontal line is higher, or lower, compared to the line which is plotted on the right of the bar. Based on this, you can judge whether the period was a bullish or a bearish one.

Thus, firstly, it would be time consuming and, secondly, if you make a mistake while identifying the details of the bars then that could lead to unnecessary trading errors.

Therefore though a bar chart has all the four price fields, it is not very helpful in quickly assessing what's going on. To find a solution to this problem we have the third type of chart which is known as a candlestick chart.

Candlestick Charts

If you look at the chart in Figure 8.5, you will find that the periods are denoted by a combination of hollow and filled oblong / rectangular bodies. These bodies look just like candles which we light in our homes or on birthday cakes.

(Powered By: www.precisiontechnicals.com)

Figure 8.5: **Monthly candlestick chart of Nifty**

Let us understand how these candlesticks are formed.

For a candlestick to form, we need the four price fields that we have already discussed, namely open, high, low and close. Once you have these four price fields, you can plot a candle. These candles tell you what is happening to the price, whether the bulls are stronger, or the bears, or whether both are confused and cannot make up their minds. Let us understand this by first learning to plot a candle.

There are basically two types of candles as shown in Figure 8.6 — black (filled) candles, and white (hollow) candles.

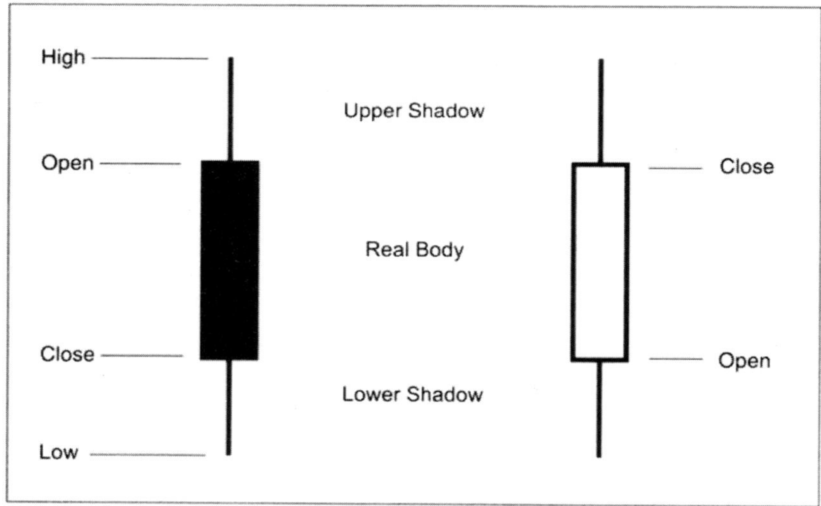

Figure 8.6: **Difference between black and white candles**

The essential difference between the two types of candles is the same as in the case of bars, namely the open and the close levels. When the close is higher than the open, then we have a white candle; when the close is lower than the open, we have a black candle. With the high of the period always being the top end of the candle and the low being bottom end. Thus:

- White or hollow candle = Close is higher than open.
- Dark or filled candle = Close is lower than open.

Let us see how these candles are formed by understanding the plotting of candlesticks. Though simple, this is very important because once you understand how a candle is plotted you will understand the price itself. Understanding the price means understanding the psychology of the buyers and sellers. Since technical analysis is all about reading the price, therefore understanding how a candlestick is formed will help you apply technical analysis better.

Plotting Candlesticks

For plotting a candlestick; we need the four price fields — open, high, low and close. Let us consider some examples.

Example 8.1: Bullish Candle

Open = 100, High = 130, Low = 90, Close = 120.

To plot a candlestick for the above price fields, we need to do the following:

1. Plot a small horizontal line for the open price on a vertical scale where the value reduces going down and increases when going up.
2. Then plot a second small horizontal line, parallel to the earlier horizontal line, for the closing price. Whether the second horizontal line is above or below the earlier line, would depend on whether the close is higher than the open, or lower in the period concerned.
3. Now mark the high and the low on the price scale.
4. Join the horizontal lines plotted for the open and the close prices. This will now become the body of the candle.
5. Join the high and the low with the body of the candle to form the sticks or shadows of the candlestick.

After joining all the price fields we will be able to see a candlestick like the one displayed in Figure 8.7.

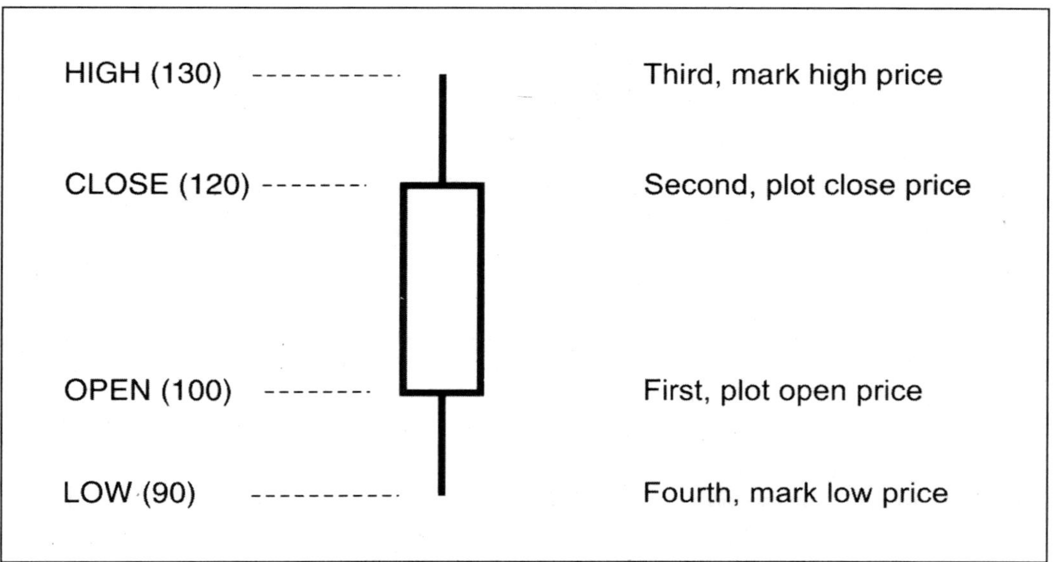

Figure 8.7: **Plotting a white candle**

~

One important thing to always remember is that when the closing price is higher than the opening price, it shows that the price has risen during that particular period. Prices go up because of buying, or demand. So for us to easily and immediately interpret that there is buying, or demand, we keep this candle body either hollow or white. Thus, when you see a white candle it means that the period represented by the candle was a bullish one during which there was net buying; in other words, during this period the buyers were stronger than the sellers.

Example 8.2: Bearish Candle

Open = 120, High = 130, Low = 90, Close = 100.

The plotting method will remain the same as in Example 8.1, which means that we will first plot a small horizontal line at the open, then another one at the close, and then mark the high and the low. We will join the open and the close to form the body of the candle, and join the high and the low to the body to form the two sticks, or shadows, of the candle.

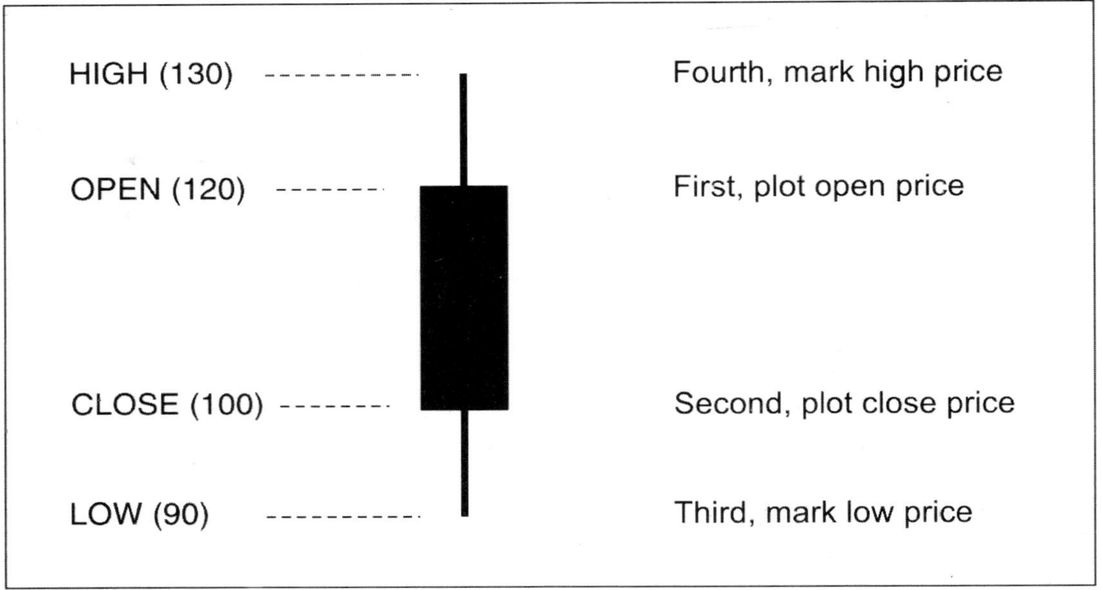

Figure 8.8: **Plotting a black candle**

~

So the plotting method remains the same but with one major change. In the earlier example the close was higher than the open but in this case the close is lower than the open. Prices move up and down because of demand and supply. If the demand is more, prices tend to rise, while with greater supply, prices tend to go down. In this case the close is below the open, which means there was excess supply, or that there was net selling because of which the price came down to close below the open. In other words, in this case the sellers were stronger than the buyers. Since this is something which we need to identify immediately, in the case of such candles we fill up the body, or colour it black. So when you look at a black candle it immediately tells you that selling dominated in that particular period. Such a candle would look like the one in Figure 8.8.

So, in simple terms:

1. White candle = Bullish, demand, buying candle.
2. Black candle = Bearish, supply, selling candle.

As the values of price fields change, so will the shape and colour of subsequent candles. Every candle will tell us whether the buyers or the sellers were stronger in the period each candle represents — or whether both were indecisive. We get to know all this instantly, just by looking at the chart.

Let's see an example so that we understand whether we really are able to obtain a visual interpretation very fast when using candlestick charts. Check the chart in Figure 8.9 to try and identify the buying and selling candles.

When you see a white candle, you immediately know that this is a buying candle, and when you see a black candle you know that it is a selling candle. This logic helps in a very quick visual interpretation. This is an advantage that the candlestick chart has over the line chart or the bar chart. It's for this reason that we prefer using candlestick charts for our analysis.

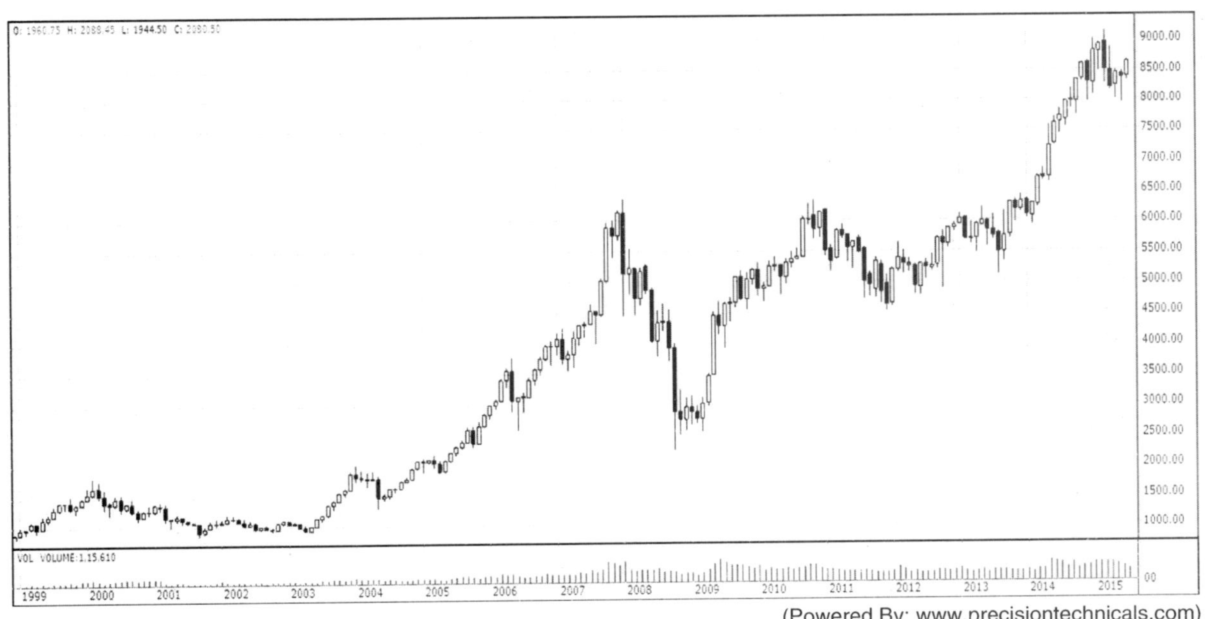

(Powered By: www.precisiontechnicals.com)

Figure 8.9: **Monthly candlestick chart of Nifty with white (hollow) and black (filled) candles**

We will discuss these types of charts in more detail and also use them in later chapters. For now, let's practice plotting a few candles and, along with it, let's also try and judge if we can understand whether they tell us what's happening with the price.

Candle Plotting Exercise

This exercise is designed to help you understand the plotting of candlesticks and also understand how to interpret them visually. This exercise will prove helpful when analysing charts using candlesticks for price plotting. With this exercise you will also understand that every candle has an interpretation. When you are analysing candlestick charts, in a way they are talking to you, explaining to you the demand and supply situation in a stock. Fill in your interpretation for each of the following candlesticks, whether it is bullish or bearish one.

Candle No. 1

- Open = 100
- High = 140
- Low = 90
- Close = 130

Interpretation: This candle is . . .

Candle No. 2

- Open = 130
- High = 140
- Low = 90
- Close = 100

Interpretation: This candle is . . .

Candle No. 3

- Open = 100
- High = 120
- Low = 80
- Close = 100

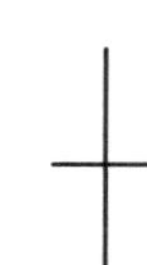

Interpretation: This candle is . . .

Candle No. 4

- Open = 100
- High = 100
- Low = 70
- Close = 100

Interpretation: This candle is . . .

Candle No. 5

- Open = 100
- High = 140
- Low = 100
- Close = 100

Interpretation: This candle is . . .

Candle No. 6

- Open = 100
- High = 140
- Low = 70
- Close = 110

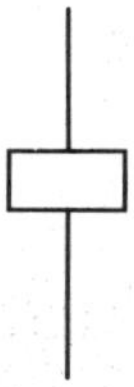

Interpretation: This candle is . . .

Candle No. 7

- Open = 100
- High = 140
- Low = 100
- Close = 140

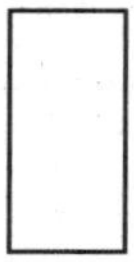

Interpretation: This candle is . . .

Candle No. 8

- Open = 120
- High = 120
- Low = 100
- Close = 100

Interpretation: This candle is . . .

Answers

Candle 1: Bullish candle with shadows

Candle 2: Bearish candle with shadows

Candle 3: Neutral / Indecision

Candle 4: Neutral / Indecision

Candle 5: Neutral / Indecision

Candle 6: Neutral / Indecision

Candle 7: Bullish candle without shadows

Candle 8: Bearish candle without shadows

Quiz: Price Charts

Questions

1. A line chart is plotted using all the four price fields: Open, High, Low and Close. (True /False?)
2. Which type of chart provides very quick visual interpretation? Line chart, bar chart, or candlestick chart?
3. OHLC helps in understanding the demand and supply situation. (True / False?)
4. Is a white candle bullish or bearish?
5. Is a black candle bullish or bearish?

Answers

1. False
2. Candlestick chart
3. True
4. Bullish
5. Bearish

INTERPRETING THE DEMAND AND SUPPLY SITUATION USING A CANDLESTICK CHART IS EASY AND FAST.

Chapter 9

~

Important Lessons from the Dow Theory

THE DOW THEORY ORIGINATED AS A SERIES of editorial articles by Charles H. Dow (1851-1902), the founder and first editor of the *Wall Street Journal*. Mr Dow never represented these articles as a way to invest or trade in the stock markets, and neither did he coin the term Dow Theory. This term came into existence after his passing away. The articles that he had written collectively became Dow Theory. Volumes of work have since been done on this theory. We can say that technical analysis of today borrows a lot from it. As such, Charles Dow is also known as father of modern day technical analysis. His seminal contribution includes discovering the trending nature of prices, the identification of trends, and how price movements discount, namely anticipate, forthcoming events in advance.

Back then there were two main sectors which were helping the United States to grow; the industrial sector which comprised heavyweights; like textile mills and automobile companies, and the railroads (railways) or transportation sector.

To effectively monitor these sectors, and also to monitor the stock market's movements, Mr Dow came up with the idea of developing the following two indices for the New York Stock Exchange (NYSE):

1. Dow Jones Industrial Average (DJIA).
2. Dow Jones Transportation Average (DJTA).

The DJIA and the DJTA came into existence around 1896. Even today we monitor the stock movements in NYSE based on DJIA.

During the intervening period of more than one hundred years since this theory was born in the form of articles and now, we have seen the stock markets change in so many different ways, including in India. I remember the days when I first started investing in 1995. The market was then controlled by just a few operators, with little transparency, high transaction charges, lack of liquidity and poor depth. In the next twenty years, the Indian stock markets witnessed major changes, particularly from the year 2000 onward. Today the Indian markets are transparent, much more liquid, and have far greater depth. Such changes keep happening as the markets and participants mature. Let us now summarily review the Dow Theory and take some important learning points which we can use for the purpose of our analysis.

Basics of Dow Theory

Price Discounts Everything

This is the basic understanding on which technical analysis works. As we have discussed in Chapter 7, price is the result of different views. It is formed by hundreds of thousands of people coming together to buy or sell a stock. Each buyer or seller has his own view about the stock's price. Some people may have a bullish view, and therefore they come and buy the stock. Others with a bearish view at the same time may be selling the same stock. These views could have been formed by their own study of technical or fundamental analysis, or because they may have heard of the stock on television, or based on an SMS from their broker or from a friend, and so on. At times, the views may even be based on a "gut feeling" that a stock is going to go up or down. So there are various views which create a price. This is what is meant when we say that the price discounts — namely takes into account — everything. It reflects all the different, and contradictory, views that people may have about a stock.

Price Movements Comprise of 3 Trends

Primary Trend

This trend is the main direction in which the price is moving. It signifies the long term trend in a stock's price. This trend is said to remain intact till there is a clear reversal signal.

The primary trend starts when investors begin to build bullish expectations. This marks the start of the first phase of the primary trend. As there is improvement in the company's earnings, the expectations turn out to be true. This is the second phase in the primary trend when the stock starts attracting investors in plenty. In this stage, the volume of trading starts rising sizeably and the stock price also starts moving quite smartly.

The third and last stage of the primary trend is when everybody realises that the stock is an opportunity because of its ongoing move and anybody and everybody wants to then start buying that stock. The stock also starts being widely discussed in the media. This is a stage of euphoria and generally this is also the extreme point of the trend. The primary trend usually lasts anywhere from one to three years.

Secondary / Intermediate Trend

This trend is an intermediate, or a corrective, trend within the primary trend. As it is a corrective move, therefore this trend is always in the direction opposite to that the primary trend. An intermediate trend normally lasts anywhere between three weeks to three months.

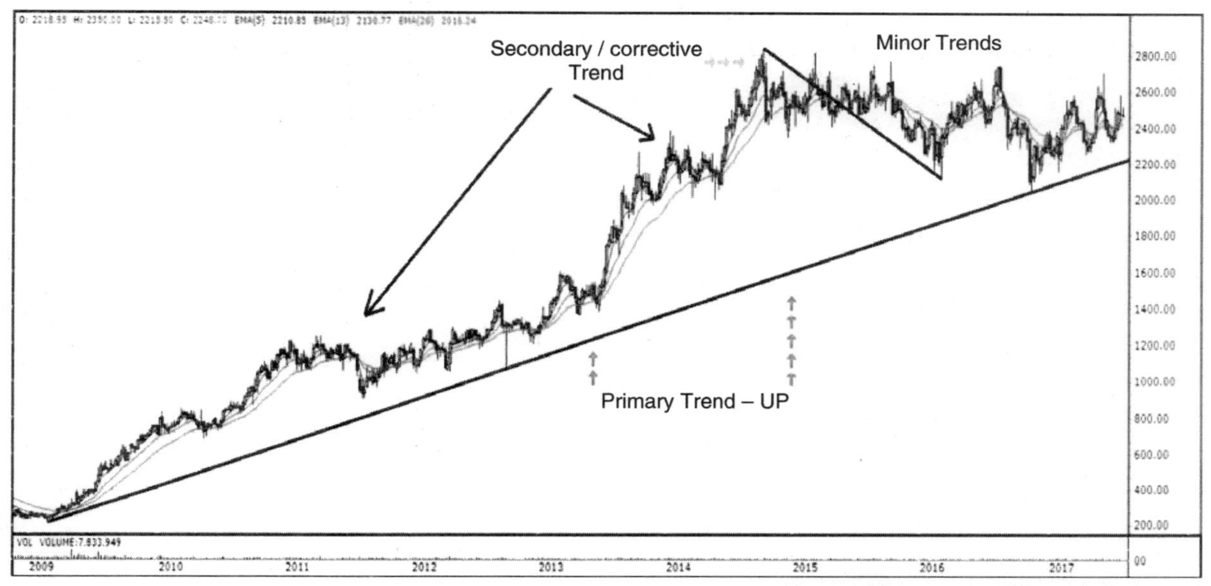

(Powered By: www.precisiontechnicals.com)

Figure 9.1: **Weekly chart of Tata Consultancy with the three trends highlighted — namely primary, secondary and minor trends.**

~

Minor Trend

These are the short term corrective moves which happen within the secondary or the intermediate trend. These trends normally last anywhere between a few days to three weeks. The Dow Theory suggests that minor trends can be misleading as the price can be volatile in the short term.

We will discuss the different forms of these trends, namely the up trend, down trend and the sideways trend in Chapter 10. We will also discuss the strategies which one can use to trade these trends.

Volume

Volume has an important role to play in all the trends. It does so in two aspects:

- Volume helps in confirming the price trend.
- It also helps in identifying a change of trend or a reversal signal.

~

Quiz: Dow Theory

Questions

1. How many trends can be seen on the price chart?
2. A trend can stay intact if it continues to get help from volumes? (True / False?)
3. The Intermediate trend is a correction in the primary trend? (True / False?)
4. Volume plays an important role in all the trends? (True / False?)

Answers

1. 3	2. True
3. True	4. True

DOW THEORY IS A STUDY OF PRICE TRENDS.

Chapter 10

~

Trading the Trend

PRICE MOVEMENTS DEPEND ON EXPECTATIONS which investors and traders have from a stock or the market. If the expectation is that the price will move up, investors would buy the stock. If investors expect the price to move down, they will sell the stock. These expectations lead to stock prices moving in trends. The trend continues so long as the expectation holds; the moment the expectation changes, the trend too changes. Every trend tells us about the expectations which investors and traders have from a particular stock, or the market. Each of the three trends postulated by the Dow Theory can, in turn, be of three types.

3 Types of Trends

As we've already learnt, the price has a habit of moving up and down. When it does so, it tends to move in trends:

1. Up trend.
2. Down trend.
3. Sideways trend.

Up Trend

In the chart in Figure 10.1, you can see that Nifty is moving upward, and that as it moves up it makes successive higher tops and higher bottoms. When the price moves in this way, then technically we term this as an up trend.

Up trend = Price moving up making higher tops and higher bottoms

In an up trend, one should try and stay long at all lower levels rather than staying short at higher levels. The reason is that since the overall trend is up, the price would have more of a positive undercurrent. Even if you are stuck at a wrong level, the stock's trend will ensure that you sail out of the stock smoothly because of the bias of the tide.

(Powered By: www.precisiontechnicals.com)

Figure 10.1: **Daily candlestick chart of Nifty displaying an up trend, with successive higher lows and higher highs**

~

Important takeaways:

- Price is strong till the trend remains up.
- An up trend suggests a bullish view.
- In an uptrend, avoid shorts and do not trade against the trend.

Down Trend

In the chart in Figure 10.2, you can see that the price of JP Associates is moving downward. In doing so, the price is making successive lower tops and lower bottoms. When the price moves in this way, then technically we term it as a down trend.

Down trend = Price moving down making successive lower tops and lower bottoms

During a down trend, one should try and stay short at all higher levels rather than going long at lower levels. This is so because when the overall trend is down, the price would face difficulty on every up move, and will eventually again fall. Even if you are stuck at a wrong level, the price trend of the stock will ensure that you will sail out of the trade smoothly because of the downward bias of the tide.

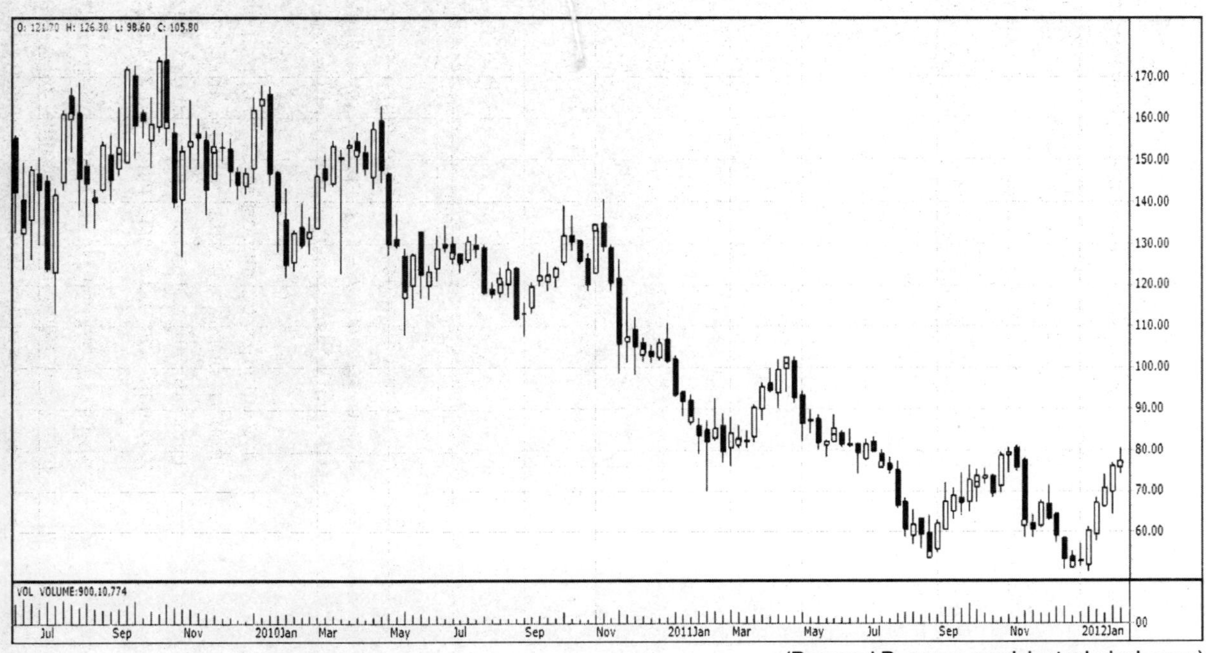

(Powered By: www.precisiontechnicals.com)

Figure 10.2: **Weekly candlestick chart of JP Associates displaying a down trend**

~

Important takeaways:

- Weakness is signified so long as the trend remains down.
- Avoid longs and do not trade against the trend.
- A down trend suggests a bearish view.

Sideways Trend

In the chart in Figure 10.3, you can observe that the price of Ashok Leyland is moving in a range, namely its movement is confined between two price levels. To highlight this we have drawn two horizontal lines, one at the upper horizontal line resistance level and the second at the lower horizontal line support level. So, in this case the price is moving between a lower level of ₹64 and a higher level of ₹76. The price continued to trade within this range for a period of five months from mid-February to mid-July. The difference between the two levels is approximately 19%.

(Powered By: www.precisiontechnicals.com)

Figure 10.3: **Daily candlestick chart of Ashok Leyland displaying a sideways trend, with a range of about 19%**

~

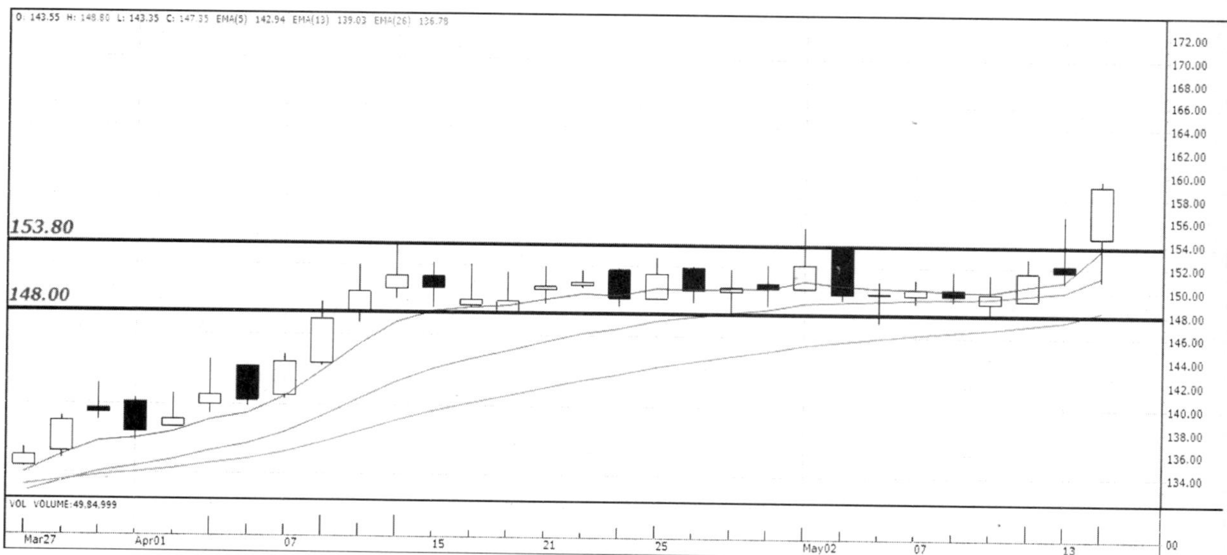

(Powered By: www.precisiontechnicals.com)

Figure 10.4: **Daily candlestick chart of NMDC displaying a sideways trend, with a narrower range of about 4%**

~

In the chart in Figure 10.4, you can observe that the price of NMDC is also moving in a range, much like the price of Ashok Leyland in Figure 10.3. But in this case there are two differences:

- One is the time period of the consolidation or the range bound move, and
- The second is the price difference between the two levels.

The higher end of the range is at ₹154 levels and the lower end is at ₹148 levels. This means that the band of the range is approximately 4%. The time period of the consolidation is also shorter when compared with that of the chart in Figure 10.3.

~

Let us now understand the reason why a price trades between a range. We have seen that stock prices move up and down based on demand and supply. As we have learnt, higher demand pulls prices up, while higher supply drags prices down. Now when the demand and supply are nearly equal, prices tend to go into a sideways trend.

So, basically, a sideways trend tells us that traders and investors as a whole are confused about the direction of the stock or the market, during this period. They are not able to make up their minds as to where the price would be heading next — whether up or down. This typically happens when investors and traders are awaiting some decisive announcements or developments from the company or the economy, etc.

Here, some questions come to mind.

Can the charts tell us whether a stock will enter a sideways trend before it actually does special?

One of the safest ways of generating returns without having to learn anything or take any risk is bank fixed deposits. If a stock generates anything more than the return generated by fixed deposits, and that too in a very short time frame, then people would naturally like to book profits. This is the normal thing which most market participants do. Yes, there are ways of trailing and partial profit bookings and we will discuss those in later chapters. But what we need to understand here is that when you buy a stock at ₹100 and the price reaches, say, ₹140 in a very short time, you do not need to be a rocket scientist to understand that it is a good time to book profits. As the price rises, a number of people who were looking at the price as an opportunity when it was trading at ₹100 automatically lose interest. The momentum takes the price higher till profit booking overpowers the fresh longs initiated in the stock and the price then automatically takes a pause. The buying and selling are nearly equal at that stage and the stock price moves into a sideways trend.

One way of anticipating if a stock may enter a sideways trend is to see whether there has either been a recent sharp rally, or a sharp fall, in the stock's price. The probability of such stocks moving into a sideways trend is high.

What happens after a sideways trend?

As we have discussed, a sideways trend indicates that market participants are unable to make up their mind whether the stock price is likely to go up or go down. Give a thought to this — would the stock price remain in such a state forever? Obviously not. At some time or the other, the price has to either make an upward breakout, meaning it could move above the higher end of the range / resistance, or the price can give us a downward breakout and move below the lower end of the range / support.

In other words, a sideways trend presents market participants a big future opportunity.

How to Trade a Sideways Trend

A sideways trend can be traded in two ways as explained below.

Important Eligibility Criteria for a Sideways Trend to be Valid

A consolidation is insignificant if the price stays range-bound for less than five candle periods before moving out of the range. Such a trend cannot be called a sideways trend. This is so because a price can move in a trend, then pause for two to four candles, and again start moving in the same direction. This type of a move cannot be considered as a sideways trend. **Therefore the consolidation needs to have a minimum of five candles. Longer the consolidation, better the subsequent move.**

Trading Within the Range

This opportunity depends on the size of the range, namely the price difference between the two levels of the sideways trend. In the charts in Figure 10.3 (Ashok Leyland) and Figure 10.4 (NMDC), we saw that the price ranges were different in the two cases. In the case of Ashok Leyland, the range between the two levels was approximately 19%. In such a case, a short term investor or a positional trader can initiate longs on support, i.e. at the lower end of the range, and initiate shorts at resistance, i.e. at the higher end of the range. When trading at a support or at a resistance, the risk reward odds are always in favour of the trade. So when the price is trading between a range of sufficient width, trades can be initiated based on whether the price is at a support or at a resistance.

But if we look at the second case (Figure 10.4, NMDC) you may decide not to enter a trade with this logic as the difference between the two levels is just 4%. The narrow range in this stock may not allow you to enter and exit a trade with positive gains.

Therefore the price difference between the higher end and the lower end of the range in a sideways trend will help you decide whether you should trade between those levels, or simply wait for a clear breakout from the range.

Trading on a Breakout

After being restricted in a range, the price will eventually break out of the range it. This could be either a move above the resistance, or below the support. **A trade in the direction of the breakout can then be initiated.**

Remember — enter a trade on confirmation and not on assumption. In other words, do not enter a trade merely in anticipation of a breakout. Do so only after an actual breakout occurs. It is always safer to enter a trade with a confirmation.

Trading Breakouts on a 5-Minute Chart (Figure 10.5)

- An opportunity after a breakout from a sideways trend works nicely on a 5-minute intraday chart.
- Such an intraday trade has the potential of generating 1% to 5% returns depending on the momentum in the stock generating this breakout.

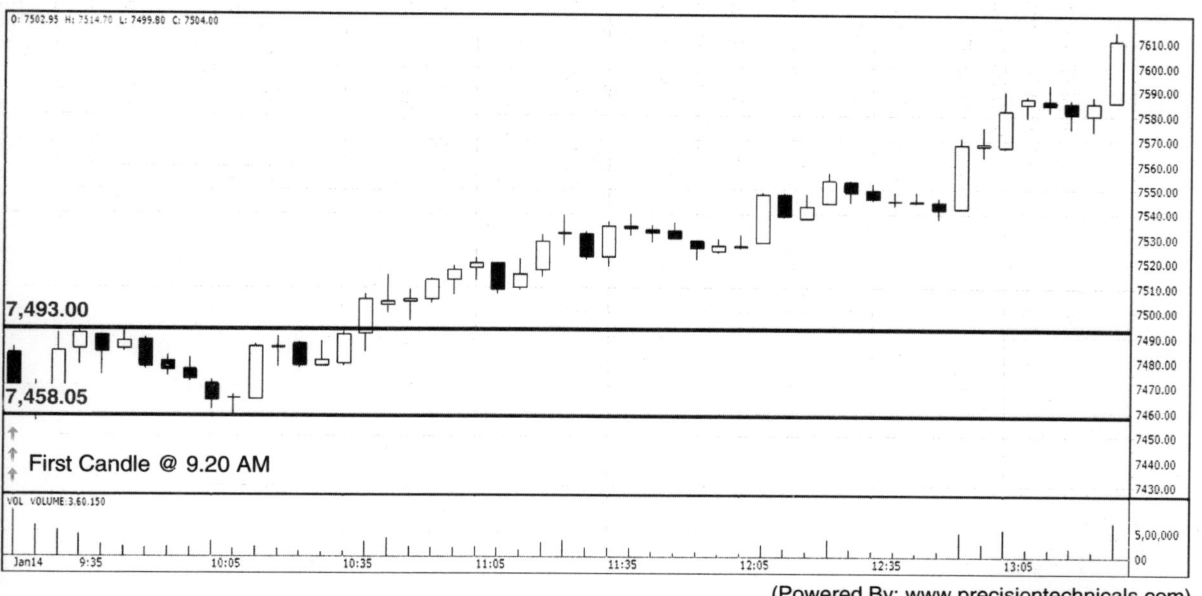

(Powered By: www.precisiontechnicals.com)

Figure 10.5: **A 5-minute chart of Nifty displaying an intraday up trend after a breakout from a sideways trend, or consolidation**

~

Trading Breakouts on Daily, Weekly and Monthly Charts

- An opportunity after a breakout from a sideways trend on a daily time period chart (*see* Figure 10.6) can generate 10% to 20% returns within 10 to 20 days.
- An opportunity after a breakout from a sideways trend on a weekly time period chart (*see* Figure 10.7) can generate 20% to 40% returns in 4 to 20 weeks.
- An opportunity after a breakout from sideways trend on a monthly time period chart (*see* Figure 10.8) can generate multibagger returns in 12 to 24 months.

(Powered By: www.precisiontechnicals.com)

Figure 10.6: **Daily chart of Vadilal industries displaying an up trend after a breakout from a sideways trend**

~

(Powered By: www.precisiontechnicals.com)

Figure 10.7: **Weekly chart of Welspun India displaying an up trend after a breakout from a sideways trend**

~

(Powered By: www.precisiontechnicals.com)

Figure 10.8: **Monthly chart of Cummins India displaying an up trend after a breakout from a sideways trend**

~

Quiz: Trading the Trend

Questions

1. What is the trend called when the price is moving up, making successive higher tops and higher bottoms?
2. What is the trend called when the price is moving down, making successive lower tops and lower bottoms?
3. What is the trend called when the price trades in a range?
4. In an uptrend one should initiate a buy trade. (True / False?)
5. In a downtrend one should initiate a sell trade. (True / False?)
6. The trend is your friend. (True / False?)

Answers

1. Up Trend
2. Down Trend
3. Sideways Trend
4. True
5. True
6. True

THE TREND IS YOUR FRIEND. YOU SHOULD TRADE WITH THE PRICE TREND TO ACHIEVE GOOD RESULTS.

Chapter 11

~

Trends and Trend Lines

Trends

Identifying the ongoing trend and trying to stay with it is the most common way of investing and trading in the stock market. As we discussed in Chapter 10, a trend can be identified by looking at the tops and bottoms the price makes:

- When the price moves upward making successive higher tops and higher bottoms, it suggests that the price is in an up trend.
- When the price moves downward making successive lower tops and lower bottoms, it suggests that the price is in a down trend.

Thus, up and down trends can be identified by looking at the levels of the successive tops and bottoms formed on a particular duration chart.

If we are able to plot trend lines, which means straight lines either inclined upwards or downwards, joining the bottoms or the tops as per the trend, then these can help us in arriving at sound buying and selling decisions. **Plotting of trend lines helps us to use trends to generate buy and sell signals.** In this chapter, we will learn about the plotting of trend lines and also learn how to use them for entering long or short trades.

Up Trend

Figure 11.1 displays the chart of Ajanta Pharma with a trend line plotted on it by connecting successive bottoms. The trend line suggests that the price is in an up trend.

(Powered By: www.precisiontechnicals.com)

Figure 11.1: **Daily chart of Ajanta Pharma displaying an up trend which also acts as a support level during the trend.**

~

Down Trend

Figure 11.2 displays the chart of BHEL with a trend line plotted on it which suggests that the price is in a down trend.

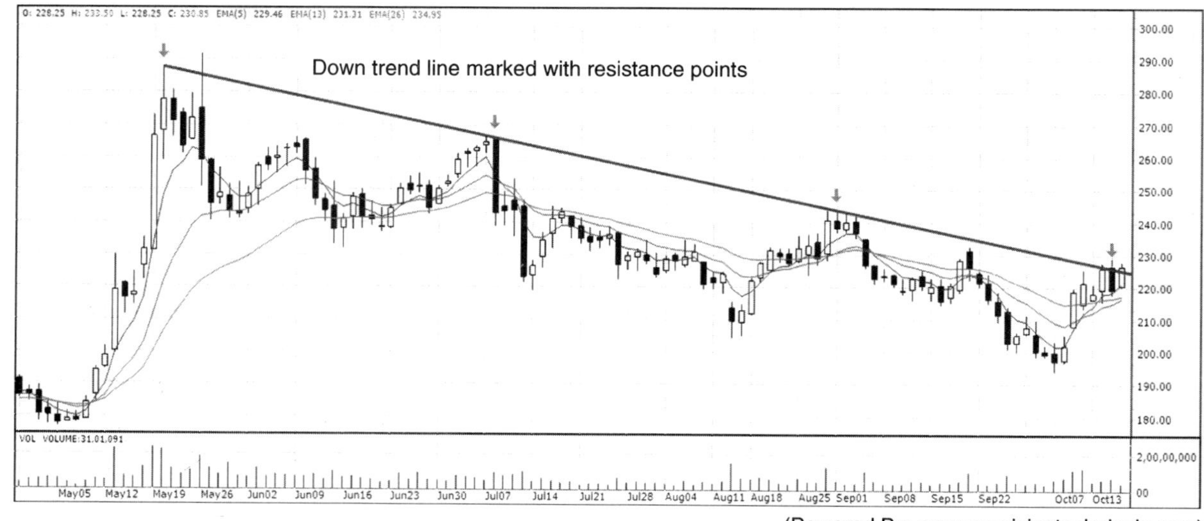

(Powered By: www.precisiontechnicals.com)

Figure 11.2: **Daily chart of BHEL displaying a down trend**

~

Validity and Confirmation of Trend Lines

Validity and confirmation are two important concepts in technical analysis.

The difference between different people interpreting the same chart differently can lead to differences in analysis as shown in Figure 11.3.

This is why you should understand the concept of validity and confirmation. You will then be able to judge what is right and what is not. It is also important to reduce the number of failure trades. As we have discussed, you can analyse to the best of your abilities but you cannot make the price move in your preferred direction. Therefore it is important to validate and confirm one's view before getting into a trade.

Now, how to validate or confirm whether your analysis is right or wrong? Who will do it?

The price itself will validate your view.

In technical analysis, the validity of a particular analysis is confirmed by the chart itself; in other words, by the stock's price. On a price chart, you may be able to plot many trend lines joining different tops and bottoms. This can also lead to confusion as to which trend line is correct or, in other words, valid.

For a trend line to be valid it should have the maximum number of points touching it. These points could be any one of the four price fields — open, high, low or the close of the price.

Figure 11.3: **Difference of opinion!**

~

So if you plot two or more trend lines and find that the number of points touched by the two lines is different, then the line which is touching a larger number points is more valid than the other.

Let us see an example of judging the validity of a trend line.

In the chart in Figure 11.4 you can see that we have plotted three down trend lines joining different price tops (highs). The difference between the three plotted lines is clearly visible on the chart in terms of the number of points each one connects with.

Line 1 connects the maximum number of points when compared with the other two lines. It joins four points, whereas Line 2 and Line 3 connect just two points each. So the question about which line is valid is answered by checking which one is touching the maximum number of points. This also means that the consensus of the market players is for the line which has the maximum number of points from where the price has reacted, or the one which the price has respected.

You must train yourself to judge the validity and confirmation of every parameter in technical analysis. Doing so will greatly help in improving your success rate when trading.

(Powered By: www.precisiontechnicals.com)

Figure 11.4: **Daily chart of BHEL with multiple trend lines plotted on it**

~

Up Trend Line as Support

Ajanta Pharma's daily chart in Figure 11.5 is an example of an up trend line acting as a support:

- An up trend line also acts as a support.
- It suggests that the price is in an up trend.
- Further confirmation is provided by rising volumes whenever the price tests the support trend line.
- Long trades should be initiated when the price is closest to the support trend line.
- This helps in reducing the risk involved in the trade as the stop loss will be below this support level.
- Risk to reward ratio is in favour of the long trade when the price is taking support on an up trend line.

(Powered By: www.precisiontechnicals.com)

Figure 11.5: **Daily chart of Ajanta Pharma: The support levels on the up trend line are marked with arrows.**

~

Down Trend Line

BHEL's daily candlestick chart in Figure 11.6 is an example of a resistance trend line:

- A down trend line also acts as a resistance.
- It suggests that the price is in a down trend.
- Further confirmation is provided by higher volumes whenever the price tests the resistance trend line.
- Short trades should be initiated when the price is closest to the resistance trend line. This helps in reducing the risk involved in the trade as the stop loss will be above this resistance level.
- Risk to reward ratio is in favour of the short trade when the price is facing resistance on a down trend line.

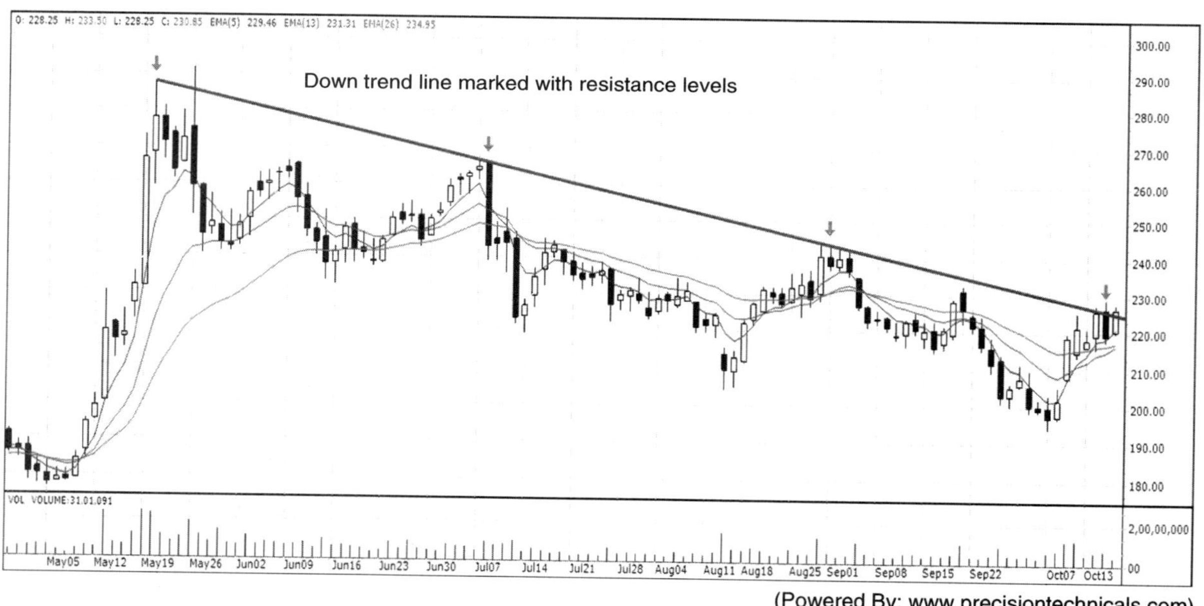

(Powered By: www.precisiontechnicals.com)

Figure 11.6: **Daily chart of BHEL showing a down trend line marked with resistance levels**

~

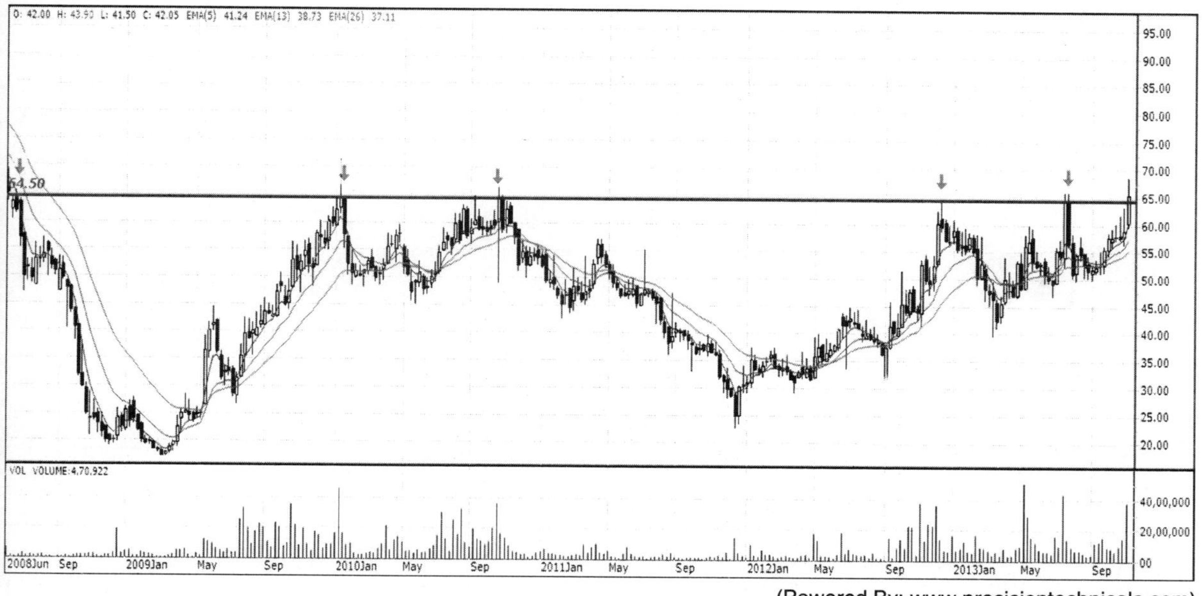

(Powered By: www.precisiontechnicals.com)

Figure 11.7: **Daily candlestick chart of Finolex Cable with the horizontal trend line marked with resistance levels**

~

Horizontal Trend Line (Sideways Trend)

The daily candlestick chart of Finolex Cable in Figure 11.7 offers an example of a horizontal trend line:

- A horizontal trend line suggests that the price is in a sideways trend.
- A horizontal trend line could act both as a resistance and as a support.
- Whether the horizontal trend line is resistance or support would be decided based on whether the price is trading above or below the horizontal line.
- For a price which is trading below the horizontal line, the line will act as a resistance.
- For a price which is trading above the horizontal line, the line will act as a support.
- Short trades can be initiated when the price is nearest to the resistance horizontal line, as indicated by the arrows in Figure 11.7.
- Long trades can be initiated when the price is nearest to the support horizontal line.
- Ultimately when the price gives a breakout, a trade can be initiated in the direction of the breakout, with a stop loss on the other side of the horizontal line.

Support and Resistance

Support and resistance are levels from where the price tends to retract back in the opposite direction.

First, let's understand resistance with the help of an example.

In the chart in Figure 11.8, you will be able to see the horizontal trend line plotted at a level of ₹64.50. As you would observe, this level has acted as a resistance for the price, which means that every time the price moved to the level of ₹64.50, it faced resistance in moving up any higher. This happens because of fresh selling which overpowers the ongoing buying and forces the price down. Resistance is marked with down arrows on the chart in Figure 11.8.

(Powered By: www.precisiontechnicals.com)

Figure 11.8: **Daily candlestick chart of Finolex Cable with horizontal trend line acting as resistance indicated by down arrows**

~

(Powered By: www.precisiontechnicals.com)

Figure 11.9: **Weekly candlestick chart of Tata Steel with the horizontal line acting as support highlighted by upward pointing arrows**

~

Now, let's consider an example of support.

In the chart in Figure 11.9, you can see a support highlighted with a horizontal line plotted at the level of ₹199.70. You would note that every time the price came down to this level, it found support and moved back up again. So the price reacts positively around this level. Put another way, investors and traders change their view to positive when the price reaches this level and the consequent fresh demand automatically overpowers the ongoing supply to take the price back up. Support levels are marked with up arrows, as in Figure 11.9.

Two Types of Support and Resistance

1. Minor level; and
2. Major level.

The main difference between the two is the number of times the price has reacted from the level in the past.

Minor Level

This is a level from where the price has reacted on only a few past occasions. It is possible, for example, that there may have been only one occasion in the past when the price has reacted from a particular level.

Major Level

This is a level from where the price has reacted several times in the past. It also means that this is a level which many people believe will either provide support, or resistance, as the case may be. When you check a long-term chart of a stock and find that the price has reacted from a level for years together, plus that the level has acted as support as well as resistance several times in the past, then that is a major level. Such a level cannot be ignored by a technical analyst. Usually, the price tends to give more respect to these levels as compared to others.

Since prices move in trends and therefore the lowest and the highest points of these trends are also always to be considered as major support or resistance levels.

Thus, for example, in the chart in Figure 11.10, you will see a horizontal level plotted at about ₹225. This level has acted as resistance as well as support numerous times as and when the price has traded above or below it. This means that it is a major level for the stock price and the chances of the price reacting from this level in the future too are high.

(Powered By: www.precisiontechnicals.com)

Figure 11.10: **Weekly candlestick chart of Godrej Industries with the horizontal line indicating a major level which has acted as both resistance and support numerous times, as highlighted by the down and up arrows, respectively.**

~

Such levels play an important role in all the three trends — namely up, down, and sideways.

When prices are trading near such levels, they provide buying and selling opportunities for investors, as well as for positional traders and day traders.

~

Quiz: Trend Lines

Questions

1. An up trend line acts as a resistance. (True / False?)
2. Does a down trend line act as support or resistance?
3. The validity of a trend line depends on the number of price points that the trend line touches. (True / False?)
4. A horizontal line will act as a ______________ when the price is trading below it.
5. A horizontal line will act as a ______________ when the price is trading above it.

Answers

1. False
2. Resistance
3. True
4. Resistance
5. Support

TREND LINES HELP IN IDENTIFYING TRENDS AS WELL AS SUPPORT AND RESISTANCE LEVELS, WHICH HELP IN TRADE ENTRY.

Chapter 12

~

Volume

VOLUME MEANS THE NUMBER OF SHARES OR SECURITIES TRADED. It is the number of shares which changes hands from sellers to buyers during a particular period. Thus, for example:

- In the case of a 5-minute chart, volume is the number of shares traded during that 5-minute period.
- In the case of a daily chart, volume is the number of shares traded during that day.
- In the case of a weekly chart, volume is the number of shares traded during the week, and so on.

As we discussed earlier in Chapter 11, validity and confirmation are two important concepts in technical analysis. These help in improving your success rate of analysis and profitable trades. As a stock market trader, investor, analyst or a broker, the most you can do is to predict a move to the best of your ability. It is not possible for you to ensure that the predicted move actually materialises. So you cannot make the price move as per your wish because price movement is governed by a variety of factors, all of which are beyond your control.

Accordingly, it is always good to limit your downside in the stock market; in other words, know the risk, and try and improve the success ratio of your analysis. Volume plays an important role in helping you achieve this.

Let me explain with an example.

Nowadays we prefer to watch movies in a multiplex. A multiplex has many screens playing different movies. Let's suppose that you don't know which screen is playing which movie, and neither are you aware of the names of the movies being played. In such a case, how do you decide which is a good movie to watch.

The answer can be found in a simple way — by watching the crowd. The screen which is more crowded is likely to be playing a popular movie. This logic is based on the reasoning that though you may have money to spend, and also free time, it does not mean that you would watch just any movie.

In the same way, when it comes to the stock market people like to trade or invest in stocks where there is some buzz. So, people like to trade stocks which are moving; they don't like to trade stocks which are relatively inactive. And as people get attracted to a particular stock, this can be observed in the form of rising volumes.

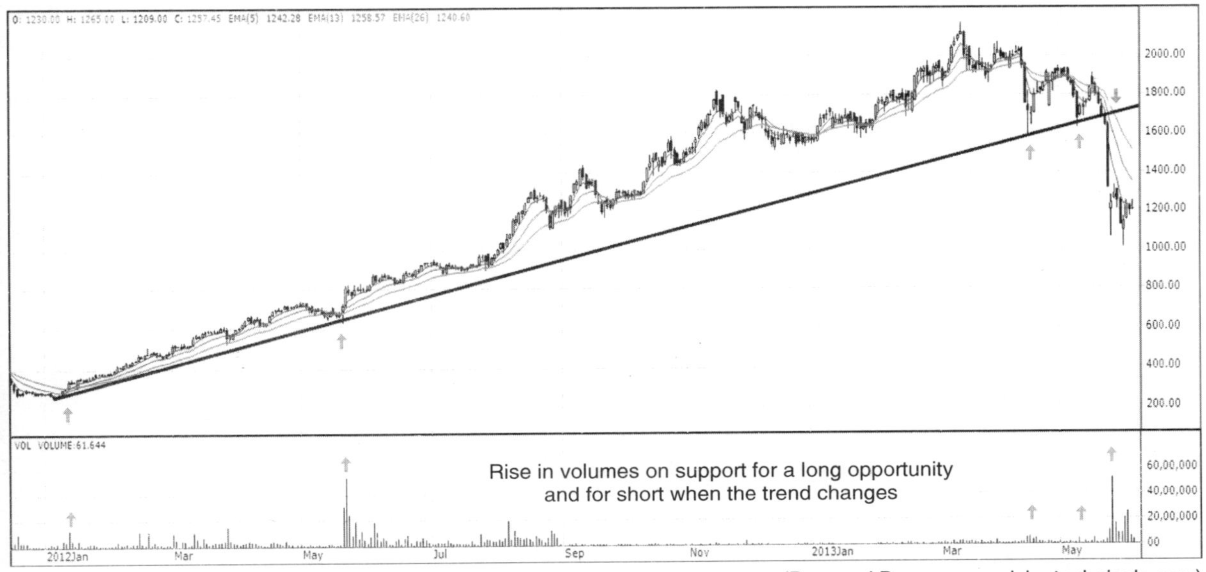

(Powered By: www.precisiontechnicals.com)

Figure 12.1: **Daily chart of Wockhardt Pharma: Note the rise in volume whenever the price takes support on the up trend line, presenting opportunities for long trades. Equally, the volumes also rise when the trend changes towards the end of the chart.**

~

Volume is not something imaginary. It is not something about which people can bluff. Like price, volume too is a fact. Volume indicates the extent of actual trading. So when a trade occurs, volume figures go up. People who trade a stock commit themselves to that trade. Thus, if an investor buys a stock he is committed to pay money for the stock he has bought, while somebody selling the same stock is committed to giving delivery of the shares which he is selling. An intraday trader is committed to the loss or profit that occurs in his account for that day, or for that trade.

Volume figures, therefore, are a fact. When compared to the past data they can tell you whether the interest in a stock is growing or reducing. This is indicated by a rise or fall in volume, respectively.

In the chart in Figure 12.1, you can see that the price is in an up trend, making higher tops and higher bottoms. This is highlighted by an up trend line which is also acting as support for the stock price.

You would also notice that every time the price nears the trend line, it finds support and moves up. It is possible for the price to do so because there is also an increase in volume at the support level. This means that there is a general consensus that the price is going to move up from that level and therefore the demand increases when compared to the supply and automatically the price takes support and moves up. This can be observed so long as the trend of the stock price remains intact.

On the right hand side of the chart you will see that the price has broken the support of the up trend line. When this happens, you can again see an increase in volumes. So volumes are not only important for a trend to stay intact, but they are also an important sign of a change of trend. If a trend has to change, then the supply has to be able to absorb all the demand, and as the supply overpowers the demand the price would be able to change its trend. So, a rise in volumes in the case of a change of trend is important.

Conclusion

- Rise in volumes + Price moving up = Higher demand.
- Rise in volumes + Price moving down = Higher supply.

~

Quiz: Volume

Questions

1. Does a rise in volume accompanied by the price moving up indicate demand or supply?
2. Does a rise in volume when the price is moving down indicate demand or supply?

Answers

1. Demand
2. Supply

TECHNICAL ANALYSIS WORKS WELL ONLY WITH LIQUID INSTRUMENTS. IT WORKS THE BEST WHEN THERE IS PLENTY OF PARTICIPATION.

Chapter 13

~

Consolidation and Correction

FUNDAMENTALS AND TECHNICALS ALWAYS HAVE TO GO HAND IN HAND. You must keep in mind that there is something which does not meet the eye whenever there is a divergence between the two. Price moves up and down based on expectations. With positive expectations, the price tends to move up while negative expectations drive down the price. Expectations create the forces of demand and supply. Price movements occur because positive expectations create demand while negative expectations create supply of the stock.

Along with the forces of demand and supply, hype can also affect stock prices. So when a stock price is moving up on positive expectations, the hype many a time ensures that the price movement exceeds expectations. This can happen both when the stock is in an up trend or in a down trend.

Whenever there occurs this kind of a divergence between the price move and the valuations, the price then moves to catch up. This catch up is called a correction or a consolidation. Such a correction, or consolidation, is further differentiated into two types:

1. Price correction; and
2. Time correction.

Price Correction or Consolidation

Let us now understand what consolidation and correction mean, how they are different from each other, and how they can help us in our analysis and trading.

While there is a slight difference between consolidation and correction, both words refer to a movement on the price chart.

Let us consider the example of a stock which moves in a trend and then witnesses a 50% price correction of the earlier move (*see* Figure 13.1).

In the chart in Figure 13.1, you can see an up trending stock. The up arrows mark the higher bottoms and the down arrows mark the rising tops of the price trend. Thus, the price is moving up making higher tops and higher bottoms. This means that every successive bottom is at a higher level when compared to the earlier one, and same is the case with every successive price top.

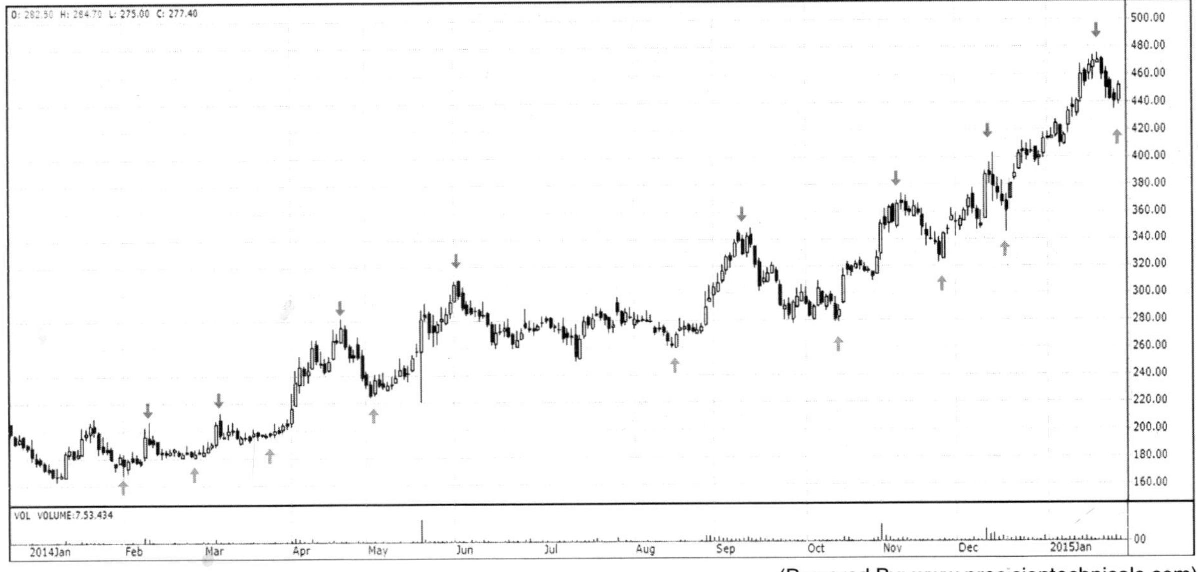

(Powered By: www.precisiontechnicals.com)

Figure 13.1: **Daily candlestick chart of SKS Microfinance showing the price making higher tops and higher bottoms**

~

Based on the way the price is moving making higher tops and higher bottoms, this is an up trending stock. On this chart the small down moves are corrections of the major trend but at no point of time has the price gone below its previous bottom.

This is something which can easily be observed visually, or you can use a technical tool to identify the same. This tool is called Fibonacci Retracements.

For identifying the various levels of retracements, we can use the following four Fibonacci retracement levels marked on the chart at:

1. 23.60%
2. 38.20%
3. 50%
4. 61.80%.

The tool has to be plotted joining the bottom and the top of the trend when you want to identify the possible levels of a downward correction in an up trend.

Conversely, it has to be plotted joining the top to the bottom of a trend when you want to identify the possible upward correction levels in a down trending stock.

When the Fibonacci Retracement tool is plotted it marks these four levels, as can be seen in the chart examples in Figure 13.2, Figure 13.3, Figure 13.4 and Figure 13.5.

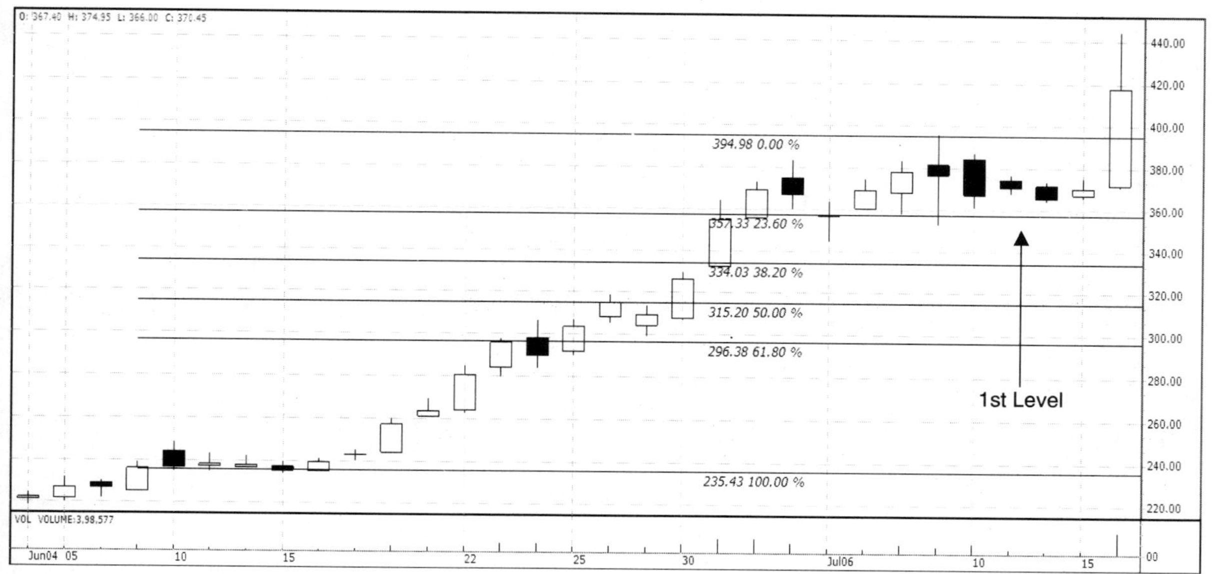

(Powered By: www.precisiontechnicals.com)

Figure 13.2: **Daily chart of Rajesh Exports with Fibonacci retracements plotted, showing the price retracing to the first Fibonacci retracement level of 23.60%.**

~

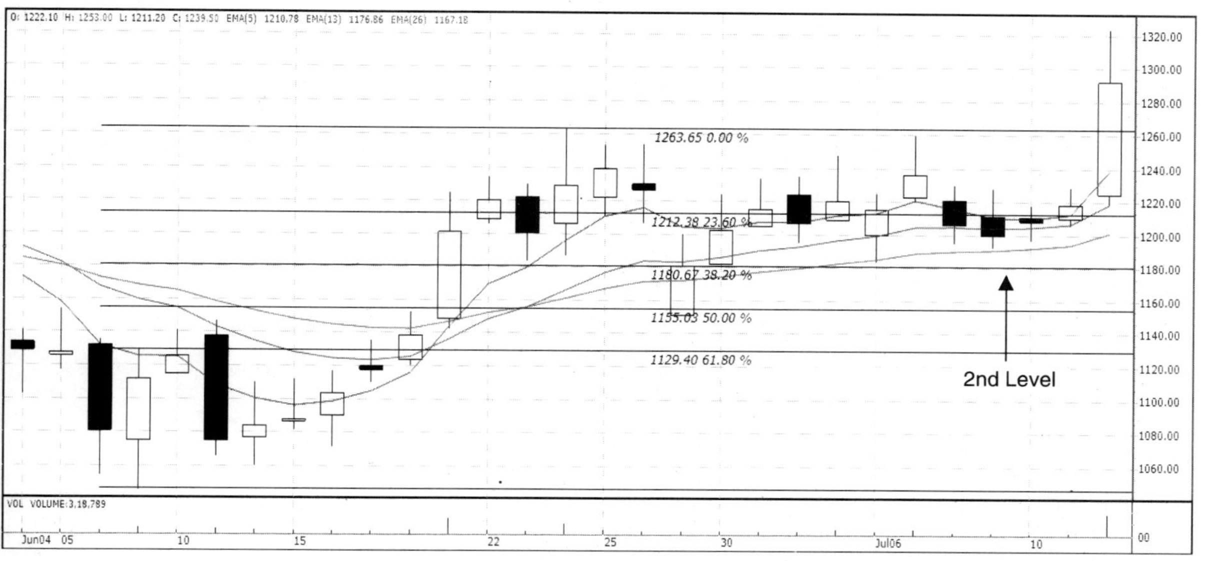

(Powered By: www.precisiontechnicals.com)

Figure 13.3: **Daily chart of Tata Elxsi with Fibonacci retracement plotted, showing the price retracing to the second Fibonacci retracement level of 38.20%**

~

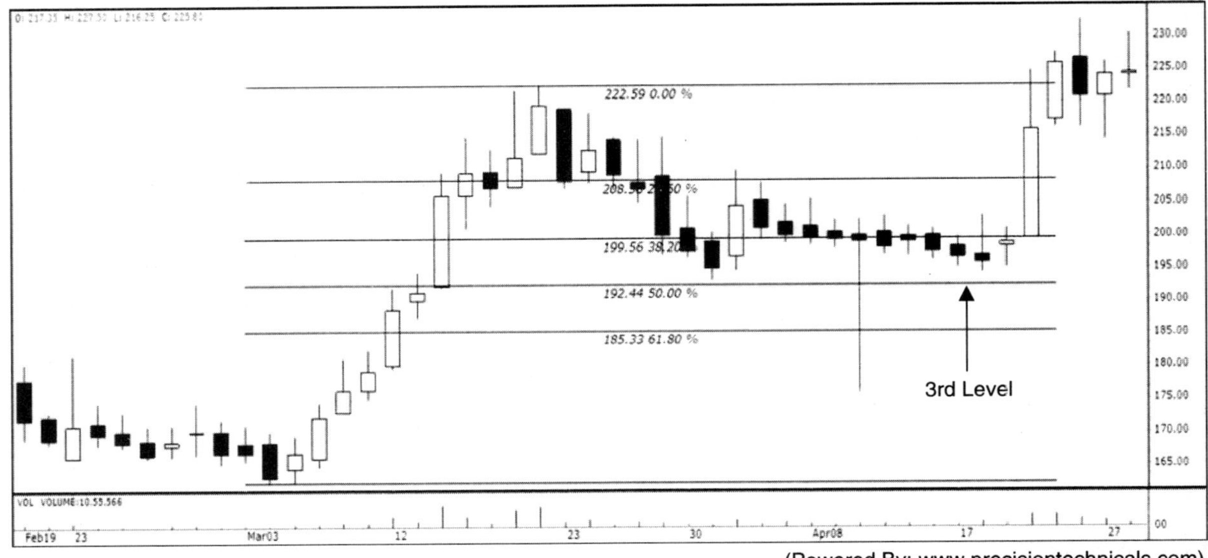

(Powered By: www.precisiontechnicals.com)

Figure 13.4: **Daily chart of Rajesh Exports with Fibonacci retracements plotted, showing the price retracing to the third Fibonacci retracement level of 50%.**

~

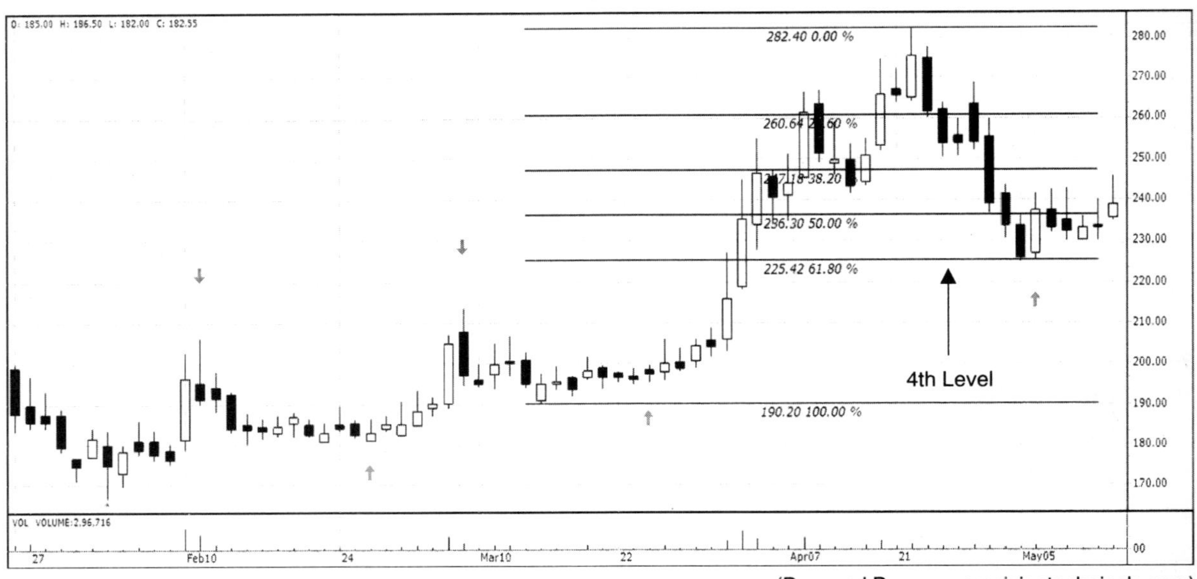

(Powered By: www.precisiontechnicals.com)

Figure 13.5: **Daily chart of SKS Microfinance with Fibonacci retracements plotted, showing the price retracing to the fourth Fibonacci retracement level of 61.80%.**

~

The price then either starts moving in the original up or down trend after the completion of a sideways trend, or reverses its earlier trend. Only when the stock price starts moving in the direction of the original trend can we judge whether it went through a correction or a consolidation. This distinction is based on the level of correction that the price completed based on Fibonacci retracements.

Consolidation means the stock price moves in the direction of the main trend after:

1. First level of Fibonacci correction, i.e. 23.60%, or
2. Second level of Fibonacci correction, i.e. 38.20%.

Correction means the stock price moves in the direction of the main trend after:

1. Third level of Fibonacci correction, i.e. 50%.
2. Fourth level of Fibonacci correction, i.e. 61.80%.

Time Correction

Every rise or fall in price is followed either by a price correction or a time correction. The way the price reacts after a rise or a fall helps us judge whether the stock is going through a price correction or a time correction.

- Price correction happens when the price runs ahead of the fundamentals, the valuations, or the expectations from a particular company or stock.
- Time correction happens when the stock price moves into a sideways consolidation after a price rise or a price fall, trading more or less in a fixed range. This occurs when the investors find that the price is quoting at the correct valuations of the business. The company's business or the valuations of the business justify the price quoted in the market. The price then starts moving in a sideways trend waiting for some new triggers of business valuations which can help the stock move either up or down.

For example, the chart in Figure 13.6 suggests that the price of IRB Infrastructure was justified by the business, or the valuation of the company, due to which the stock had been trading in a range, i.e. at a particular level, for more than four years. There are two things which can happen going forward. Either the business will improve. As and when this happens, the price will start reflecting the improvement in business and will display an up move on the chart. On the other hand; if the business deteriorate, then the price will start to again move downward to correct for the lower valuations of the business.

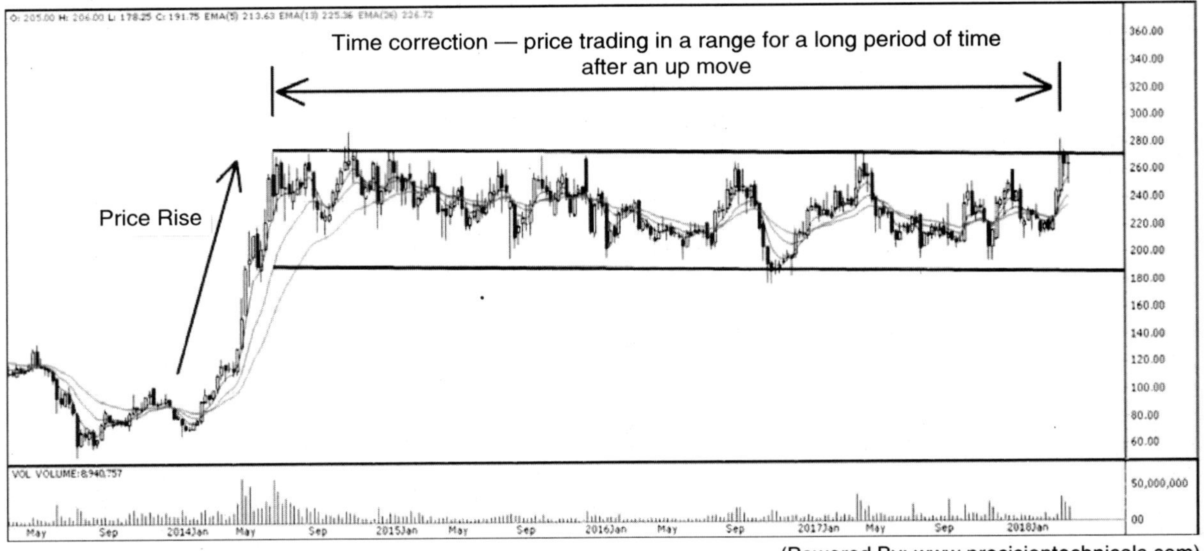

Figure 13.6: **Weekly chart of IRB Infrastructure which displays the price in a sideways consolidation move, or a time correction, after an earlier upmove**

~

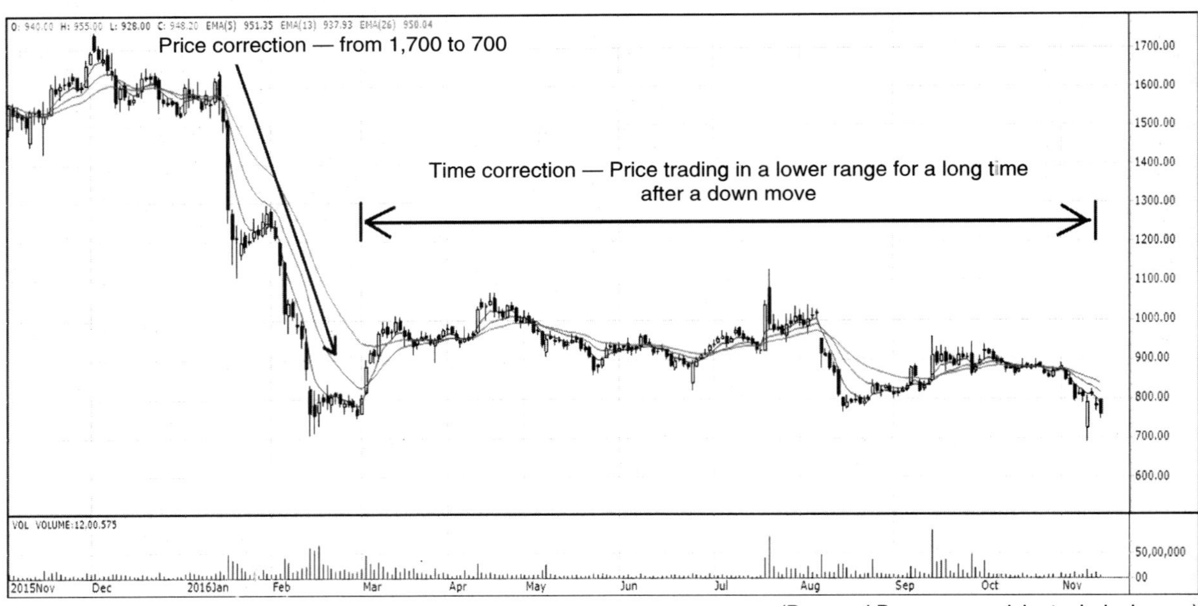

Figure .13.7: **Daily chart of Wockhardt Pharma which first displays a price correction from the level of ₹1,700 to about ₹700 and then a time correction (consolidation) around that lower level**

~

In the chart in Figure 13.7, the price of Wockhardt Pharma witnessed a down trend from ₹1,700 to ₹700, after which the price began consolidating in a range. This chart suggests that the business went down which, in turn, led to a fall in its stock price to reflect the deteriorating business valuations. The latter move, which is more of a range bound move for the price, suggests that the business has settled after deteriorating and the price is now waiting for either the business valuation to improve, or deteriorate, further so that the price can, accordingly, move up or move down.

~

Quiz: Consolidation and Correction

Questions

1. A catch up between the price and the valuations of a company is called a correction or a consolidation. (True / False?)
2. There are 2 types of corrections: price correction and time correction. (True / False?)
3. Which are the four levels of Fibonacci retracements?
4. Time correction is when a stock price trades more or less in a range for a considerable period of time. (True / False?)

Answers

1. True	2. True
3. 23.60, 38.20, 50 and 61.80	4. True

A STOCK WHICH CONTINUES ITS TREND AFTER A CONSOLIDATION HAS MORE STRENGTH THAN ONE MOVING AFTER A CORRECTION.

Chapter 14

~

Trading Strategies Using Moving Averages

IN THE EARLIER CHAPTERS WE HAVE SEEN HOW TRENDS HELP US in determining support and resistance, and also help us generate triggers for a fresh trade entry. To add to this, and to make identification of trends and triggers simpler in cases where plotting trend lines is not easily possible, we have another tool, the moving average (MA). This is the most commonly used indicator in technical analysis. The simplicity of this indicator makes it an all-time favourite of the chartists. The difference between the MA line and the trend line is that a trend line is a straight line while a moving average line is an undulating line.

The moving average (MA) line moves along with the price. It provides immediate guidance about the trend of a price, and in the simplest of ways. The response of the MA line to the price movement depends on the periodicity of the MA used. Shorter term MAs tend to respond faster as compared to longer term averages.

MA Lines of Less than 50 Time Periods

- These are short term moving averages.
- They are used to generate buy and sell triggers.

MA Lines of More than 50 Time Periods

- These are long term moving averages.
- These are useful for determining support and resistance levels.
- They help confirm the trend of a price.
- They identify the strength of the price.

Relationship Between a Trader's Profile and MA Time Period

Day Trader

As a day trader, you would want to enter a trade as soon as the prices react. For this you should use shorter term averages, such as 3-, 5-, 7-, 10-, 11-, or 13-period MAs plotted on an intraday 5-minute chart.

Short Term Investor and Swing Trader

As a short term investor, a swing trader or a positional trader, you should use averages such as 5-, 13- and 26-period MAs plotted on a daily chart.

Long Term Investor

A long term investor should use a combination of the MAs used by a short term investor, and add to that a set of long term averages, such as 50-, 100- and 200-period MAs on the weekly or the monthly chart.

Types of Commonly Used MAs

Simple Moving Average (SMA)

- SMA is the simplest to calculate.
- SMA takes the sum of the past closing prices over the relevant time period and divides it by the number of closing prices used in the calculation.
- For example, the mathematical formula for calculating a 5-period SMA is as follows:

  5 SMA = (Close on Day 1 + Close on Day 2 + Close on Day 3 + Close on Day 4
  + Close on Day 5) ÷ 5

Exponential Moving Average (EMA)

- This is the most widely used type of MA for analysing charts.
- The exponential method of calculating MA is typically used for short term moving averages.
- EMAs react faster to price movements as compared to SMAs.
- In EMAs, greater weight is given to the more recent data.

- EMA is calculated by applying a percentage of today's closing price to yesterday's moving average value.
- Calculating an exponential moving average is a three-step process:
  1. Calculating the SMA.
  2. Calculating the multiplier for weighting the EMA.
  3. Calculating the current EMA.
- The mathematical formula for calculating a 5-period EMA is as follows:

  SMA: 5 period sum ÷ 5.

  Calculating the weighting multiplier: [2/(selected time period + 1)] = [2/(5 + 1)] = 0.3333 (33.33%).

  Calculating the EMA: [Closing price – EMA(previous day)] x multiplier + EMA(previous day).

Weighted Moving Average (WMA)

- The weighted method of calculating MAs is generally used for long term averages.
- Price has a tendency to react at WMA levels; therefore WMA is widely accepted as support and resistance.
- More weight is given to the latest data and lesser weight to the older data.
- A weighted moving average is calculated by multiplying each of the previous day's data by a weight.
- The mathematical formula for calculating a 5-period WMA, looks like as follows:

  5 WMA = [(Close on Day 1 x 5) + (Close on Day 2 x 4) + (Close on Day 3 x 3) + (Close on Day 4 x 2) + (Close on Day 5 x 1)] ÷ 5 Average Period (5 + 4 + 3 + 2 + 1).

  Day 1 = latest close.

  Day 2 = previous close, so on and so forth.

Interpretation of Moving Averages

The most common interpretation is that a buy signal is generated when the price crosses above the average line, while a sell signal is generated when the price falls below the average line, as shown in Figure 14.1.

Such an interpretation, however, has its own limitations. When the price moves frequently above and below an average line, it becomes a headache for the chartist. This type of a move above and below the moving average will generate a lot of whipsaws, namely false signals, as can be observed on the chart in Figure 14.1.

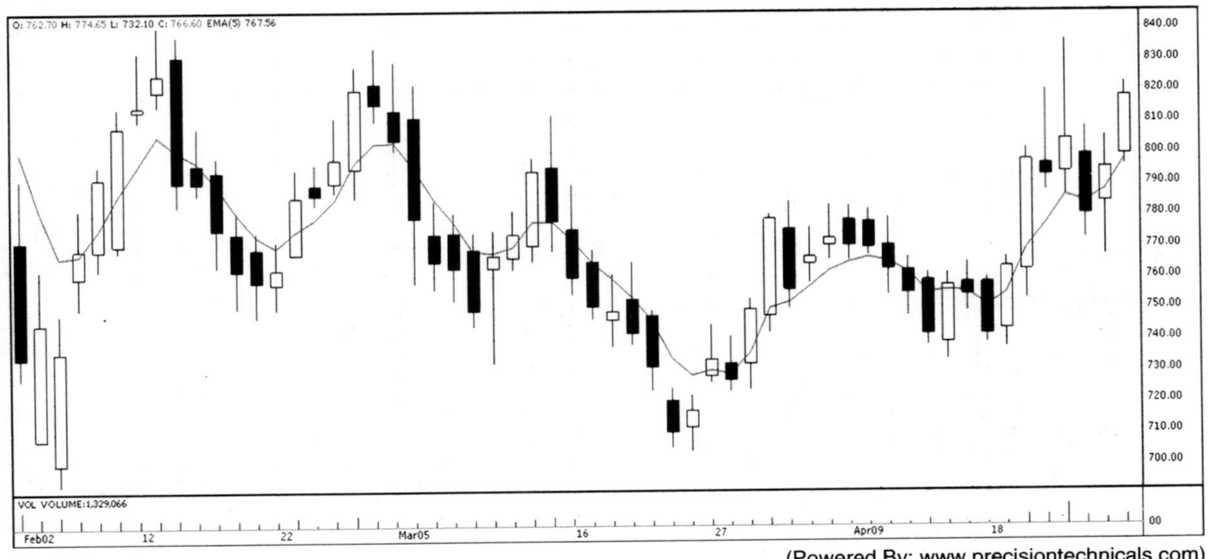

(Powered By: www.precisiontechnicals.com)

Figure 14.1: **Daily price chart of Wockhardt Pharma with a moving average plotted on it. Note the large number of crossovers, and therefore whipsaws.**

~

To overcome this limitation and reduce the large number of whipsaws, we can use multiple averages.

I prefer using a combination of 5-, 13-, and 26-period moving averages. The reason for using this combination is that on a daily time period chart a 5-day MA represents one market working week, a 13-day MA represents a fortnight, and a 26-day represents a month. So in a way we will be using a combination of the weekly, fortnightly and monthly views. Combining these three views will enable you to arrive at entry and exit decisions which will be both logical and which would also carry lower risk. This combination of averages works well for all time period charts.

Let us understand this point on price charts.

Buy Strategies

The chart of Aurobindo Pharma in Figure 14.2 displays all the three averages, namely 5-, 13-, and 26DEMAs. You need to know that when we plot multiple averages on a chart, the shortest period average is always closest to the price. As the time period of the average increases, it moves farther away from the price. When we use the combination of 5-, 13-, 26-day exponential moving averages, the 5-day exponential MA line will remain closest to the price, followed by the 13-day average line, while the longest period MA, in this case the 26-day EMA, will be at the farthest distance from the price.

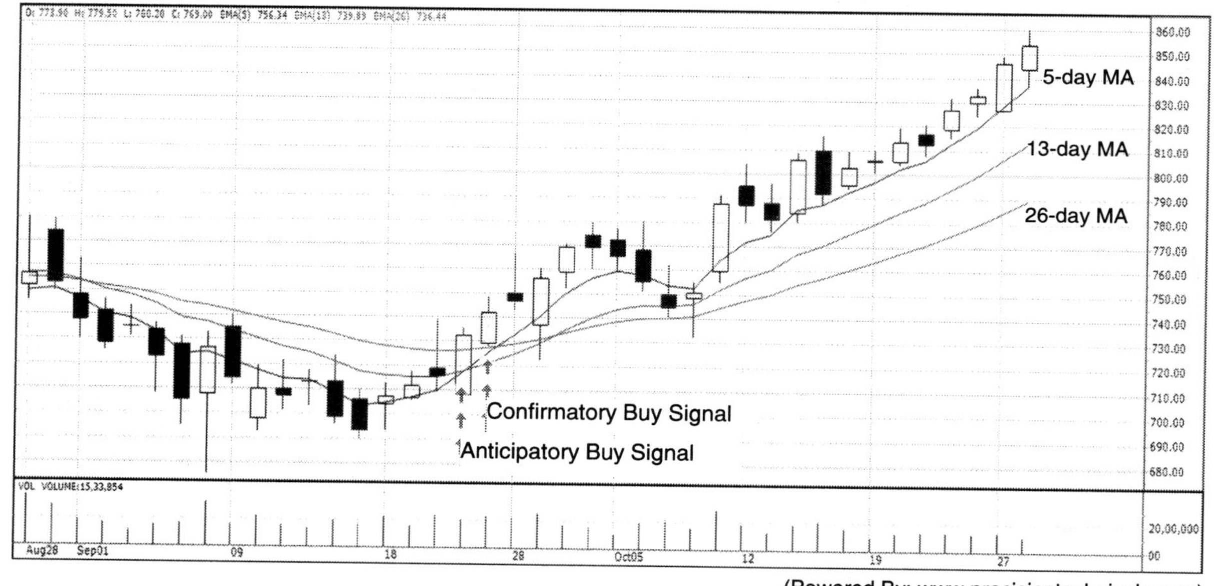

Figure 14.2: **Daily chart of Aurobindo Pharma with 5-, 13-, and 26-day exponential moving averages showing a positive crossover**

~

Now, with three different time period averages plotted on a chart, you will be able to see crossovers among these averages as the price moves up and down. Another important thing to keep in mind is that the smallest average will always cross over the other time period averages. So in this case it will always be the 5DEMA line which crosses the 13DEMA and 26DEMA lines.

When the averages cross each other and tend to move up, we call it a positive crossover (see Figure 14.2), and when they cross each other and move downward we call it as a negative crossover (see Figure 14.3).

There can be a total of three types of crossovers which can happen when we use this combination. But for us only the first two crossovers are important because signal from the third one will be a bit late for one to enter a trade.

- The first one is when the 5DEMA line crosses the 13DEMA line.
- The second is when the 5DEMA line crosses the 26DEMA line.
- The third one is when 13DEMA crosses the 26DEMA.

Let's now consider the practical use of these crossovers.

Anticipatory Crossover

The first type of crossover occurs when the price changes its trend from down to up and is called an anticipatory crossover. In this case, the 5DEMA line crosses the 13DEMA line from below and heads upward (*see* Figure 14.2). This is considered an initial buy signal, which means you should enter 30% of the total quantity you want to buy of the stock at this point. This helps in reducing the risk involved in the trade to as low as 30% if the signal fails and the stop loss is triggered. The advantage in entering 30% of the total quantity at this stage is that you get to enter the stock when it is on the verge of changing its trend.

Confirmatory Crossover

As the price moves up higher after an anticipatory crossover, the 5DEMA line then crosses the 26DEMA line generating a confirmatory buy (*see* Figure 14.2). Upon the occurrence of this crossover, we add the balance 70% quantity to the trade.

This strategy helps us in entering the trade after the trend is confirmed. To further reduce risk, use this strategy in combination with other strategies which we will be discussing in the later chapters.

Sell Signal Strategies

In the case of a sell signal strategy, too, we will be using the same combination of averages. This time they would be generating a downward crossover. This occurs when there is profit booking after an uptrend, leading the price to correct — in such a case, fall.

There are two things which could happen in a correction:

- The stock price may correct (fall) some percentage of its earlier rise or earlier up trend; or
- The price may change its trend altogether, and change into a down trend.

When such a move first starts it is difficult to judge whether it is a correction or a change of trend. Therefore, it is better for a chartist to be cautious about the nature of the price change and not jump to any premature conclusion.

Anticipatory Crossover

After an upward rally when the 5DEMA line crosses the 13DEMA line on the downside, namely from above, it generates an anticipatory sell. This is a signal suggesting that we sell 30% of the quantity we hold. This helps us in staying with the trend while waiting for further confirmation about whether this is just a correction or a complete trend change.

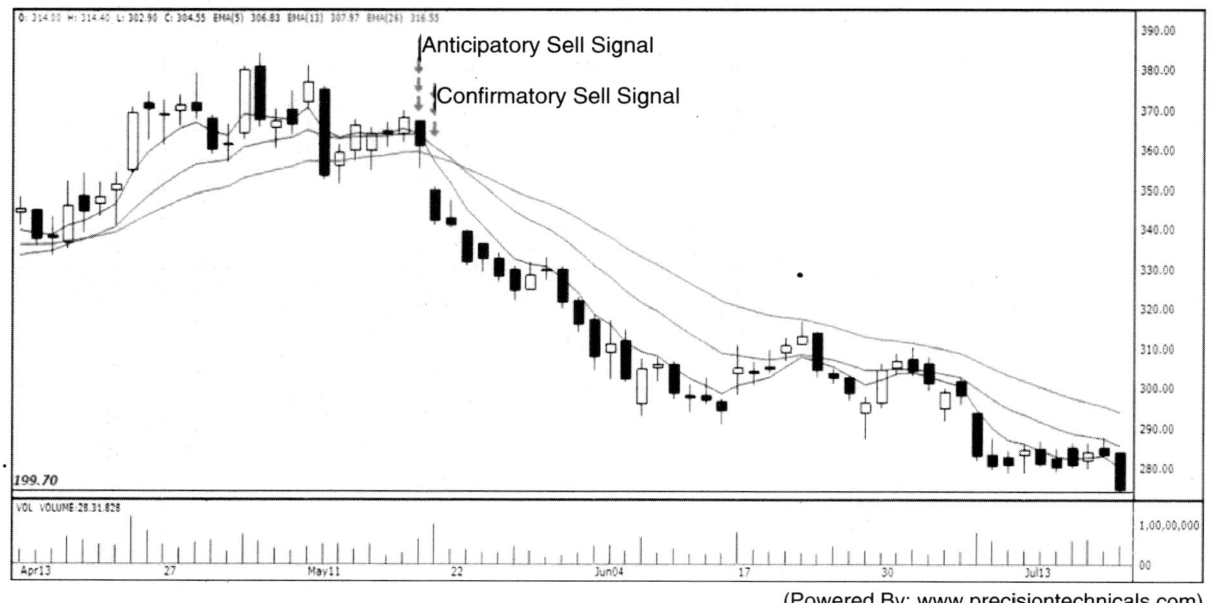

(Powered By: www.precisiontechnicals.com)

Figure 14.3: **Daily chart of Tata Steel with 5-, 13-, and 26DEMAs showing a negative crossover and the resulting anticipatory and confirmatory sell signals**

~

So even if the stock price just corrects the earlier up move, and then again starts to move in the direction of the earlier up trend, you do not lose out on the opportunity since you continue to hold the rest of the 70% quantity. This is displayed in the chart in Figure 14.3.

Confirmatory Crossover

When the 5DEMA line crosses the 26DEMA line on the downside, it suggests that the chances of the price moving down, or not immediately making a new top, are now high. This is a confirmatory crossover for the sell strategy. On this crossover, you can sell the rest of the 70% of the quantity.

If the price had displayed a big rally before such a crossover, then normally the price will tend to consolidate sideways, or downward, for an approximate period of 6 months.

Sangam (Confluence) Strategy

This strategy works on crossovers of all the three averages. Remember, in the first two strategies we considered only two types of crossovers. **The Sangam Strategy uses all the three moving average lines crossing one another at one single point or period.** This happens only very rarely, but when it does occur the price typically makes a sharp move from thereon. Buy or sell is based on the direction in which the averages are moving after the crossover. Another important point in this strategy is that we do not get the 30% and 70% entry and exit signals. Instead, the trade would have to be entered or exited with full quantity when the crossover happens. The signal of the trade will depend on whether it is a positive crossover or a negative crossover. A positive crossover would be a buy signal, while a negative crossover would be a sell signal.

Positive Sangam

All averages crossing at one point moving upwards is a Positive Sangam, as displayed in the chart in Figure 14.4.

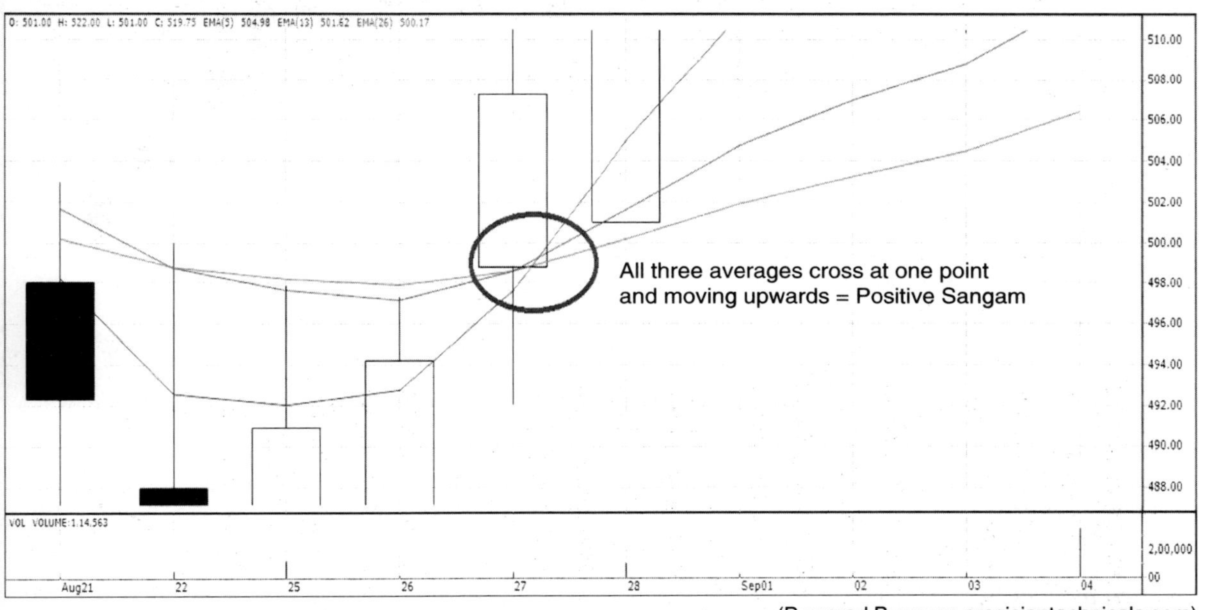

(Powered By: www.precisiontechnicals.com)

Figure 14.4: **Positive Sangam: Daily chart of Gujarat Flouro with 5-13-26 positive crossover at one point, after which the price heads up**

~

Negative Sangam

All averages crossing at one point moving downwards is a Negative Sangam. This is illustrated in Figure 14.5.

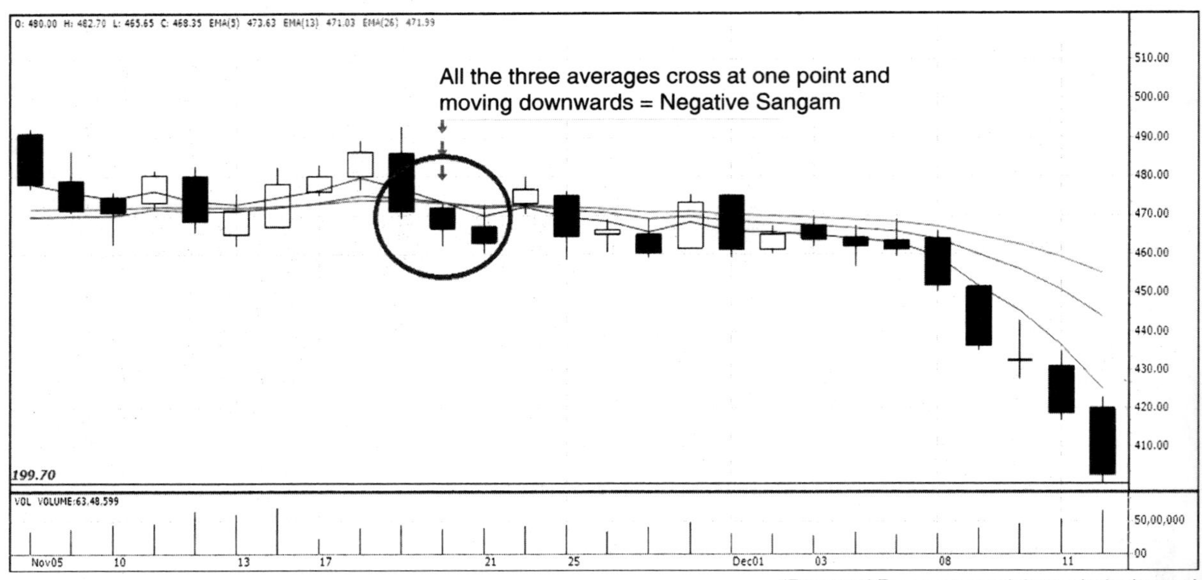

(Powered By: www.precisiontechnicals.com)

Figure 14.5: **Negative Sangam: Daily chart of Tata Steel with 5-13-26 negative crossover at one point after which all three averages head down. So does the price**

~

Quiz: Moving Averages

Questions

1. Moving averages help us judge the trend of a stock price. (True / False?)
2. Short term moving averages are those which are plotted for less than 50-time periods. (True / False?)
3. Long term moving averages can be used as support and resistance levels. (True / False?)
4. Exponential moving averages work well for short term triggers using crossovers. (True / False?)
5. What is the proven combination of moving averages used for generating buy and sell signals?
6. In an anticipatory crossover, which moving averages cross each other?
7. In a confirmatory crossover, which moving averages cross each other?
8. In Sangam strategy, all three averages meet and cross one another at a single point. (True / False?)

Answers

1. True	2. True	3. True	4. True
5. 5, 13, 26	6. 5, 13	7. 5, 26	8. True

MOVING AVERAGES CAN HELP IN GENERATING BUY AND SELL TRIGGERS AND ALSO HELP US STAY ALIGNED WITH THE PRICE TREND.

Chapter 15

~

Trading Candlestick Patterns

IN THE 16TH CENTURY, THE JAPANESE DEVELOPED A METHOD of analysing price movement in rice trading contracts. Today we know this method as the Japanese candlestick way of analysing prices.

Why Candlesticks?

As we discussed in earlier chapters, we prefer Japanese candlesticks charts over other types of charts because:

1. They are easy to use.
2. They use all the four price fields; open, high, low and close.
3. They offer immediate visual interpretation.
4. They help us read the price.
5. They help us understand the way various market participants have positioned themselves.

Basic Types of Candles

Let us briefly recap what we discussed in Chapter 8.

There are two basic types of candles — white and black. Every candle displays one period of data. These candles can be used for plotting charts of different time periods. Thus, you can plot several intraday charts, for example — 1-minute, 2-minute, 3-minute, 5-minute charts — and also end of the period charts for daily, weekly and monthly time periods. The end result of the analysis will differ depending on the time period of the chart interpreted.

White Candle

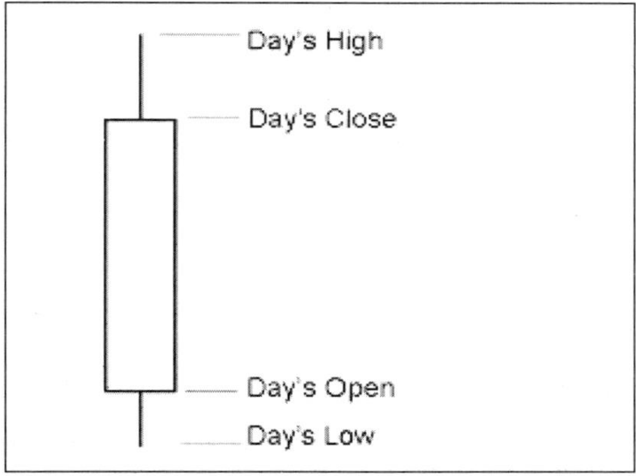

Figure 15.1: **White candle with OHLC marked**

A white candle, as displayed in Figure 15.1, is a bullish candle. It is formed in a period when the close is higher than the open. It suggests that during that period, buying was more aggressive than the selling.

The open and close help form the body of the candle. The difference between the open and low, or the close and high, is marked with a line which is called shadow or stick.

~

Black Candle

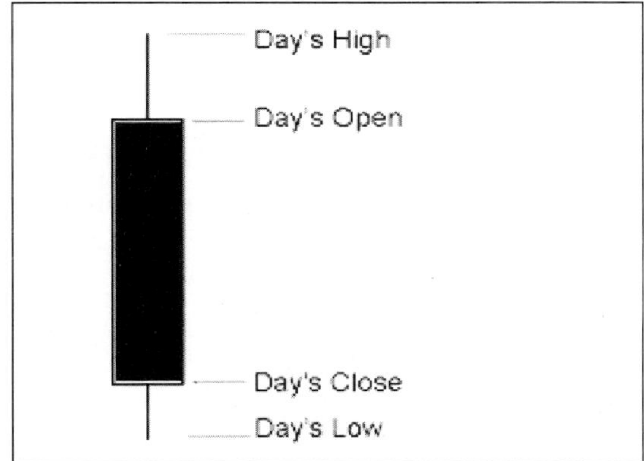

Figure 15.2: **Black candle with OHLC marked**

A black candle, as displayed in Figure 15.2, is a bearish candle. Here the close is lower than the open, indicating that selling was more aggressive than the buying during this period.

The open and close help form the body of the candle, the difference between the open and high, or the close and low, is marked with a line which is called shadow or stick.

~

Important Levels in a Candle

Every candle is shaped by, and represents, the sentiments of the buyers and the sellers. We know that every candle is made up of four price fields, namely — open, high, low and close. But when it comes to identifying the important levels in a candle, the mid-point of the body also plays a crucial role. Called the median, this level is a point where sentiments are either shifting from bullish to bearish, or from bearish to bullish. As such, this level acts as both good support and resistance, as the case may be. The five levels, namely O, H, L, C and the median strong can be identified in all candles which have reasonable sized bodies, namely a candle in which the difference between the open and the close is more than 0.5% of the stock's price.

The reasoning is that if the buyers or the sellers are strong enough then they should be able to make a sustainable move and, consequently, the price difference between the open and the close will be more than 0.5% of the stock's price. If this is not so, it would mean that neither the buyers nor the sellers were able to influence the direction of the stock's price, due to which reason the price did not create a significant difference between its open and close. But if difference between the open and close is significant, then the fifth level, which is the median, gains importance.

These five candle levels can be used as support and resistance and can also be helpful in implementing risk management as highlighted in Figure 15.3, both for a white as well as a black candle.

For a white candle, all levels below the close are support levels, while all levels above the close are always resistance levels. So:

- In the case of a white candle, we have 3 support levels and 1 resistance level.
- Just the opposite of this is true for the black candle. Thus, in a black candle we have 1 support level and 3 resistance levels.

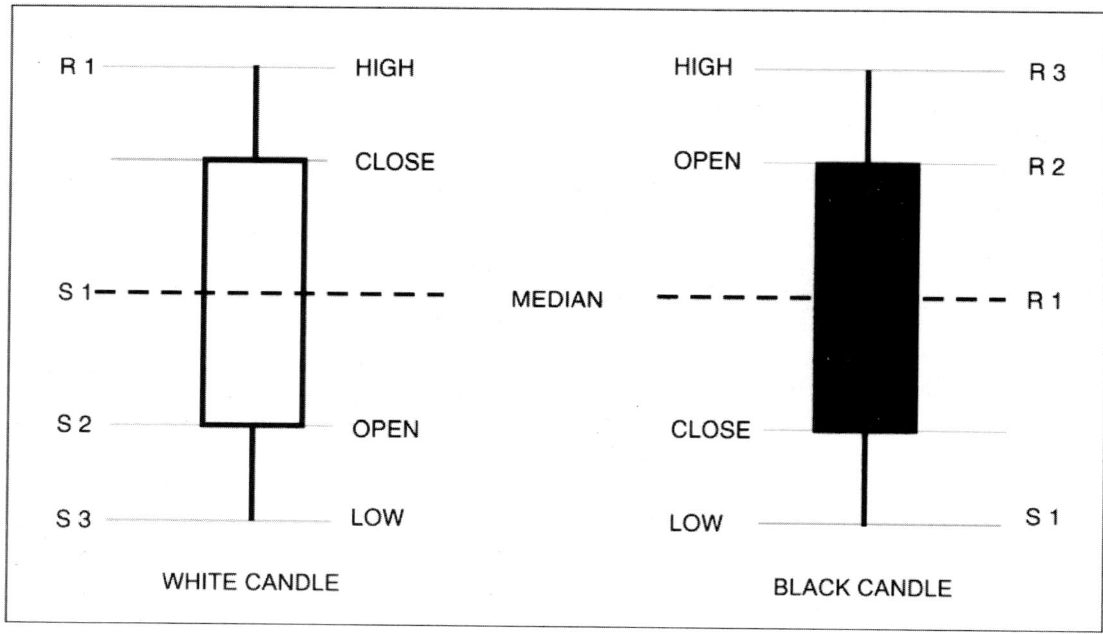

Figure 15.3: **White (hollow) and black (filled) candles with the support and resistance levels marked**

These levels can be seen in the chart in Figure 15.3, where they are marked as S1, S2, S3 for the three support levels, and R1, R2, R3 for the three resistance levels.

To summarise:

- A white / hollow / buying candle has:
  - 3 support levels, marked S1, S2, S3, respectively on Figure 15.3
  - 1 resistance level, marked R1 on Figure 15.3.
- A black / filled / selling candle has:
  - 1 support level, marked S1 on Figure 15.3
  - 3 resistance levels, marked R1, R2, R3, on Figure 15.3.

Later in the book we will learn how to interpret these levels and understand their practical utility in trading.

Interpretation of Candlesticks

The interpretation of candlesticks is based on patterns. When formed, these patterns tell us the aggressiveness of buyers and sellers in a particular stock. They also tell us about the way buyers and sellers have positioned themselves in the stock. These candlestick patterns, or formations, can be categorized as follows:

1. Neutral candlestick patterns;
2. Bullish candlestick patterns; and
3. Bearish candlestick patterns.

Neutral Candlestick Patterns

These are candlestick patterns which suggest that both buyers and sellers are unsure about the future direction of the stock price. The indecisiveness can be due to various reasons, such as a sharp rise or fall in the price, or uncertainty created by an upcoming event or development.

Important Criteria to Remember

1. **A difference of less than 0.5% between a candle's open and close price indicates indecision.** Neutral or indecision candles do not have a median. The logic is that if the buyers are strong, they should be able to take the price higher. On the other hand, if the sellers are strong, they should be able to lower the price. If neither of these two conditions are met, then the result is indecision.

2. **When a candle has shadows / sticks, whether on its top or at its bottom, which are larger than the size of its body, then again it indicates indecision.** The reason is that a shadow is a retracement of the price from a particular level. If this retracement is bigger than the size of the body, it means that there is not enough price strength for the candle to be a bullish or a bearish one.

Some neutral candles are neutral or indecision candles on a standalone basis, while others are neutral in conjunction with another candle as a pair. Below we discuss some of the important neutral or indecision candles.

Doji

When the open and the close of a candle are at the same level, then the candle is called a Doji. These candles can be of different types based on their shadows / sticks. The names of the variants of a Doji candle can be different. It is important to understand the psychology behind the formation of this candle.

Let us understand these candles by plotting them for the following price fields:

Normal Doji

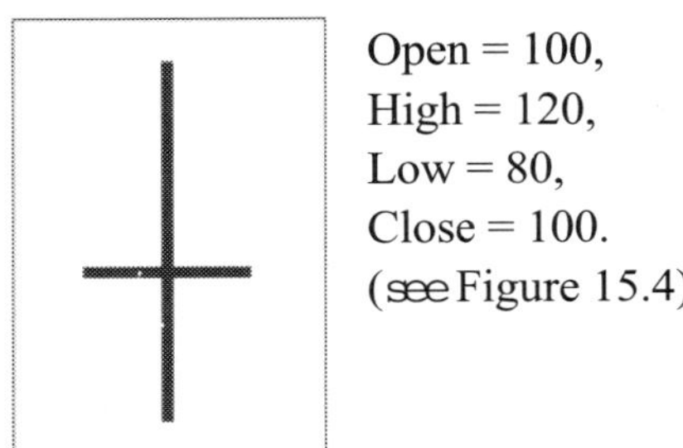

Open = 100,
High = 120,
Low = 80,
Close = 100.
(see Figure 15.4)

Figure 15.4: **Normal Doji**

Long-Legged Doji

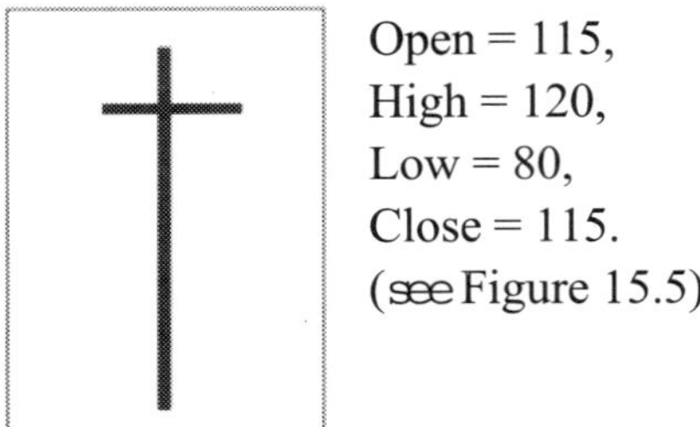

Open = 115,
High = 120,
Low = 80,
Close = 115.
(see Figure 15.5)

Figure 15.5: **Long-legged Doji**

Dragonfly Doji

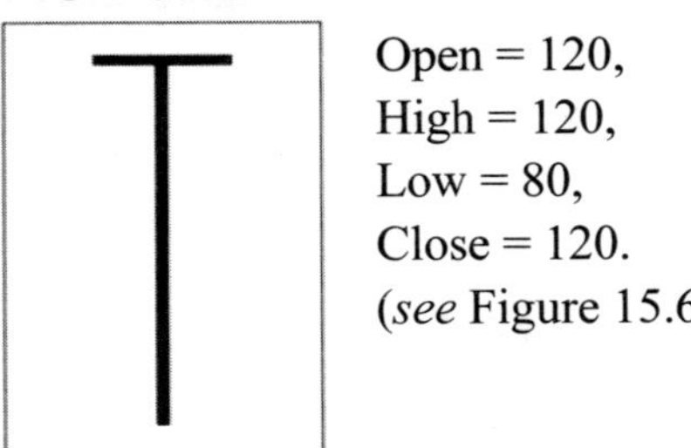

Open = 120,
High = 120,
Low = 80,
Close = 120.
(*see* Figure 15.6)

Figure 15.6:
Dragonfly Doji

Gravestone Doji

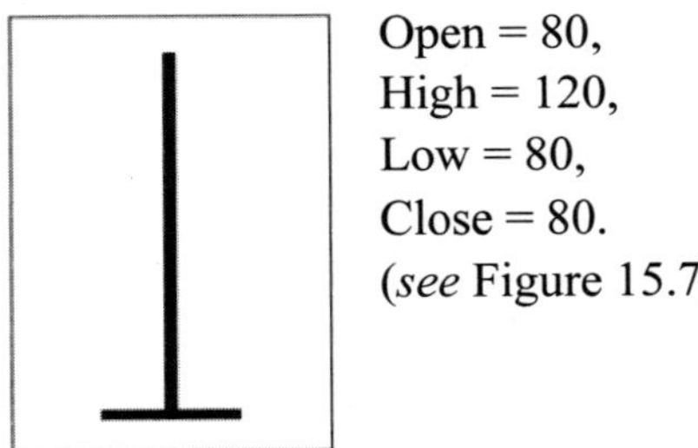

Open = 80,
High = 120,
Low = 80,
Close = 80.
(*see* Figure 15.7)

Figure 15.7:
Gravestone Doji

4-Price Doji

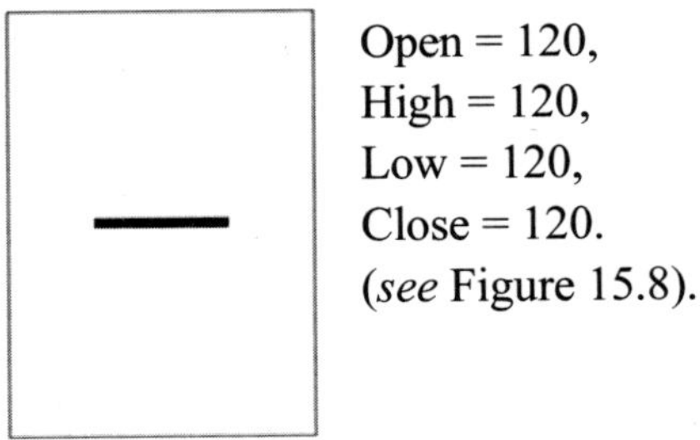

Open = 120,
High = 120,
Low = 120,
Close = 120.
(*see* Figure 15.8).

Figure 15.8:
4-Price Doji

Spinning Top

Such a candle has a small body with shadows of equal size on either side of it. Though spinning top candles have a body, they do not have a median as the difference between the open and the close is less than 0.5% of the stock price. Such a candle is called a spinning top because it looks like one, as you can see in Figure 15.9 and Figure 15.10.

The colour of the candle could be either white (*see* Figure 15.9) or black (*see* Figure 15.10). Irrespective of the colour, a spinning top is an indecision or a neutral candle.

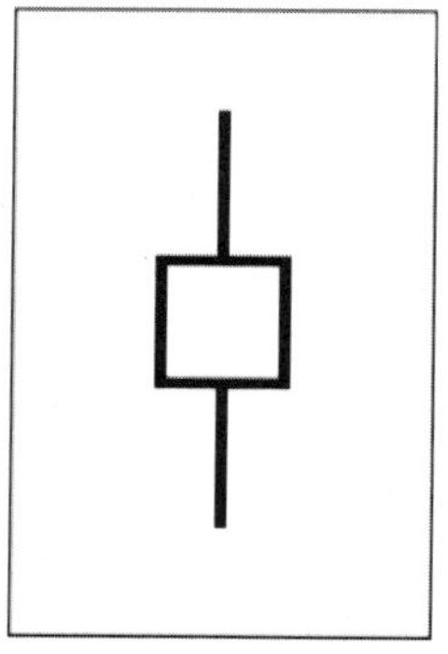

Figure 15.9: **Spinning top (white body)**

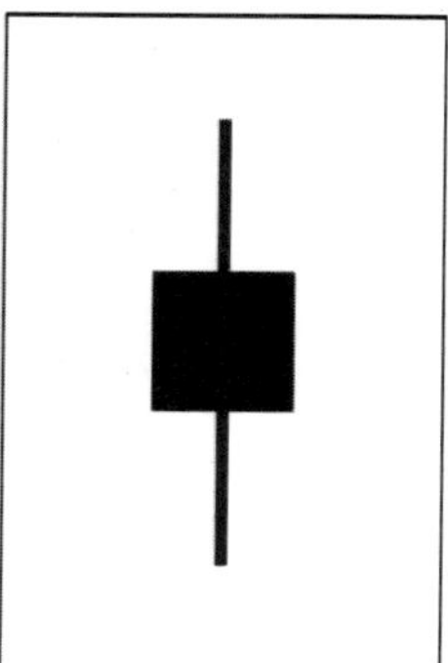

Figure 15.10: **Spinning top (black body)**

~

Long-Legged Candles

When a candle has shadows on both sides, and one of them is either equal to or is longer than the size of the candle's body, then it is a neutral candle. You would recall that the body of a candle is the difference between the open and the close prices. The shadow of a candle tells us that the price had first moved higher, or lower, and later retraced from that level. When the size of the shadow is equal, or longer, than the size of the candle's body, it suggests indecision, as in this case of a long-legged candle.

Figure 15.11 displays candles where the shadows at the bottom of the candle's body are equal to or bigger than the body (white or black) of the candle.

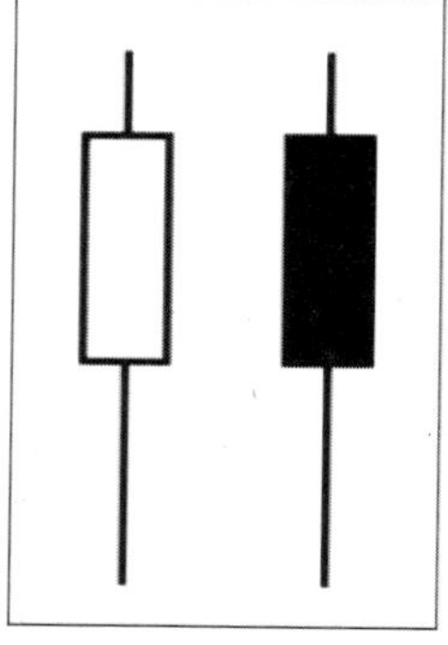

Figure 15.11: **Long-legged candle**

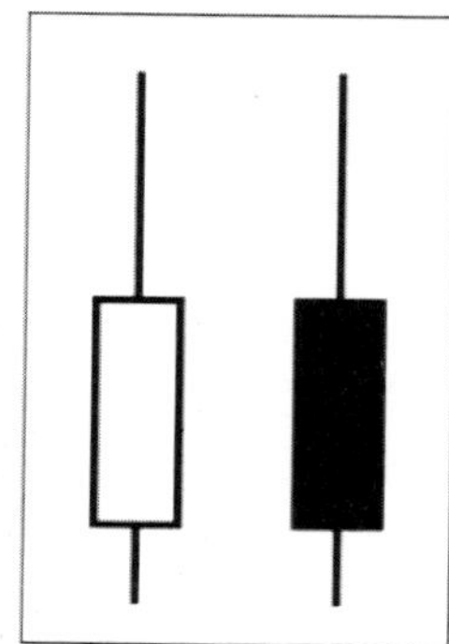

Figure 15.12: **Long-legged candle**

~

Figure 15.12 displays candles where the shadows at the top of the candle's body (white or black) are equal to or bigger than the body of the candle.

Important Levels in Doji Candles

Before we move on to the next indecision candle pattern, let's discuss the important levels in the case of the Doji variety of indecision or neutral candles.

As described earlier, normally there are five important levels in a candle which act as support and resistance: open, high, low, close, and the median. These levels act as support and resistance for the immediate next period. They are helpful on all the different time period charts that traders analyse.

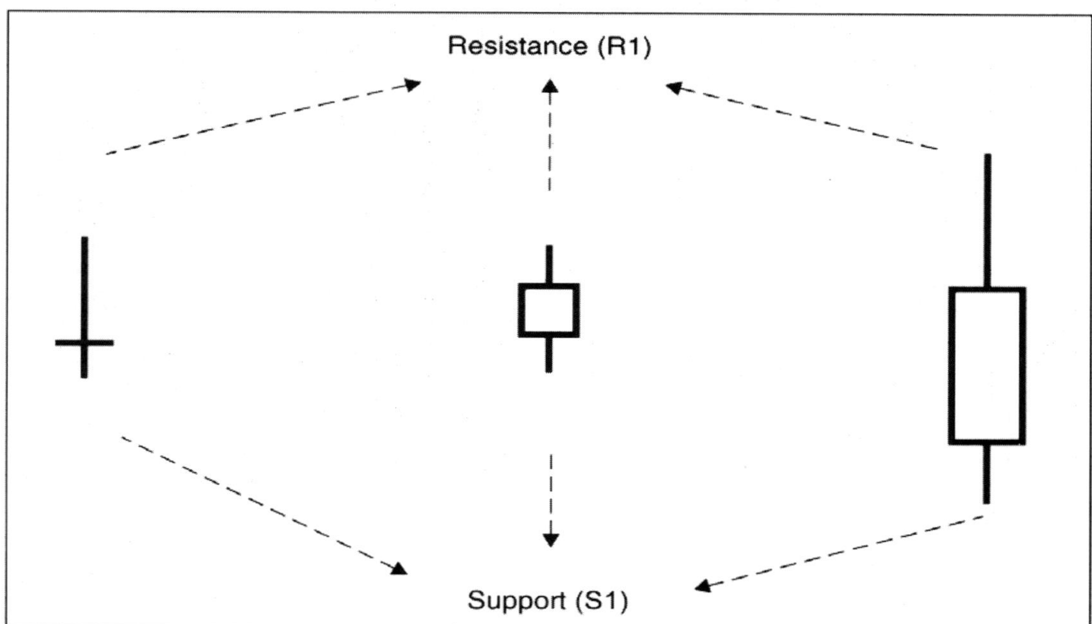

Figure 15.13: **There are only two support and resistance levels for neutral candles, the high and the low**

~

It is important to know that in the case of Doji indecision or neutral candles there are only two important levels, namely the candle's high and its low. So the candles that we have seen so far, namely spinning tops and the long legged candles, which belong to the doji family of candles, all have two important levels, which are the high and the low as shown in Figure 15.13.

The support and resistance levels are a bit different in case of the Harami pattern, which we shall consider next.

Harami Candles

Harami in Japanese means pregnant. This formation is a combination of two successive candles. When seen in combination the two candles have the appearance of a woman carrying a baby in her womb, and therefore the name.

In the Harami candle formation, the first candle's body will always be bigger than that of the second candle. The open and close of the second candle will be within the open and close of the earlier candle. The body of the second candle lies entirely within the range of the earlier candle's body. The colour combinations of the candles could be white-black, white-white, black-white, or black-black as shown in Figure 15.14.

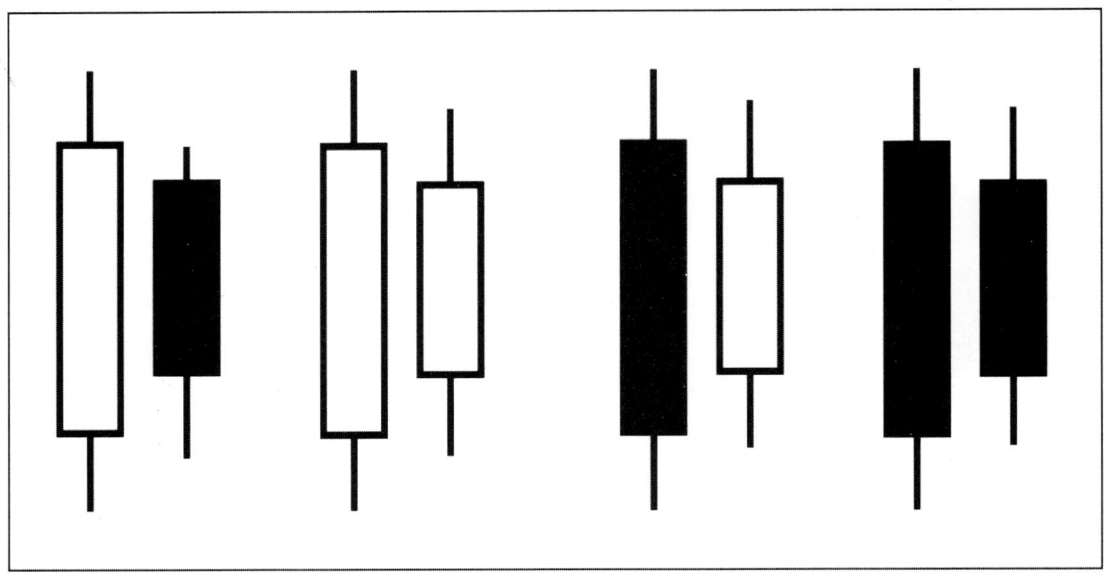

Figure 15.14: **Four different Harami candle combinations**

~

Conditions for Harami Candle Formation

1. The main body of the Harami pattern candle should be sizeable — bigger in comparison to the regular candles.
2. The Harami candle should have significantly higher volume when compared to its own historical volumes; four times or more than the regular volumes.
3. The body of the second candle should be smaller and contained within the first / main candle's body. This means that the open and close of the second candle should be within the open and close span of the first candle's main body.

4. It does not matter if the sticks / shadows of the second candle are longer than both the bodies. What is important is that the size of the second candle's body must be smaller, and its span contained within the open and close of the first candle.

Support and Resistance in Harami Formation

As discussed earlier, neutral candles have two important levels which act as support and resistance. Normally these are the high and the low of the neutral candles but in case of the harami pattern these levels are the open and close of the main body or the bigger / main candle. Irrespective of whether the main candle or the first candle is white or black, the upper level is the resistance and the lower level is the support as shown in Figure 15.15.

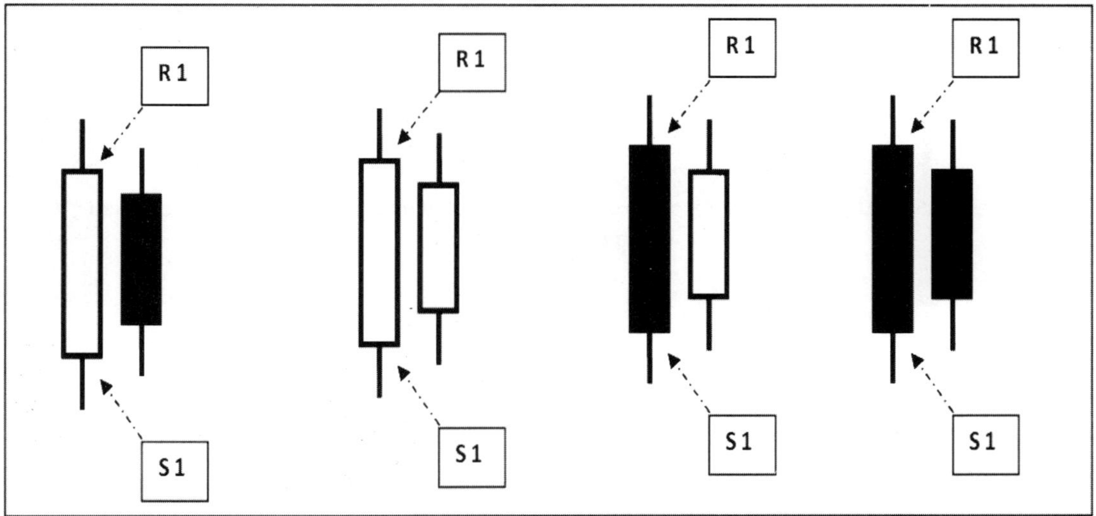

Figure 15.15: **Support and resistance displayed on the four different Harami candle combinations**

~

Trading Neutral Candlestick Patterns

Neutral candle patterns can be used for executing swing or positional trades.

A neutral pattern means that the market's view on the stock concerned is indecisive for the buyer as well as the seller. The logic behind executing a trade using neutral patterns is that the stock price cannot stay neutral, or indecisive, forever. Sooner or later, a future direction emerges and, whenever it does, it offers us an opportunity to enter a trade in that direction.

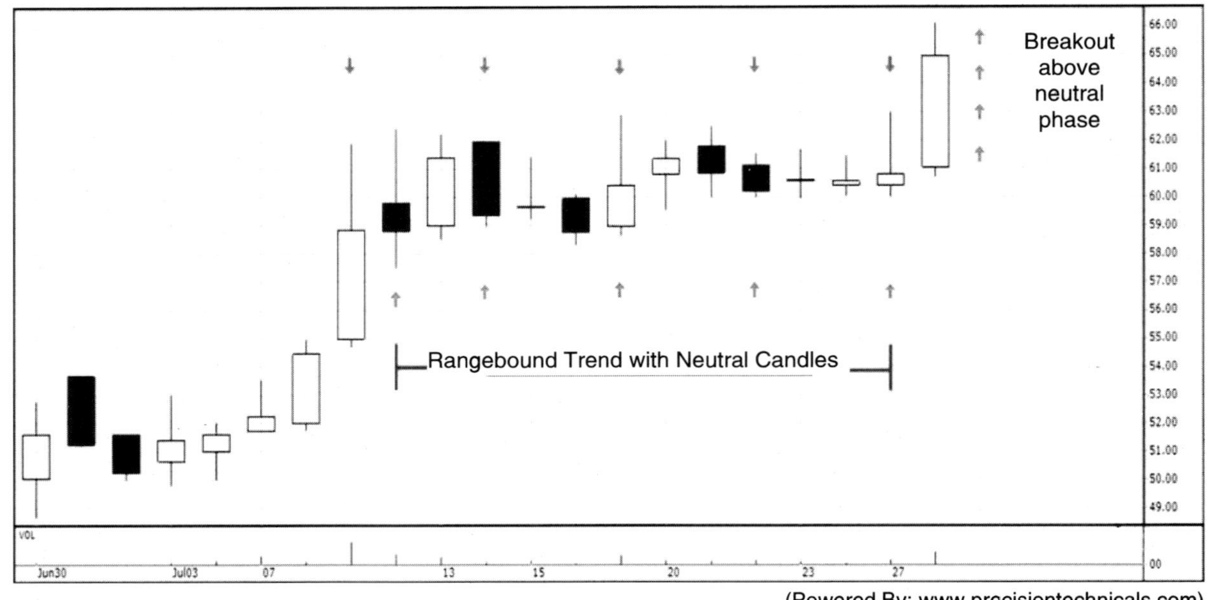

(Powered By: www.precisiontechnicals.com)

Figure 15.16: **Daily candlestick chart of Time Techno with indecision candles, followed by an upward breakout**

~

Let's consider some examples.

In the chart in Figure 15.16 you can see a period labelled "Rangebound Trend with Neutral Candles." This period has also been highlighted using arrows pointing upward and downward, a period where the price is moving sideways with most of the candles being neutral. After this phase, you will notice a white candle which has moved above the neutral range. This means the price has now gathered the strength to move upwards after having gone through a phase where buyers and sellers were indecisive. Finally, thus, the buyers have overpowered the sellers. Execution of a long trade at this point would carry a known and calculated risk.

~

In the chart in Figure 15.17 you can clearly see the sideways trend during which most candles were neutral. In the chart this period is labelled as "Rangebound Trend with Neutral Candles." Finally, the price decides to head down, signifying that after an indecisive phase the sellers have overpowered the buyers to generate a downward breakout. This becomes an opportunity to initiate a trade on the short side with calculated and known risk.

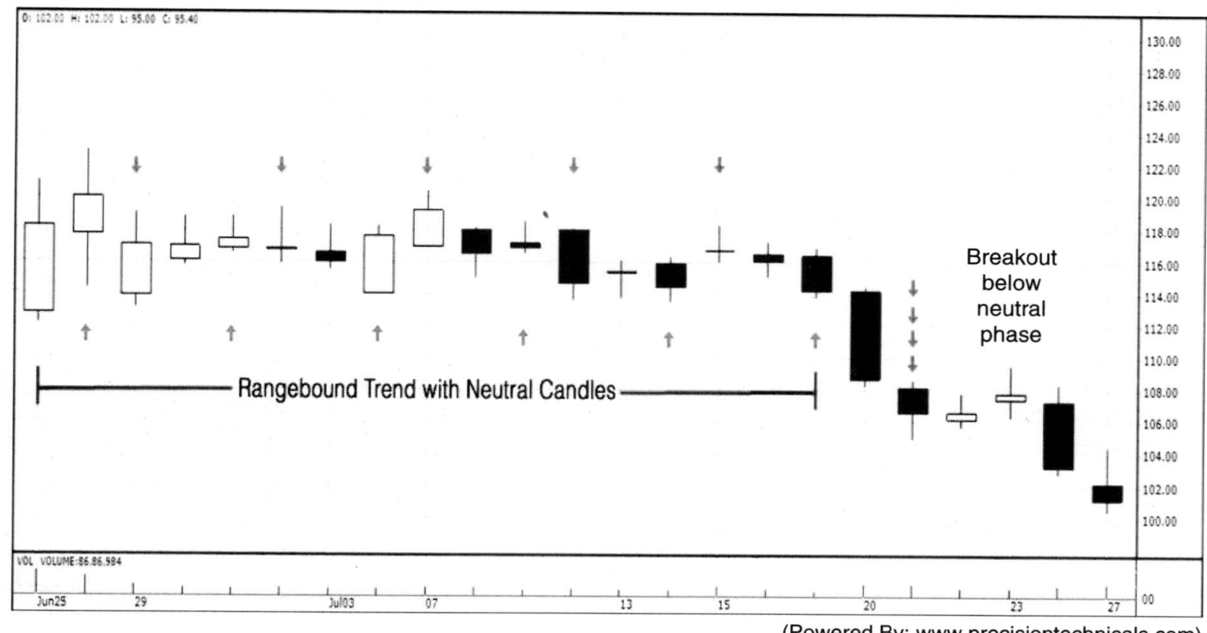

(Powered By: www.precisiontechnicals.com)

Figure 15.17: **Daily candlestick chart of DLF with indecision candles followed by a downward breakout**

~

The strategy displayed in Figure 15.16 and Figure 15.17 is suitable for trading when regular neutral candles are formed for consecutive periods one after the other. **The strategy works very nicely for a day trader on the 5-minute chart, for a positional trader and short term investor on a daily time period chart, and for an investor using weekly and monthly charts.**

~

Another candlestick formation which can be used for positional trading and short term investment is the Harami pattern. There is a small difference, though, in the way a harami pattern is traded. Let us understand the strategy with the help of an example.

In the chart in Figure 15.18, you can see the price of Adani Enterprises rising from levels of ₹200 to make highs of approximately ₹400. Then, on the last candle, there is an abnormal rise both in price and trading volume. The stock price on that day jumped up by approximately 25% and the volume by a factor of ten over the average historically traded volumes. Normally, you would take this to be an extremely bullish day as can be seen in the chart.

The chart in Figure 15.18 shows only the first day of the Harami pattern, represented by the big white candle on the extreme right. Remember, the Harami pattern is made up of two candles and so long as the second candle does not form within the body of the first candle you don't yet know whether this may become a Harami. For that confirmation, we need to wait for the next candle to form.

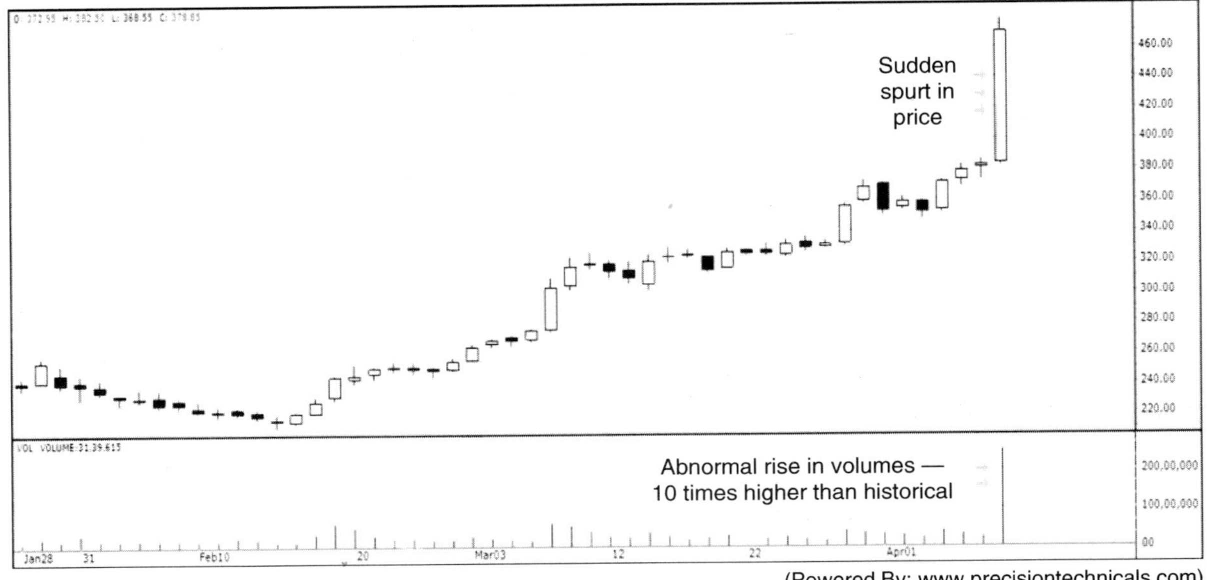

Figure 15.18: **Daily candlestick chart of Adani Enterprises. The candle on the extreme right is the first of the two Harami candles.**

~

Important: Always build a cautious outlook on a chart when the price displays this kind of an abnormal move — a big price rise accompanied by an abnormal rise in volumes. Many a time this can happen due to short covering plus panic buying by those who feel that they have missed an opportunity. Don't, therefore, be tempted to jump into a trade when you see something like this happening on the price chart, without waiting for a proper confirmation.

When trading starts the next day, market participants are confused as to whether the rally will continue further or fizzle out. This leads to participants not being able to make up their mind, and the next candle which comes up looks like the last one in the chart in Figure 15.19.

In the chart in Figure 15.19 you can clearly see that the last candle is a small black candle which has opened and closed within the span of the open and close of the earlier candle. Now this is clearly a Harami pattern.

Your eureka moment of finding a pattern like this is only after you have validated and confirmed it on the chart. For this, you need to check the following two things:

1. The first / main candle must be a big candle with abnormal volumes.
2. The body of the second candle should be contained within the first candle's body. Volumes on the second candle need not be monitored.

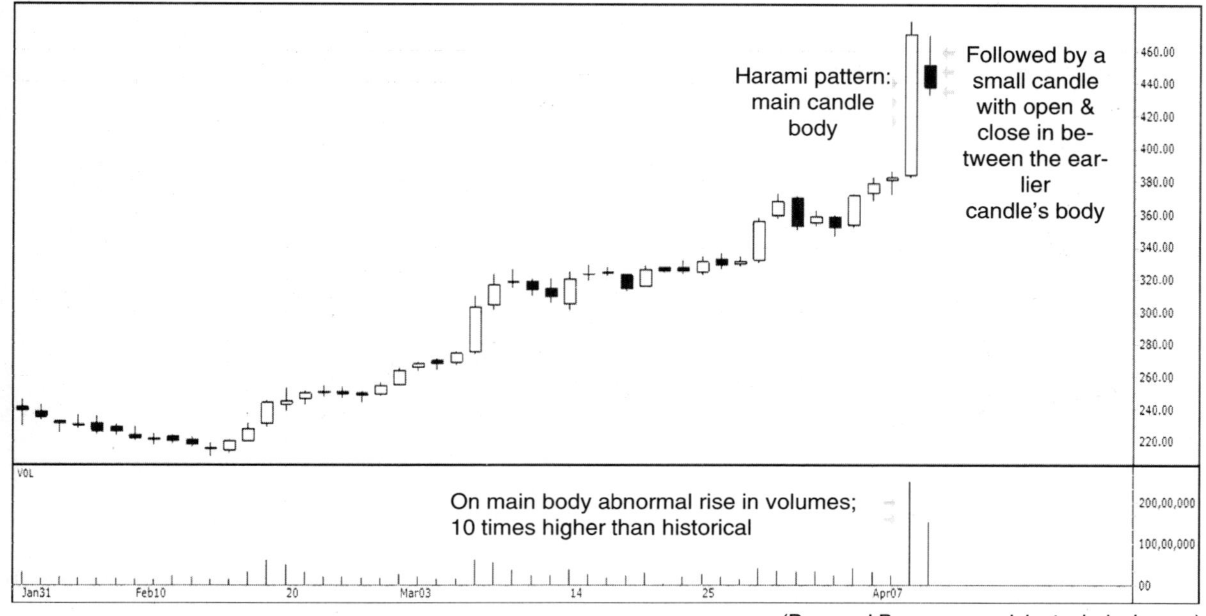

(Powered By: www.precisiontechnicals.com)

Figure 15.19: **Daily candlestick chart of Adani Enterprises which displays the Harami pattern — first, an unusually large candle, followed by a candle smaller than the first candle's body, both accompanied by obviously large volumes.**

~

These two criteria confirm a Harami pattern. You might be wondering why I have been referring to this as a eureka moment. You will understand this when I show you the opportunity which this pattern offers to day traders, positional and swing traders, as well as to short term investors.

But let us first see another example of the Harami pattern.

~

In the chart in Figure 15.20, you can see that the last candle is a big black candle, suggesting that the price has witnessed a sharp fall. The second thing that can be observed is the abnormal rise in volume on that candle.

Important: Looking at a big black candle with abnormal volume should make you cautious rather than immediately bearish. **Normally after a big move, the next candle which comes up is usually a neutral candle.** This means that when you see something like this on the price chart, you should wait for the second candle to form before you arrive at a conclusion.

In the chart in Figure 15.21, you can see that the body of the second candle that has formed is confined within the span of the first big candle's body. This is now a Harami pattern. But, remember, your eureka moment is only after this confirmation.

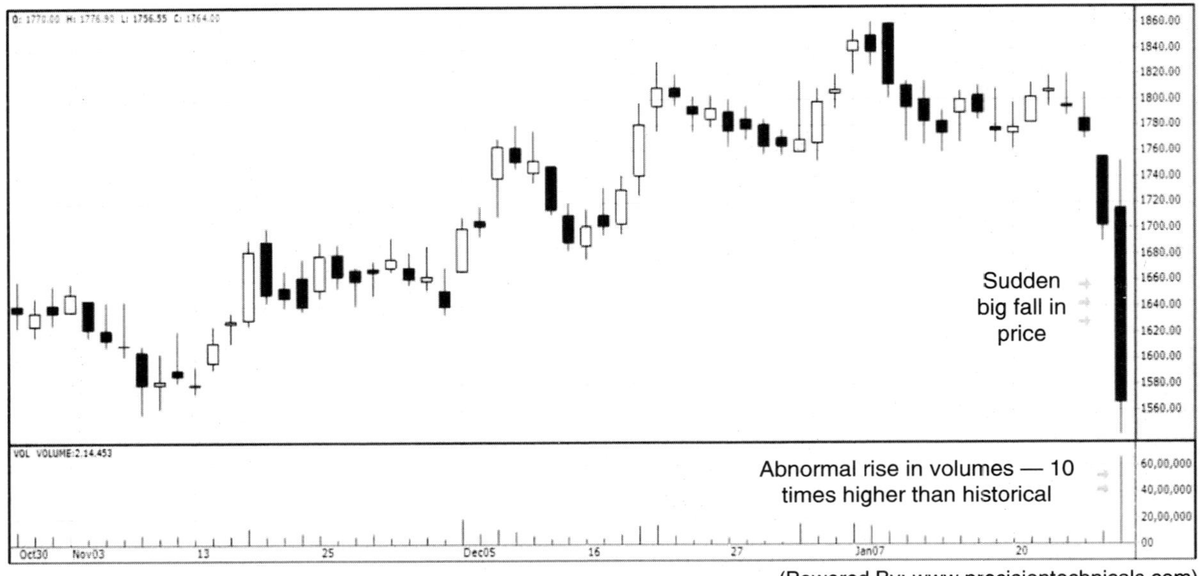

(Powered By: www.precisiontechnicals.com)

Figure 15.20: **Daily candlestick chart of Maruti which displays the first candle of the Harami pattern at the extreme right.**

~

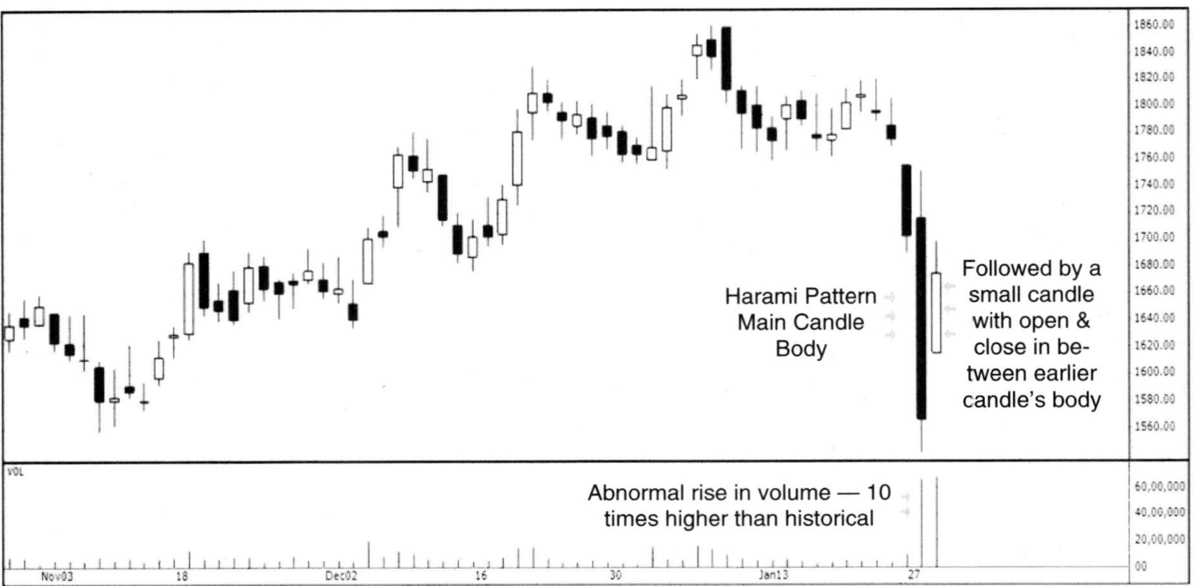

(Powered By: www.precisiontechnicals.com)

Figure 15.21: **Daily candlestick chart of Maruti which displays the completed Harami pattern.**

~

(Powered By: www.precisiontechnicals.com)

Figure 15.22: **Daily candlestick chart of Maruti showing the Harami pattern with horizontal lines indicating the resistance at support levels, at R1 and S1, respectively.**

Trading a Harami Pattern

When a Harami pattern is confirmed with the help of the criteria discussed above, the next thing you need to do is mark the pattern's resistance and support, namely mark the levels R1 and S1, with horizontal lines. In the chart in Figure 15.22, you will be able to see two levels marked using horizontal lines — one for resistance and the second for support.

The next thing that you have to do is wait for the price to decide its direction by way of a breakout and close either above the resistance or below the support. On a daily time period chart, this usually occurs anytime between 10 to 40 trading sessions after the Harami pattern's formation.

Important: Earlier we have discussed that when we are looking at a price which is trading between a range we can go long on supports and go short at resistance levels but this logic does not apply to the Harami pattern. The reason is that in the case of the Harami pattern the mood of the buyers and sellers remains confused till the price gives a breakout. The movements of the price between these levels are also very choppy and it is advisable to keep watching the candles patiently, waiting for a breakout to happen.

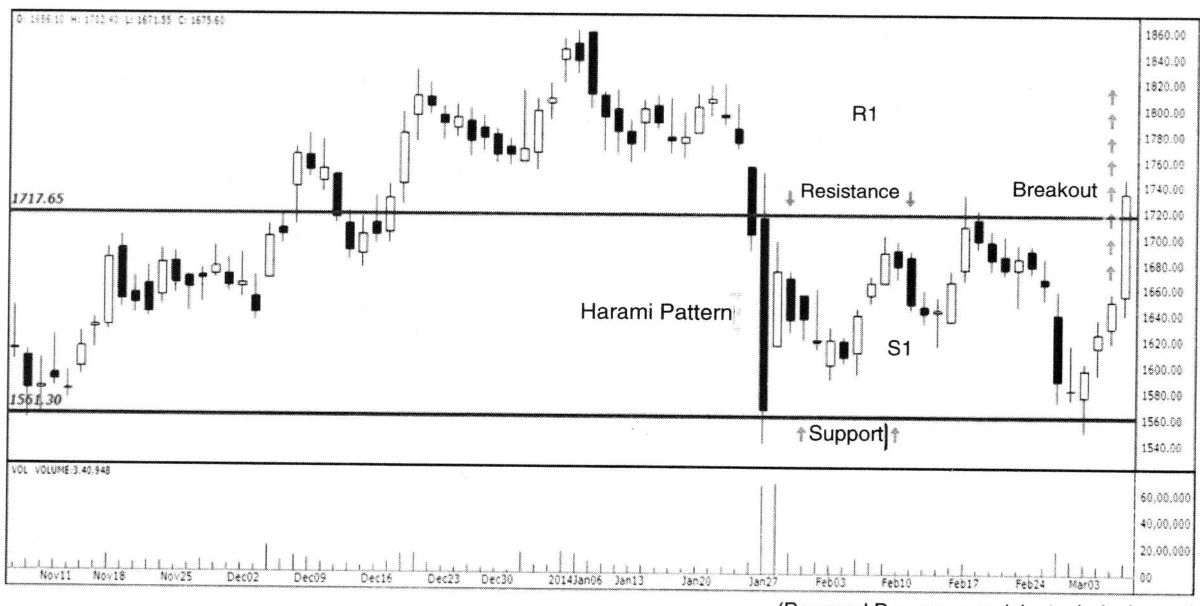

Figure 15.23: **Daily candlestick chart of Maruti showing the Harami pattern with horizontal lines indicating the resistance and support levels at R1 and S1 respectively, followed by an upside breakout.**

~

A few periods later, as the indecisive mood phases out and the price decides upon a direction, the chart would look like the one in Figure 15.23.

In Figure 15.23 you can see the last candle has closed above the resistance, suggesting a breakout. Again, as we have discussed validity and confirmation are two important aspects to always look out for before taking action. The confirmation of a valid breakout in such a case will be based on volumes. This means we need to check the volume on the breakout candle and compare it with those on the earlier three candles. If the volume has increased it would mean that it is not only you who is viewing this candle as a breakout but others too are seeing at it as such. With this confirmation, you now have a real eureka moment for initiating a trade using a Harami pattern.

The same logic is applicable if we have a breakout on the lower side, namely below the support. Again you follow the same procedure and then arrive at a decision whether to go short in the stock, or avoid a trade.

This is a complete, different perspective on trading a Harami pattern.

Of course, risk management is important and must be implemented after initiating a trade. We will discuss this in Chapter 18.

With a Harami pattern we have an entry point, or an invitation to get into a trade, but the question which then arises is where to exit the trade. The answers to all these questions will be discussed in the later chapters, and at the end of the book we will also implement all the points discussed in the Trade Selection Ready-Reckoner for arriving at an action plan.

Bullish Candlesticks and Patterns

These are candlesticks and combinations of candles that suggest that the mood of the market participants is bullish, or is turning bullish. At times such a pattern can be in the form of a single candle; at other times it may be in form of multiple candlesticks. These candlestick formations tell us that the buyers are stronger, or that the stock is in demand. The meaningful candles in this type will always have a median, which also means that they would mostly have a sizeable body.

It is also important to understand and remember that bullish candle patterns are especially important when they form either at a possible bottom in a trend, or at an important breakout level.

Prices keep moving up and down all the time, plus they keep moving up and down in trends over a period of time. Due to this, the price creates tops and bottoms when we see a historical chart. This is useful in determining if the price has reacted at an important level, or if it is just a normal movement.

Let us now see the important bullish candlestick patterns.

White Candle (With Sticks / Shadows)

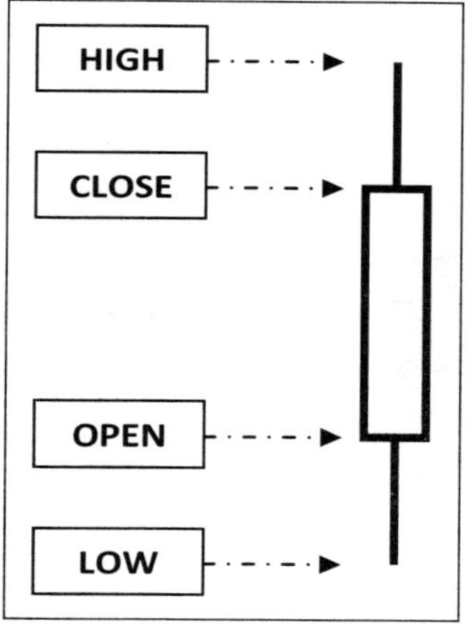

Figure 15.24: **A white / bullish candle with sticks (shadows)**

A white candle, as shown in Figure 15.24, symbolizes buying or demand. It means that buyers have overpowered the sellers and have taken the price up. Since the close is higher than the open, it makes for a white or hollow-body candle. Whether or not this candle has shadows or sticks on the top or at the bottom of the body, it remains a bullish candle.

When we have a white candle, like the one plotted in Figure 15.24, accompanied by an increase in volumes, and if it forms on a crucial support or at an important breakout level, then the importance of the candle increases.

White Candle (Without Sticks / Shadows)

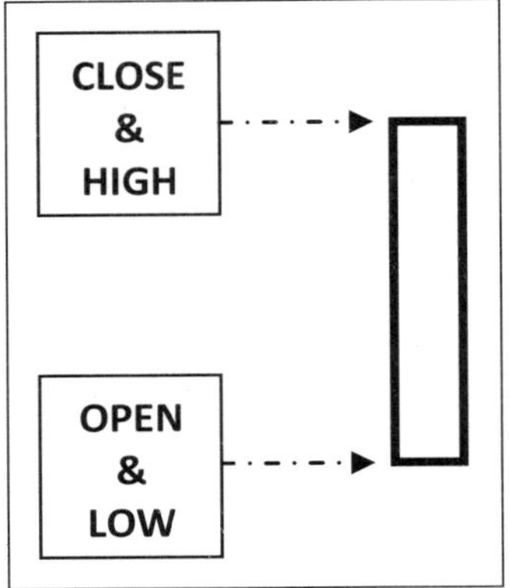

Figure 15.25: **A white / bullish candle without sticks (shadows)**

Such a candle, as shown in Figure 15.25, also symbolises bullishness. As it does not have shadows, this candle is much more bullish than the one in Figure 15.24.

This kind of a candle will form when the price starts moving up from the open without making any new low. So in such a candle the open itself is the period low and then it closes at the period's high. This means that the buyers were strong enough to overpower all the selling during this period. The buyer strength did not allow the price to retrace at all, indicating extreme bullishness.

Bullish Piercing Candle Pattern

If in a down trend we have a white candle which pierces the body of the earlier black candle, namely it closes above the previous black candle's median, it is called bullish piercing (*see* Figure 15.26). This pattern is more effective when it occurs at the end of a down trend, or when it occurs at a crucial support level, or at a breakout level.

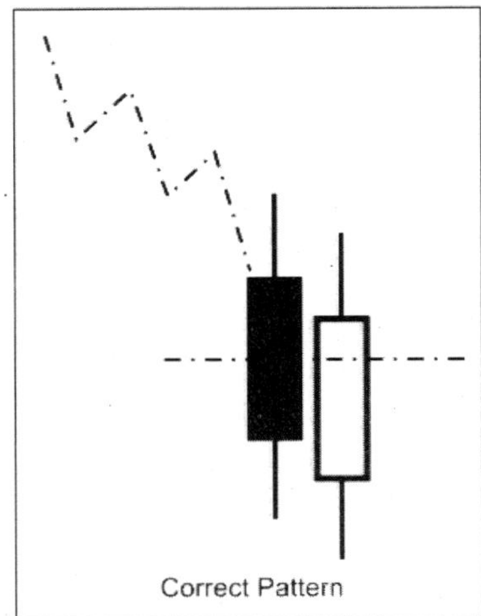

Figure 15.26: **Bullish Piercing (Valid Pattern)**

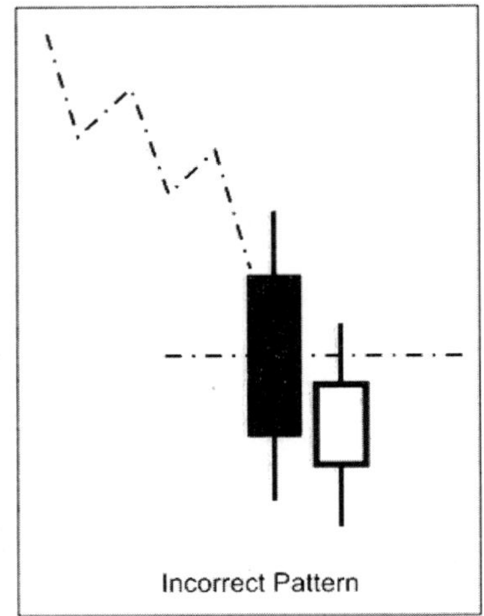

Figure 15.27: **Bullish Piercing (Invalid Pattern)**

Owing to the down trend, selling brings the price down. Then one day the price opens at or below the previous black candle's close, and buying overpowers the selling to take the price back up. Finally, the price closes in between the median and open of the previous black candle.

This means that the bulls have pierced the bears. Remember, however, this logic will work only if the white candle closes above the median, as in Figure 15.26.

If the price fails to close above the median, then the pattern is invalid. This can be seen in Figure 15.27.

Criteria

1. Open of the white candle has to be at or below the close of the earlier black candle.
2. Close of the white candle has to be between the median and the open of the black candle.
3. Higher volume needs to validate the pattern.

Bullish Engulf

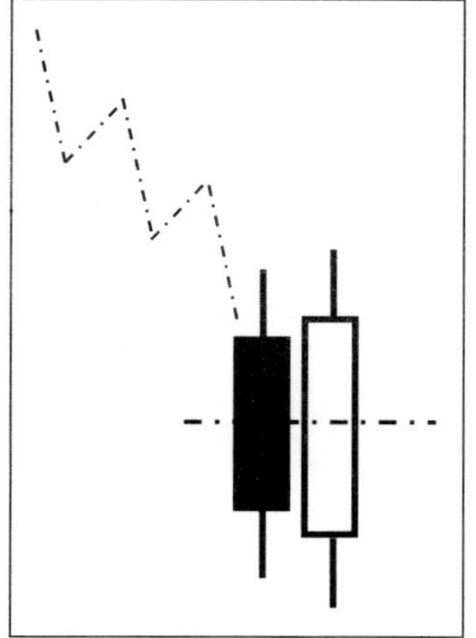

Figure 15.28: **Bullish Engulf**

If, during a down trend, we have a white candle which engulfs the whole of the earlier black candle as shown in Figure 15.28, it is called a bullish engulf.

A bullish engulf can occur anywhere in a trend but is more effective when it forms at the bottom of a trend, or at a crucial support level, or at a breakout level.

This pattern shows that the ongoing selling is forcing the price down. Then one day, even as the price opens at or below the previous day's close, the buying overpowers the selling to take it higher where it closes above the open of the earlier black candle.

In other words, the bulls have engulfed the bears and so the white candle has engulfed the whole of the earlier black candle.

Criteria

1. Open of the white candle has to be at or below the close of the earlier black candle.
2. Close of the white candle has to be above the open of the black candle.
3. Higher volume must validate the pattern.

Hammer at Bottom

This candle is called a hammer because it looks like one, as can be seen in Figure 15.29. As shown in Figure 15.30, such a candle suggests that the price had fallen to a level where it found support and moved up again. For this candle to be effective, it has to be at the bottom of a trend.

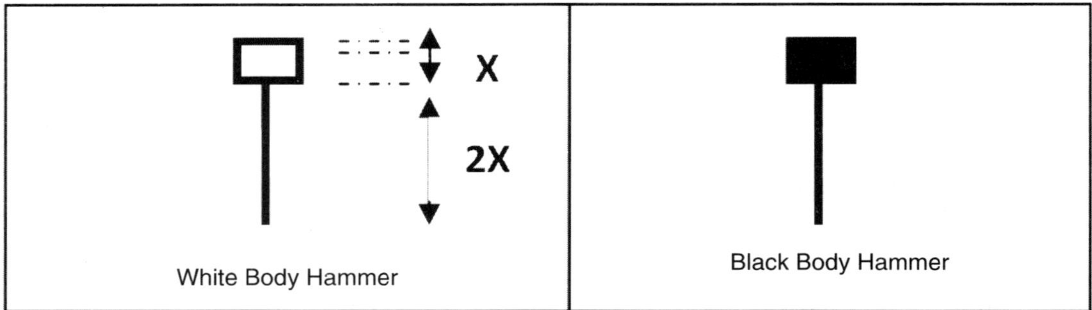

Figure 15.29: **Hammer at bottom**

~

The pattern in Figure 15.31 is invalid because the candle which looks like a hammer does not fulfil the criteria of the stick or the shadow being at least double the size of the body.

Criteria

1. Size of the stick, or shadow, has to be at least double the size of the body for the candle to be valid, as shown in Figure 15.30.
2. Longer the stick, the better is the candle pattern.

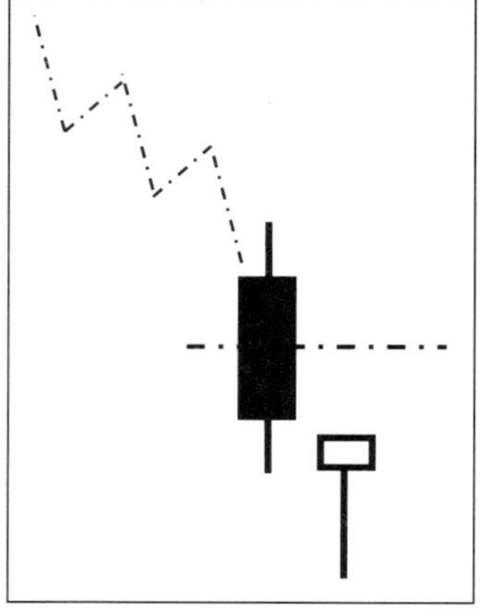

Figure 15.30: **Hammer at bottom (Valid Pattern)**

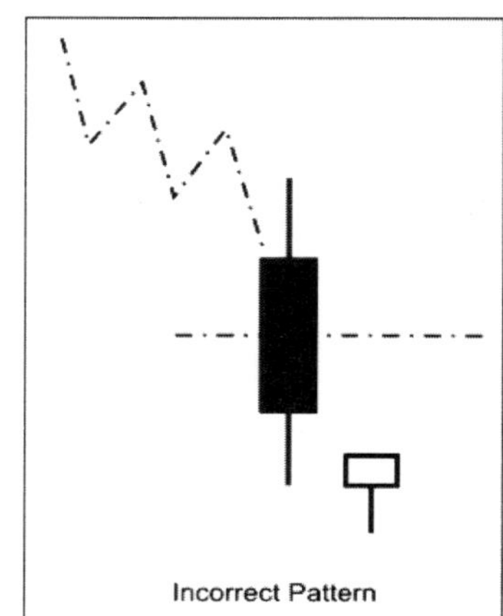

Figure 15.31: **Hammer at bottom (Invalid Pattern)**

~

3. The colour of the body could either be white or black.
4. There should be no stick or shadow on the top of the body, otherwise it will become a neutral candle.
5. Increase in volumes must confirm the importance of that level and candle formation.
6. An effective hammer is one which happens at the end of a down trend.

Morning Star Formation

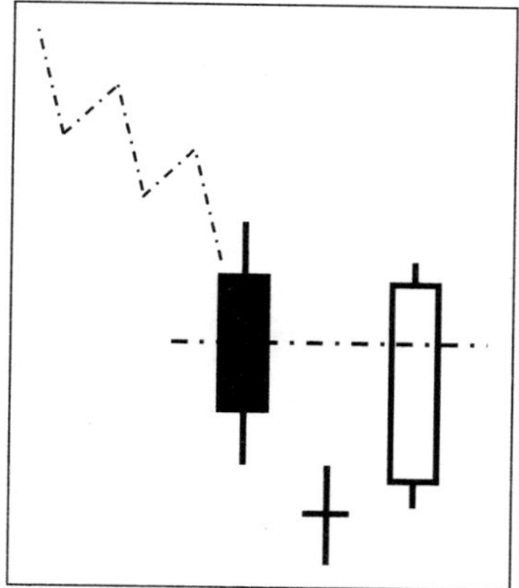

Figure 15.32: **Morning Star**

This pattern comprises of three candles as shown in Figure 15.32. In this pattern we first have the price moving in a down trend. Then there is an indecision or a neutral candle, because the buyers and sellers are confused as to whether the price will bounce back from this level or continue to fall further. After the neutral candle we have a white candle which opens at or below the close of the first black candle and then starts moving up to close above the median of that black candle. This tells us that the sellers are now tired and buyers are regaining strength and could help the stock start an upward move.

Dark candles / black candles symbolize the night, i.e. bad days as the price is falling, while white candles symbolize good days and daylight. So this pattern means that the night is now gone, the neutral candle means the sun has now started to rise, and the white candle is the start of the good day(s).

Criteria

1. Morning star is a three-candle pattern.
2. At the end of a down trend, there has to be a black candle, followed by a neutral candle.
3. The third day's candle opens at or below the close of the first black candle.
4. Close of the white candle (third candle in the three candle formation) has to be above the median of the first black candle.
5. Volumes on the last candle have to validate the pattern.

Bearish Candlestick Formations

These are candlesticks which suggest that the mood amongst market participants is bearish, or is turning bearish. At times this can happen in the form of a single candle, while at other times it can be a multiple candle formation. These candlesticks tell us that there is weakness in the price due to the supply being greater than the demand. The meaningful candles of this type will always have a median, which also means that they would have a sizeable body.

It is important to keep in mind that **bearish candles and bearish candle formations play an important role when they form at possible tops of a trend.**

Let us now see the major candles in the category of bearish candlestick patterns.

Black Candle (With Sticks / Shadows)

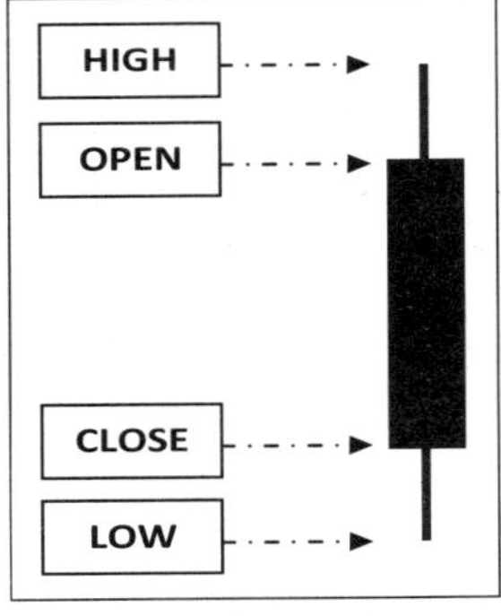

Figure 15.33: **Black / bearish candle with sticks / shadows**

A black candle, as shown in Figure 15.33, stands for selling or supply. A black candle indicates that sellers have overpowered the buyers due to which the price has fallen. A black candle's close is lower than its open and this logic makes it black in colour, or a candle with a filled body. Even if this candle has shadows or sticks on the top and bottom of the body, it continues to be bearish.

This type of a candle becomes particularly important when it forms at the end of a trend, or near a resistance or at a breakout level.

Black Candle (Without Sticks / Shadows)

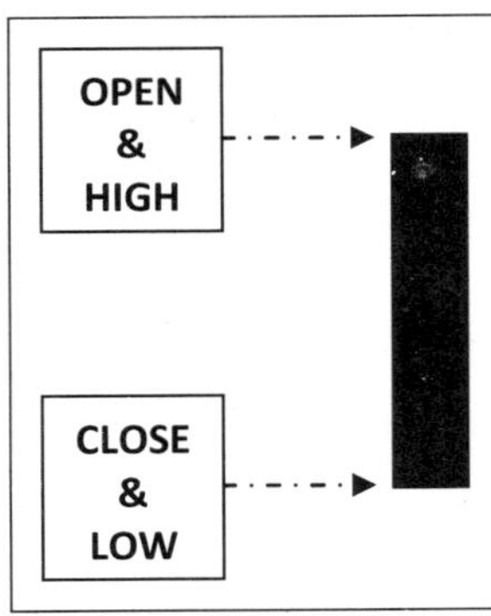

Figure 15.34: **Black / Bearish candle without sticks / shadows**

Such a candle, as shown in Figure 15.34, also symbolizes bearishness. The candle in Figure 15.34 is more bearish when compared to the one in Figure 15.33 as it does not have shadows.

This kind of a candle will form when the price opens at a particular level and then starts moving down without making any new high. So the open itself is the period's high price, and it closes at the day's low. This means that the sellers have overpowered the buyers with strength as there is no retracement in the price during that period. It thus symbolizes extreme bearishness.

Bearish Piercing

When we have a black candle forming in an up trend which pierces the body of the previous white candle on the downside, as shown in Figure 15.35, it is called bearish piercing. Such a candle is more powerful when it occurs at the end of an up trend.

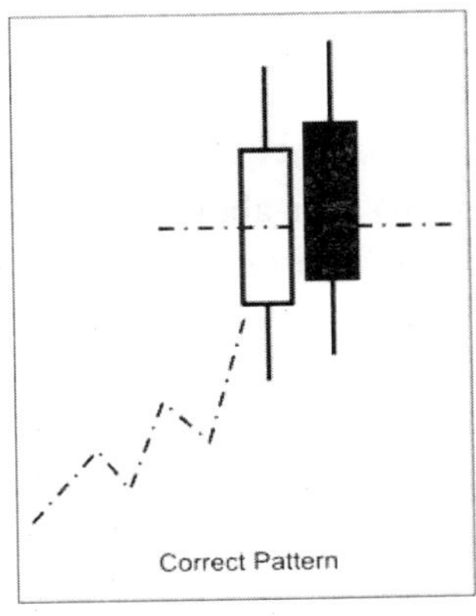

Figure 15.35: **Bearish Piercing (Valid Pattern)**

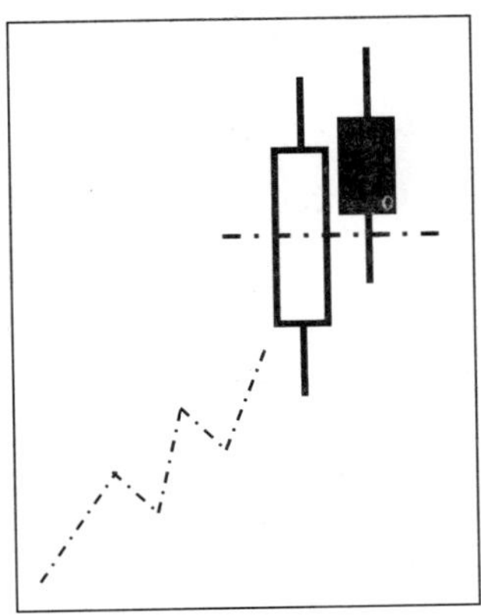

Figure 15.36: **Bearish Piercing (Invalid Pattern)**

~

This pattern shows that the buying, or demand, first took the price up. The next day the price opens at or above the earlier candle close. The selling then overpowers the buying and brings the price down to close in between the median and open of the previous white candle. This signifies that the bears have pierced the bulls.

Please note that this logic will work only if the black candle closes below the median of the earlier white candle. If the price fails to close below the median, the pattern is then not valid (see Figure 15.36).

Criteria

1. Open of the black candle has to be at, or above, the close of the earlier white candle.
2. Close of the black candle has to be between the median and open of the white candle.
3. Volume has to validate the pattern.

Bearish Engulf

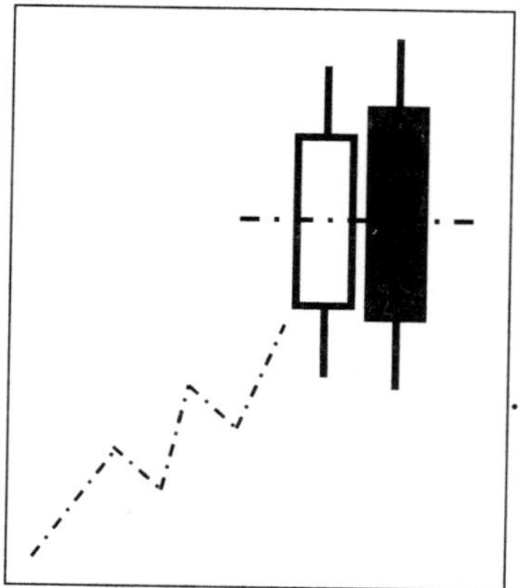

Figure 15.37: **Bearish Engulf**

A bearish engulf occurs when a black candle engulfs the whole of the previous white candle while the price is in an up trend. This is shown in Figure 15.37. A bearish engulf can occur anywhere in the trend but is more effective when it forms either at the top of the up trend, or at a crucial resistance level, or at a breakout level.

In a bearish engulf the price is originally moving up, after which the price opens at, or above, the previous white candle's close. The selling then overpowers the buying to bring the price down. The closing of such a black candle is below the open of the earlier white candle. Thus the black candle engulfs the whole of the white candle. This means that the bears have engulfed the bulls.

Criteria

1. Open of the black candle has to be at or above the close of the previous white candle.
2. Close of the black candle has to be below the open of the previous white candle.
3. Volumes have to validate the pattern. Volume validation is covered in Chapter 12.

Inverted Hammer at Top

This candle is called as an inverted hammer because in this case the hammer candle is upside down and looks like the one shown in Figure 15.38.

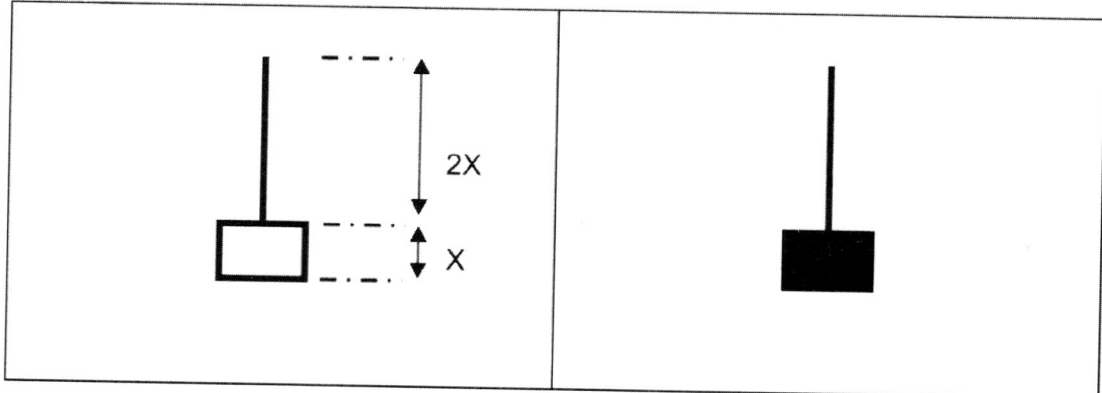

Figure 15.38: **Inverted Hammer**

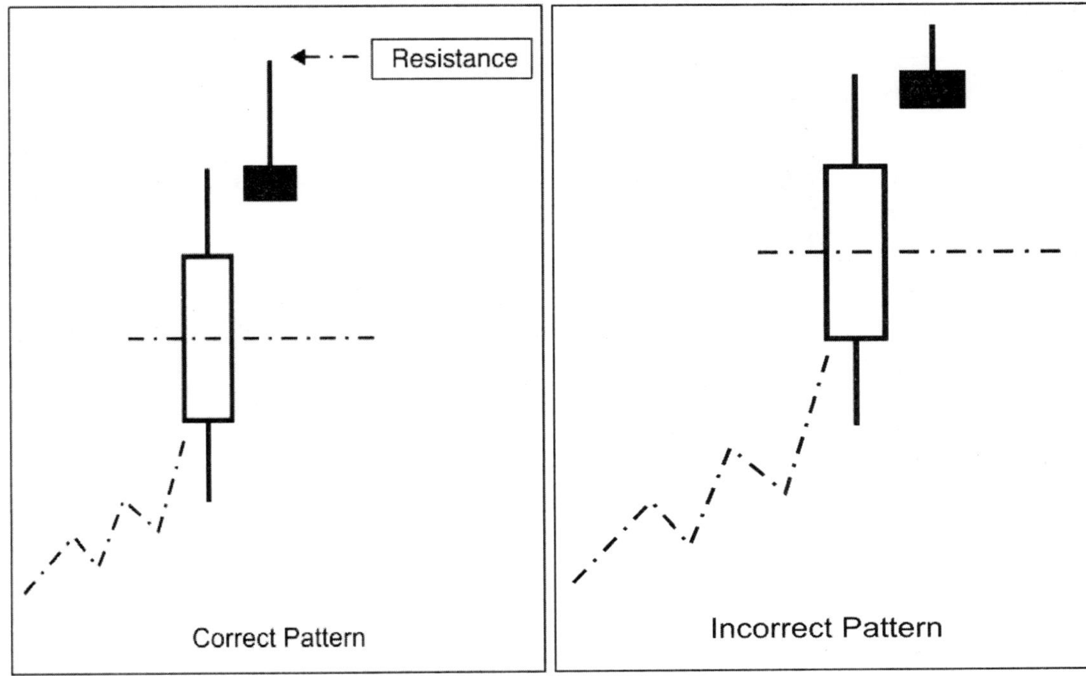

Figure 15.39: **Inverted Hammer at the top (Valid Pattern)**

Figure 15.40: **Inverted Hammer at the top (Invalid Pattern)**

An inverted hammer candle suggests that the price has rallied upward to reach a level where it is now facing resistance. As a result, selling then forces the price down after it has made a high. For such a candle to be effective, it has to be at the top of a trend (*see* Figure 15.39).

The pattern in Figure 15.40, is incorrect. Though the candle looks like a hammer, it does not fulfil the criterion of the stick or the shadow being double the size of the candle's body.

Criteria

1. The size of the stick or the shadow has to be at least double the size of the body, as shown in Figure 15.38.
2. The longer the stick, the better the candle formation.
3. The colour of the body could be either white or black.
4. There should be no stick or shadow at the bottom of the body, otherwise it becomes a neutral candle.
5. There must be an increase in volumes to confirm the importance of the resistance level formed by the high of the inverted hammer and candle formation.
6. An effective inverted hammer is the one which forms at the end of an up trend.

Evening Star: 3-Candle Formation

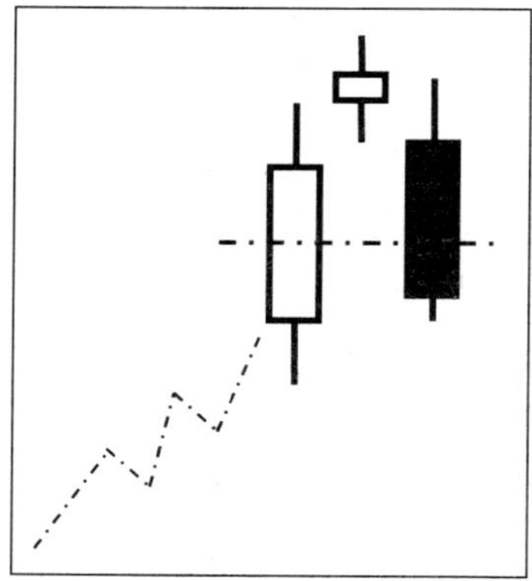

Figure 15.41: **Evening Star**

The evening star pattern is made up of three candles as shown in Figure 15.41. This pattern occurs with the price moving in an up trend. Thus, the first candle is white. Then there is an indecision or neutral candle. This occurs because at the top of a trend participants get confused as to whether the price will continue to rally or enter a correction. The neutral candle is followed by a black candle which opens at, or above, the close of the first white candle, and then starts moving down to close below the median of the first white candle.

The evening star tells us that the buyers are now tired and sellers are gaining in strength which will help the stock to start a downward move.

White candles symbolize daylight, or good days, while black candles symbolize bad days for the price. So this pattern indicates the sun has now set and the night is starting.

Criteria

1. The evening star is a 3-candle pattern.
2. At the end of an up trend there has to be a white candle followed by a neutral candle.
3. On the third day the candle opens at or above the close of the first white candle.
4. Close of the black candle has to be below the median of the first candle (white) in this three candles formation.
5. Volumes have to validate the pattern.

Hanging Man

This pattern can be confusing if you are not careful. Normally, a hammer is a bullish pattern but when it forms at the top, as shown in Figure 15.42, it can be deceiving.

A hammer normally suggests that the price witnessed selling after the opening which brought it down to a level where it found support, whereupon buying overpowered the selling to take the price up again. If a hammer is formed when the price is already in an up trend, then one needs to be careful. Such a pattern can often be deceptive as the price can as well start falling from the next candle. Looking at the bullish candle, people who jump into the stock get stuck when the price falls, in a way symbolizing their being hanged!

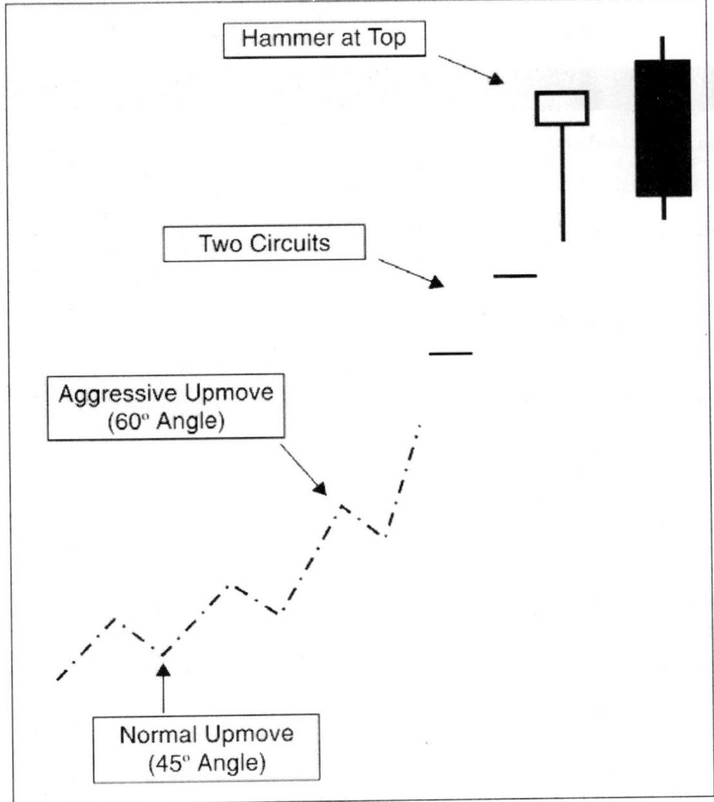

Figure 15.42: **Hanging Man**

~

Criteria

1. Ongoing normal up trend in the stock price with approximately a 45-degree angle.
2. Followed by an aggressive up move with approximately 60-degree angle.
3. Then, the stock price hits a few circuit filters. The circuit filter is a level till which the price can move up or down in a day (not valid for stocks traded in the futures and options segment).
4. This is followed by a hammer at the top. The colour of the hammer can be either white or black.
5. A hammer must be followed by a black candle.
6. Increase in volumes on the last candle helps to validate the pattern.

~

Quiz: Candlestick Patterns

Questions

1. Candlesticks provide a quick visual interpretation of price movement. (True / False?)
2. White candle = Bullish candle. (True / False?)
3. Black candle = Bearish candle. (True / False?)
4. In a white candle, the close is greater than the open. (True / False?)
5. In a black candle, the close is lower than the open. (True / False?)
6. In a white candle, the median acts as a support. (True / False?)
7. In a black candle, the median acts as a support. (True / False?)
8. The Doji is either a bullish or bearish candle. (True / False?)
9. Harami is either a bullish or bearish candle. (True / False?)

Answers

1. True	2. True	3. True	4. True	5. True
6. True	7. False	8. False	9. False	

CANDLESTICK CHARTS HELP IN IDENTIFYING TRADE ENTRIES. THEY ALSO HELP IN IMPLEMENTING RISK MANAGEMENT AT THE CORRECT LEVELS.

Chapter 16

~

Trading Price Patterns

EVERY STOCK PRICE CHART GOES THROUGH A LIFE CYCLE. Even apart from overall market variations, the business of a company does not remain constant at all times. When business is subdued, it is reflected in the price chart with the price moving sideways. Then, as business starts improving, the price starts moving up. Investor sentiment is also reflected on the chart. When people start feeling that the business is overvalued, or that it is not performing as it had in the past, the stock price starts reacting in the downward direction.

As expectations of investors and traders change about a particular stock, the price correspondingly moves up or down forming distinct patterns on the chart in the process. So, in short, price patterns are formed due to changes in investor expectations. Before we discuss price patterns in detail, it is important to understand the typical cycle of a stock's price chart as depicted in Figure 16.1.

When the company's business is not doing well, its price moves in a down trend. As the business starts to improve, the price forms a reversal pattern at the bottom and then changes its trend to up. Thus, from a down trend it starts moving in an up trend. As this trend change is underway, people want to reconfirm that a change is indeed happening and, therefore, in between you will find continuation patterns wherein the price often moves into a consolidation before resuming its move in the direction of the new trend. After a few days, months, or years, the performance of the company hits a plateau, or the company is unable to continue growing at the same pace. You will then see a slowdown in its price movement. Then as the business performance starts deteriorating, you will see a reversal pattern whereupon the price again changes its trend from up to down. The only variation among the charts of different companies could be the time duration after which such changes occur. In some stocks this may happen in a month, in some cases in six months, and in others over an even longer period.

The chart in Figure 16.1 will help you understand that reversal patterns are effective when they form at the top and at the bottom of a trend. Since price constantly moves up and down, you may see a price pattern very often. It is, therefore, important to know as to when these patterns might work — and when they may not.

Thus, when the price is moving in a trend you will see continuation patterns and not reversal patterns. Once you understand this, you will not be frustrated at not seeing reversal patterns as often as continuation patterns.

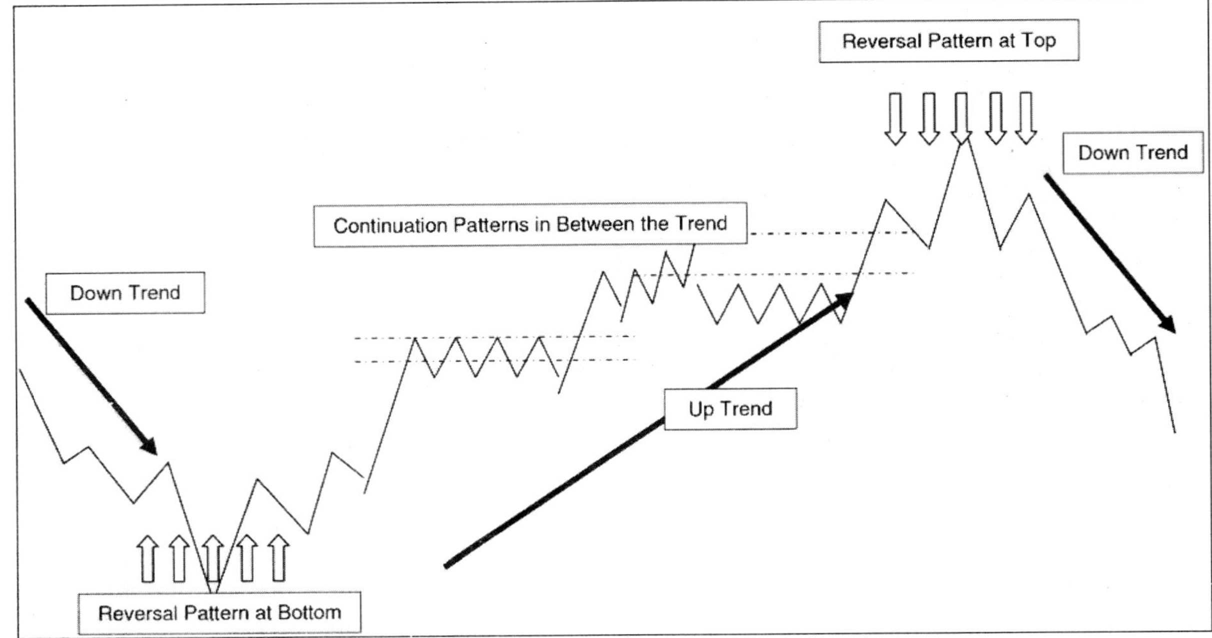

Figure 16.1: **Life cycle of a stock's price movement**

~

Another important point to be kept in mind is that the price moves up and down in trends, and this can be deceptive in that it can display false price patterns. Therefore, it is important for you to clearly grasp the conditions which confirm these patterns, and their formation, on price charts.

Price Discounts Everything

In technical analysis, price patterns work better than any other parameter. This is because a price pattern is a direct representation of price behaviour, while all other parameters, or indicators, are shadows of the price in that they are derived from it. Price patterns help you judge the way buyers and sellers have positioned themselves in a stock, the relative equilibrium of their positions, and the direction in which they are applying their force. Price is nothing but a result of demand and supply in play. To fully grasp how and why price movements work better than other tools or theories, we need to understand the psychology at work behind price movements and pattern formations.

Prices move up and down based on expectations. A price is created by the combined action of all the people trading in a particular stock or market. These people trade with different ideas and views. Some use fundamental analysis, others technical analysis, some astrology, some rely on gut feeling, some on tips, some on news; thus, people generate their buy and sell signals using various approaches. Then you have individual investors and traders, HNI investors and traders, FIIs and DIIs who help in price creation. All of them come to the market to trade — and their collective interaction creates a price. Price therefore discounts, i.e. takes into account, all sentiments, analyses, emotions and everything else involved in a trade.

Are you not surprised by the fact of the stock price going up even before a company announces good numbers, while there is profit booking after the actual announcement? Conversely, even before any negative news is aired or printed in the media, the price is already in a down trend. Why and how does this happen?

It happens for the simple reason that we are all in a hurry to be the first to enter a trade — and also exit it before anybody else can. All market participants have the urge of buying a stock at the lowest possible price, and exiting at the highest price. Whether we are successful or not is a completely different story. This is the reason why stock markets discount, namely anticipate, upcoming events and act accordingly before they actually happen, sometimes by as much as three to six months.

Let's look at an example.

Say you are the owner of a company which is going to get an order worth ₹1,000 crore. What would your priority be — informing the media, or first clinching the deal? Obviously, any business owner would first want to lay his hands on the deal and get the money into his bank; whether to spread the news or not is a completely different decision altogether.

Also, a company may not immediately divulge such news due to compliance requirements. Thus, for example, insider trading regulations may not allow the company to do so. Or, it may not inform the media as it might affect the stock price. Nevertheless, there would be a lot of people connected directly and indirectly with the development. Some of them might buy the company's shares. The broker, who knows about your connections, may spread the news to his clients and buying interest automatically comes in and is eventually reflected on the chart in the form of price action and increasing volumes. As an investor I may not have access to the directors, owners or the decision makers in a company. It may also not be necessary to have some friend in the know of a crucial deal which a company is getting into. I may not even know which stock the institutions are buying or selling. But I do have access to the price chart, which tells me that something is indeed cooking. I may not understand the exact reasons for the growing interest, and may not get to know in the immediate future the reason behind this price action.

All that doesn't matter. Price patterns help in identifying such opportunities much before everybody in the stock market comes to know about them.

Advantages of Price Patterns

1. Price patterns give us tentative price targets.
2. Price patterns give us tentative time targets.
3. Price patterns generate major moves.

4. Price patterns create opportunities for intraday traders, positional and swing traders, short term investors and long term investors.
5. Price patterns can be used on different time period charts, namely 5-minute, daily, weekly and monthly charts.

Types of Price Patterns

Price patterns can broadly be divided into the following two categories.

1. Reversal patterns; and
2. Continuation patterns.

As we discuss these price patterns, we will also be looking at the following important points:

1. Pattern identification;
2. Pattern confirmation;
3. Pattern validity;
4. Pattern price target; and
5. Pattern time target.

Which Price Patterns Work Best On Which Charts

Price patterns suggest the occurrence of a change in a stock's fundamentals. This change can happen in the short term or over the long term. The time period of the chart on which these patterns are formed tells us whether the change is going to impact the price for the short term or for the longer term. For example, short term changes could be triggered by USFDA regulatory issues which come up in the case of Indian pharma companies and have an impact on the price movement of these stocks in the short term, and in some cases in the medium term. Then there are policy decisions which can impact stock prices in the long term. Real change of fundamentals or a business event have an impact on the price change on the long term chart.

We will be discussing price patterns which work, but remember that all these price patterns may not work in the same efficient way on different time period charts. This is highlighted in Table 16.1.

Table 16.1

Which Price Patterns Work Best on Which Charts

Time Period of Chart	*Price Patterns That Work Best*
5-Minute Chart	1. Sideways breakouts, 2. Trend change breakouts, 3. Flag formations.
Daily Chart	1. Flag formations, 2. Double top or bottom formations, 3. Head and shoulders, 4. Trend change breakouts.
Weekly Chart	1. Flag formations, 2. Double top or bottom formations, 3. Head and shoulders, 4. Trend change breakouts.
Monthly Chart	1. Flag formations, 2. Rounding bottom formations.

Reversal Patterns

As the name suggests, these are patterns whose formation indicates a change in the ongoing price trend. They are most effective when they form either at the bottom or at the top of a trend. These are important patterns which suggest that the fundamentals of a company are changing, either from good to bad when they form at the top of a trend, or from bad to good when they form at the bottom of a trend. We will be looking at each of these situations separately under the headings, "Reversal Patterns at Bottom" and "Reversal Patterns at Top," respectively.

Reversal Patterns at the Top

These price patterns suggest that the fundamentals of the company are changing from good to bad. After the formation of these patterns, the price trend changes from up to down. Thus, these price patterns present you an opportunity to go short in a stock, or drop the stock from your portfolio.

Important reversal patterns at the top are:

1. Head and shoulders;
2. Double / triple top; and
3. Trend change downward breakout.

Head and Shoulders Pattern

As the name suggests, this price formation looks like the head and shoulders of a person standing upright. This is a reversal pattern at the top and suggests that the fundamentals of the company are changing from good to bad. After the formation of this pattern, the price trend changes from an up trend to a down trend, thus presenting an opportunity to either go short in the concerned stock, or sell the stock if you are holding it in your portfolio.

Pattern Identification

Let's look at the chart in Figure 16.2. The up trend is clearly visible on the left and centre of the chart, with the price making higher tops and higher bottoms, marked on the chart with "B" standing for "Bottom," "HT" for "Higher Top," and "HB" for "Higher Bottom." The last candle at the extreme right in the chart suggests that the price has made a higher bottom and will now be moving towards the level of the earlier top, and because the price has been trading in an up trend, ideally the price should now make a new higher top.

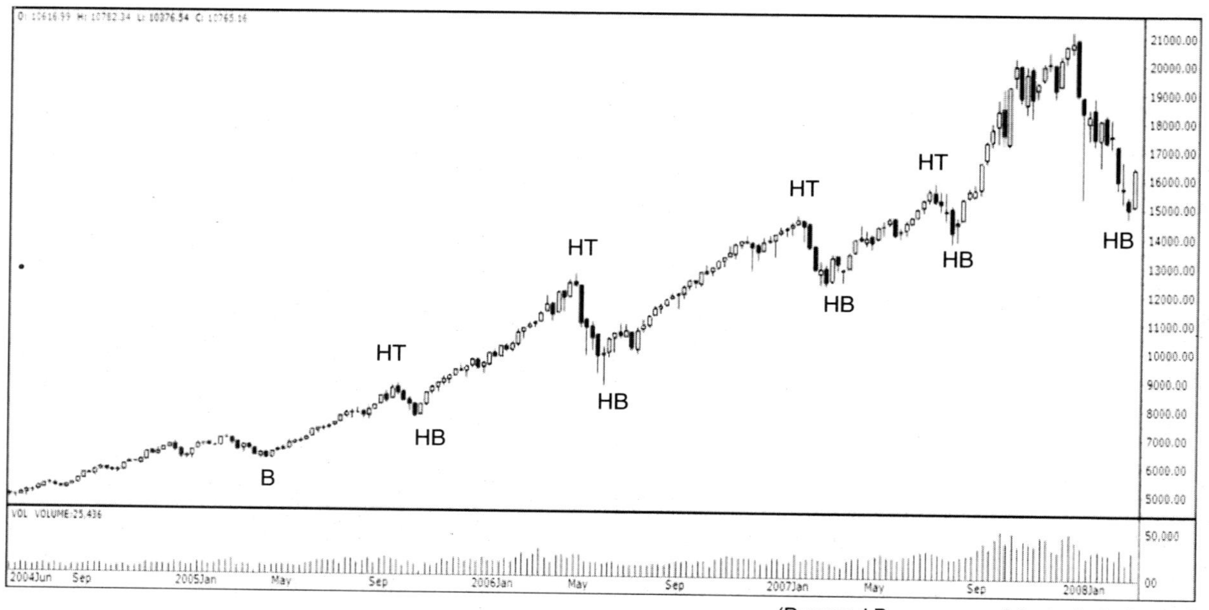

(Powered By: www.precisiontechnicals.com)

Figure 16.2: **Weekly candlestick chart of BSE Sensex making higher tops and higher bottoms. ("B" stands for bottom, "HB" is higher bottom, and "HT" is highter top)**

Thus, this chart formation suggests that the price will now move higher to test the earlier top at 21,000 levels as can be seen on the price scale on the right hand side of the chart. If the price has to continue its up trend, then it should also make a new top higher than the earlier one. So till now the sentiment is bullish as the price continues to move in an up trend.

Now let's look at the same chart with some more candles added on its right hand side as the price continues to move in the up trend. In the chart in Figure 16.3, you will be able to see the way the price has moved up after making a higher bottom. This confirms that the stock is indeed in an up trend and is now heading towards the earlier top to make a new high (marked with up arrows).

Now look at the chart in Figure 16.4. The price movement after this point will surprise you. In Figure 16.3, the price looked to be moving in an up trend but in the next chart in Figure 16.4, the price seems to be in a mood to change its trend. The price has started to move downward as indicated by down arrows on the price chart in Figure 16.4.

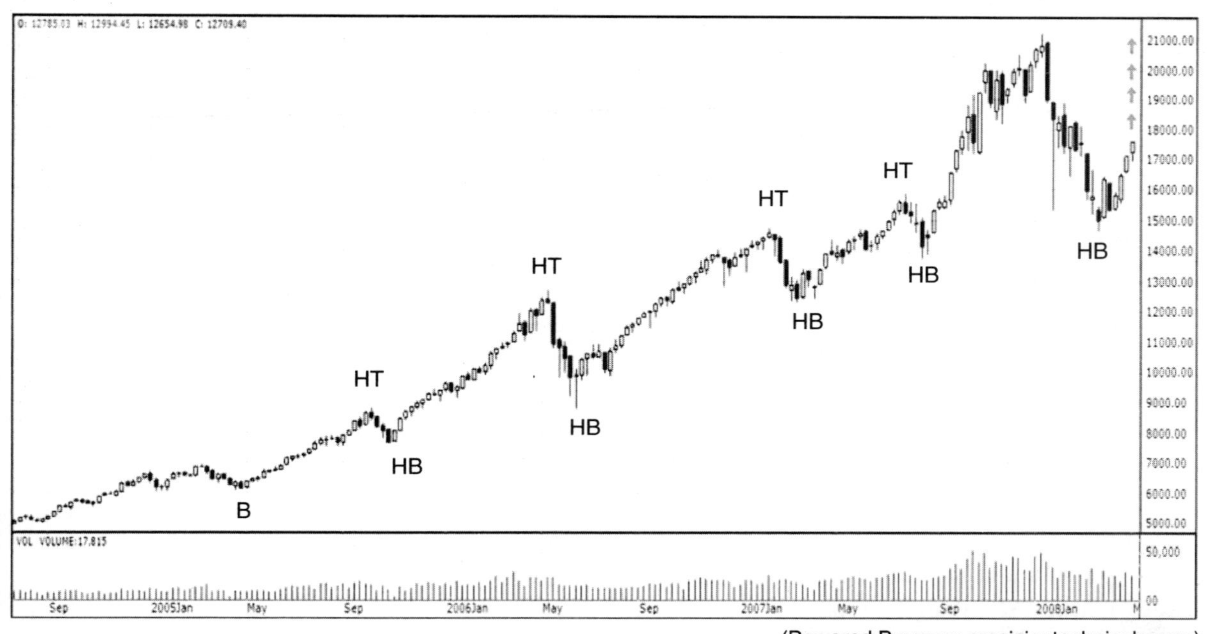

(Powered By: www.precisiontechnicals.com)

Figure 16.3: **This weekly candlestick chart of BSE Sensex shows the price moving up after making a higher bottom**

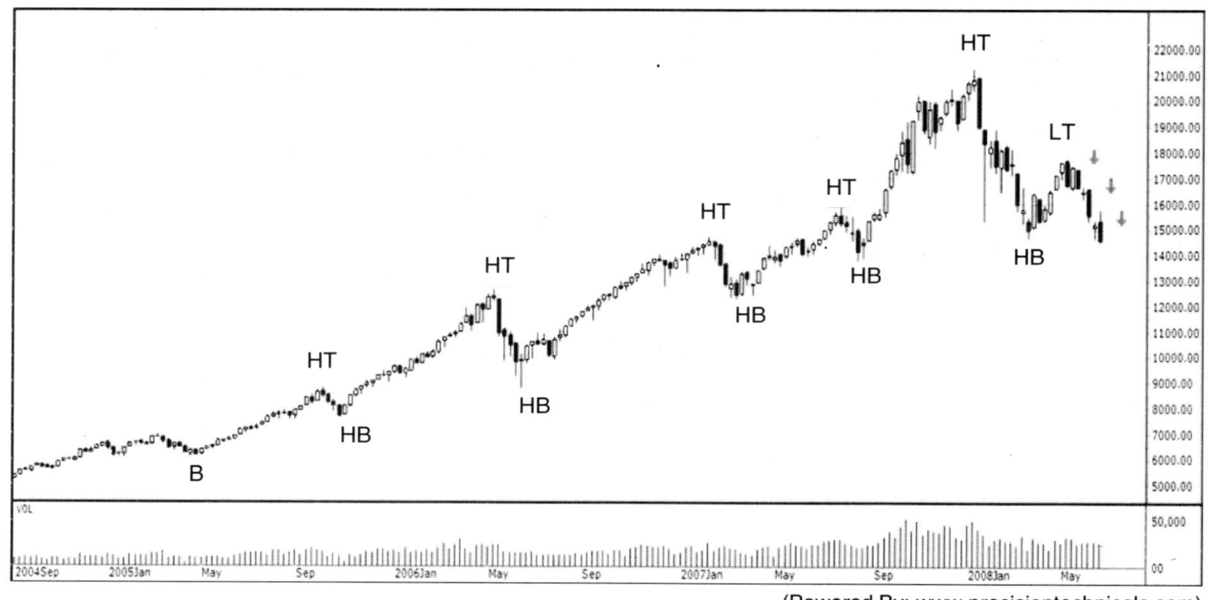

(Powered By: www.precisiontechnicals.com)

Figure 16.4: **Weekly candlestick chart of BSE Sensex showing the price moving down**

~

When you see a chart like the one in Figure 16.4, it will trigger the first doubt in your mind about the prevailing trend. Till a few days back the stock was in an up trend, but suddenly the price has changed its direction and is now moving downward. It also seems that the price has now formed a lower top (marked "LT" in the chart in Figure 16.4), and so it is possible that the stock could change its trend. To confirm a down trend we need both a lower top as well as a lower bottom. This may or may not happen. So, for now, we need to wait for a confirmation. This is also the exact point where we are able to see a head and shoulders-like formation on the chart. The head and the two shoulders are marked on the chart in Figure 16.5.

In the chart in Figure 16.5, you can see that the topmost point is the head, the earlier top is the left shoulder (Shoulder 1 on the chart), and the lower top after the head is the right shoulder, marked Shoulder 2 on the chart.

The line chart in Figure 16.6 shows the head and shoulders formation more clearly.

Whenever you have difficulty in identifying a head and shoulders formation, plot straight lines like the ones plotted in Figure 16.6. They will help you in clearly visualizing the pattern.

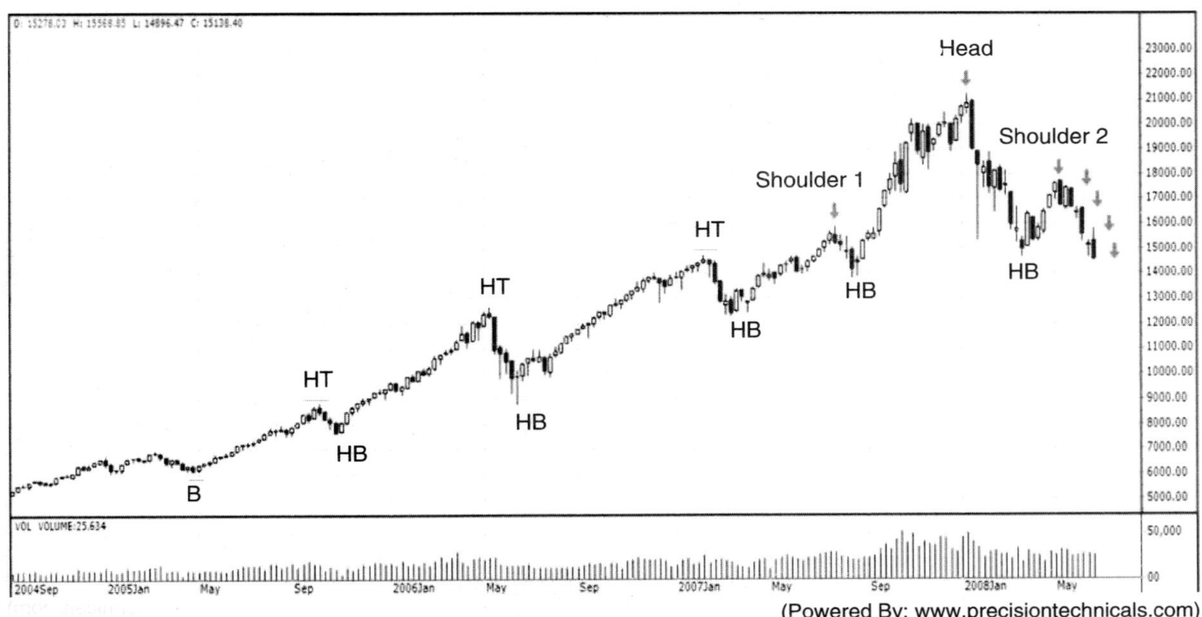

Figure 16.5: **Weekly candlestick chart of BSE Sensex with a head and the two shoulders marked**

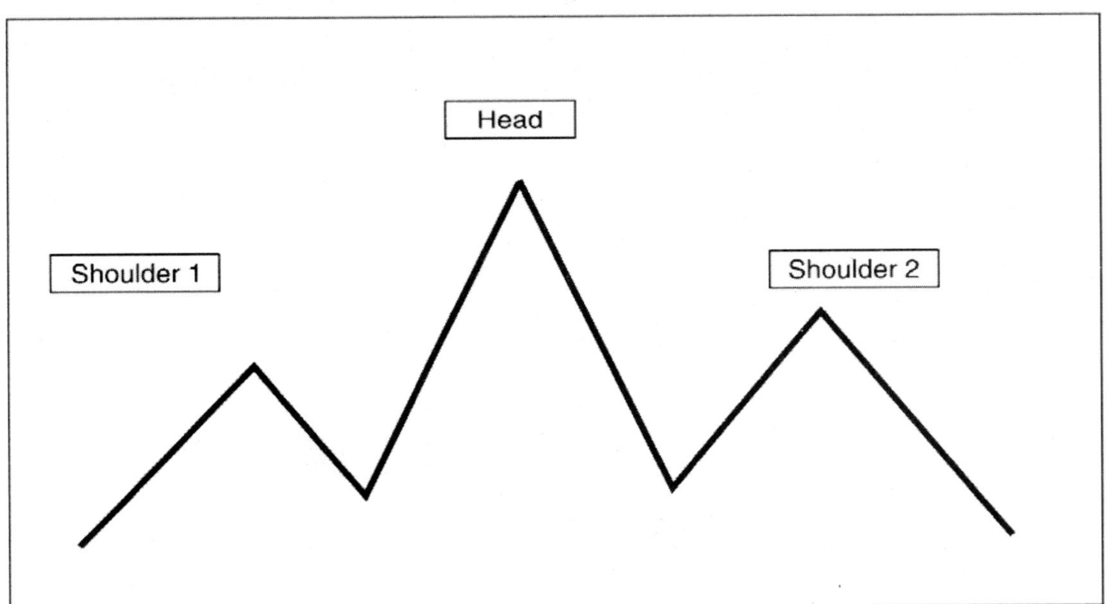

Figure 16.6: **Plotting lines help identify the head and shoulder pattern**

(Powered By: www.precisiontechnicals.com)

Figure 16.7: **Daily candlestick chart of Reliance Industries with the price movement showing multiple up and down trends**

~

Pattern Confirmation

As the price moves in trends, you may see apparent head and shoulders patterns every now and then. The chart in Figure 16.7 displays price trends on the chart of Reliance Industries. As the price is moves, you may wrongly interpret these up and down trends to be a head and shoulders pattern. It is important, therefore, for you to be able to pick the valid pattern and avoid mistakes. For this, you need to confirm and validate the pattern that you are looking at on the price chart.

Whenever you feel that you have identified a head and shoulders pattern, the next important thing for you to do is plot a neckline. This has to be plotted by joining the lowest points between the head and the two shoulders. These will be the first and second neck points, by joining which a neckline is plotted.

So we need to have a head which is higher than the two shoulders, plus a neckline. It should look like a normal person standing upright. Human shoulders are not above the head, and neither should they be in the case of this pattern. So there should be one head with two shoulders which look like those of a normal human being. The pattern can be vertical, or tilted slightly to the right, or to the left, as in Figure 16.8, Figure 16.9 and Figure 16.10, respectively:

- The correction in the price from the top of the head to the second neck point should not be less than 50% of the earlier move from the first neck point to the high of the head.
- The second neck point should not be more than 30% below the first neck point.

You will normally come across patterns as displayed in Figure 16.8 and Figure 16.9. The one shown in Figure 16.10 is rarely observed.

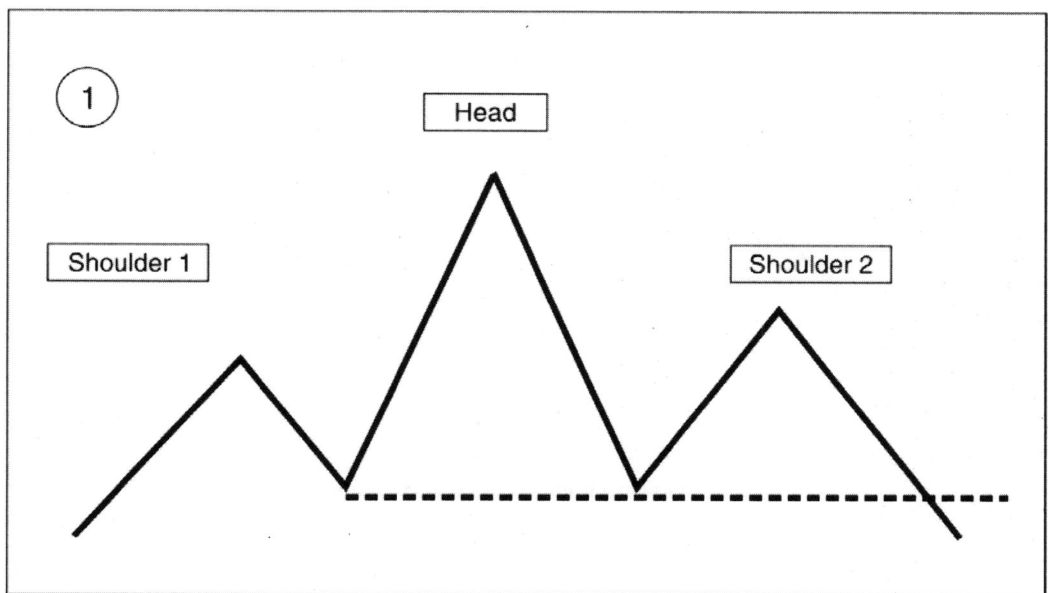

Figure 16.8: **Horizontal head and shoulder pattern**

~

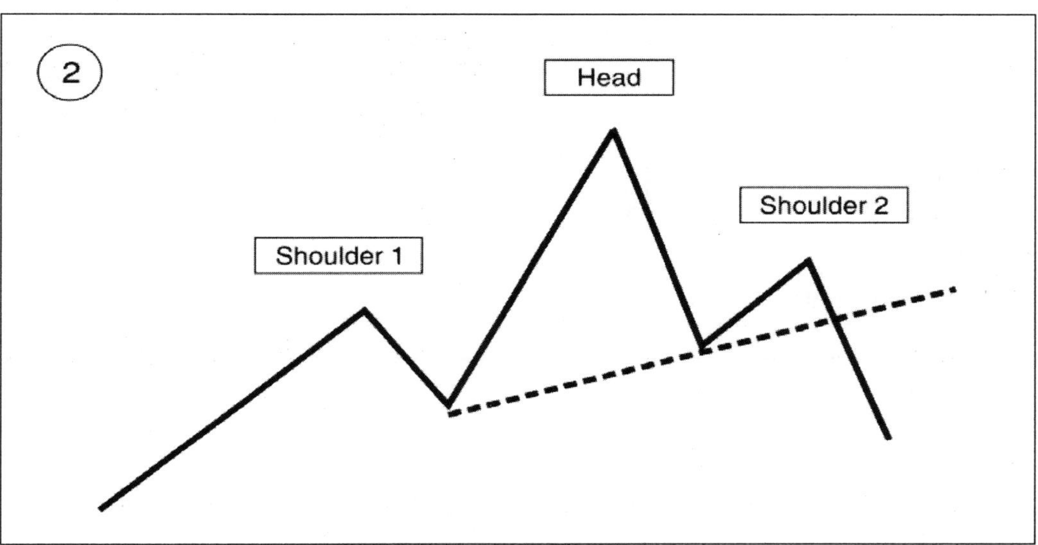

Figure 16.9: **Upward inclined head and shoulder pattern**

~

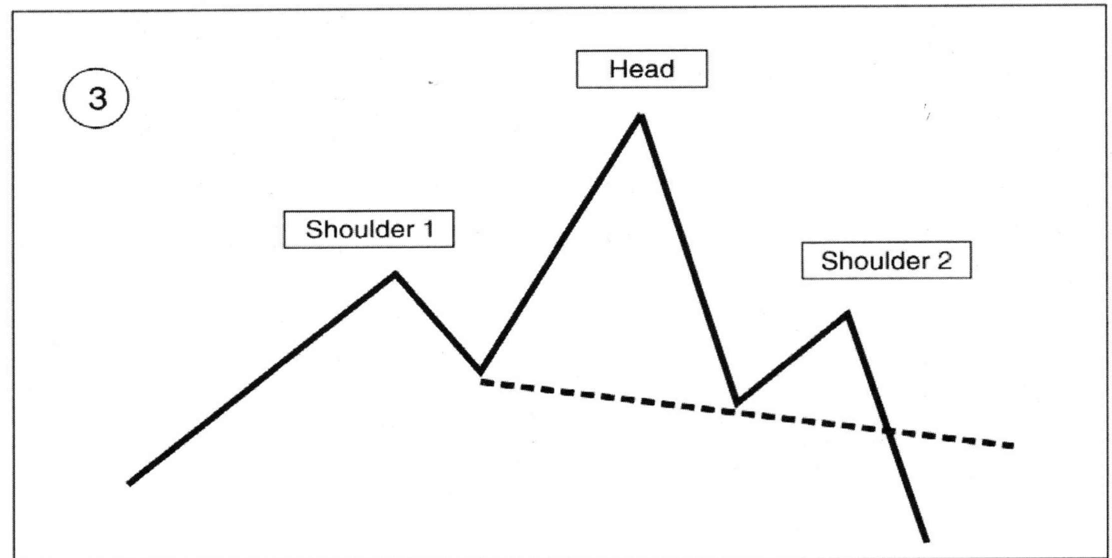

Figure 16.10: **Downward inclined head and shoulders pattern**

~

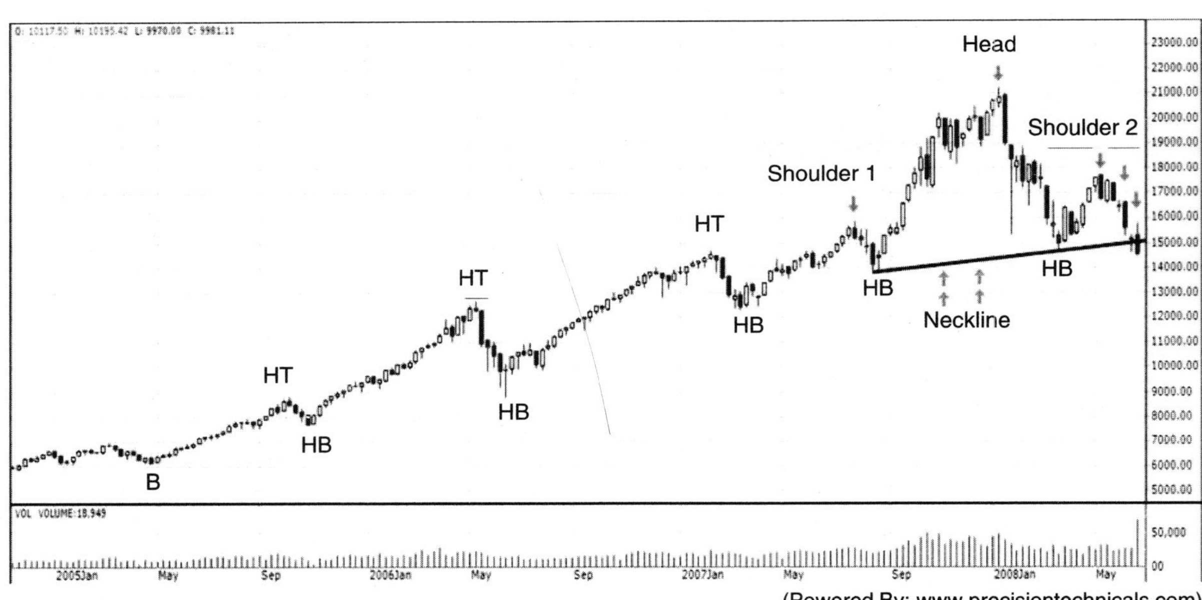

(Powered By: www.precisiontechnicals.com)

Figure 16.11: **Weekly candlestick chart of BSE Sensex with head and shoulders and neckline highlighted**

~

Once you have managed to plot the neckline you will be able to see the head and shoulders pattern but **it will be confirmed only when the neckline is broken on the downside.**

Remember: Never enter a trade on an assumption; do so only upon confirmation. So, in this case you should not enter a trade assuming that we will get a downward breakout going forward. History has proven that such trades involve high risk.

Now, let us plot a neckline on the BSE Sensex chart in Figure 16.11. In this chart, you will be able to see the neckline plotted by joining the lowest points between the head and the two shoulders. The last candle on the chart suggests that the price has closed below the neckline. With this breakdown we can now say that the price pattern stands confirmed. Further, the price has also made a lower bottom compared to earlier one suggesting a change of trend.

We now need to check the validity of this price pattern.

Pattern Validity

After obtaining a confirmation for the pattern, the next important step is checking its validity. This is important in order to reduce whipsaws, namely false breakouts. As we have discussed earlier, confirmation and validity together help us in reducing the risk involved in a trade.

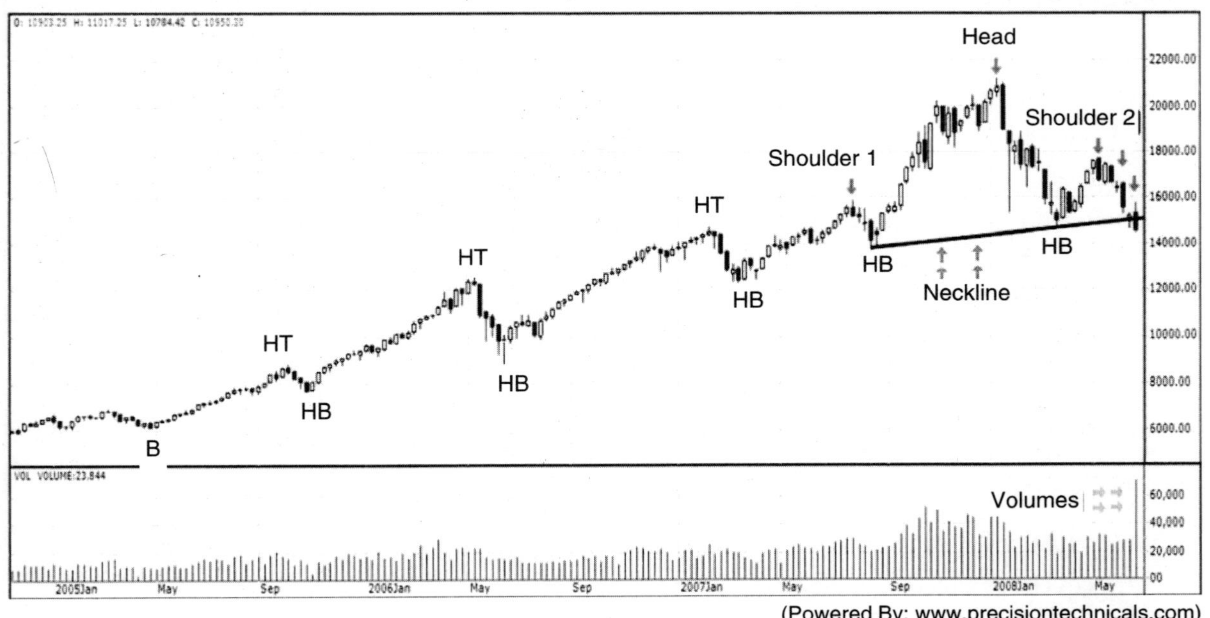

(Powered By: www.precisiontechnicals.com)

Figure 16.12: **Weekly candlestick chart of BSE Sensex with volume plotted in the lower panel**

The validity of a pattern is confirmed by considering the trading volumes. The logic of this is that a single individual cannot create a meaningful price move. But if a larger number of people trading a stock are on the long side, then the price will go up, while if a larger number of people trading a stock are on the short side, the price would move downwards.

Remember the multiplex example in Chapter 12?

A similar logic applies in the stock market. You would want to trade a stock which presents an opportunity. This also implies that when a stock price breaks out, thousands of people should see the breakout as an opportunity. If it is valid breakout then it is but natural that volumes for the breakout period should be high because a large number of traders would see an opportunity around the same time.

Thus, the validity of a pattern is confirmed by higher volumes, as can be seen in the chart displayed in Figure 16.12.

In this chart, you will see that the price has given a breakout below the neckline, and that this breakout is accompanied by high volumes. When a stock qualifies on both confirmation as well as validity, you can then get ready to trade this view.

Pattern Price Target

In the case of Figure 16.12, we now have both confirmation and validity, and the view suggests that one can go short. The next set of parameters which we need are:

- Risk management,
- Price target, and
- Time frame.

Risk management will be discussed at length later in Chapter 18. For now, let us discuss the tentative price target and a tentative time frame for the price to reach its target.

When we trade a price pattern we are directly trading the shift of sentiment between the bulls and the bears. This means that both sides are executing trades in their respective directions, but only one of them is going to win. The winner is going to be decided by the direction, confirmation, and validity of the breakout.

In the case of a price pattern, there are two forces which come into play after a breakout.

- If we have an upward breakout:
    1. First, there is genuine buying which helps in generating the breakout.
    2. The initial genuine buying is followed by both further follow-up buying as well as short covering, which help the price rally higher.
- If we have a downward breakout:
    1. First, there is the genuine selling which helps generate the breakout.
    2. This is followed by further follow-up selling as well as longs squaring off, both of which help the price move down further.

A pattern's price target is important to understand in order to know the level where one needs to either exit the trade, or book full or partial profits. Thus, for example, you are comfortable with a bank fixed deposit because you are aware of the returns that your investment is going to generate after the pre-defined tenure. Defining a tentative price target similarly helps provide comfort to a trader. And when you are at ease, it is easier to stay on in a trade.

For calculating the price target in the case of a head and shoulders formation, you need to do the following:

1. Measure the vertical distance between the high of the head to the neckline.
2. Subtract the value derived as above from the breakout point on the neckline to arrive at the target.

This target calculation is shown in the chart in Figure 16.13, where you can see the price line plotted on the chart.* The vertical distance between the high of the head and the neckline is 6,804.03, and after deducting this value from the breakout point on the neckline, the target is 8,324. The closing on the breakout candle is 14,571, which means the price is expected to fall by more than 6,000 going forward.

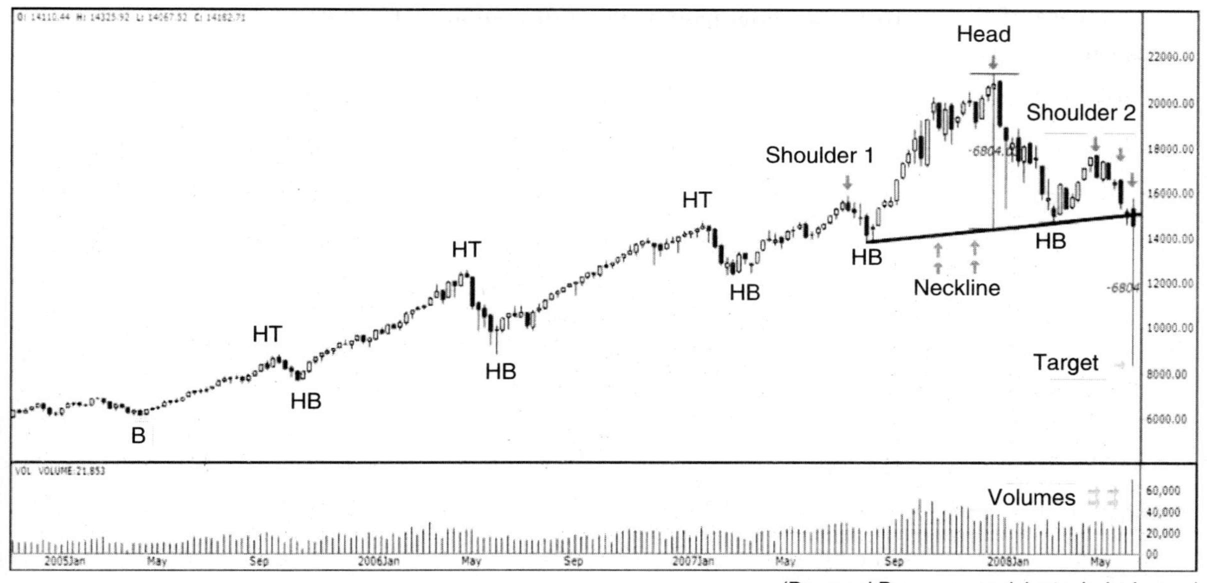

(Powered By: www.precisiontechnicals.com)

Figure 16.13: **Weekly candlestick chart of BSE Sensex with head and shoulder pattern price target calculation.**

~

* In Profision software you can automatically calculate the value using the price line. Or, you can do so as explained.

As discussed earlier, price patterns have the potential to generate big moves and big opportunities.

Remember, this pattern resembles a person standing upright. If such a person's neck is cut or slit open, like the price breakout seen on the chart, the person would die and fall to the ground. The same thing happens to the price when the neckline is broken.

Pattern Time Target

Calculating the pattern time target is important, just as calculating the pattern price target is. You will better understand the importance of calculating the pattern time target in later chapters when we discuss trading plans. It helps in assessing whether a particular stock fits in your profile. It also helps in gauging the strength of the stock, and in implementing partial profit booking.

In the head and shoulders pattern in the chart in Figure 16.14, you will be able to see that the price has changed its trend in the span of the last seven trading candles. This is a short time frame for traders to shift over their positions from bullish to bearish. This occurs because the ups and downs in the market often make people wait in hope. Due to this, experience shows

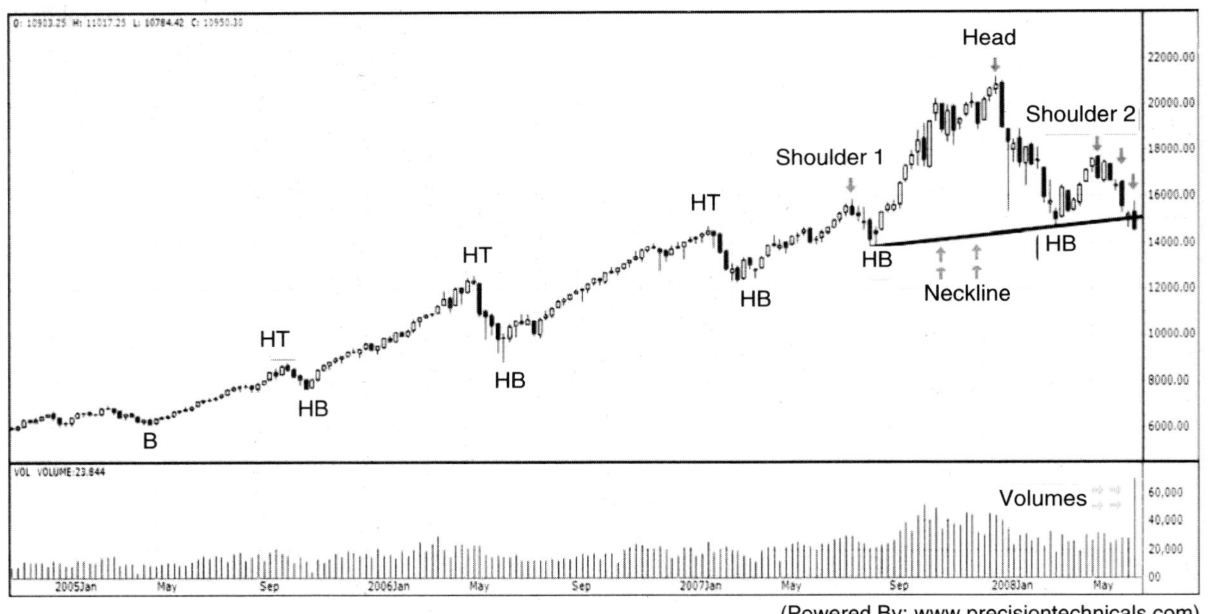

Figure 16.14: **Weekly candlestick chart of BSE Sensex with head and shoulders pattern and the break down on the down side**

that for the target to be achieved the price usually takes one-third of the time that it took for the pattern to form from the first neck point to the breakout level. So the calculation is simple; count the number of candles in between these two points, and divide that number by 3.

Let us consider the example shown in Figure 16.15.

In this chart, you will be able to see the candle count* tool plotted on the price chart, which displays the number of candles between the first neck point and the breakout candle, showing the figure "45," meaning that there are 45 candles between these two points. In this case, then, the time target would be one-third of 45.

Time Target = One-third of the total number of candles from the first neck point to the breakout candle. $= 45 \div 3 = 15$

Time Target = 15 candles.

Thus, we expect the target to be achieved in the time represented by approximately 15 candles.

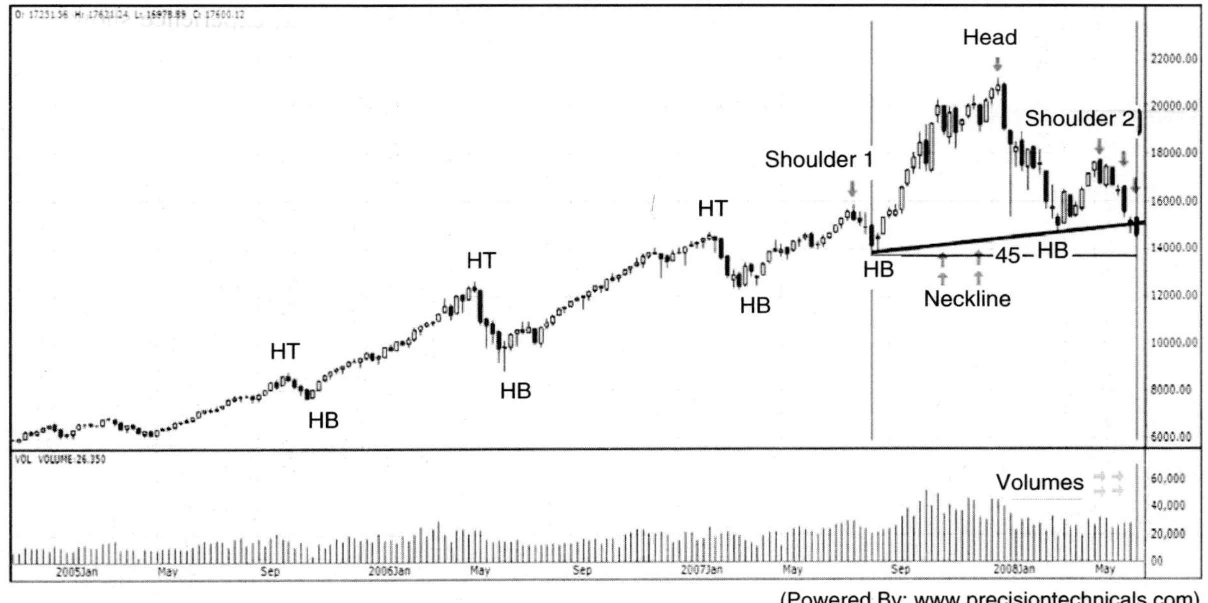

(Powered By: www.precisiontechnicals.com)

Figure 16.15: **Weekly candlestick chart of BSE Sensex with the candle count tool plotted**

~

* In the Profision software you can automatically calculate the number of candles in a pattern using the Candle count tool. Else, you can do so as explained.

Double Top Formation Pattern

As the name indicates, in this pattern the price forms two tops at about the same level suggesting that it is facing resistance here. This pattern can have an impact on the price both in the short term as well as the long term. Every trending stock price has to reach the earlier top before it can make a new one. Therefore, it is possible that you may see a lot of double tops forming as the price moves in an up trend.

Let us now consider an example.

In the chart in Figure 16.16 the price is in an up trend making successive higher tops and higher bottoms. As we can see, the last candle on the chart does not give any sign of the price facing resistance at the level of the earlier top. So this chart does not show us any signs of a double top formation. It is quite possible that if the momentum continued, the price would have gone on to make a new top confirming that the up trend was intact.

You need to be aware of this possibility so that you do not get stuck in a wrong trade.

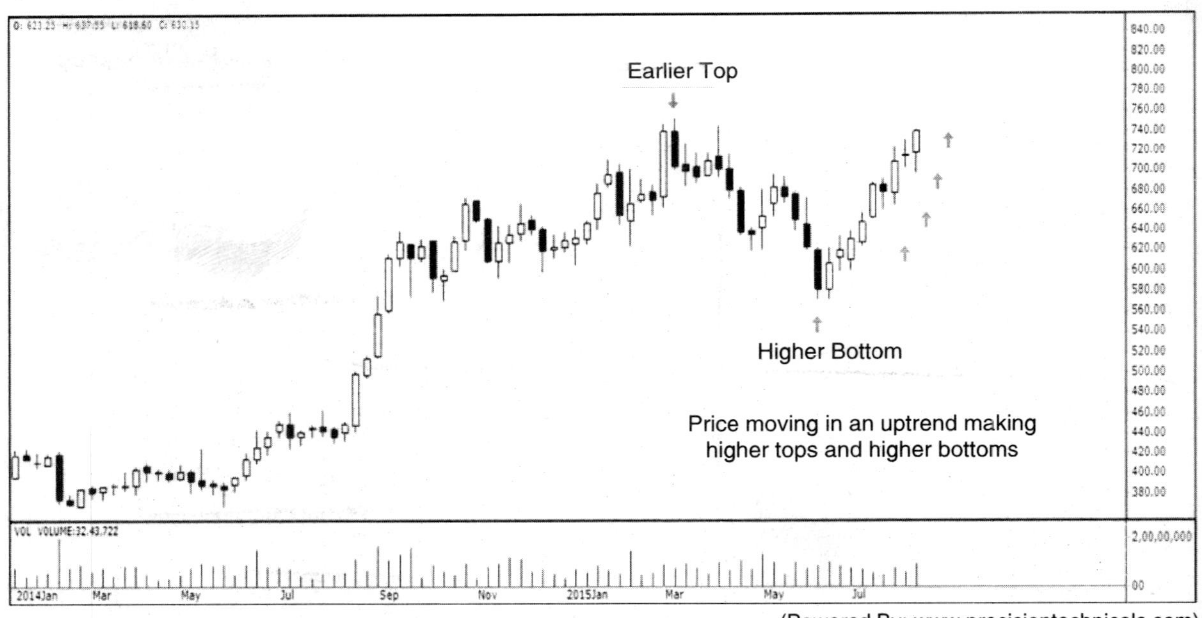

(Powered By: www.precisiontechnicals.com)

Figure 16.16: **Daily candlestick chart of Cipla with the price in an up trend making higher tops and higher bottoms**

To help pick the correct double top, the following elements are required:

- Pattern identification,
- Pattern confirmation, and
- Pattern validity.

Once a double top forms, it suggests an intermediate down trend in the price. It is an opportunity to either go short in the concerned stock, or exit the stock if you are holding it in your portfolio. If you wish, you could buy it back later when it gives you a buy signal.

Pattern Identification

The stock price is moving in an up trend. It reaches a level from where we witness a correction. Being in an up trend, the price manages to make a higher bottom as marked in Figure 16.17, and again starts moving upward. As it reaches the earlier top it faces resistance and then moves into an intermediate down trend. This happens because the momentum in the price has failed to generate a breakout above the earlier top marked by the horizontal line in Figure 16.17. Had this breakout occurred, the stock would have made a higher top after a higher bottom, and could have continued its upward trend. But because it faced resistance at the level of the earlier top it did not make a new one and therefore the chances that the price may enter a sideways trend are now high.

(Powered By: www.precisiontechnicals.com)

Figure 16.17: **Daily candlestick chart of Cipla with double top formation**

~

Let us consider the example in Figure 16.17.

In the chart in Figure 16.17, the price of Cipla moved from ₹380 levels in May 2014 to make highs of approximately ₹750 in March 2015. After that the price witnessed a correction, moving down from ₹750 to ₹575 levels in the next three months. This suggests that the price made a higher bottom compared with the earlier one. On moving up, it then faced resistance at that same level where it had made the earlier top due to an increase in selling pressure.

The fact of the price facing resistance at the level of the earlier top in the ongoing up trend will help in identifying a double top pattern. But to enter a trade, we still have to confirm and validate the pattern.

Pattern Confirmation and Validity

Once the stock price fails to cross the level of the earlier top, the confirmation of this pattern rests on the following factors:

1. The two tops have to be at the same level, which can be identified by plotting a horizontal line.
2. The candle at the second top should generate a sell signal as per candlestick patterns.
3. Volume on the sell candle at the double top level should be higher compared to the previous three candles.

The chart in Figure 16.18 meets all the three criteria for confirming and validating a double top pattern.

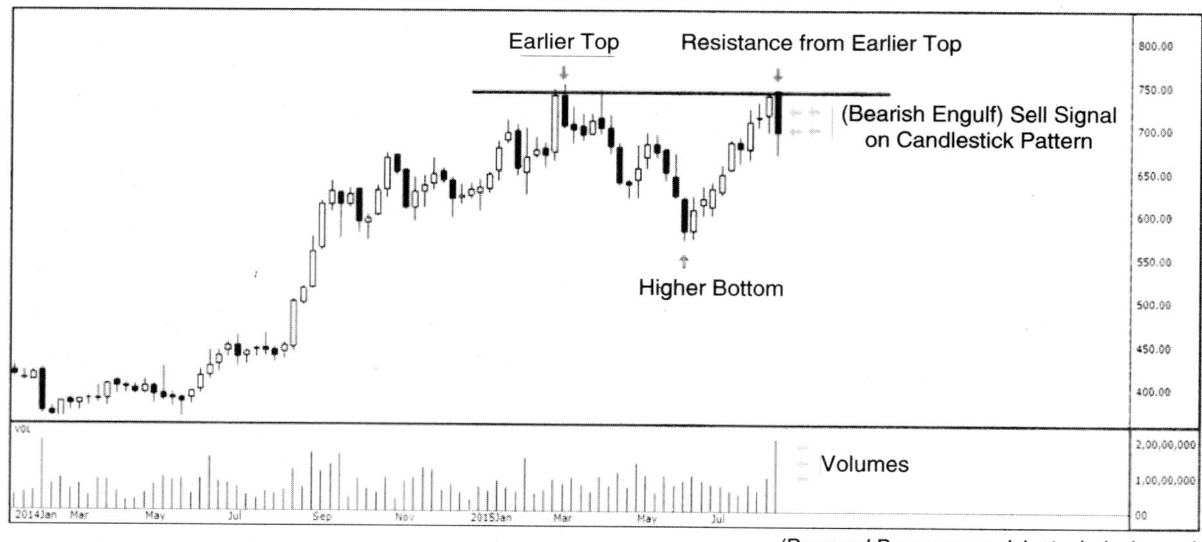

(Powered By: www.precisiontechnicals.com)

Figure 16.18: **Daily candlestick chart of Cipla confirming and validating a double top pattern**

This means that now you can either short this stock, or sell it.

Pattern Price Target

In case you are selling a stock, you need to know the level where you should book profits in the trade, or a level where you can cover your position. In the case of a double top formation, the price usually travels half of the distance between the lowest point between the two tops, and the double top level. The calculation for arriving at a target in this case is thus as follows:

1. Measure the difference from the double top level to the lowest point in between the two tops.
2. Price is expected to fall half of this distance from the double top level.
3. So divide this difference calculated in Point 1 above by 2, and then deduct it from the double top level.

The chart in Figure 16.19, displays the price difference as being ₹172.88 using the price line tool inbuilt in Profision*. So the price will travel a minimum of half of this distance, as marked on the chart.

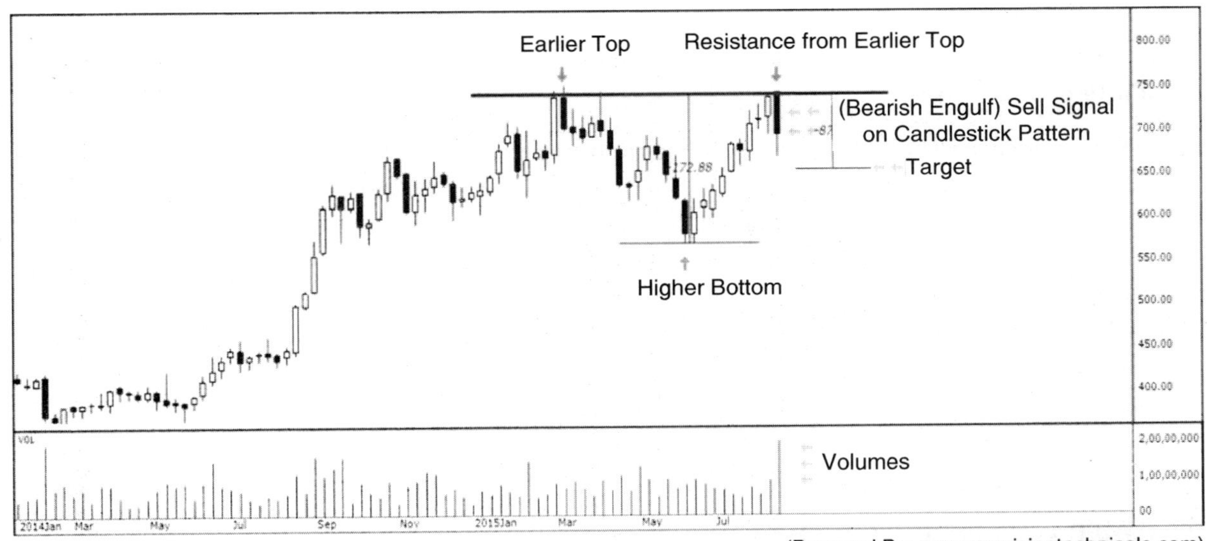

(Powered By: www.precisiontechnicals.com)

Figure 16.19: **Daily candlestick chart of Cipla displaying the double top formation and the price target calculation**

~

* In the Profision software you can automatically calculate the value using the price line. Or, you can do so as explained.

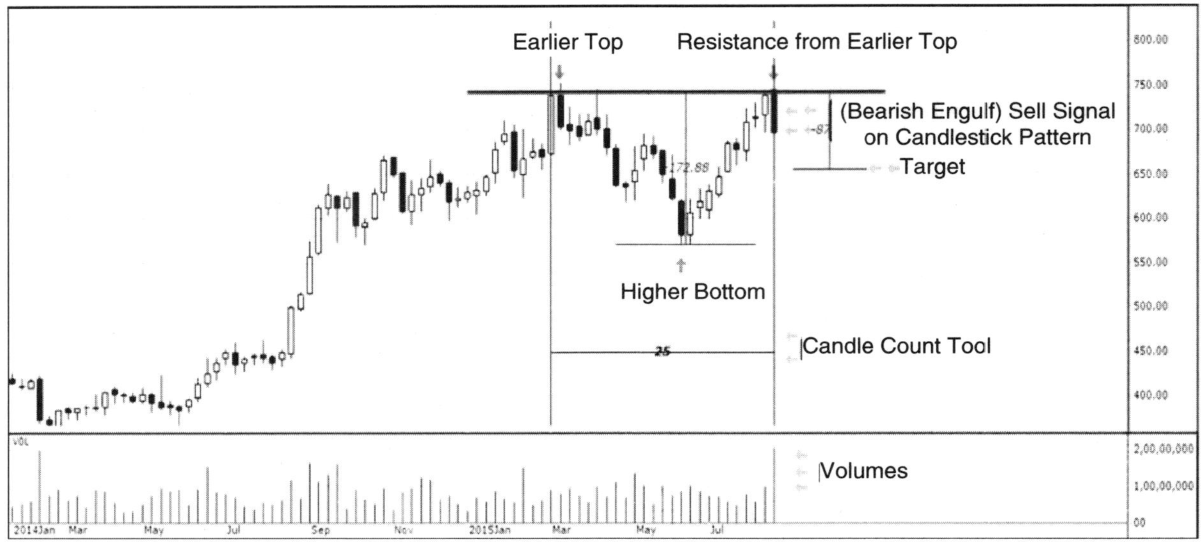

Figure 16.20: **Daily candlestick chart of Cipla displaying the double top formation and with the candle count tool plotted on the chart to calculate the time target.**

~

Pattern Time Target

The importance of this has been explained in the earlier head and shoulders pattern and is applicable for all price patterns. Thus, you need to count the number of candles from the first top to the last candle in this formation, and then divide that number by three to arrive at the time target. The chart in Figure 16.20 displays the candle count tool being used for counting the candles, making it easy and fast.

In the chart in Figure 16.20, you can see the candle count as 25. This means that the target price is expected to be achieved in 25 divided by 3 = 8.33 candles. We cannot have decimals when counting candles, therefore we take the higher side figure for safety, so in this case it would be 9 candles.

Triple Top Formation Pattern

If the price continues to show strength after making a double top formation, then it is possible that it may move up again to test the same resistance for a third time, thus making a triple top. This is a situation of extreme strength and this pattern usually forms only when some positive outcome is expected in the future.

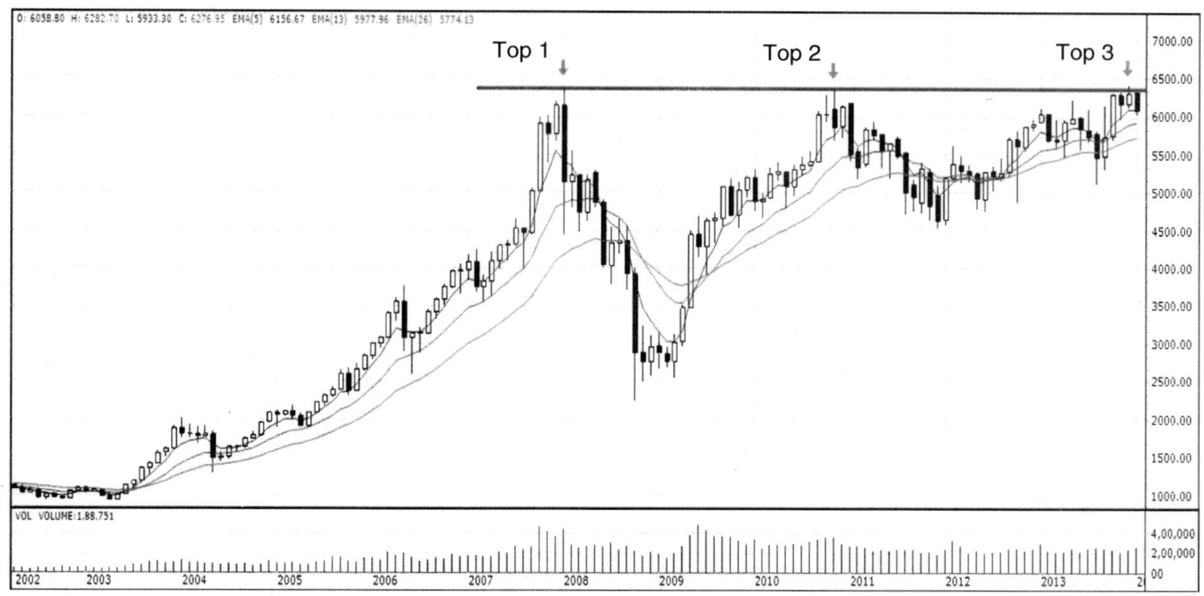

(Powered By: www.precisiontechnicals.com)

Figure 16.21: **Monthly candlestick chart of Nifty with a triple top formation**

~

Important: Instead of trading a triple top on the short side, it is better to wait for the price to give us a breakout above this triple top level because the downside opportunities may not be much when compared to the upside potential of the stock after the upward breakout.

The above comments are contradictory but they work because the pattern itself suggests a strong undercurrent helping the price test the same resistance multiple times. **This pattern is rare but whenever it does form you should be on the right side of the trade**.

The chart in Figure 16.21 shows that in 2008 the Nifty made a high of 6,357.10 (Top 1), then in 2010 it made a high of 6,338.50 (Top 2), and in 2013 a high of 6,415.25 (Top 3). Overall, the price failed to move above the level marked with a horizontal line. This is a triple top formation.

When the price displays a tendency of going back to the resistance level more than twice it means there is a positive undercurrent. Instead of using this as an opportunity to go short, one should wait for an upward breakout above this triple top level. **Such a pattern suggests that the price is getting ready to move to a completely new level after the breakout. It could also mean that the stock is being re-rated.** Thus, if the chart in Figure 16.22 is that of a company then the business will get re-rated, and if it is an index, such as Nifty as in this case, it means the overall market is getting re-rated.

(Powered By: www.precisiontechnicals.com)

Figure 16.22: **Monthly candlestick chart of Nifty showing the price movement after the triple top breakout**

~

The chart in Figure 16.22 displays the price movement after the breakout:

- The breakout is signalled when the price manages to close above the horizontal resistance line plotted on the chart.
- Confirmation is based on the breakout candle being a white candle, either with small sticks or without sticks / shadows.
- Validity is based on an increase in volume suggesting that it is a widely perceived breakout and that there are plenty of people trading it.

In such patterns, the price has the potential to double from the breakout level in 3 to 5 years. **Remember that though we have included this pattern among reversal patterns at the top, this pattern should be used to trade on the long side and not for trading on the short side.**

The pattern suggests that the stock or index is moving into a completely new zone. Correlating this fact with the fundamentals would suggest that the company is shifting into a new business level. This re-rating could be due to business expansion or some positive breakthrough which warrants re-rating of the stock price.

Downward Trend Change Breakout

This pattern occurs when the stock fails to live up to the extremely bullish expectations of investors and traders. After moving in an up trend the price then gets into a sideways trend, i.e. it becomes range bound. This usually happens when there is some positive undercurrent in a stock's price.

The direction of breakout after the sideways trend is important. An upward breakout means that the price would continue in the direction of the earlier trend. But many a time the direction of the breakout is downward, which means that the positive expectations in the stock have now failed. The stock then gives a downward breakout after the sideways trend, and then continues to move further down.

This creates a sell signal on the chart which can be used by both investors as well as traders depending on which time period chart the pattern forms on. Investors can exit the stock if they are holding it in their portfolio, while traders can go short and capitalize on the opportunity. Let us see this with the help of the example in Figure 16.23.

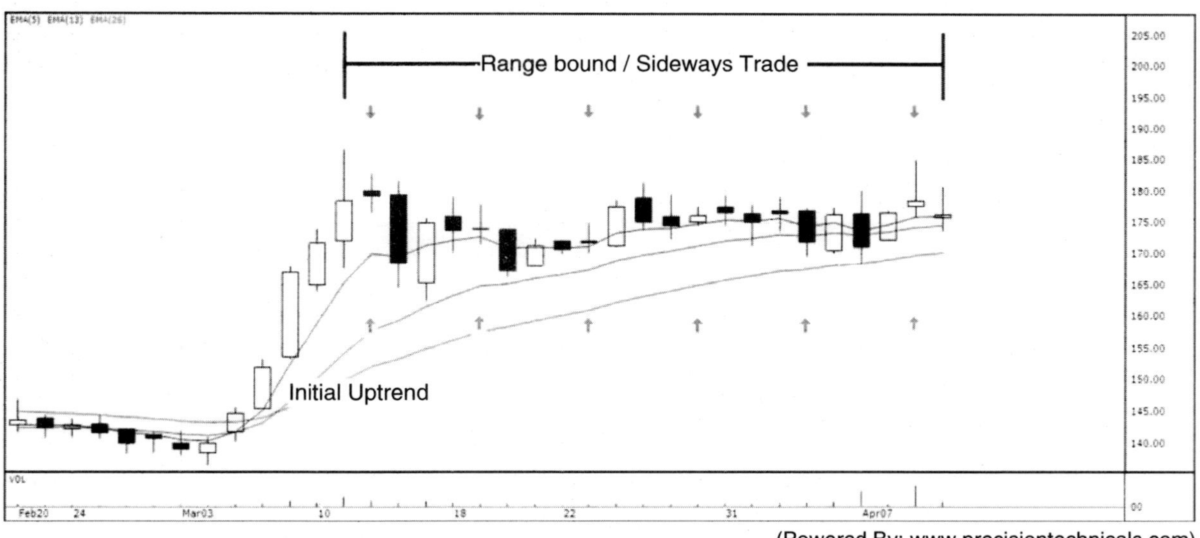

(Powered By: www.precisiontechnicals.com)

Figure 16.23: **Downward trend change breakout pattern on DLF daily candlestick chart after a sideways trend**

~

In the chart in Figure 16.23, the price moved up from ₹136 levels on 4 March 2014, to make a high of approximately ₹186 on 11 March. After this, the stock entered an overall sideways trend for the next 22 trading sessions. The range of the sideways trend is highlighted in the chart and also marked with up as well as down arrows.

This type of a formation can be traded in two ways.

The first way is to trade the price between the two levels: Go long when the price comes near the support levels with a stop loss below the support; and go short when the stock nears the resistance level with a stop loss above the resistance level.

Second, the formation can be traded on a breakout. The stock price of DLF generated a downward breakout after a sideways trend of 22 trading sessions. This breakout helps us in identifying it as a downward trend change breakout pattern.

The name of the pattern suggests that the price was originally in an up trend, it then moved into a sideways trend, and finally the price trend has changed to down.

After the pattern is identified, the next important thing is its confirmation and validation. The confirmation of this pattern is based on the breakout having a good black candle closing below the support level or the range, and is validated by the breakout being accompanied by a rise in volume when compared to the earlier three candles.

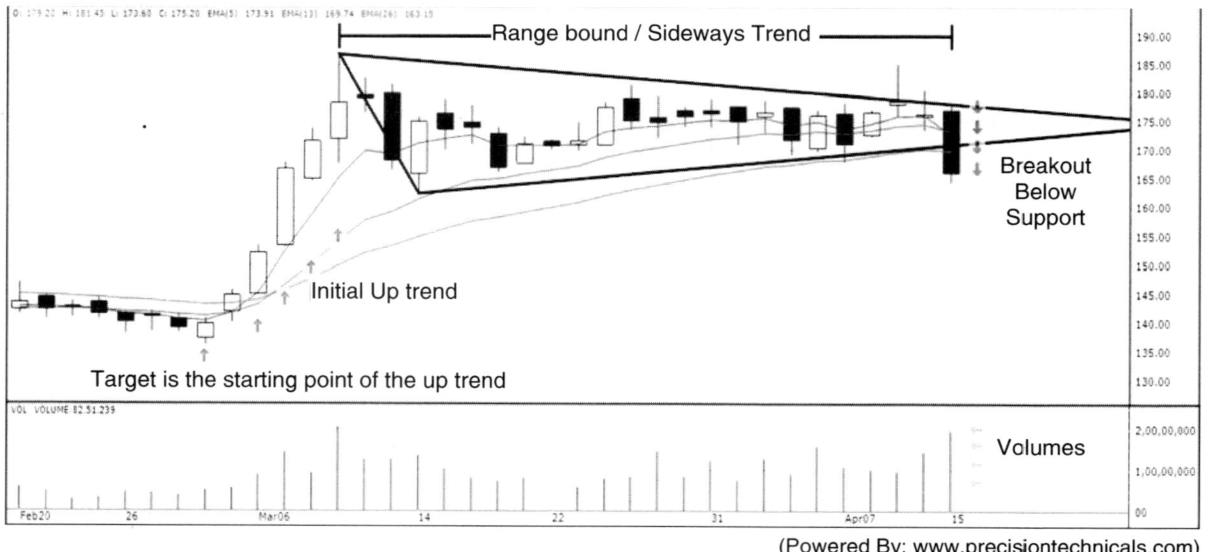

(Powered By: www.precisiontechnicals.com)

Figure 16.24: **Daily candlestick chart of DLF with a downward trend change breakout**

The chart in Figure 16.24 shows that the stock price qualifies in the identification, confirmation as well as the validity of a downward trend change breakout pattern.

Before you enter a trade, you need to complete the analysis by estimating both the price target and the time target. A downward trend change breakout suggests that you either go short in the stock, or exit the stock if it is a part of your portfolio.

The price target for this pattern is the lowest point (starting point) of the original up trend. In this case, as marked on the chart in Figure 16.24, you can see that the original up trend which prevailed, before the sideways trend started, began from a level of ₹136. This now becomes the target for the stock price after the breakout.

The next important thing is to determine the time target, the calculation of which remains the same for all patterns. We need to count the number of candles from the start of the up trend till the pattern breakout candle (last candle), and then divide that number by 3.

In the chart in Figure 16.25, you will be able to see the candle count tool plotted on the chart which displays the count as 29 candles between the two points. So the time target is 29 ÷ 3 = 9.66. We round it off higher to 10 candles. That is the time target.

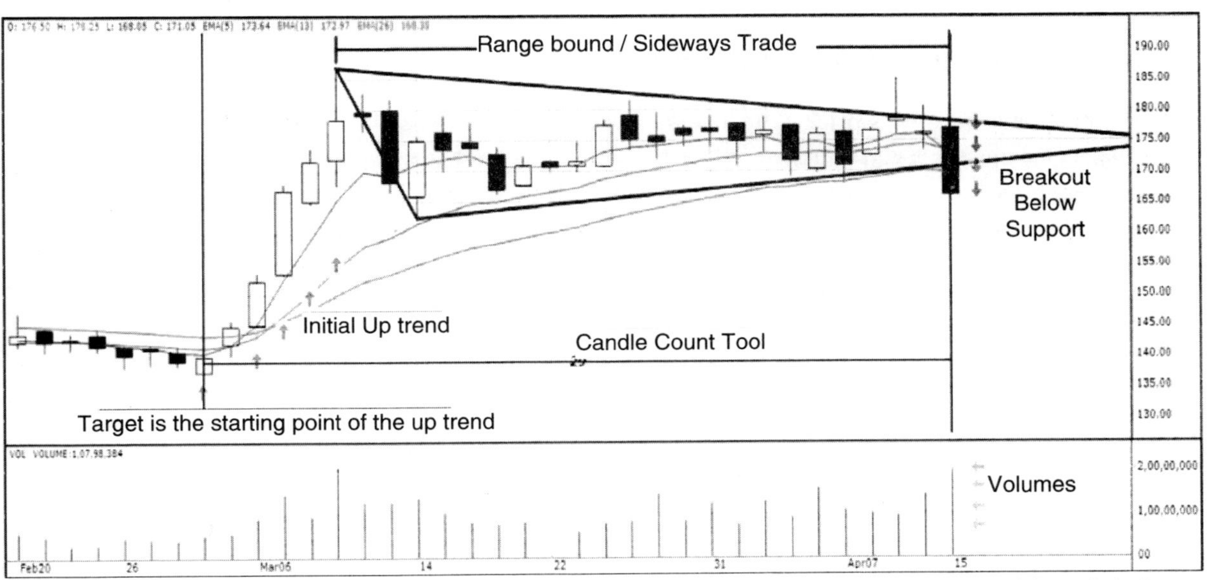

Powered By: www.precisiontechnicals.com

Figure 16.25: **Daily candlestick chart of DLF with the candle count tool plotted on the chart**

Reversal Patterns at the Bottom

These price patterns suggest that the fundamentals of the company are improving, namely changing from bad to good. After the formation of such patterns the price trend changes from down to up. This means that these price patterns present you an opportunity to go long in a stock, both with a short term as well as with a long term view. These patterns also have the potential of generating multibagger returns in your portfolio.

Let us now understand the psychology, identification, confirmation, validity, price target and time target when analysing these patterns.

The important reversal patterns at bottom are:

1. Inverted head and shoulders;
2. Double or triple bottom;
3. Rounding bottom;
4. Upward trend change breakout; and
5. Listing breakout pattern.

Inverted Head and Shoulders Pattern

As the name suggests, this price formation looks like a person doing a headstand (yogic *sheer-shasana*). This is a reversal pattern at the bottom. It suggests that something good or positive is happening with the company's fundamentals which is likely to become publicly known in the near future. After the formation of this pattern, the price trend changes from down to up. Obviously, then, this pattern presents an opportunity to go long.

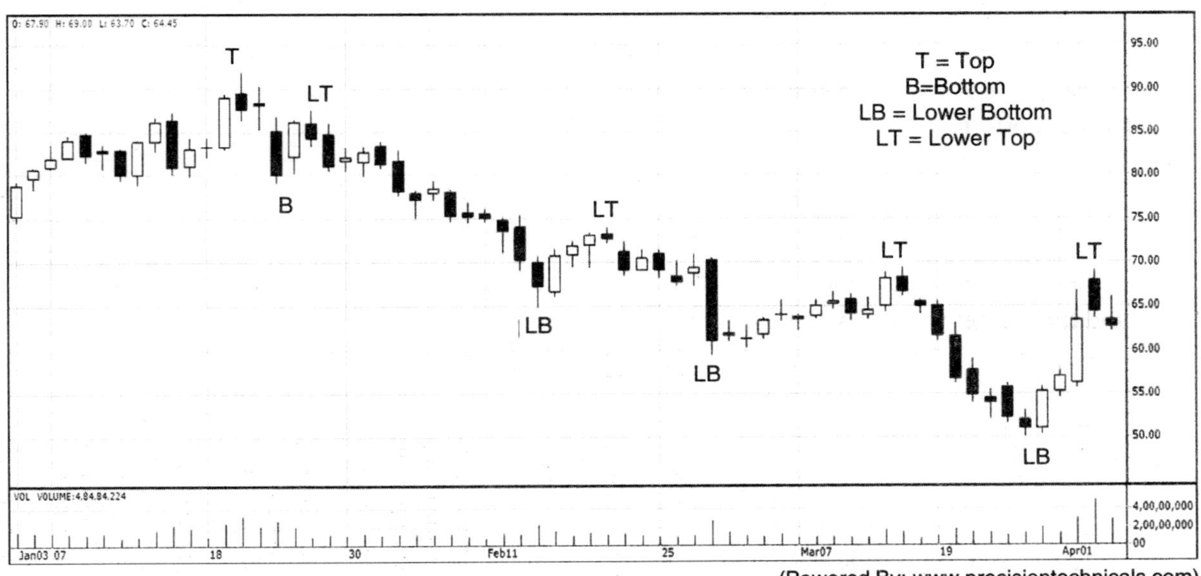

(Powered By: www.precisiontechnicals.com)

Figure 16.26: **Daily candlestick chart of RCOM with successive lower tops and bottoms marked**

~

Pattern Identification

In the chart in Figure 16.26, you can see the price making lower tops and lower bottoms. This suggests that the price is in a down trend. Looking at the current chart set-up one would say that after making a lower top, the price now seems to be heading for a new lower bottom. In the series of charts that follow we will understand the process by which you will be able to identify the formation of an inverted head and shoulders pattern.

In Figure 16.27, there are four additional candles on the right hand side of the chart and a change of view is clear. In this chart we can see that the price suddenly made a higher bottom and also made a new high after making lower tops and lower bottoms for many days.

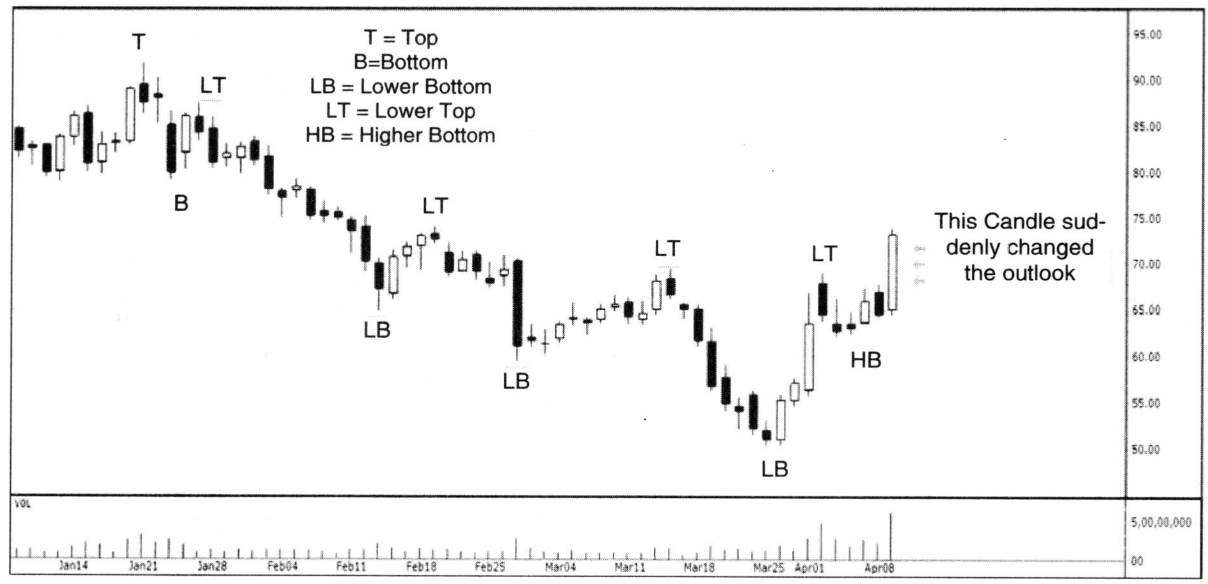

(Powered By: www.precisiontechnicals.com)

Figure 16.27: **Daily candlestick chart of RCOM with tops and bottoms marked on the chart — see how the last candle changes the outlook**

~

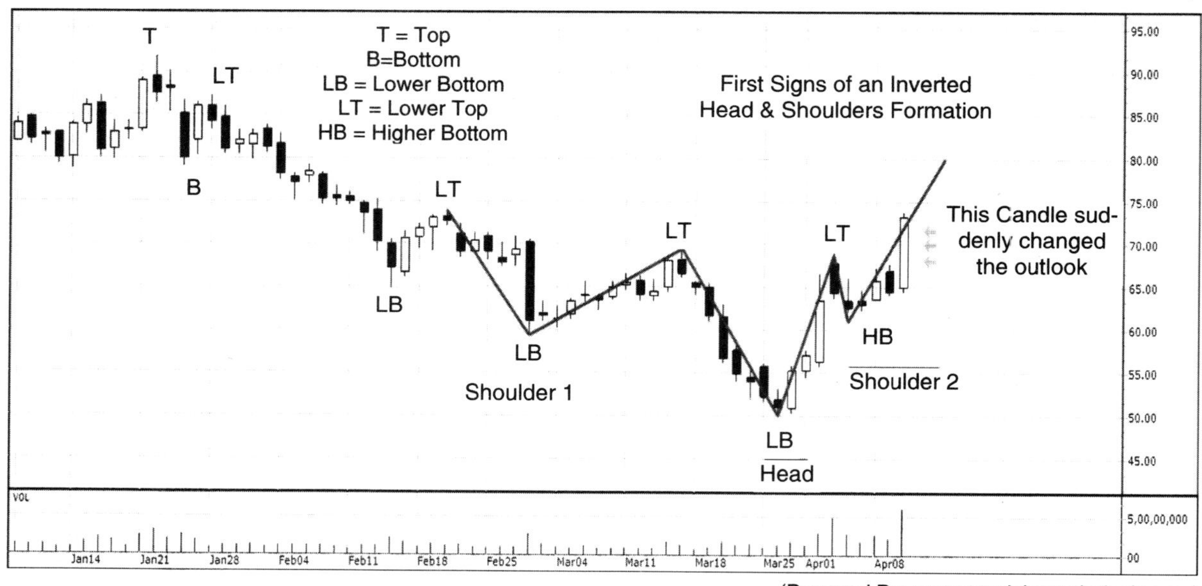

(Powered By: www.precisiontechnicals.com)

Figure 16.28: **Daily candlestick chart of RCOM with one inverted head and shoulders pattern highlighted with solid lines**

~

This is the first time after many days of a down trend that there is a change in the trend. Once the candle is formed you will be able to see an inverted head and shoulders forming on the chart. Let us mark the pattern so that we will be able to see it clearly. In the chart in Figure 16.28, the inverted head and shoulders is identified by solid lines.

Pattern Confirmation

In the chart in Figure 16.29, we have plotted the neckline joining the highest points between the head and the shoulders. As you can see, the last candle has given us both a break-out and a close above the neckline suggesting that an inverted head and shoulders pattern has formed.

As this pattern resembles a person standing upside down, we should have a head and one shoulder each on either side of the head, at a higher level than the head. This pattern can have either a horizontal neckline or a slanted one. **None of the shoulders should be below the head; otherwise the pattern is not valid.**

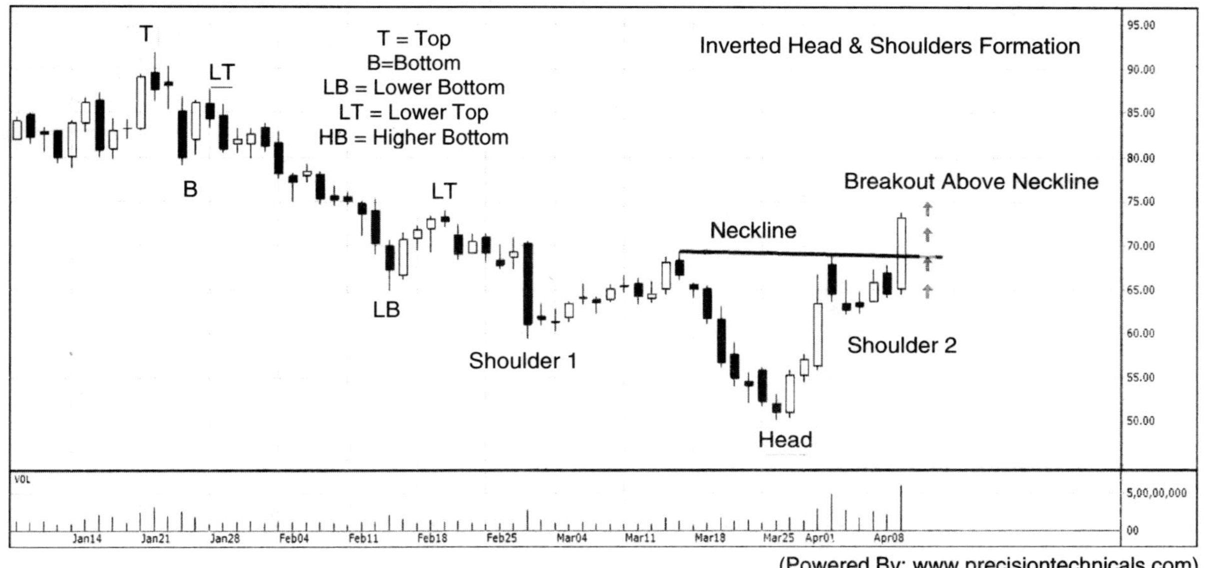

(Powered By: www.precisiontechnicals.com)

Figure 16.29: **Daily candlestick chart of RCOM with the neckline plotted on it**

~

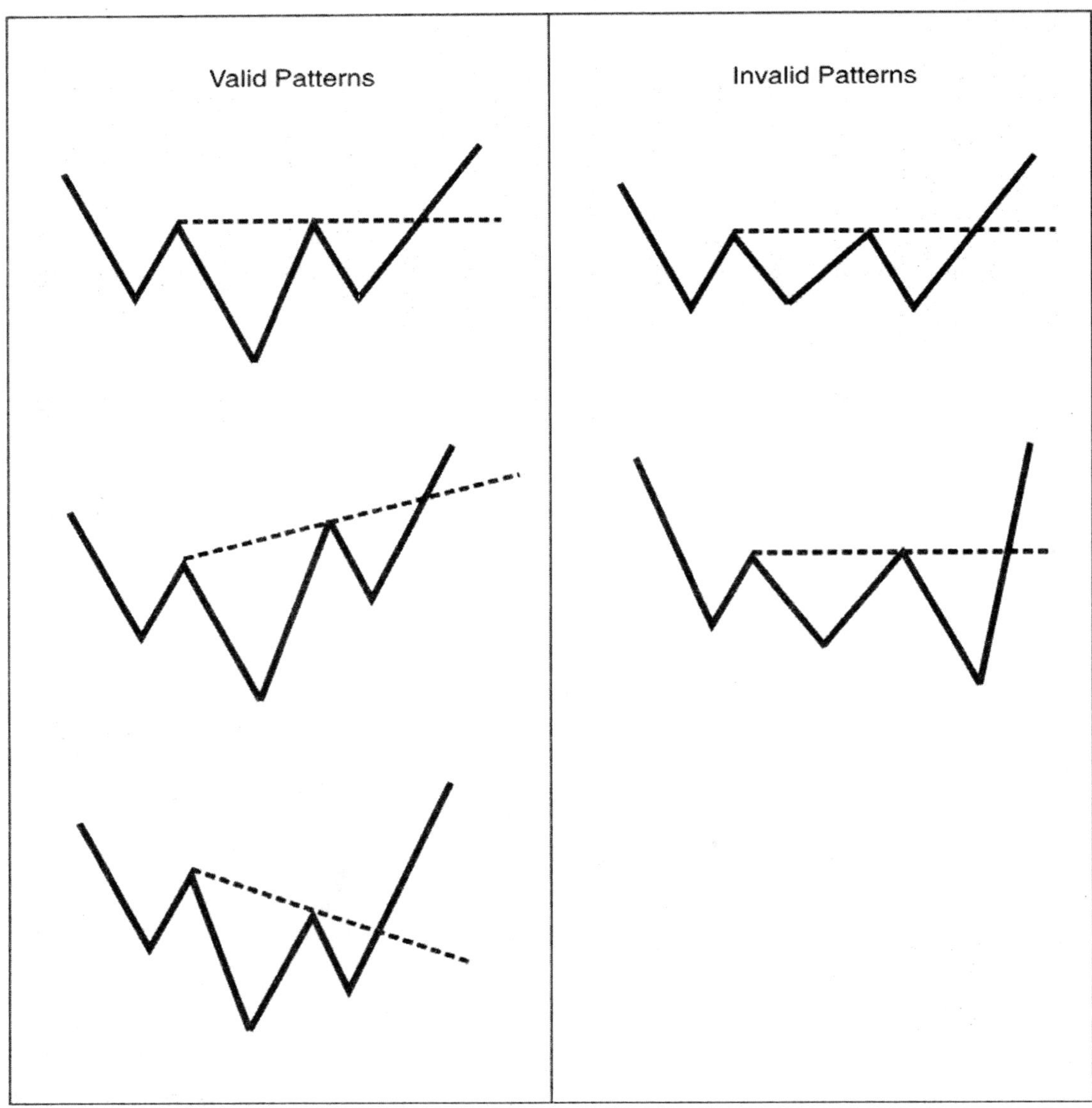

Figure 16.30: **Valid and invalid inverted head and shoulders patterns**

~

Let us look at Figure 16.30 which displays some examples to understand the differences between valid and invalid inverted head and shoulders patterns.

Remember: Do not enter a trade in anticipation of the neckline being broken in the future. This would be presuming that the price will give a breakout above the neckline, which also acts as a strong resistance. History has proved that such trades involve high risk and when using technical analysis it is best to trade only on a confirmation and not in anticipation.

Pattern Validation

After confirming the pattern, the next important step is its validation. This is important in order to reduce the number of losing trades, whipsaws or false breakouts. As has been highlighted right through, pattern confirmation and validation are most important for reducing the chances of a wrong analysis.

The validity of a pattern is confirmed by volumes. A single individual can neither create nor significantly influence price moves. Only when a strong consensus, evidenced by higher volumes, exists on the long side will the price go up; if the strong consensus is on the short side, that will make the stock move downwards.

The chart in Figure 16.31 displays how the higher than normal volumes help us in validating the price pattern.

In this chart you can see that the price has given us a breakout above the neckline and this is accompanied by high volumes. Once a stock qualifies for both confirmation as well as validity, one should trade this breakout.

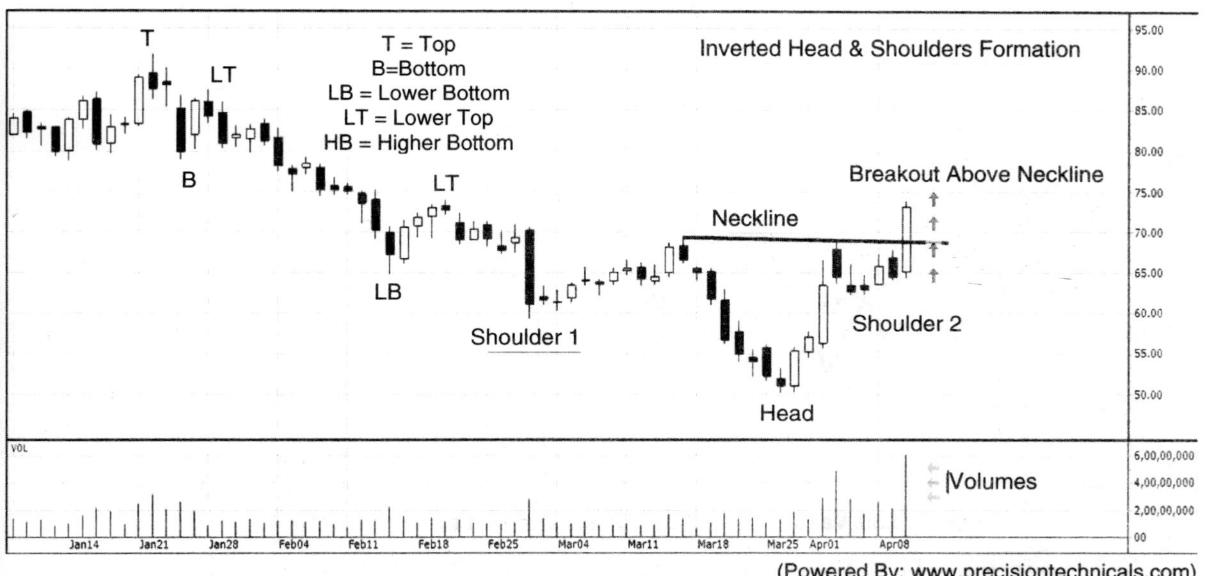

(Powered By: www.precisiontechnicals.com)

Figure 16.31: **Daily candlestick chart of RCOM showing the breakout above the neckline plotted on the chart**

~

Pattern Price Target

We now have both a confirmation and a validity for the breakout pattern on the chart in Figure 16.31. The view suggests that one can now go long. The next set of parameters we should consider are risk management, price target, and time frame. We will discuss risk management at length in Chapter 18 later in the book. For now, let us discuss how to set up a tentative price target and a tentative time frame.

When we trade a price pattern, we are directly trading the sentiments of the bulls and the bears. This means that both sides are executing trading positions in their respective directions, but only one of them is going to win. The winner is decided by the direction, confirmation and validity of the breakout.

Also, as discussed earlier, in the case of a price pattern there are two forces which come into play after a breakout:

- In the case of an upward breakout:
    1. Genuine buying first helps in generating the upward breakout and, then, the subsequent follow up buying helps the trend to continue.
    2. Subsequent short covering by traders caught on the wrong side helps the price rally up further.
- In the case of a downward breakout:
    1. Genuine selling first helps in generating the downward breakout and, then, the subsequent follow up selling helps the trend to continue.
    2. This spurs the longs to square off, which forces the price move down even further.

Pattern price target is important in order for the trader to understand the level where one needs to either exit the trade, or book full or partial profits. Remember, you are comfortable with a fixed deposit investment because you are aware of the returns that your investment is going to generate after the pre-defined tenure. Defining a tentative price target can similarly help you feel comfortable in the trade.

In the case of an inverted head and shoulders formation you need to do the following to calculate the price target:

1. Measure the vertical distance between the low of the head and the neckline.
2. Add the same value from the breakout point on the neckline.

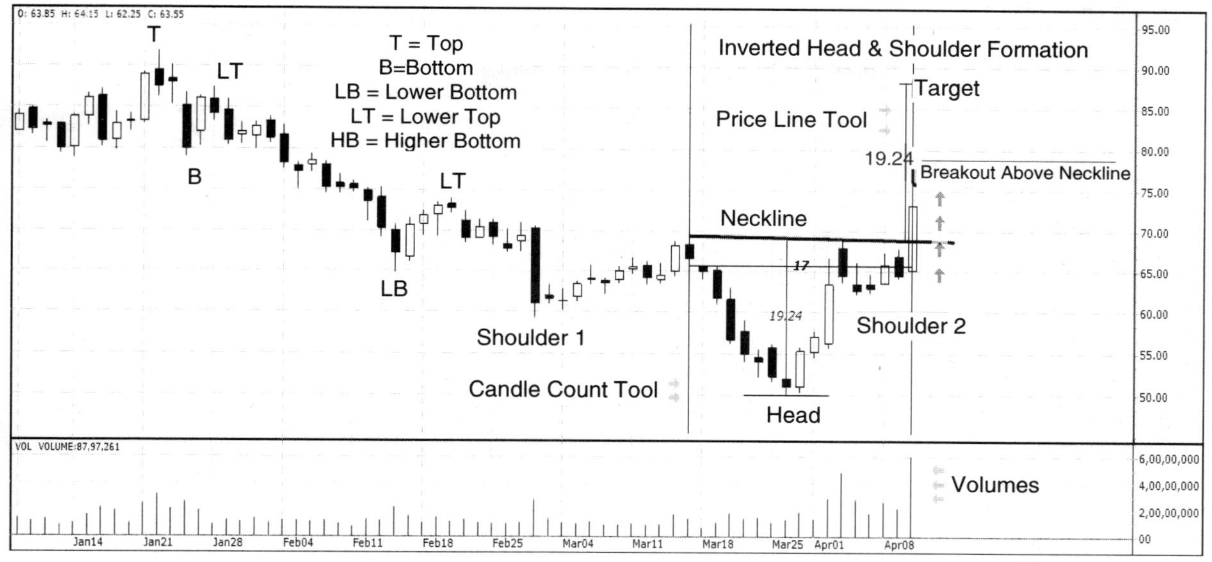

(Powered By: www.precisiontechnicals.com)

Figure 16.32: **Price target calculation in the daily candlestick chart of RCOM with the price line tool plotted and the price target calculation figures displayed. The vertical distance between the low of the head and the neckline is at ₹19.24, and after adding the same value in the breakout point on the neckline the target as displayed is ₹88.20. The current closing is ₹73.20, which means the price is expected to rally up by approximately 19% in the days to come.**

~

The price target calculating is shown in Figure 16.32.

As discussed earlier, these patterns generate big moves and big opportunities.

Pattern Time Target

Just like the pattern price target, calculating the pattern time target is also important because it helps in assessing whether the particular stock fits in your investment profile or positional trader profile. It also helps in assessing the strength of the stock and in implementing partial profit booking.

As discussed earlier, the price usually takes one-third as much time to reach the target as it had taken for the pattern to form from the first neck point to the breakout level. So the calculation is simple; count the number of candles in between these points, and divide that number by 3.

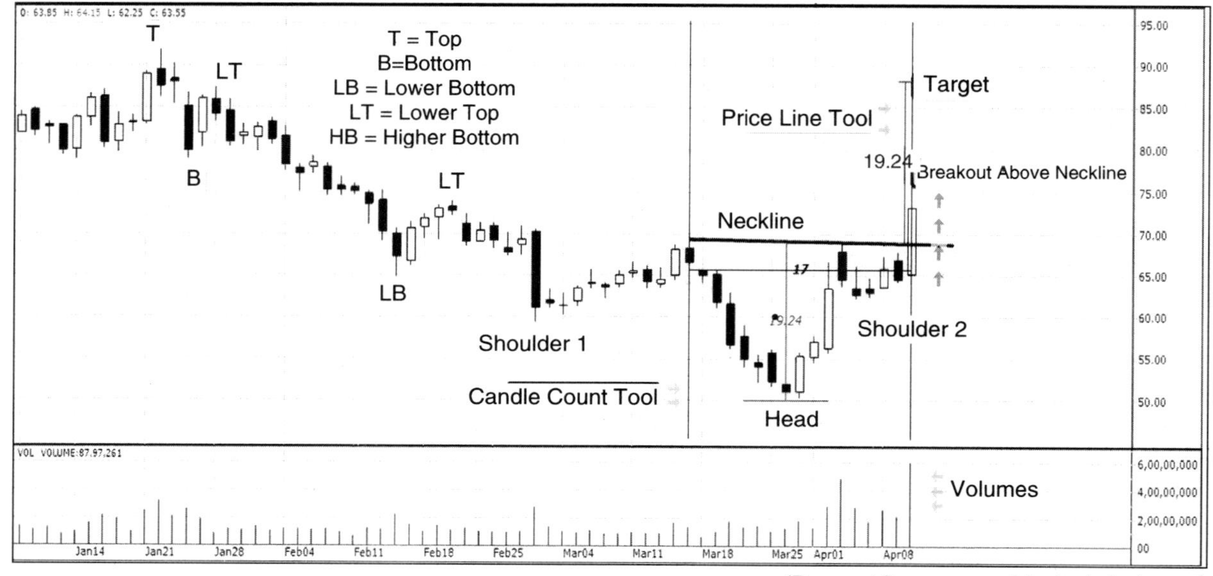

(Powered By: www.precisiontechnicals.com)

Figure 16.33: **Inverted head and shoulders formation in the daily candlestick chart of RCOM with the candle count tool plotted**

~

The chart in Figure 16.33 displays the candle count tool* which is showing the number of candles between the first neck point and the breakout candle as 17, meaning that there are 17 candles between these two points. So the time target would be one-third of 17.

Time Target = Number of candles from the first neck point to the breakout candle.

= 17 ÷ 3 = 5.67

Time Target = 6 Candles (rounded upwards as we cannot have decimals when counting candles).

We expect the price target to be achieved in approximately 6 candles.

---

* In the Profision software you can automatically calculate the number of candles in a pattern using the candle count tool. Or, You can do so as explained here.

Double Bottom Formation

This pattern is a mirror opposite of the double top formation. To start with, the price is in a down trend. It then finds support at a level from where it rallies upward but the move fails to sustain. The price again falls to the lows made earlier. This can be observed in the chart in Figure 16.34, where you can clearly see the weakness in the price which is continuously heading downward. The chart is suggesting that the price could even go on to make new lows. Now, however, if you see the follow up chart in Figure 16.35, we have a white candle which has come up at the end.

This is the first hint that there may be a double bottom taking shape, because after witnessing a sell-off the price has managed to take support at the same level as that of the earlier bottom.

In the chart in Figure 16.36, a horizontal line has been plotted to check whether the double bottom identified is both confirmed and valid.

(Powered By: www.precisiontechnicals.com)

Figure 16.34: **Weekly candlestick chart of JSW Steel showing the price in a down trend.**

(Powered By: www.precisiontechnicals.com)

Figure 16.35: **Follow up weekly candlestick chart of JSW Steel showing the price trending down but a white candle has formed at the end of this chart.**

~

(Powered By: www.precisiontechnicals.com)

Figure 16.36: **Weekly candlestick chart of JSW Steel following on from Figure 16.34 and Figure 16.35 with the double bottom level marked by a horizontal line.**

~

For validation and confirmation we need to check whether the stock fulfils the following criteria:

1. First, the two bottoms should be marked by using a horizontal line. A difference of up to 0.5% between the two bottoms is fine, but no more.
2. We need to have a buy signal from the candlestick pattern at the second bottom.
3. There must be an increase in volume on the last candle compared to the volumes of the earlier three candles.

The buy signal by the candlestick pattern, along with increased volumes at the double bottom level suggest that the price has taken support at the level of the earlier bottom.

If the price formation fulfils the above criteria then we can call this pattern as a double bottom formation. This is a reversal formation at the bottom, suggesting that the price which was earlier in a down trend will now change to an up trend after this formation (*see* Figure 16.37).

(Powered By: www.precisiontechnicals.com)

Figure 16.37: **Weekly candlestick chart of JSW Steel with the double bottom marked by a horizontal line and increase in volume highlighted, showing how the last candle suddenly changes our view of what the chart is telling us.**

~

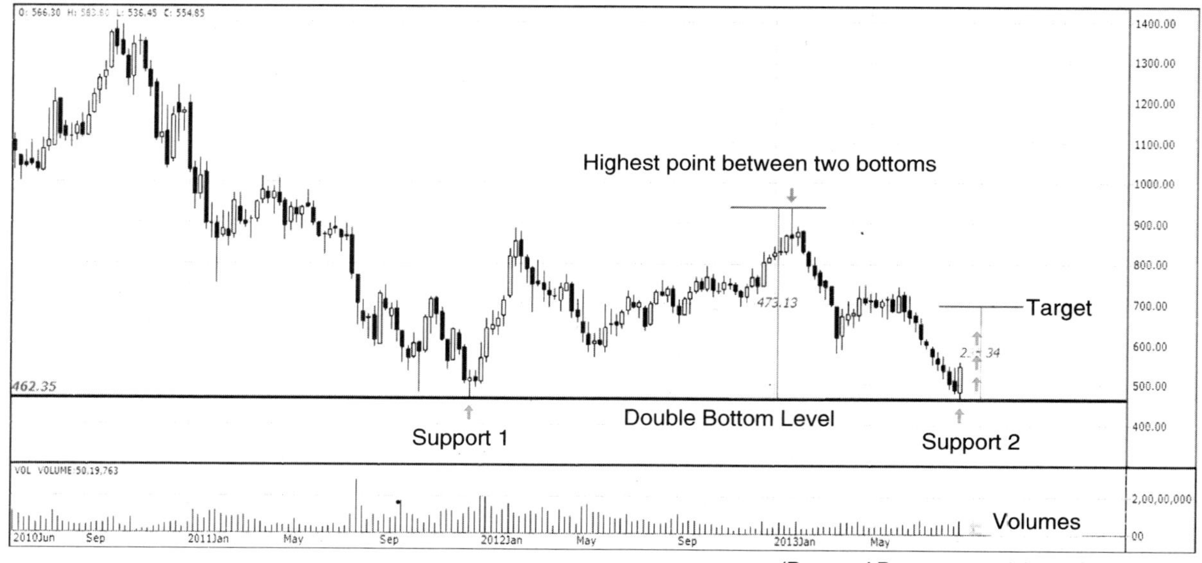

(Powered By: www.precisiontechnicals.com)

Figure 16.38: **Calculating the price target in the weekly candlestick chart of JSW Steel. The price target is marked on the chart.**

~

After identifying, confirming and validating the pattern, the next task is to work out the price target and the time target for the price.

For arriving at the price target we do the following, as shown in Figure 16.38:

1. Calculate the difference between the double bottom level and the highest point between the two bottoms.
2. The price is expected to rise a minimum of 50% of this difference from the double bottom level.

For arriving at the time target, we count the number of candles between the two bottoms, and divide the number by 3.

In the chart in Figure 16.39, you will be able to see the candle count tool identifying the number of intervening candles as 88. The time target would be this number divided by 3.

Now, 88 ÷ 3 = 30 (rounded off)

So the price target is expected to be achieved over the time span of 30 candles.

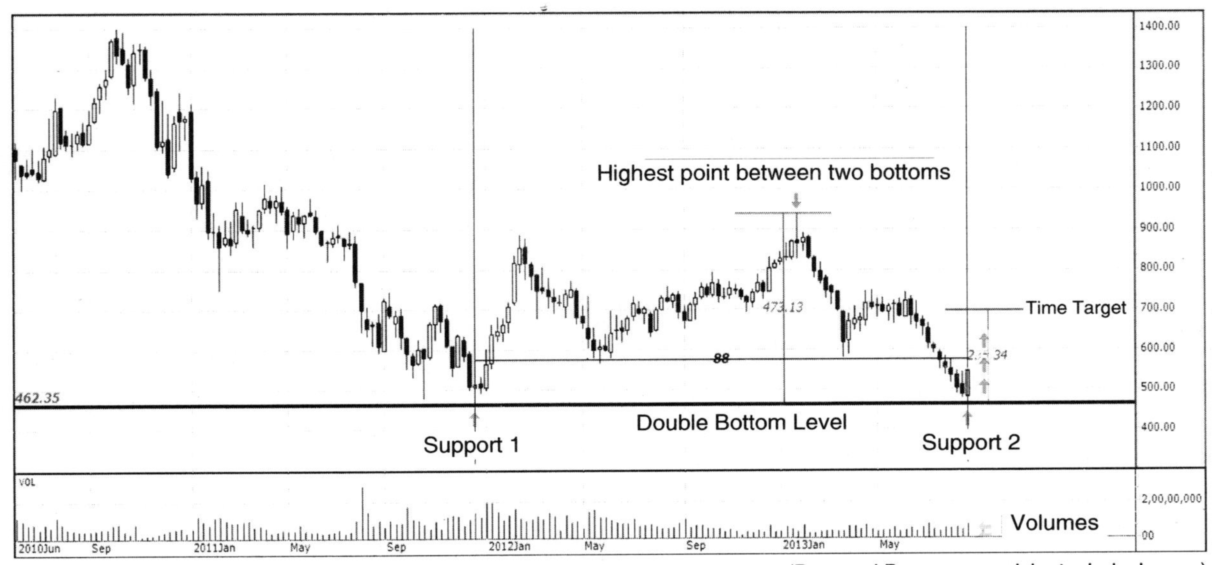

(Powered By: www.precisiontechnicals.com)

Figure 16.39: **Weekly candlestick chart of JSW Steel with the candle count tool plotted to arrive at the time target**

~

Triple Bottom Formation Pattern

This pattern is just the opposite of a triple top formation. As the name suggests, it occurs at the bottom of a down trend and is similar to a double bottom formation except for the addition of one more bottom, making it three bottoms in all. This pattern is very rarely observed. Its important points, such as its identification, confirmation, validity, price target and time target are all similar as in the case of a double bottom formation pattern. This pattern forms at the bottom of the trend and also at the bottom of a business cycle. In short, this pattern is formed when investors are hopeful of the business reviving.

Rounding Bottom Formation Pattern

This is an interesting price pattern, useful for long term investors who want to buy into multi-bagger stocks. Before going into the details of this pattern, let us try to understand the psychology behind this formation. The formation of this pattern is a good example of technicals and fundamentals going hand in hand. I will be showing you a way wherein with the help of the price chart you can also understand the fundamentals of a company.

Figure 16.40: **Monthly candlestick chart of Whirlpool displaying a price correction**

~

The chart in Figure 16.40 displays that the price of Whirlpool fell from its highs of ₹237.50 in September 1994 to lows of ₹15.50 in December 1997. This is called a price correction.

For a moment let's consider that you are the promoter of this company. The stock price of your company has fallen from ₹237.50 to ₹15.50 in three years. In a way this chart is revealing the condition of your company's fundamental health. Now, here's the question for you:

What do you feel is going on in your company? Is its condition good or bad?

The falling share price from 1994 to 1997 tells us that the fundamentals of this company turned from good to bad. For three years the stock price remained in a down trend till finally the management woke up as the price reached alarmingly low levels.

As the management / promoter finally wakes up, there arises our next question for you:

As a good promoter of this company what would your plan of action be?

You may have many possible answers rushing to your mind. You may think of buying back shares of your own company from the market because they are available cheap, but then if the company's fundamentals are not sound it means that there also must be a cash flow problem which may not allow you to buy back shares. You may even think of selling off and exiting the company, but that is not always an easy thing to do. When the business is not performing well, you may not easily find a buyer. Plus, the question is addressed to a good promoter, which means a person who would not like to run away but one who would stand firm like the captain of a ship in a crisis till he ensures that the ship has weathered the storm. Therefore your answer to this question would be that you would make all efforts to revive the company.

What could be the different steps or efforts to revive the company?

Among the first things could be cost cutting, changing the business strategy, changing people, employing good management, infusing funds, launching new products, looking out for mergers and acquisitions, etc.

So as the management and the promoter start making efforts to revive the company's business, the stock price goes through a phase of consolidation. Market players and investors had earlier witnessed the fundamentals of the company deteriorating and they would like to confirm and reconfirm any positive changes before they seriously start investing in the stock. This consolidation, called time correction, can be observed in the chart in Figure 16.41.

As the management works hard and starts making efforts to bring the company back into the green, and also achieve positive performance with consistent growth, the stock price witnesses a consolidation. This consolidation, or sideways trend, can, at times last for weeks, and in some cases it can even continue for years together. The chart in Figure 16.41 shows that in this case the company witnessed a consolidation for 13 years! This time correction is indeed important for the price. The longer the duration of this consolidation, better are the later results.

(Powered By: www.precisiontechnicals.com)

Figure 16.41: **Monthly candlestick chart of Whirlpool displays a time correction, or consolidation phase, which lasted thirteen years**

~

There is obviously no fixed time period in which a company can be turned around. Some promoters may be able to do so in two years, while other cases may take much longer.

How much time would you as a promoter of this company require to turn around your loss making or non-performing company whose stock price has fallen in the last 3 years from ₹237.50 to ₹15.50?

The following are some clues for arriving at an answer to this question.

As you start making efforts to revive your company, you would implement new initiatives, make a lot of changes, and continuously check whether they are working. So you implement a strategy, then check whether the new strategy is working in terms of business improvement, or in terms of its quarterly earnings. You would want to see consistency in earnings for some consecutive quarters. Otherwise you could strike lucky in one of the quarters and then be back to where you had started off from. Also, some changes may not work and you may need to modify or reverse them after a few quarters, and then again wait and see if the new change works.

Due to such reasons, the likely time period is a minimum of eight quarters, which means two complete years. So technically for a time correction or price consolidation to be a good one, and for the stock to fit into this price pattern, this phase should last for a minimum of two years. Essentially, the longer the consolidation, better the eventual results.

(Powered By: www.precisiontechnicals.com)

Figure 16.42: **Monthly candlestick chart of Whirlpool displaying a time correction or consolidation phase — the consolidation is clearly visible and highlighted by two horizontal lines**

Price consolidation is clearly visible in the chart in Figure 16.42 and is highlighted by two horizontal lines, one at approximately ₹14.50 and the second one at ₹61. In 1996-1997, the company's management realized that they needed to start making efforts when the stock price fell to levels of approximately ₹14.50. The turnaround efforts went on for thirteen years during which period the price continued to trade between this range of consolidation or time correction.

The next question that arises is: when would it be clear that the efforts of the promoter or the management have started to work and that tnis could be a possible turnaround story? How does one identify, confirm and validate this pattern?

In the case of a rounding bottom, you should enter only after the pattern's formation is confirmed. If you enter a trade during consolidation, then it would be a gamble wherein you would be taking a bet on the management action before you know whether it is going to be successful or not. It is better to enter a trade only when the chart tells you to do so with some certainty. Remember, markets anticipate events well before they actually happen; so the chart will tell you well in advance if a turnaround is going to happen. Let's understand how this works (*see* Figure 16.43).

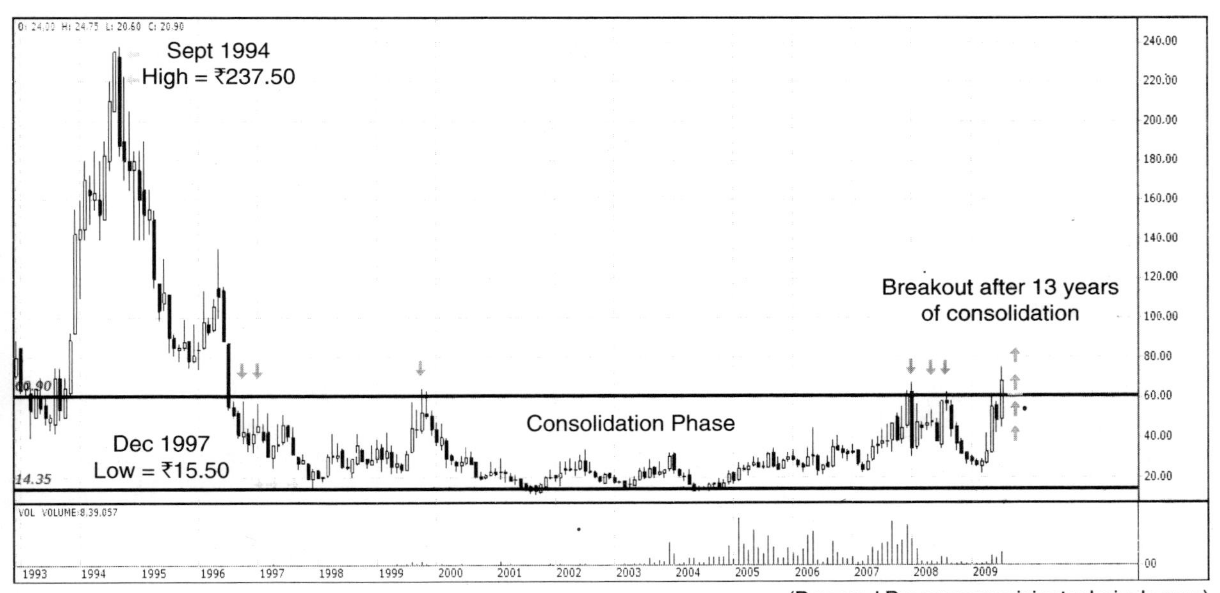

(Powered By: www.precisiontechnicals.com)

Figure 16.43: **Monthly candlestick chart of Whirlpool displays the breakout above the consolidation phase, the point for trade entry**

After the consolidation phase, the price finally breaks out and closes above the consolidation range. This is the first technical sign which suggests that the fundamentals are going to improve. This is the moment when long term investors can initiate a long trade in this stock.

As a promoter, you would know that your efforts to revive the company have by now started working out. You would see the business improving, orders starting to flow in and, at the same time, the price chart giving a breakout above the consolidation phase.

So, as a promoter of this company you are now a happy man. But is this enough reward for all the efforts that you have made, or would you expect something more from your business? Let's look at the chart in Figure 16.43 once again.

As a promoter you had witnessed the price fall from ₹237.50 in 1994 to ₹15.50 in 1996, then witnessed a consolidation in the price between ₹15 and ₹60 for thirteen long years, until it broke out, suggesting some major changes occurring in the business. As you get the first signal of some positive change happening in the fundamentals of your company, would you as promoter have some kind of a target for the efforts that you have taken to revive your company? Look at the chart in Figure 16.43 and then answer the question.

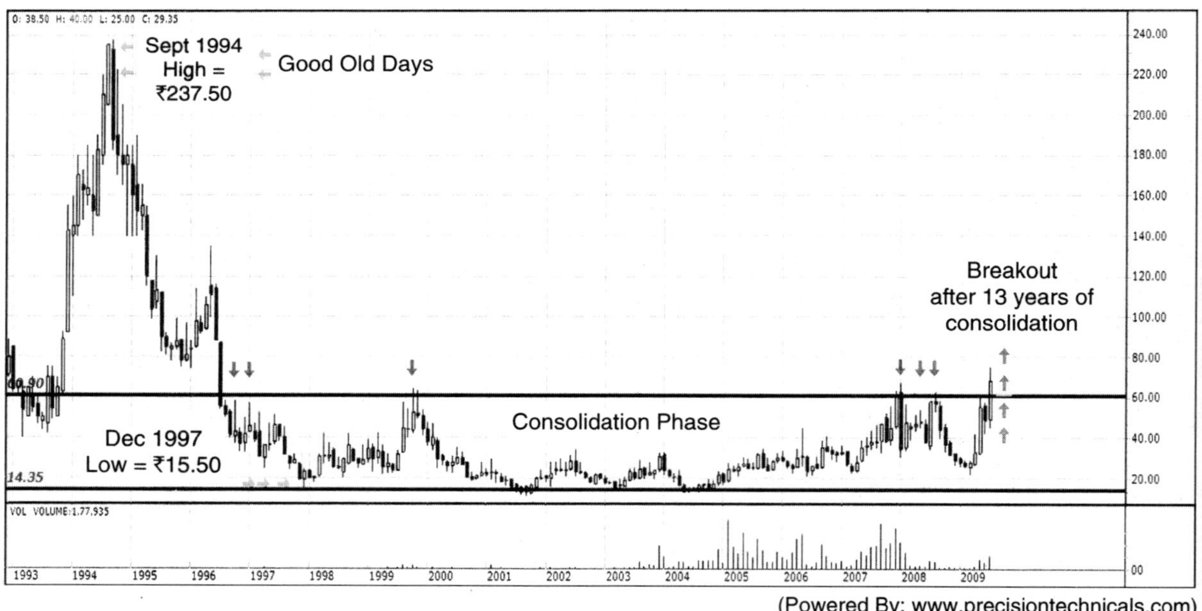

(Powered By: www.precisiontechnicals.com)

Figure 16.44: **Monthly candlestick chart of Whirlpool displays the rounding bottom formation and a subsequent breakout after a 13-years consolidation phase. The target will be the level of the "good old days" of September 1994 which can be seen in the top left area of the chart.**

~

Think about it. As a good promoter who has made efforts to revive your business, you would want to take the business back to its high levels, i.e. the levels it was trading in the good old days before the downfall. While a promoter can't directly influence the stock price, but the efforts that you make to improve the business will finally reflect in the stock price movement.

Mirroring the same sentiments on the price chart, you would want your company's price to go back to those earlier, higher levels where it was before a downfall in the business started. Considering that earlier highs were good days for the business, you would want the price to go back at least to its level of the good old days. In Figure 16.44 the "good old days level" is marked at ₹237.50 which was the peak for the price. So this, then, becomes the target for the price after the breakout.

For a promoter, business growth is an acknowledgement that the efforts taken to revive the company are taking effect. This gets reflected on the price chart with the price rising towards the target level of the good old days.

In the chart in Figure 16.45, you can see the target being achieved suggesting that the management and promoters took the right steps, and made the right changes which enabled the company to come back into the green.

This formation is called a rounding bottom formation.

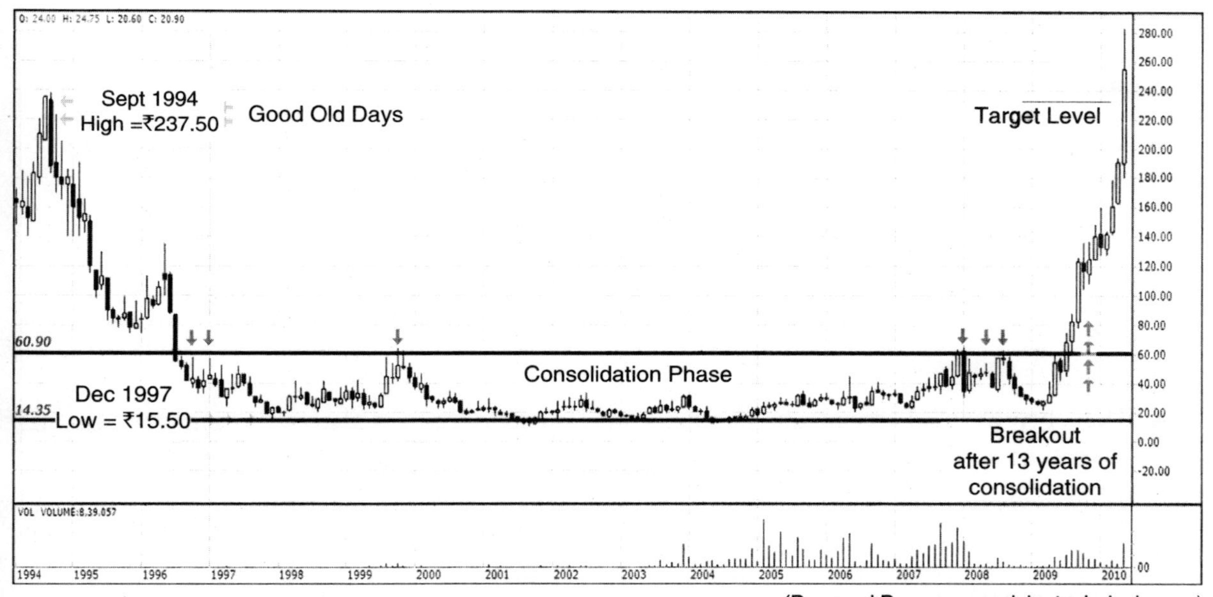

(Powered By: www.precisiontechnicals.com)

Figure 16.45: **Monthly candlestick chart of Whirlpool displays how the target is achieved after breakout from the rounding bottom formation**

Criteria

- First, a decline in the stock price suggesting the business going from good to bad, namely price correction.
- Then a consolidation in the price for a minimum of two years, namely time correction.
- Price then breaks out and closes above this consolidation phase, signalled by the close being above the resistance level plotted at the higher end of the consolidation.
- The breakout needs to be validated by an increase in volumes when compared with the earlier three candles.

Price Target

After the breakout, the price target is the price prevailing in the earlier "good old days," which means the past peak price from where the business had fallen.

Time Target

The price is expected to achieve its target in one to three years.

Important

- **Do not look for the rounding bottom price pattern on a daily or a weekly chart for the simple reason that businesses do not turn around in a matter of days or weeks.**
- If the time correction lasts less than two years, it does not qualify for this price pattern.
- These patterns work nicely on monthly time frame charts. A business turning around is a longer time process, therefore the results also take time. These patterns usually achieve their targets in one to three years.
- Though you would be entering a trade for the long term, risk management is important because such companies are also prone to risk as they are on the verge of a turnaround.
- The maximum weightage of your portfolio should be invested in such stocks for the following two reasons:
  - These stocks have inherent strength, therefore they are not linked to what is happening in the rest of the stock market. The index may fall but a stock where a change in fundamentals is underway would be far less affected. When the market falls, people tend to shift their investments to safe bets, and turnaround stocks qualify in this category.

Turnaround stocks have the potential to generate multibagger returns. Even if there are failures in some stocks, the returns that the rest of your stock portfolio generates will ensure that your portfolio gains handsomely. These stocks thus help in capital appreciation.

Upward Trend Change Breakout Pattern

This pattern is the opposite of the downward trend change breakout pattern that we considered earlier in the chapter. In this case, the price is falling to start with, after which it reaches a level where it enters a consolidation, and then the breakout occurs on the upward side. In this pattern, thus, the bearish sentiment changes to a bullish one due to positive future expectations.

This creates a buy signal on the chart which can be used by both investors and traders. These signals are generally more effective on short term charts. Let's look at some practical examples.

As you can see in the chart of Yes Bank in Figure 16.46, after making a high at ₹366.35 on 21 January 2014 the price witnessed a sell-off which brought it down to a low of ₹291.40 on 4 February. After this, the stock witnessed a sideways trend wherein the price traded between a resistance at approximately ₹313 and a support at approximately ₹294. This sideways trend continued for one month and can be seen highlighted on the chart by two horizontal lines. The overall sideways trend suggests that the buying and selling during this period remained equal, and therefore this neutral phase.

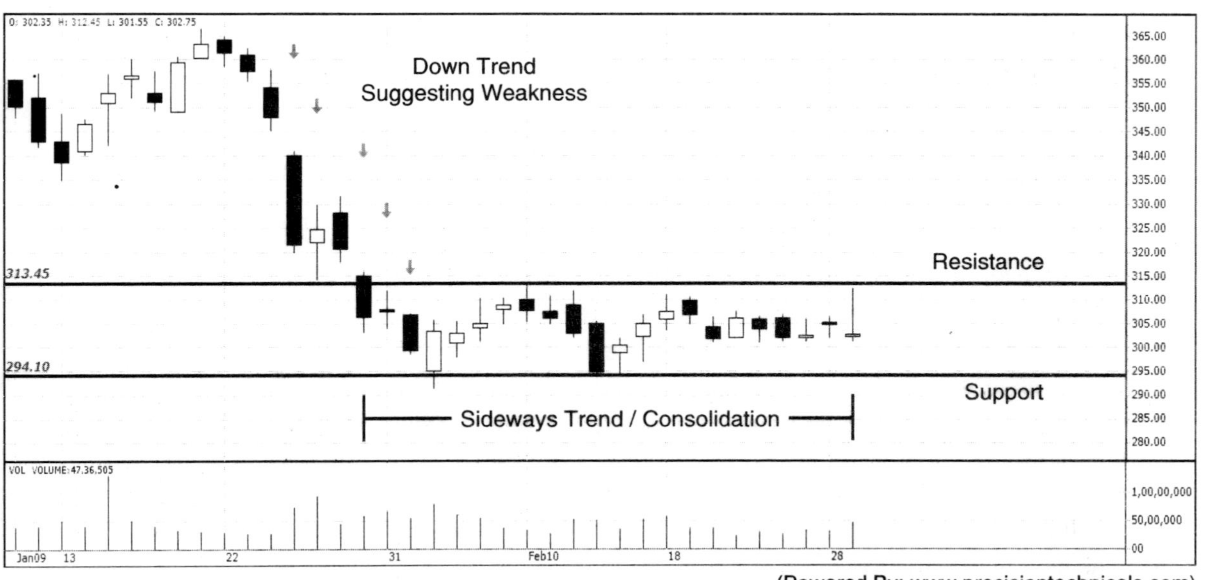

(Powered By: www.precisiontechnicals.com)

Figure 16.46: **Daily candlestick chart of Yes Bank showing price consolidation**

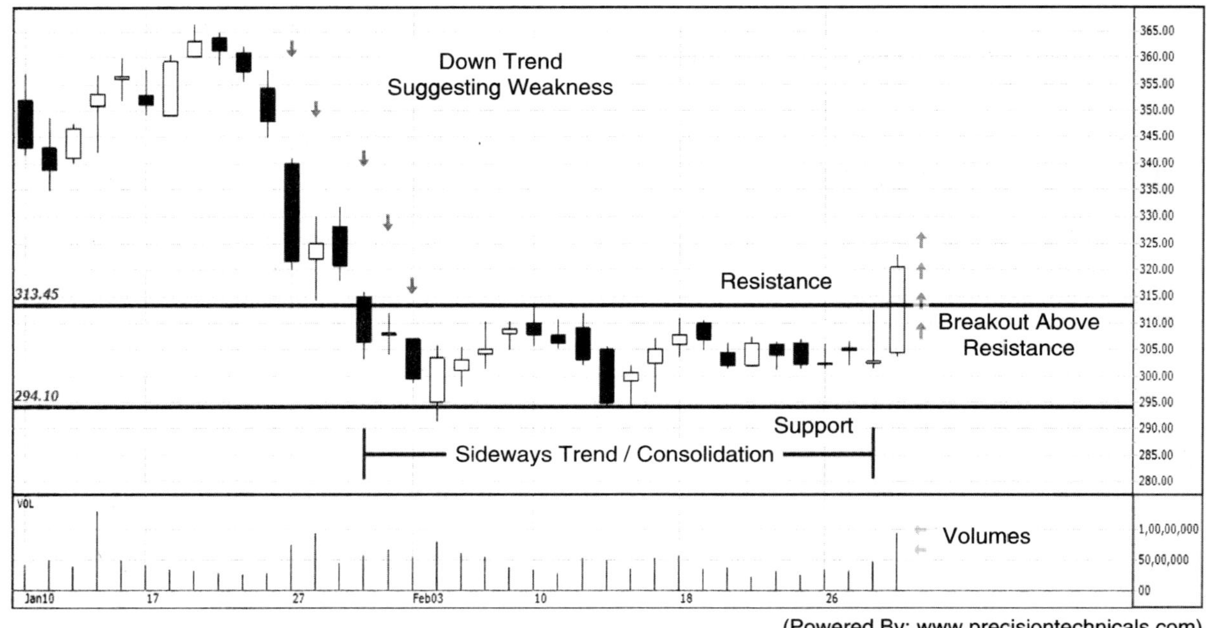

(Powered By: www.precisiontechnicals.com)

Figure 16.47: **Upward trend change breakout pattern: Daily candlestick chart of Yes Bank with price breaking out above the consolidation range**

~

Upward Breakout

The chart in Figure 16.47 shows an upward breakout after a consolidation in Yes Bank. This breakout is confirmed as the closing of the last candle is above the resistance level, and this is also validated by an increase in volumes when compared with the earlier three candles.

To summarise: The original trend was down, after which the price went into a sideways trend and, later, the price trend changed to up, therefore we call this as an upward trend change breakout pattern.

This pattern initiates a buy signal for the stock.

Now, when we are buying a stock we need to know the price target for the prospective trade. The price target in case of this pattern is the price at the start of the initial down trend; in other words, the highest point from where the price started to fall. In this case, the level is ₹366.35 — the high of the candle after which the down trend started. You can see this marked on the chart in Figure 16.48.

The next important thing to work out is the time target. To determine this, we need to count the number of candles from the start of the down trend till the pattern breakout candle / last candle, and then divide that number by 3.

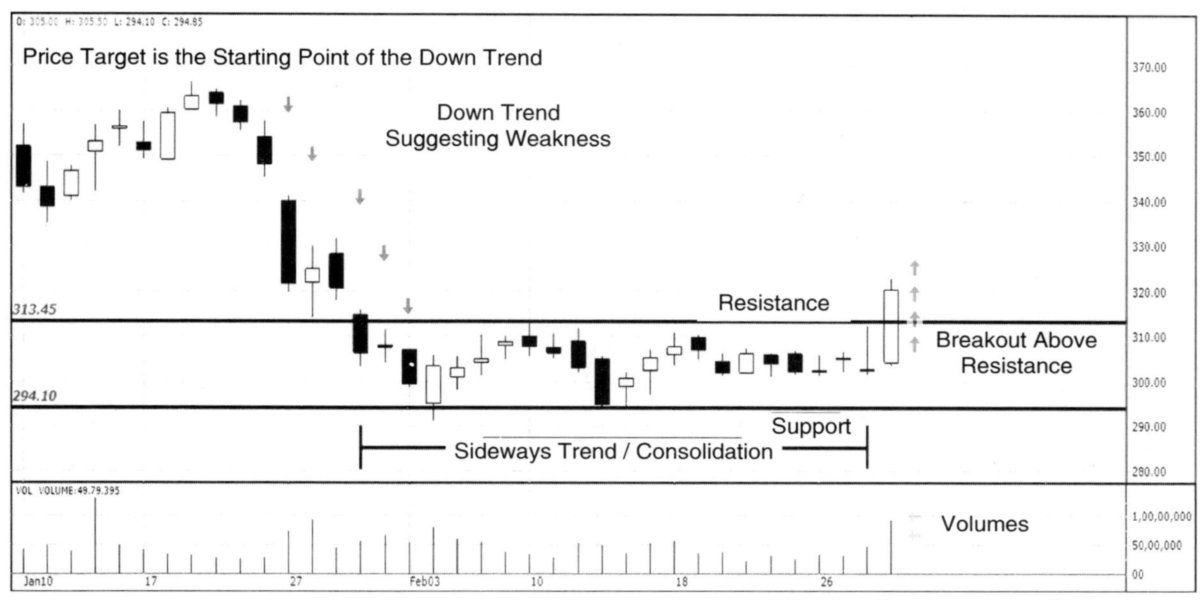

(Powered By: www.precisiontechnicals.com)

Figure 16.48: **Upward trend change breakout pattern: Daily candlestick chart of Yes Bank with price target highlighted for the upward trend change breakout**

~

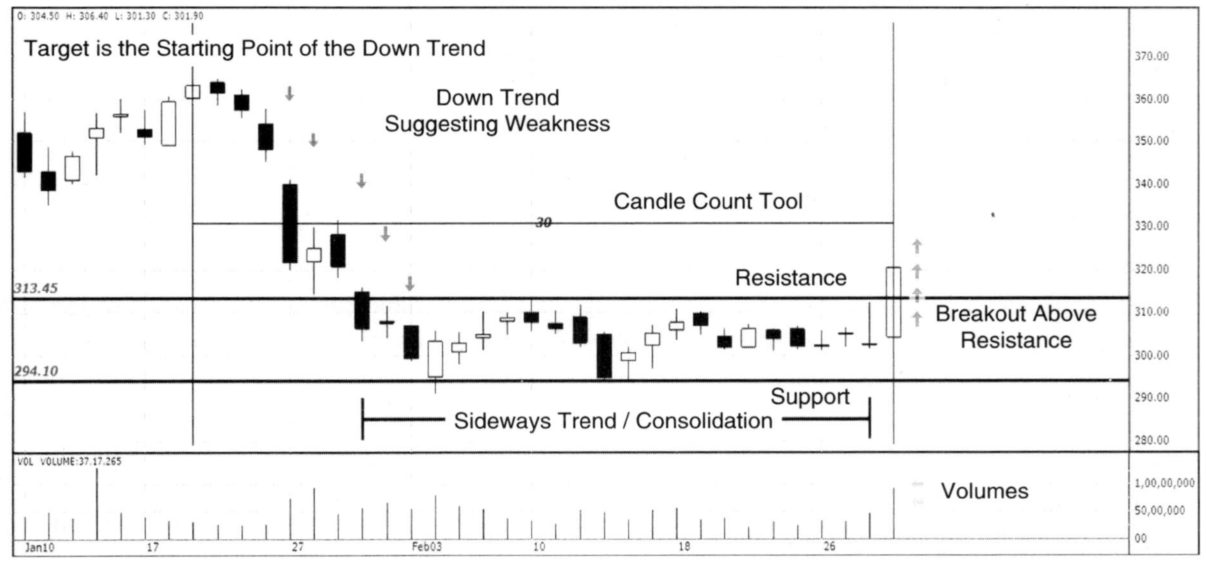

(Powered By: www.precisiontechnicals.com)

Figure 16.49: **Daily candlestick chart of Yes Bank with candle count tool plotted in order to determine the time target in case of an upward trend change breakout pattern**

~

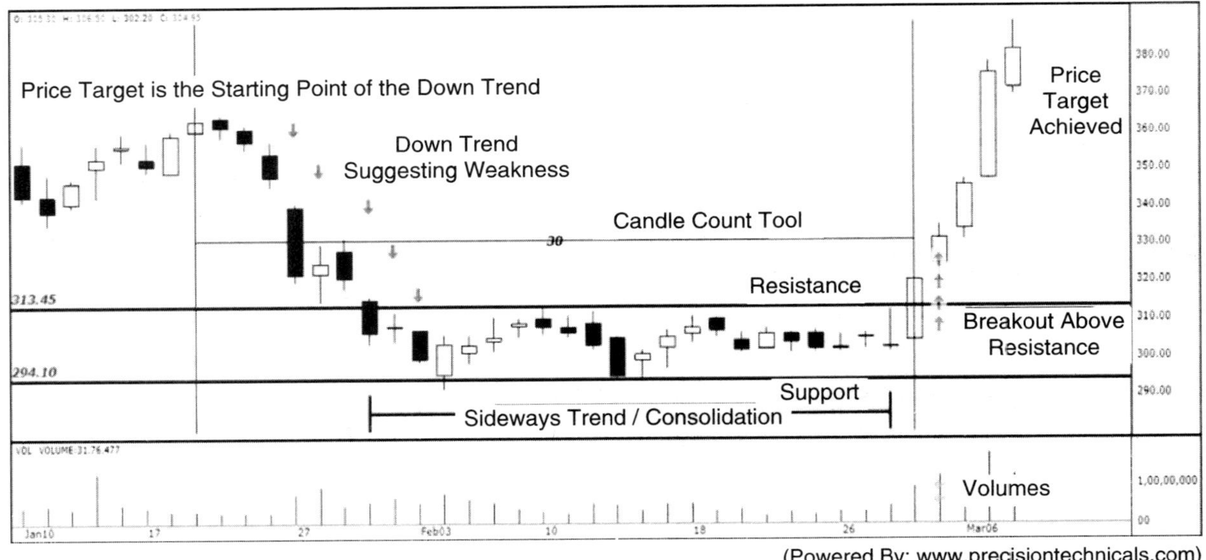

(Powered By: www.precisiontechnicals.com)

Figure 16.50: **Daily candlestick chart of Yes Bank illustrating the price move after the breakout**

~

In the chart in Figure 16.49, you can see the candle count tool plotted on the chart which shows the count as 30 candles between the two points. So the target is 30 ÷ 3 = 10. The time target for the stock price is thus ten candles.

As explained earlier, these patterns are effective when formed on a short term chart.

The price move after the breakout is displayed in Figure 16.50.

Listing Breakout Pattern

Now I introduce a unique pattern which you won't find in any other book in the world. This is a pattern which should be of interest to the long term investor and can be observed in stocks which have a listing history of at least ten years. **It presents a multibagger opportunity for anyone who is ready to stay invested with a long term view.** Let us consider the behaviour and psychology underlying this pattern.

A company decides to file for an IPO listing in order to raise funds for the expansion and growth of its business. The price band for an IPO is decided by its lead managers, book building managers and merchant bankers along with the management of the company based on valuations of business along with some future forecast. Once this is finalized, filed and approved by SEBI, the book building process is done on the given dates. An IPO may be undersubscribed, subscribed fully, or oversubscribed, based on the potential of its business, the pricing, and the prevailing market sentiment at the time of the IPO.

(Powered By: www.precisiontechnicals.com)

Figure 16.51: **Weekly candlestick chart of Persistent Systems with the listing breakout pattern highlighted**

~

The chart in Figure 16.51, which is a weekly candlestick chart of Persistent Systems.

The stock is valued at ₹310 and the IPO gets oversubscribed. The sentiment in the market is good, plus the company has a good name in its industry. The share may list at par — meaning at the same price as of the IPO, or at a premium — meaning at a price higher than the IPO price, or at a discount — meaning at a price lower than the IPO price.

In this case the stock was listed on the exchange at a premium, and closed at around ₹406 level on the listing day. Some people who received the stock booked profits as they were making good gains on listing, as can be observed on the chart highlighted by Caption 1 inset inside the chart in Figure 16.51. There were also people who had missed out either in applying for this IPO, or who had applied but who were not allotted any shares. When the stock lists at a premium, they look at it as a missed opportunity. This feeling of having been left out makes them jump into the stock as the price starts moving up again, and this can be observed on the chart in Figure 16.51 as highlighted by Caption 2 and Caption 3 when the price moves from about ₹360 level to about ₹500 levels.

Thus, we have a stock which, based on future valuations, had a price tag of ₹310, but got listed at ₹406, and two months later was trading at nearly ₹500. At this time the price does not justify the business valuation and investors, domestic funds, foreign institutional investors, etc. realize that the stock is now overpriced. The higher demand *vis-à-vis* the supply during this period took the price to the level of about ₹500. But as the market players realize that the stock is overvalued, the price starts drifting downwards as highlighted by Caption 4 in Figure 16.51. While there is no major selling but because the investors have lost interest in the stock due to its high valuations, the price starts drifting downwards. The price then falls to a level where investors again find value. In the chart in Figure 16.51 you will be able to see that after drifting downwards for two years, the price finally regained its original value, a level where the price justified the business valuations. This can be observed with Caption 5 in Figure 16.51. For the next eight to ten months, the price then traded at this level.

As the business fundamentals start to improve, the chart shows investor interest coming back and the price starts moving upward. This can be observed in the chart at Caption 6 in Figure 16.51. The price keeps moving up as the management of the company works hard to improve the business.

Finally, the stock price once again reaches the all-time high level which it had created after its listing on the exchange. This is an important period and is highlighted by Caption 7 in Figure 16.51. This is a phase which every technical analyst needs to be aware of. As you know "technical analysis is a study of the past price movements which help in deciding the course in the future." Once the price regains its previous high level of approximately ₹500, it faces resistance at first. The price has regained this level after a period of two years and is facing resistance, which means that at this level supply has overpowered demand.

This resistance is mainly because of the exit trades / sell trades executed by investors who had jumped onto the stock in the euphoria after the IPO listing and were stuck in the stock for the next two years while the price drifted deep down below their buying price. As the stock again approaches their buying price, such investors heave a sigh of relief at being able to exit the stock and sell it in order to recover their original investment. This selling continues for a while till all such investors have exited. Meanwhile, the business continues to improve and finally the stock price gives us a breakout above this resistance as highlighted by Caption 8 on the chart in Figure 16.51.

We get a confirmation of this pattern when the price closes above the resistance and it is validated by increasing volumes as compared to the earlier three candles.

This pattern is called listing breakout pattern. **The price has the potential to double in the next one to two years after a listing breakout pattern is formed.** This happens as the business is growing, which is now validated by market players. This pattern confirms that a positive change is going to happen on the fundamental front in the future. The chart in Figure 16.52 shows the way the price moved after the pattern formation.

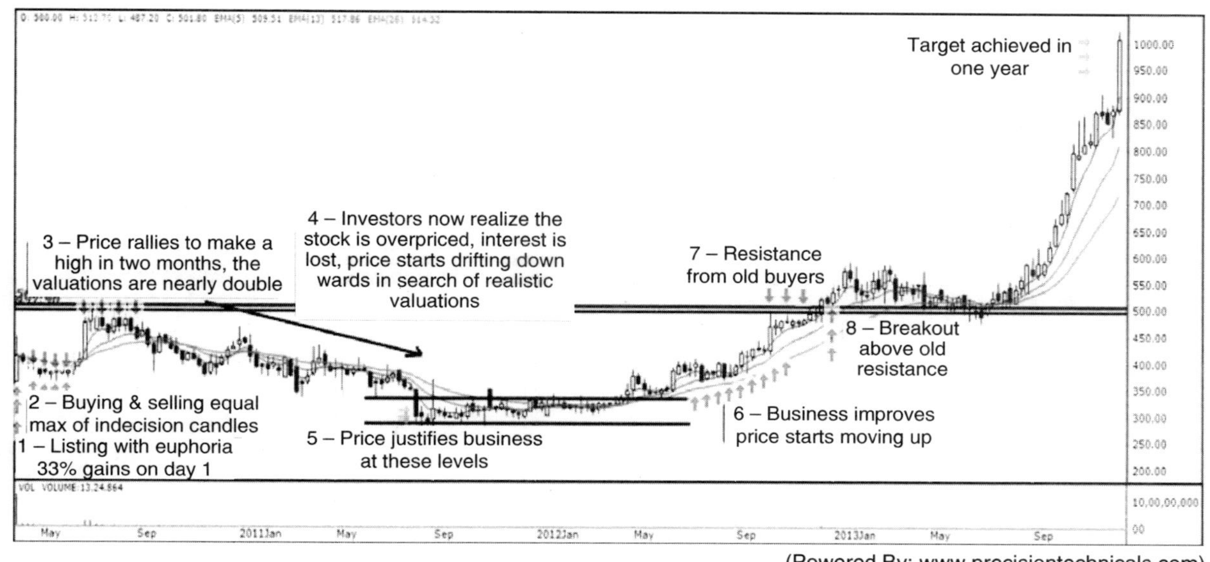

(Powered By: www.precisiontechnicals.com)

Figure 16.52: **Weekly candlestick chart of Persistent Systems highlighting the price move after the listing breakout pattern**

~

Continuation Patterns

If you refer to the life cycle of a stock price chart discussed at the start of this chapter, you will realize that reversal patterns occur when a trend is changing. Thus, they form at the top and at the bottom of a trend. In between a trend we have continuation patterns which help us enter a trade. Continuation patterns are observed far more frequently as compared to reversal patterns.

As the name suggests, the price continues to move in its earlier trend after the formation of these patterns. **Continuation patterns work very well on intraday, short term, medium term as well as long term charts. Also, continuation patterns form in both directions — up as well as down.**

Price formations are created due to a change in the expectations of investors and traders in the market. So long as the same expectations hold, the trend continues. But people like to confirm the trend from time to time, as the price changes its levels. These continuation patterns are formed when people are in the process of reconfirming a particular trend.

These patterns are useful for:

- Intraday traders if formed on a 5-minute chart,
- Positional and swing traders when seen on a daily chart, and
- Investors when they form on a weekly or a monthly chart.

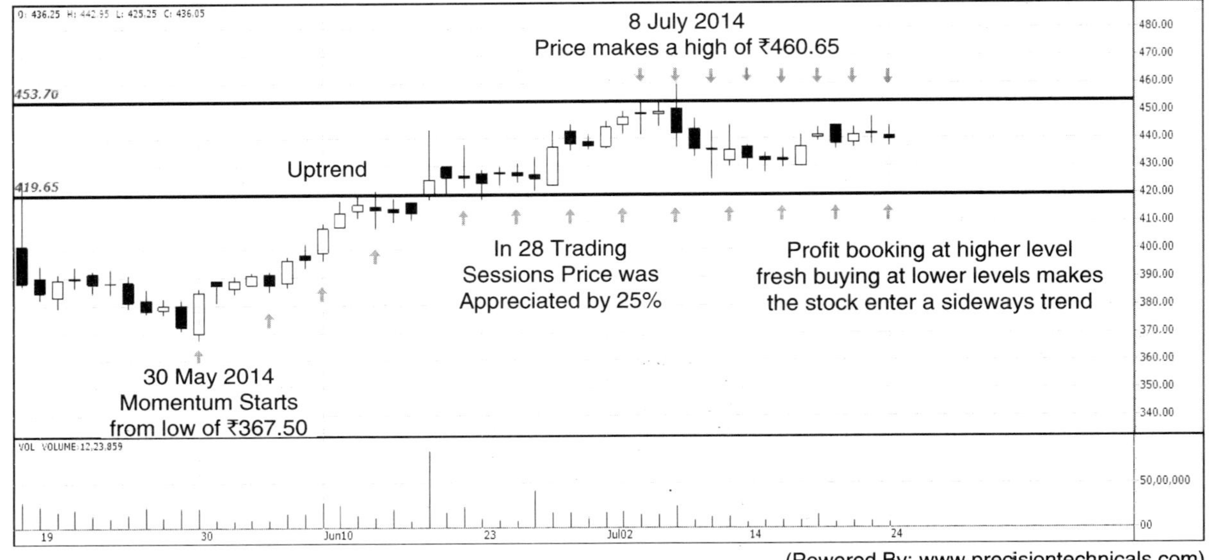

(Powered By: www.precisiontechnicals.com)

Figure 16.53: **Daily candlestick chart of Cipla with the price stuck in a range after an up trend**

~

Up Flag Formation

This is a formation which occurs when the price is moving in an up trend. Let's understand the forces that affect these formations and the psychology behind this pattern with the help of an example.

In the chart in Figure 16.53, the price of Cipla started an up trend on 30 May 2014 from its lows of ₹367.50. The up trend came to an end on 8 July at a high ₹460.65. In 28 trading sessions the price had witnessed a rally of 25%, a phenomenal return for a short term trade. Let us see it this way — you invested in the stock, maybe not at the lowest point but, say at ₹380, in which case you made 21%, or at ₹390, in which case you made 18%, or maybe at ₹400, in which case you made 15%.

Now when people make such good gains in a short term, most investors would book profits. There is nothing wrong in doing so; booking profits is a good thing.

Had this been true in this particular case though, then the stock would have faced selling pressure which would normally have brought the price down. However, instead of the price coming down in a big way, it went into a sideways trend.

This is possible only when the selling and the buying are equal. This can continue for days or weeks, and, at times, even for months (*see* Figure 16.54).

If the buying were to overpower the supply, then eventually we would get a breakout in the upward direction as displayed in the chart in Figure 16.55.

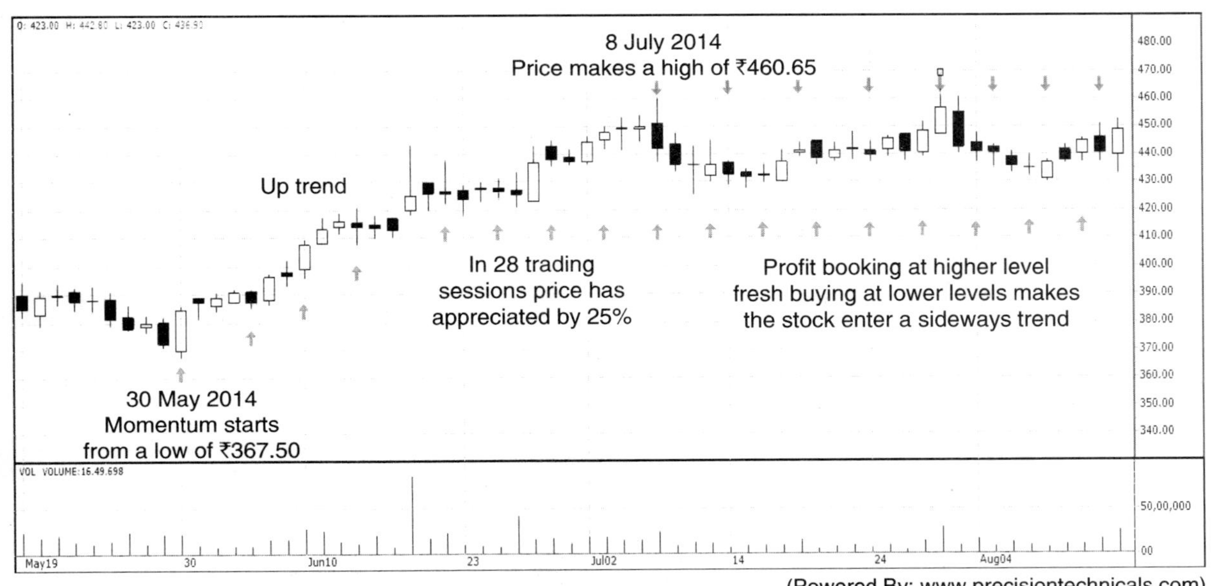

(Powered By: www.precisiontechnicals.com)

Figure 16.54: **Daily candlestick chart of Cipla with its price trading in a range**

~

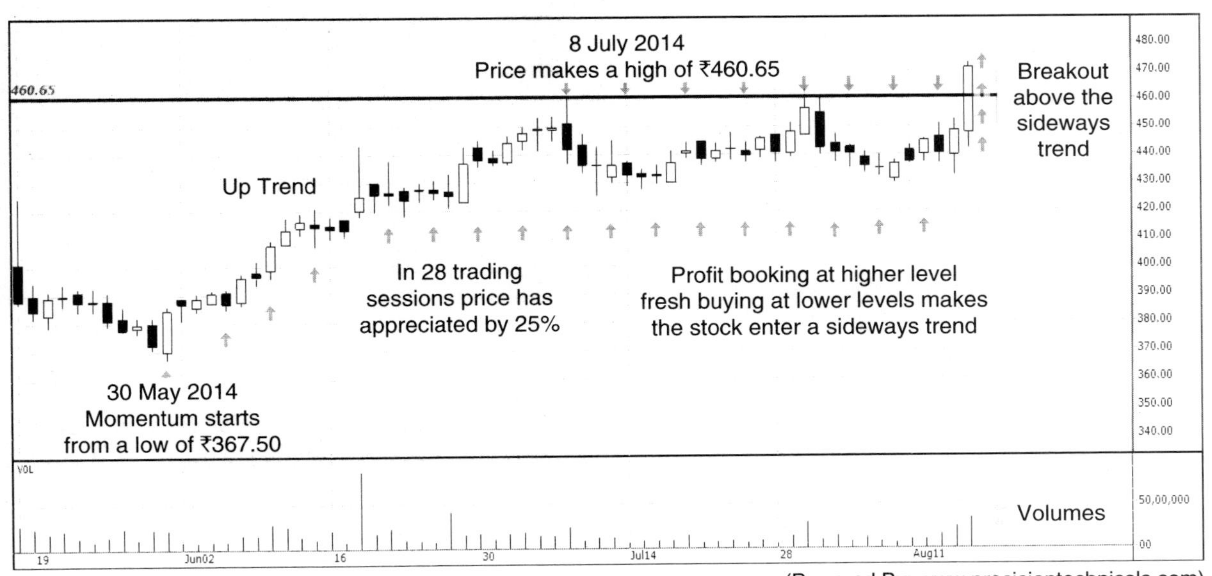

(Powered By: www.precisiontechnicals.com)

Figure 16.55: **Daily candlestick chart of Cipla with an upward breakout after the sideways trend**

~

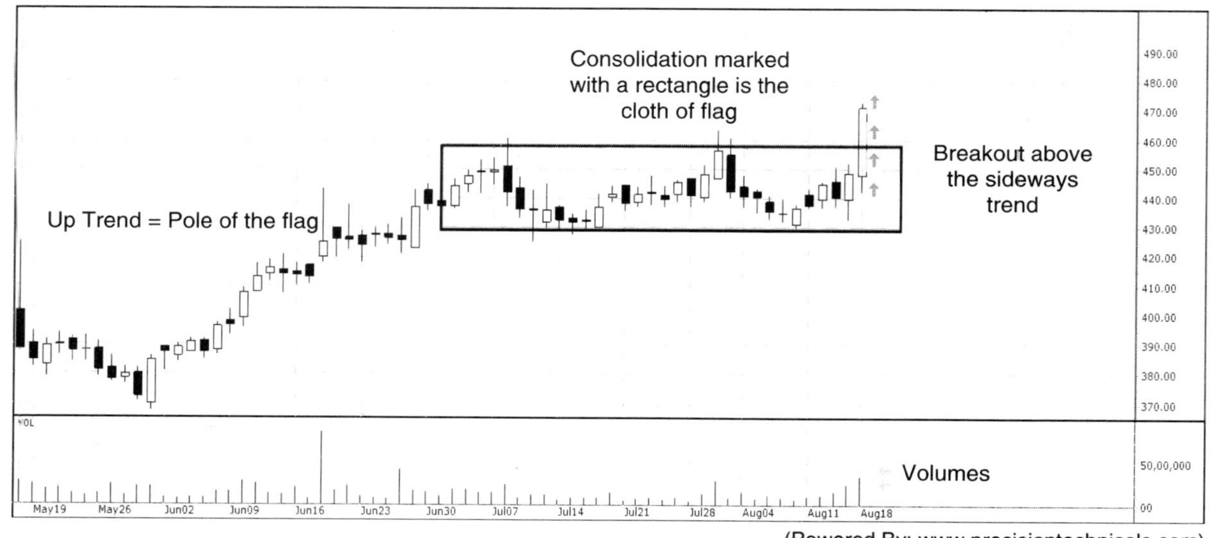

(Powered By: www.precisiontechnicals.com)

Figure 16.56: **Daily candlestick chart of Cipla with an up flag formation. The price till to trend was up the flag formation, and again breaks out of the flag in the upward direction.**

~

The last white candle in the chart in Figure 16.55 has signalled a breakout and closed above the sideways trend. This breakout is validated by strong volumes. Such a formation is called an up flag formation, since it looks like a flag flying on a flagpole. The initial up trend forms the pole of the flag and the subsequent sideways trend, or consolidation, is the fabric of the flag. This has been marked on the chart in Figure 16.56 to help you understand it visually.

With this breakout, the chart is suggesting that the price is likely to continue in the direction of the earlier up trend. We now have confirmation as well as validation for the pattern and therefore this becomes a buy signal for us. Now, if you decide to go long, you need to determine the price target and the time target for the trade.

To arrive at the price target in the case of a flag we need to measure the distance of the pole and add that number to the low of the consolidation, or the low of the fabric / rectangle.

For determining the time target we need to count the number of candles from the start of the pole to the breakout candle and divide that number by three.

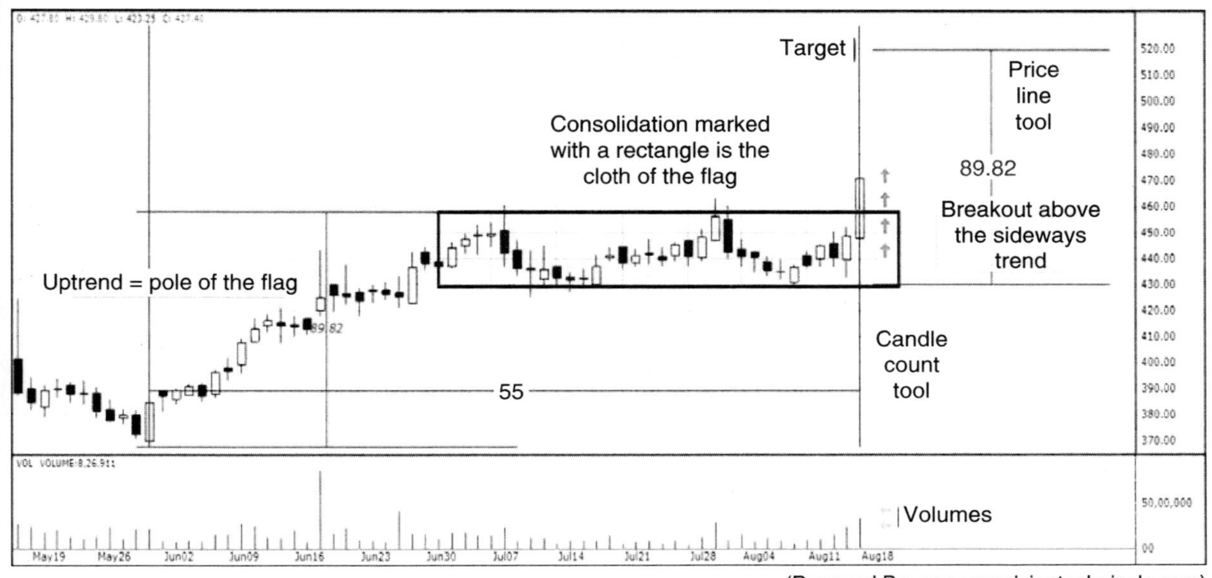

(Powered By: www.precisiontechnicals.com)

Figure 16.57: **Daily candlestick chart of Cipla with candle count and price line tool plotted**

~

The price target can be plotted using the price line tool in-built into Profision and the time target is plotted using the candle count tool. This can be observed in the chart in Figure 16.57.

The price target is ₹520 and the time target is 19 candles.

Criteria

- An ongoing up trend is needed to form the pole of the flag.
- The subsequent consolidation or sideways trend must last for a minimum of 5 days. If the consolidation is for fewer than 5 days, then it does not qualify as an up flag pattern, since the price can take a pause and start moving again without consolidation. Longer the consolidation, better the results after the breakout.
- The breakout and close must be above the consolidation.
- Breakout must be accompanied by higher volumes as compared to the earlier three candles.

Important

- A flag can be identified by marking the consolidation using a rectangle as well as triangle.
- In some consolidations the price moves between two levels, while in others the price can move in a narrowing range.
- The calculations for the price target and the time target for both remain the same.
- In a rectangular flag, the pole distance is added to in the low of the rectangle, while in a triangle flag the pole distance is added to the low of the triangle on the vertical axis of the breakout candle.

An example of a triangle flag with price target plotted can be seen in Figure 16.58.

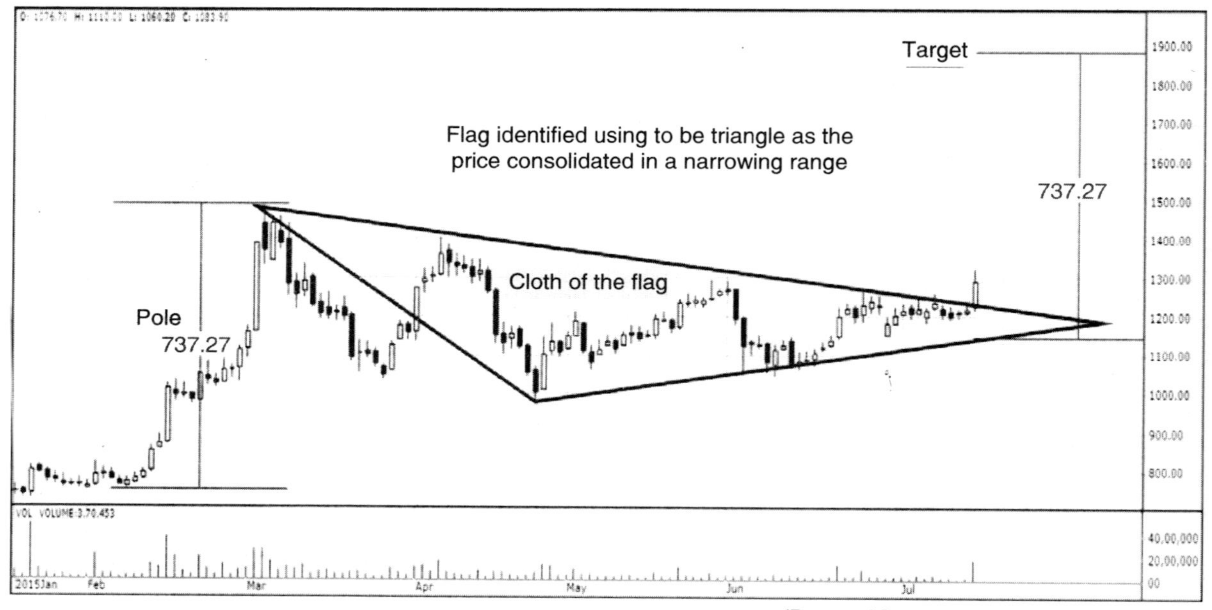

(Powered By: www.precisiontechnicals.com)

Figure 16.58: **Tata Elxsi daily candlestick chart with a triangle up flag with price and time targets marked on it**

Down Flag Formation

This pattern is just the opposite of an up flag formation. In a down flag formation, the price is originally moving in a down trend which forms the pole. Then we have the price consolidating in a sideways trend and, finally, there is a downward breakout. This pattern therefore generates a sell signal.

Let us consider an example.

The chart in Figure 16.59 shows that the price moved into a sideways trend after falling from levels of ₹200 to ₹140. This happens when there are many people trading a stock with different ideas and objectives; for example, someone may be booking profit made in a short trade, some others could have a view that the price can give a bounce back after the fall, and there could be yet others who expect the price to fall even further.

Due to these different sentiments, the price moves into a sideways trend, wherein the buying and selling is essentially equal as seen in the chart in Figure 16.59.

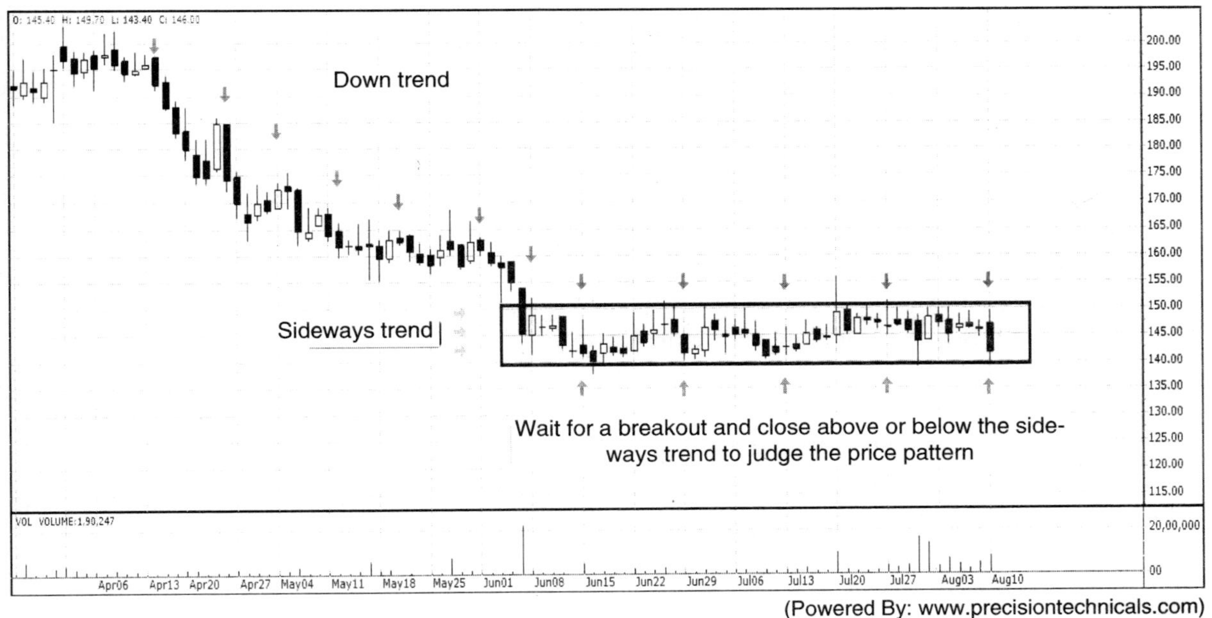

(Powered By: www.precisiontechnicals.com)

Figure 16.59: **Daily candlestick chart of IL&FS Transport with the price consolidation highlighted on the chart**

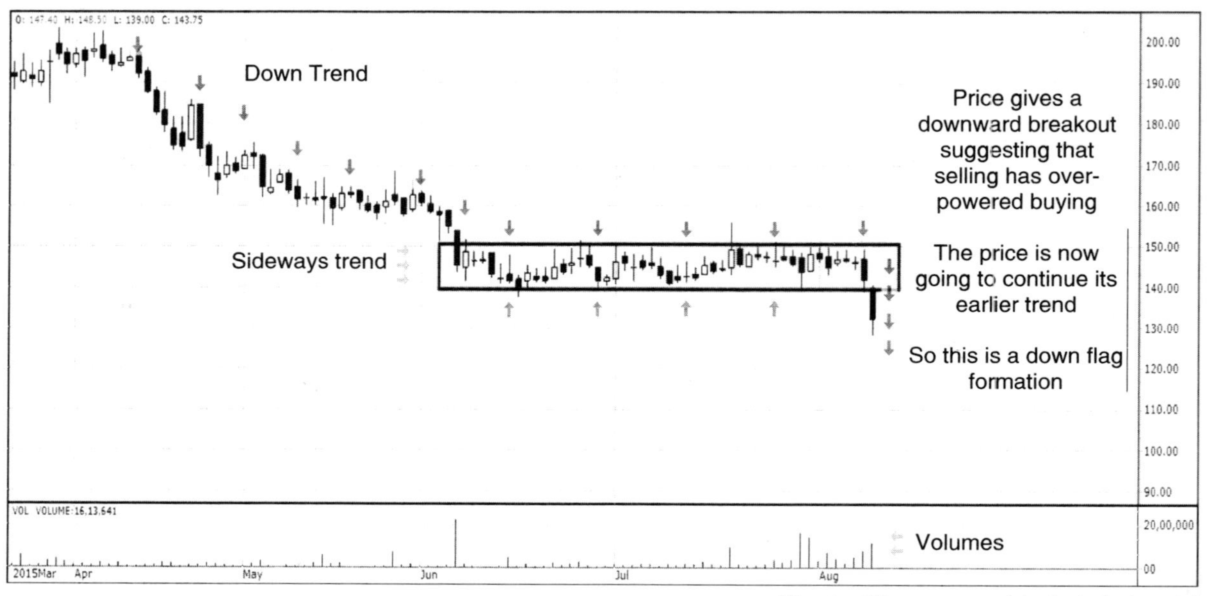

Figure 16.60: **Daily candlestick chart of IL&FS Transport with a downward breakout after the consolidation**

~

The subsequent chart in Figure 16.60 suggests that the selling has overpowered the buying, which means that the price will now continue its earlier down trend. This is a continuation pattern known as a down flag. With a closing below the sideways trend, we have confirmation for this pattern. With increasing volumes on the breakout, we can also validate this price formation to be a down flag formation. This, now, is a sell signal. Investors who are holding this stock in their portfolio, and who had not exited earlier, can do so now with this confirmation and validity in hand. Positional and swing traders, as well as intraday traders, can make use of this formation to enter fresh short trades.

Next we need to figure out the price target, the stop loss, and the tentative time that would be taken for this pattern to complete its formation.

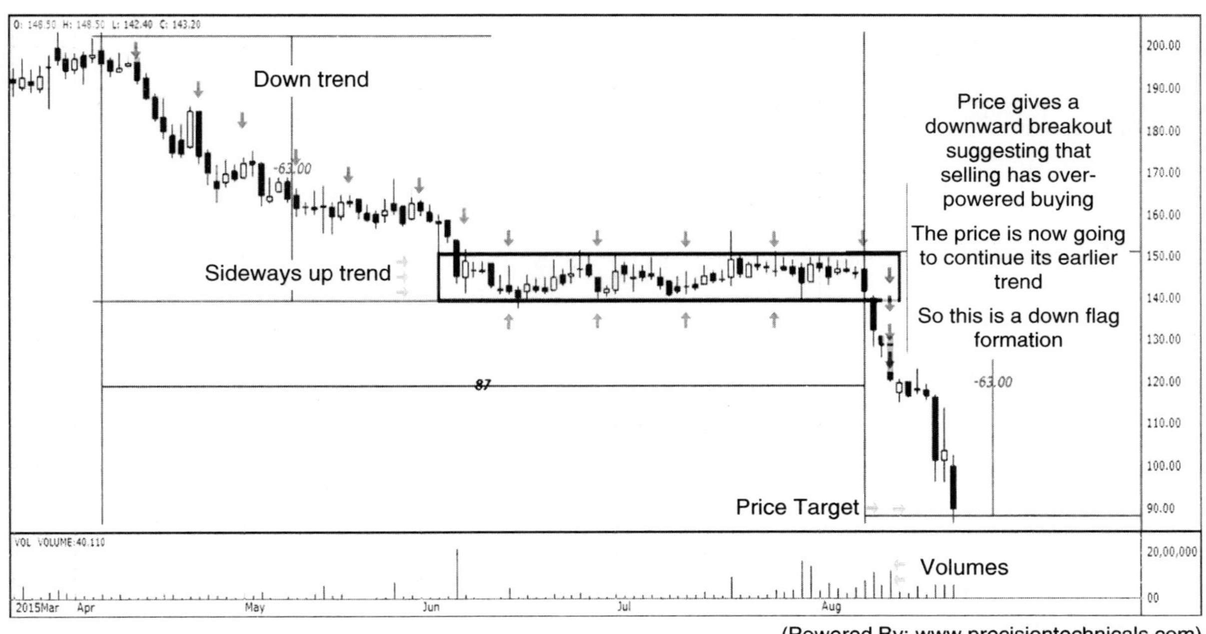

(Powered By: www.precisiontechnicals.com)

Figure 16.61: **Daily candlestick chart of IL&FS Transport with a down flag formation with the price and time targets indicated**

~

On the chart in Figure 16.61, you will be able to see the price target marked with the help of the price line tool. Using the candle count tool we have also calculated the number of candles in the total formation. The price target is ₹88.50 and the candle count suggests 87 candles in the formation, which means that the target will be achieved in one-third this time period, namely in 29 candles. The closing of the breakout candle is at ₹132. Risk management / stop loss for the down flag formation will be discussed separately in Chapter 18.

~

Quiz: Price Patterns

Questions

1. Price patterns help generate tentative price targets. (True / False?)
2. Price patterns help generate tentative time targets. (True / False?)
3. Price patterns help generate big moves. (True / False?)
4. Price patterns are categorized into two types — reversal patterns and continuation patterns. (True / False?)
5. Head & Shoulder is a reversal pattern at the bottom? (True / False?)
6. Inverted Head & Shoulder is a reversal pattern at the bottom? (True / False?)
7. Double Top is a reversal pattern at the top? (True / False?)
8. Rounding Bottom pattern helps in judging a change of fundamentals in a company. (True / False?)
9. Price patterns display the sentimental change happening in a stock price. (True / False?)

Answers

1. True	2. True	3. True	4. True	5. False
6. True	7. True	8. True	9. True	

SENTIMENTAL SHIFTS BETWEEN THE BUYERS AND SELLERS (DEMAND AND SUPPLY) ARE IDENTIFIED USING PRICE PATTERNS. THIS MAKES PRICE PATTERS IMPORTANT IN TECHNICAL ANALYSIS.

Chapter 17

~

Trading Oscillators

OSCILLATORS ARE TECHNICAL INDICATORS that help in measuring a stock's momentum and strength. The scale on which oscillators are plotted is normally displayed in a separate panel on the price chart bounded by an oversold zone at the bottom of this panel and an overbought zone at its top. Oscillators also generate buy and sell signals as they display crossovers suggesting a change of trend for the price.

We will be discussing two types of oscillators — range bound oscillators and centred oscillators.

Range Bound Oscillators

In range bound oscillators, we will learn about:

- Relative strength index (RSI); and
- Stochastic oscillator (Stochastic).

As the name suggests, these oscillators are bounded in a range on a scale from 0 to 100. The scale is ascending with the oversold zone at the bottom and the overbought zone at the top:

- In the case of RSI, the oversold zone is between 0 and 30, and the overbought zone is between 70 and 100.
- In case of the stochastic oscillator, the oversold zone is between 0 and 20, and the overbought zone is between 80 and 100.

In the case of RSI, the pair of 14-day RSI line and 9-day RSI line is normally used to generate triggers in the form of crossovers, whereas in case of the stochastic the triggers are generated by crossovers between the %K and %D lines.

These two oscillators are also known as leading indicators.

We can generate different results by changing the time periods in these oscillators. The time periods mentioned above are optimised and will help you in all the different market conditions.

As we have discussed, we should have a limited and useful set of tools and indicators for analysis. Another important thing is that you should not be dependent on any single tool or indicator, nor should you give 100% weightage to any single indicator or tool as every tool, indicator or analysis fails at some time or the other. Therefore, it is good to stay with a simple and limited set of tools which can help you in all the different market conditions.

Formulas for calculating all the oscillators discussed here are widely available on the Internet and we will not be discussing them in this book. Our objective is to interpret these oscillators in the right way for our analysis and trading.

Relative Strength Index (RSI)

RSI is a momentum oscillator that measures the speed and change in price movements. RSI oscillates between a scale of 0 and 100. Traditionally, RSI is considered to be in overbought zone when above 70, and in the oversold zone when below 30. Signals can also be generated by looking for divergences, failure swings, and centre line crossovers. RSI can also be used to identify the general trend of the price.

In the chart in Figure 17.1, you can see the RSI plotted in a panel above the price chart. The solid black line is the 14-day RSI and the dotted or lighter line is the 9-day RSI. Horizontal lines are marked on the scale at 30 and at 70. The zone between the scale of 0 to 30 is the oversold zone, while the zone between 70 to 100 is the overbought zone.

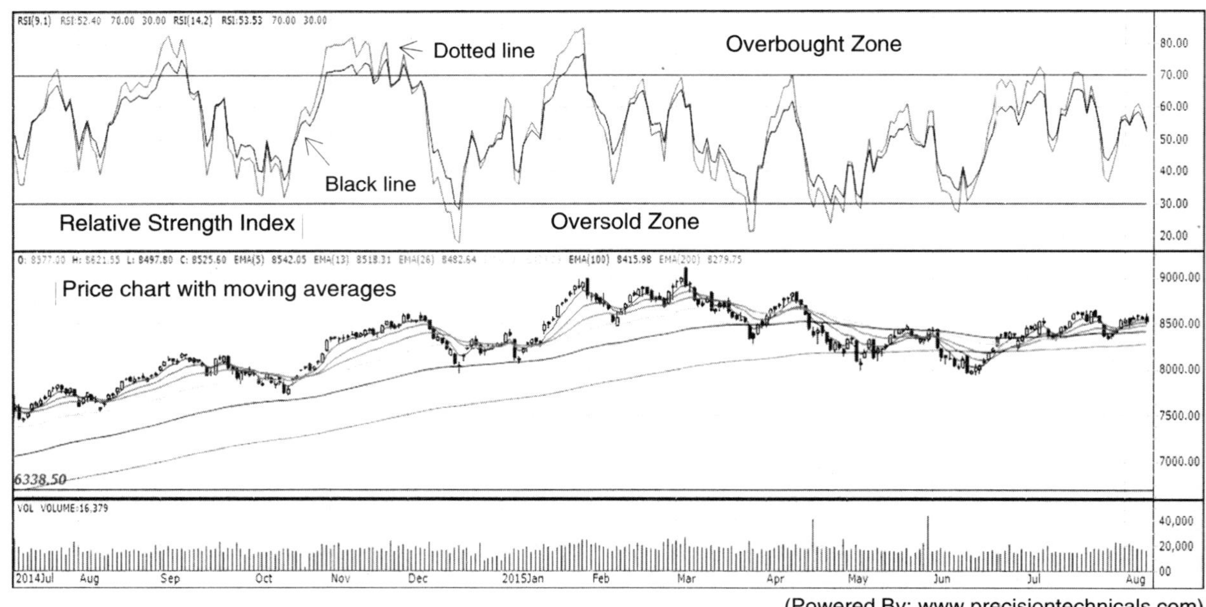

(Powered By: www.precisiontechnicals.com)

Figure 17.1: **Daily candlestick chart of Nifty with the RSI plotted in the upper panel**

Stochastic Oscillator

The stochastic oscillator is a momentum indicator that shows the location of the closing price relative to the high-low range over a set number of periods. It doesn't follow volume or anything like that. Instead, it follows the speed, or momentum, of the price. **As a rule, momentum changes direction before the price does. As such, bullish and bearish divergences in the stochastic oscillator can be used to anticipate reversals.** Because the stochastic oscillator is range bound, it is also useful for identifying overbought and oversold levels.

Stochastic oscillator can be categorised into three different categories based on the time periods used, namely fast, slow, and full. We use the full stochastic oscillator for our analysis purpose.

Fast stochastic uses the normal time periods (5, 3) for plotting whereas the slow stochastic smoothens the normal time period with an additional 3-period SMA (5, 3). The full stochastic oscillator is a fully customisable version of the slow stochastic oscillator and uses further smoothening (5, 3, 3).

You can see the stochastic plotted in the upper panel of Nifty's daily candlestick chart in Figure 17.2.

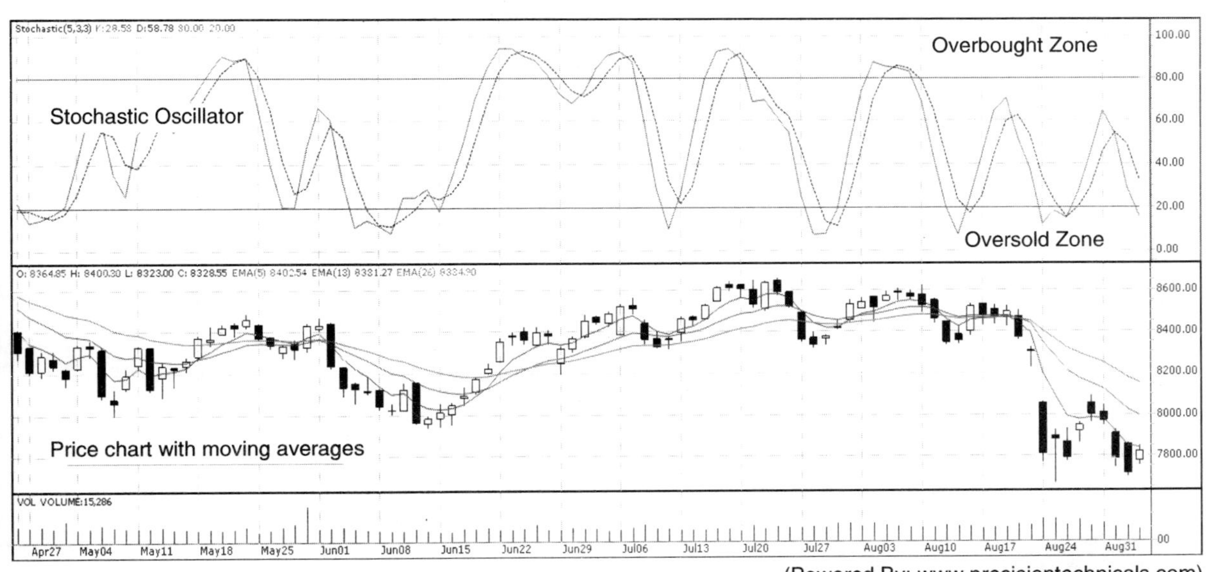

(Powered By: www.precisiontechnicals.com)

Figure 17.2: **Daily candlestick chart of Nifty with the stochastic oscillator plotted above the price chart**

~

Centred Oscillator: Moving Average Convergence Divergence (MACD)

MACD, on the other hand, is a centred oscillator and falls under the category of lagging indicators. MACD is pronounced as either "Mac-Dee" or "M-A-C-D."

The reason for using MACD in our analysis is to get a view from various parameters to generate signals in different market conditions. In MACD, the scale is divided into two parts — a positive scale and a negative scale, with a horizontal line at zero. This is the reason that we call it a centred oscillator. MACD hovers between the positive and negative scale, moving up and down between the positive and negative zones based on the stock's price trend.

MACD is also made up of two lines, the MACD line, and the trigger line. The two lines help in generating crossover triggers for arriving at buy and sell conclusions. MACD is calculated by subtracting the 26-period exponential moving average (26EMA) from the 12-period exponential moving average (12EMA), with a 9-period exponential moving average of the MACD being used as the trigger.

The moving average convergence divergence oscillator (MACD) is one of the simplest and most effective momentum indicators available. The MACD turns two trend-following moving averages into a momentum oscillator by subtracting the longer moving average from the shorter moving average. As a result, **MACD offers the best of both worlds — trend following and momentum.**

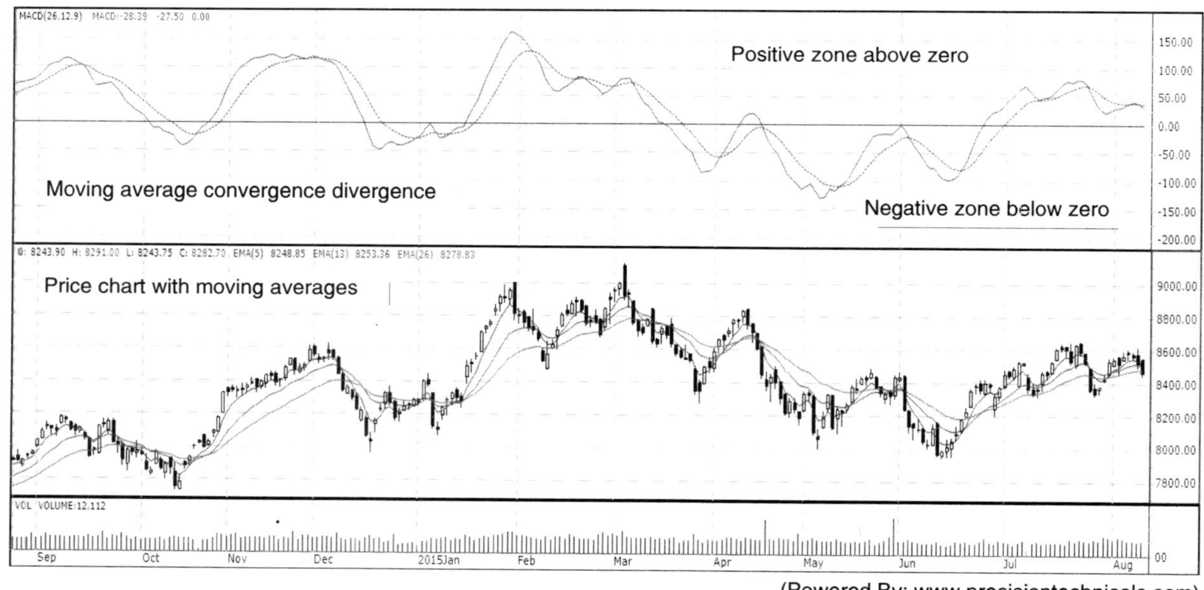

(Powered By: www.precisiontechnicals.com)

Figure 17.3: **Daily candlestick chart of Nifty with the MACD plotted above the price chart**

~

The MACD fluctuates above and below the zero line as the moving averages converge, cross, and diverge. Traders can look for signal line crossovers, centre line crossovers and divergences in order to generate signals. However, because the MACD is unbounded, it is not particularly useful for identifying overbought and oversold levels.

The values of 12, 26 and 9 are the typical settings used with the MACD. Other values can, however, be substituted depending on your trading style and goals.

You can see the MACD plotted in the upper panel of the daily candlestick chart of Nifty in Figure 17.3.

Interpretations of Oscillators

We will now look at these oscillators with their commonly used triggers and also discuss an improvised way of using them in our strategy. We will also discuss the reasons for not using the common triggers, but the improvised way of generating signals from these additional tools.

Some of the triggers which can be used with improvisations are also mentioned.

1. Divergence;
2. Crossover;
3. Oversold and overbought; and
4. Positive and negative zones.

The common triggers, and reasons for not using them in our analysis, are listed below.

Divergence

When the price and the oscillator move in opposite directions, they are said to be at divergence with each other. The common understanding is that these divergences give a directional lead for us to judge how the price will move next.

There are two types of divergences which can be observed — positive divergence and negative divergence.

Positive Divergence

- When the oscillator is moving up and the price is moving down, it is termed as a positive divergence (*see* Figure 17.4).
- The normal understanding in such a case is that the price would soon follow the oscillator, and will also move up.

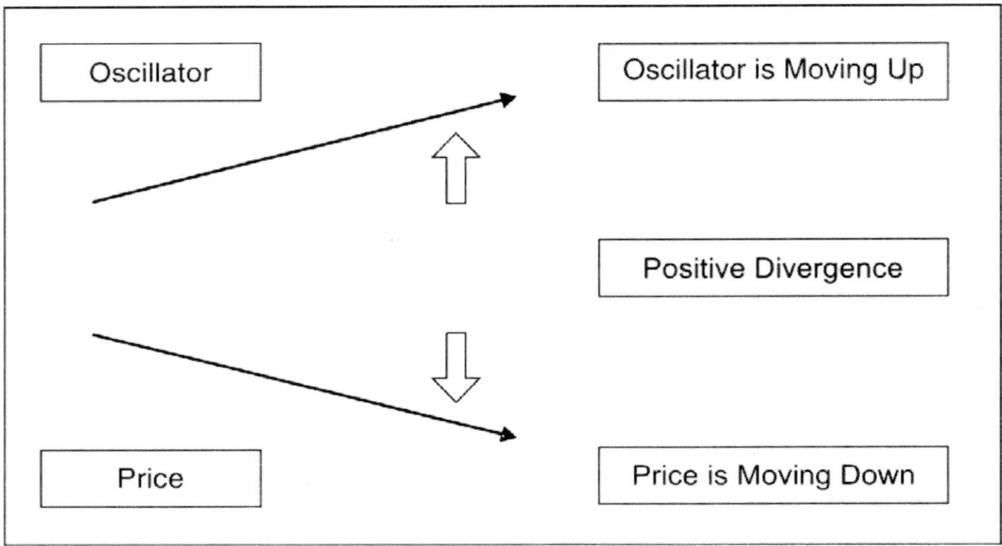

Figure 17.4: **Positive divergence when oscillator is moving up and the price is headed down**

~

Negative Divergence

- If the oscillator is moving down while the price is going up, it is termed as a negative divergence, (*see* Figure 17.5).

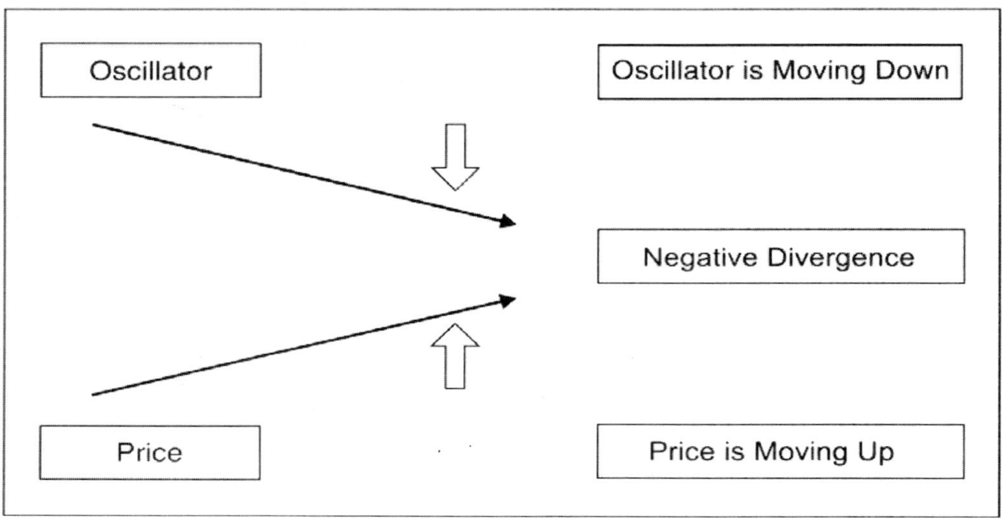

Figure 17.5: **Negative divergence when the oscillator heads down but the price is moving up**

~

- The normal understanding is that in such a case the price would also soon follow the oscillator and move down.

  It's important to keep in mind that:

- The oscillator does not create the price; it is the price which creates the oscillator.
- A divergence can also be nullified by the oscillator moving in the direction of the price, in which case the buy or sell indications will fail, which is why I do not use it as a trigger.

Crossovers

As we have seen, an oscillator has two lines which oscillate on a scale. One line is the main line of the oscillator and the second one is the oscillator's trigger line. There are crossovers between these two which can be used as signals for long or short trades. Accordingly, they are termed as positive and negative crossovers, respectively.

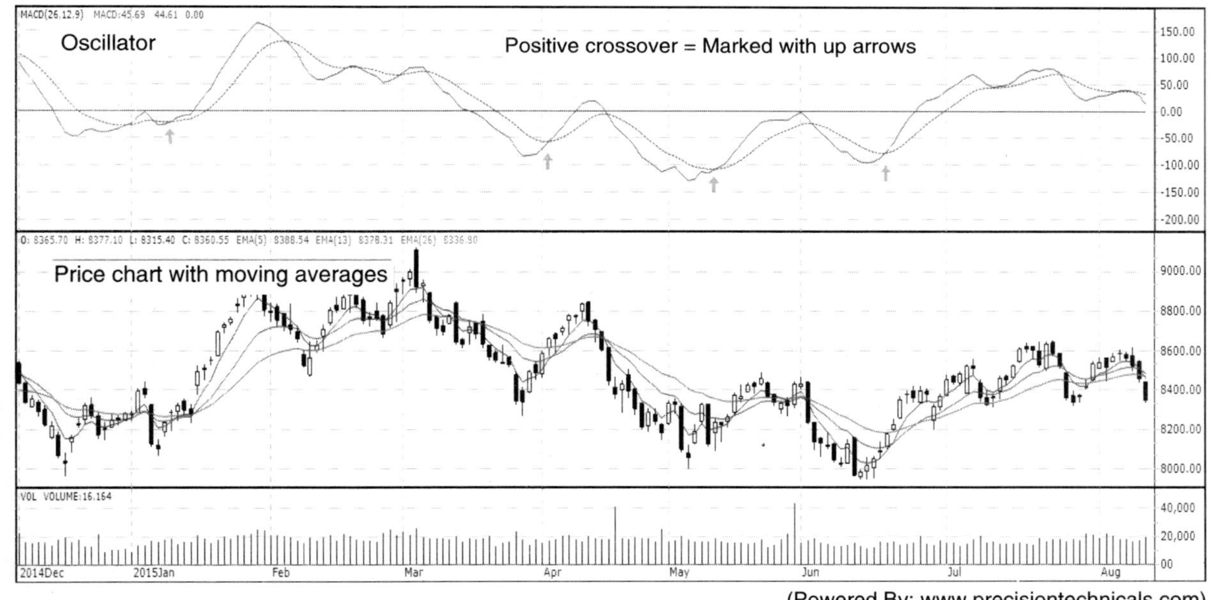

(Powered By: www.precisiontechnicals.com)

Figure 17.6: **Positive crossover triggers in the oscillator plotted above the price chart are marked with up arrows**

~

Positive Crossover

- This occurs when the two lines of an oscillator cross each other and move upward as can be seen in Figure 17.6 which has the crossovers marked by up arrows.
- A positive crossover also occurs when the trigger line crosses the main line of the oscillator in the upward direction.

Negative Crossover

- This occurs when the two lines of an oscillator cross each other and move downward, as can be seen in Figure 17.7 marked by down arrows.
- It also occurs when the trigger line crosses the main line of the oscillator in the downward direction.

Note: Many a time high frequency of signals or crossovers on a chart may lead to the chartist losing interest in them.

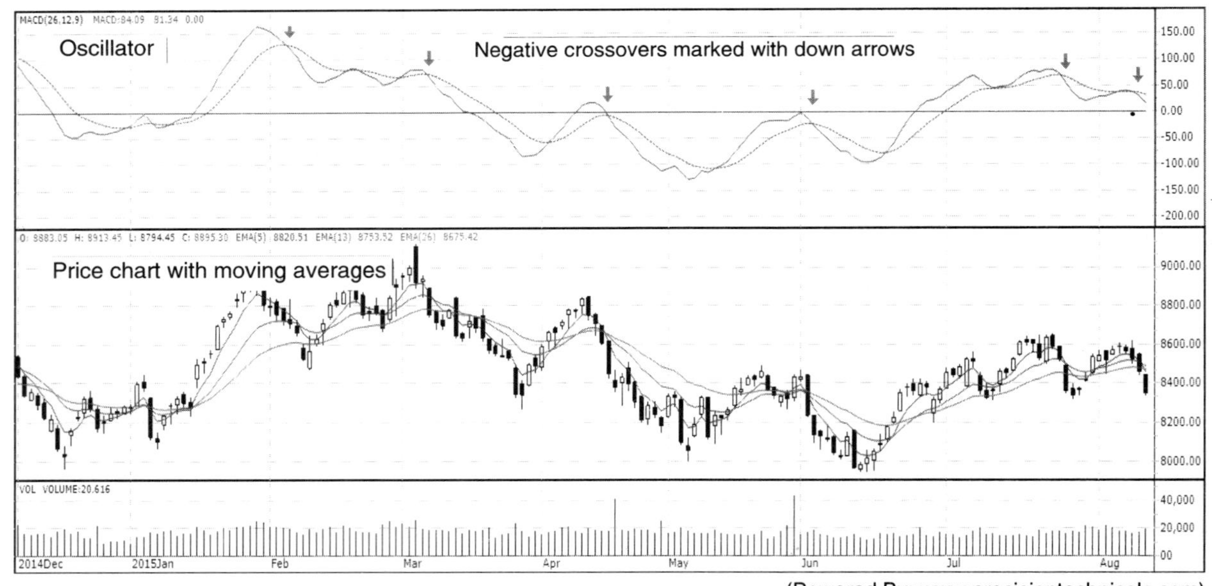

(Powered By: www.precisiontechnicals.com)

Figure 17.7: **Negative crossover triggers in the oscillator plotted above the price chart are highlighted with downward pointing arrows**

~

Improvisation

Crossovers cannot be considered important by themselves for the simple reason that when a stock goes into a sideways trend the oscillator will generate plenty of false signals. The oscillator will generate positive as well as negative crossovers one after the other so long as the stock continues to trade in a sideways trend. Accordingly, the signals need to be monitored along with either the price, or the zone that they are crossing at. This will become clearer in Part 2 of the book.

- **In the Case of RSI and the Stochastic:**
  - Positive crossover and a price pattern = Buy trigger.
  - Negative crossover and a price pattern = Sell trigger.
  - Positive crossover in oversold zone and a price pattern = Buy trigger.
  - Negative crossover in overbought zone and a price pattern = Sell trigger.
- **In the case of MACD:**
  - Positive crossover in a positive zone and a price pattern = Buy trigger.
  - Negative crossover in a positive zone and a price pattern = Sell trigger.

Oversold and Overbought

There can be periods when the price moves in one direction without any corrections. The price normally does not sustain this kind of a trend. The reason is simple — once a person is making profits in a long or a short trade he or she tends to square off the trade. This profit booking in a trade after an upward rally, plus value buying which can be seen after the price has fallen significantly, are what make prices react and move in trends. When the price moves in one direction without a correction or profit booking, then the oscillators tend to move into zones which suggest that the price movement is now stretched and the chances of a correction become high. These zones are indicated by the relative strength index (RSI) and the stochastic oscillator.

Oversold Zone

If the prices fall without a correction, whether due to profit booking or fresh selling, they drive the oscillator to a level which suggests an imminent bounce back in the stock price. This being the common understanding, it makes people believe that when a stock is trading in an oversold zone, it is a buy signal (*see* Figure 17.8).

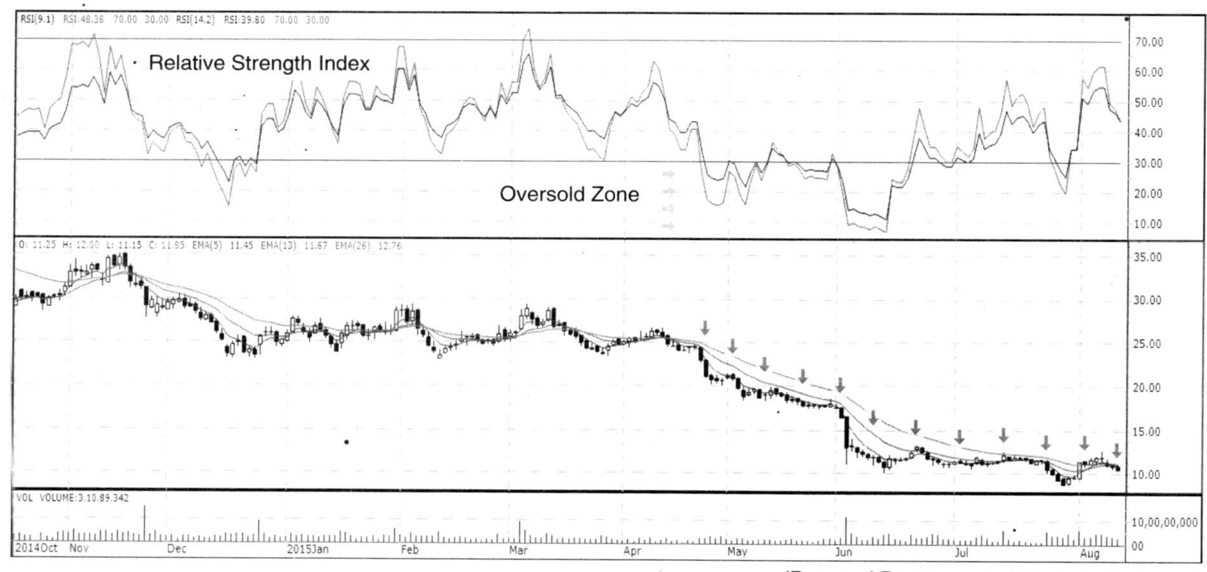

(Powered By: www.precisiontechnicals.com)

Figure 17.8: **RSI trades in the oversold zone but the price keeps falling. RSI later moves out of the oversold zone but the price continues to trend down**

~

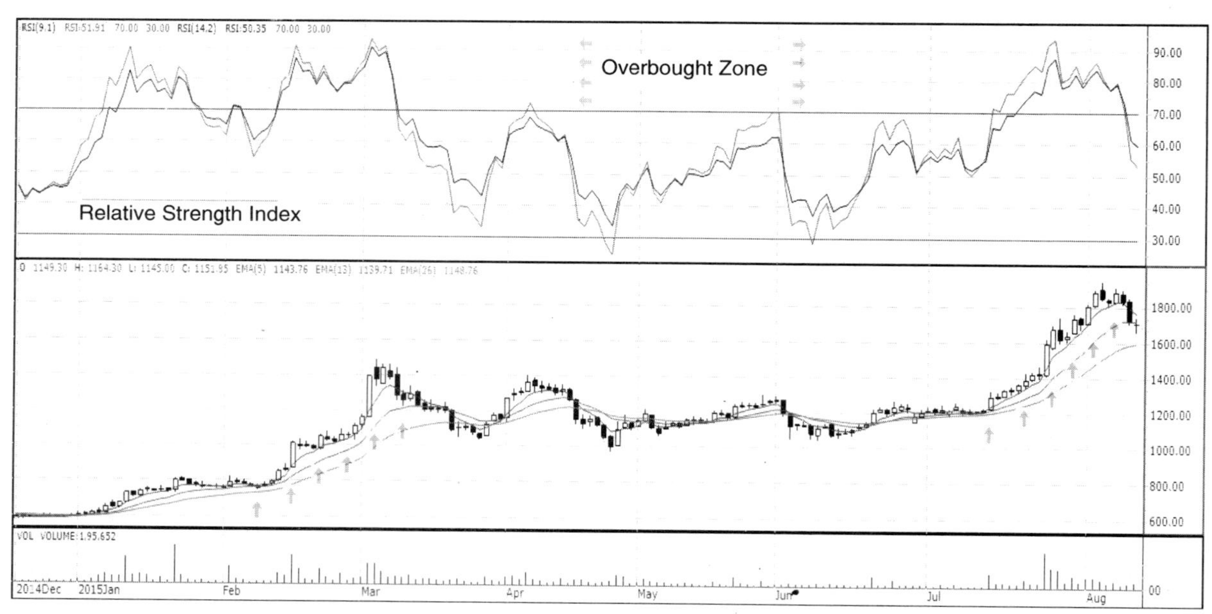

(Powered By: www.precisiontechnicals.com)

Figure 17.9: **RSI trades in the overbought zone but the price keeps rising**

~

Overbought Zone

This is a zone where the prices rise without a correction or profit booking, pushing the oscillator to a level which suggests an imminent downward correction in the stock price. This being the common understanding, it makes people believe that when a stock is trading in an overbought zone it is a sell signal (*see* Figure 17.9).

Alert

- A stock can continue to fall with the oscillator staying in the oversold zone for a long period, as in Figure 17.8.
- A stock can continue to rise with the oscillator staying in the overbought zone for a long period, as in Figure 17.9.

Improvisation

Oversold and overbought zones may thus not be effective on a stand alone basis but can yield good results if they are used along with crossovers and price pattern triggers.

In the case of RSI and stochastic:

- Positive crossover in an oversold zone with a bullish price pattern as a buy trigger will help generate better results.
- Negative crossover in an overbought zone with a bearish price pattern as a sell trigger will help generate better results.

Positive and Negative Zones

The MACD hovers between positive and negative zones above and below a zero level marked in the centre with a horizontal line. It also generates crossovers as it hovers up or down.

The chart in Figure 17.10 displays the MACD moving between these positive and negative zones.

MACD Crossover Triggers

- When MACD gives a positive crossover in the positive zone, it is a good buy trigger.
- When MACD gives a negative crossover in the negative zone, it is a good sell trigger.

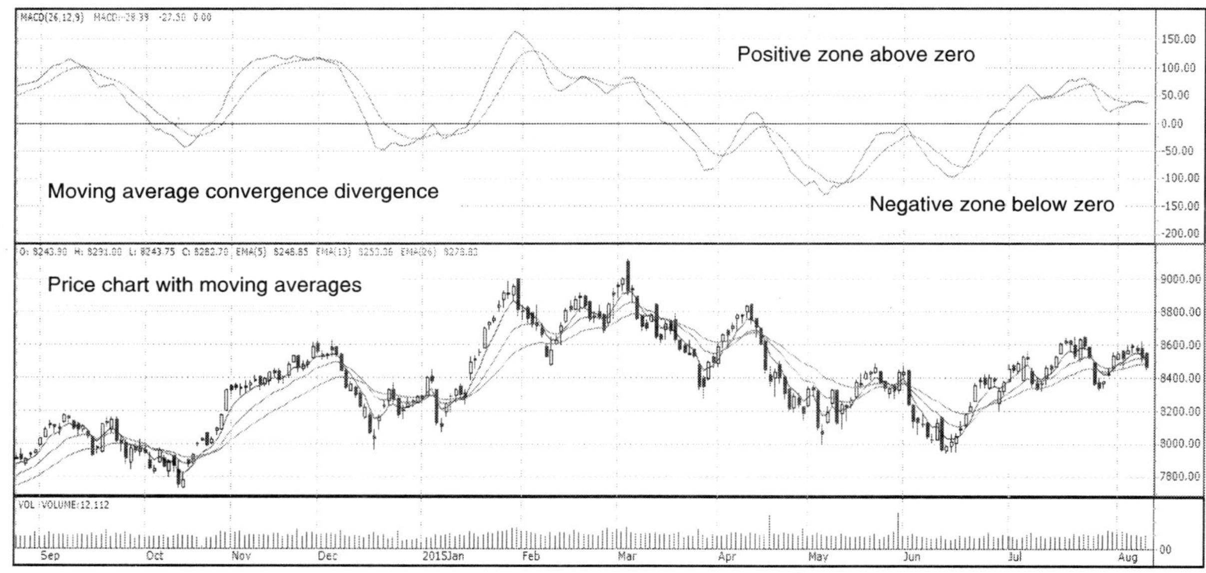

(Powered By: www.precisiontechnicals.com)

Figure 17.10: **MACD hovers in between the positive and negative zones displaying crossovers**

~

Key Points about Oscillators

1. An indicator or oscillator does not move the price; it is the price which makes the indicator or oscillator move. This is the reason for using indicators / oscillators as supportive tools.

2. In the extreme short term, oscillators can be used by themselves for generating triggers but remember when you reduce the time frame, the number of whipsaws increases, and the consequent number of failing trades means that the risk also increases.

3. Every parameter, every tool, every analysis has its limitations, its advantages and disadvantages. Each one also fails at some time or the other and you should therefore not give undue weight to any single indicator or oscillator.

4. We need to have a select set of tools and parameters which can be useful in different market conditions. They should be able to tell us when one should be trading or investing in the markets, and also tell us when one needs to stay away from the markets.

5. There are hundreds of indicators / oscillators or parameters developed over the long years of stock market history throughout the world. They were not developed in a day. Thus, some years back there may have been a hundred parameters or indicators. Then somebody came up with an idea for the 101st indicator, maybe because the person was not comfortable with the existing ones or maybe because he did not have faith in them, or, possibly,

they were not generating the kind of results he was expecting or, maybe, he thought he had a much better idea. The same logic is applicable to all the indicators / oscillators developed in the world till date. So, the thousand plus indicators / oscillators that are available today have all been born of such thinking.

The irony is that they did not have faith in the existing ones, while we tend to fall a prey to all of them!

Also, you must be aware that redundant indicators / oscillators are often touted by sales persons who want to sell you their software by showing you glowing reports for select time periods when their indicators / oscillators may have worked well. Remember, it's a selective, best-foot-forward part of the story.

~

Finally, success in the markets is determined only 20% by your strategy. Painstaking effort is required for achieving the sustained discipline which is 80% of what it takes to succeed. Therefore, keep your strategy as simple as possible.

~

Quiz: Trading Oscillators

Questions

1. Price creates the oscillator. (True / False?)
2. Oscillator creates the price. (True / False?)
3. MACD is a range bound oscillator. (True / False?)

Answers

1. True	2. False	3. False

INDICATORS AND OSCILLATORS ARE SHADOWS OF THE PRICE AND YOU SHOULD THEREFORE USE THEM AS SUPPORTING TOOLS.

Chapter 18

~

Risk Management

STOCK MARKETS ATTRACT INVESTORS AND TRADERS because they believe here they can make money very fast. Indians have an inclination towards gambling, a habit of placing bets right from childhood. The bet could be over a chocolate when young, and about whether the class teacher would be on leave on a particular day. As they grow up, the bets change to money. And this change happens before you realize it, and by the time you do, you have already started enjoying the change.

It is an irony that when people look at the stock markets they do so from a gambling point of view. They come here to become multi millionaires without even giving a thought that such an attitude could, instead, take everything away — their money, peace of mind, family life, etc.

They then pay a consultant or an advisor in order to get investing and trading tips. Having paid the advisor they believe that he should be able to generate stock picks which will always work.

In all this one thing is forgotten, namely that all stock picks come with risk. **What's most important in the stock market is for us to manage the risk. You must enter a trade** not for the likely returns but **only if the risk is acceptable to you. The returns will then automatically follow.**

Before we get into the details of risk management, let us clearly understand certain points:

1. You should participate in the stock market only if you have the courage to accept your mistakes. In other words, when necessary you should be able to accept that a stock has not worked as per your expectation and therefore you need to exit.

2. The biggest and the best of stock market investors have become big, and are called wise, because they learnt this art of accepting their mistakes early in life.

3. Accepting a mistake and exiting a stock will give you a small loss but it can help preserve your precious capital for profitable future trades. As they say, "Taking a small loss now and then is better than being hit by the mother of all losses."

4. When you don't accept your mistakes, or don't exit a trade which does not work as per your expectations, then you are stuck with a loss making stock in your portfolio. Not only are your funds stuck in such a case but you could also lose your confidence and self-belief in making profits in the stock markets.

I have seen people buy a particular stock at ₹2,000 and average it at ₹1,000, average it further at ₹500, and still further average the stock at ₹200, at ₹100, at ₹10, at ₹3, and finally at ₹1. As of 14 August 2015, that stock traded at a price of 90 paisa. The price of ₹2,000 was quoted in the year 2000, and 90 paisa in 2015. Though I have not mentioned the name of the stock, I am sure you too must be aware of many such examples.

Just imagine the mental torture that people must go through when they continue to hold such stocks in their portfolios. They would have been left with no confidence in themselves thereafter. They would also forever be busy cursing the stock market and giving it a bad name simply because they did not accept their mistake and exit a losing stock.

Your money is hard earned and therefore you must husband it wisely. There are a lot of methods of learning sound investing and trading. You need not do so by committing unnecessary mistakes. It is always cheaper and easier to learn from others' mistakes — and if you have the right attitude, you will be able to do so in quick time.

Let me explain this in a different way. You may be doing a job or you may be running a business. In your profession you tend to know your limits, you know what you are good at, you know things which you can do and things which you cannot. In the same way, it is important for you to know your limits in the stock markets.

Risk management is nothing but implementing a stop loss to limit your risk or limit your loss.

Suppose you have a portfolio in which you are holding two stocks. Both the stocks have been bought at the same price, say, ₹100. A few days later Stock A trades at ₹120 and Stock B trades at ₹90. You need funds for something and therefore need to sell one of the stocks. Which stock would you sell — Stock A or Stock B?

If your answer is Stock A, then you need to read this chapter very thoroughly and imbibe its lessons so that you never forget the importance of risk management.

Be a Farmer in the Stock Market

In the stock market, you should consider yourself to be a farmer. Here is why.

A farmer ploughs his field, while an investor filters the stocks traded on the exchange.

Once the field is ploughed, the farmer starts seeding it; the investor starts buying stocks in his portfolio.

The farmer waters his farm and takes care of it on a periodic basis. Correspondingly, the investor monitors his investments. Just as the crops grows in the farm, the stocks also start appreciating in the investor's portfolio.

Now comes the moment when both the investor and the farmer are confronted with a problem.

The farmer finds that there are weeds growing alongside the good crop. The investor too finds that side by side with stocks which are appreciating, there are some stocks which are not performing well — or are generating losses.

If the farmer does not act on this problem and does not remove the weeds in time, he will end up with a destroyed crop. Similarly, if the investor does not restructure his loss-making stocks, these may end up having a negative effect on his overall portfolio even though it also contains positively performing stocks.

The farmer decides to remove the weeds from his farm. He then again waters his good crop to ensure that he has a healthy harvest which can fetch him handsome profit. The efforts which he made turn out to be successful.

This should be an important learning for the stock market enthusiast.

What does the typical stock market investor do, instead?

He books profit in stocks which are generating positive returns, but continues to hold the loss making stocks in the hope that they would, ultimately, come back in the green and he would then be able to book profits in those stocks, too. Many investors even average such loss-making stocks with a view that a small rally in the stock price would help them exit the stock profitably. In doing so, they tend to forget that they are putting their good money to chase bad money. If the strategy does not work, and the stock does not appreciate, then even the fresh funds get stuck and eventually the investor loses his confidence as well.

Just imagine the change if the investor had decided to take a farmer-like approach.

Like the farmer who pulls out the weeds from his farm, suppose the investor decides to exit stocks which are not performing and replace them with stocks which are expected to gain. Just as the farmer had to make efforts to remove the weeds from his farm, the investor would have to bear some initial losses. But once non-performing stocks are replaced with stocks which are expected to perform, or even if the investor merely sticks to the performing stocks which are already in his portfolio, he would end up in profit.

Stock market trading is a business much the same as most other businesses, where loss and profit are an ongoing process. If you do not have the mindset for facing losses, then you are not built for the stock market. There is no magic wand for generating only profits.

You need to understand that money lost today can be regained tomorrow, but if losses make you lose your confidence, then gaining that back is a very difficult task.

Let me tell you another story about implementing risk management in stock markets.

Ramji decides to start investing in the stock market. He meets a couple of friends for advice. We all have friends who like to give lots of free advice, don't we? So, Ramji got plenty advice from his friends who caution him that while the stock markets are a good thing, but he must take care of the risk involved in this business.

Being new to this field, Ramji asked how he should manage this risk. He should decide his limits, his friends told him, and that he should also decide the amount of money after losing which he would stop trading for the day, or exit a particular trade. Ramji was somehow not convinced by this advice. Why accept loss in a trade, he wondered. If he were buying a stock for profit, would it not be better to wait for the stock to start making profits before squaring off?

Ramji's friends managed to convince him that the stock price rises and falls due to its demand and supply balance, and no one should expect the price to move as per one's own expectation. The best one can do is predict the probable move, but you can't make the price move as per one's you wish. Ramji agreed with this risk management logic of pre-defining a limit for any single day or trade loss. Friends also advised him that if he started with an amount of ₹1 lakh and kept a risk limit of ₹1,000 per day, then it would take 100 days, or 100 trades to lose the whole capital. And, surely, not all trades would fail. Traders who do not set a clear limit, however, can lose their capital in a short time.

Ramji felt happy with this advice. He felt he now had a winning formula in hand for making it big in the market. He opened a trading account, deposited the requisite margin money with his broker, and selected a good day to start his venture. Based on his study using various media, the Internet, print and television, Ramji selected a stock to trade. He called his broker as the market opened, talked to the dealer who had taken his call, and told him to buy 1,000 shares of the stock he had selected. Soon the dealer confirmed on a recorded phone line that 1,000 shares had been bought at ₹200 per share. As he was about to disconnect the call, Ramji remembered the valuable piece of advice about risk management that his friends had given him. Immediately he told the dealer who had executed his order that he wanted to place a stop loss one rupee below his buying price. The logic behind this was his decision of a maximum loss limit of ₹1,000 for a day. Since he had bought 1,000 shares, a one rupee fall would mean a loss of ₹1,000 — therefore the stop loss one rupee below the buying price. The dealer placed the stop loss and informed Ramji about it.

A little later Ramji checked the price of the stock which he had bought and, to his pleasant surprise, the stock was trading 9% up for the day. He was happy. In fact, he was very happy that he had decided to enter the stock market, and applauded his intelligence in picking the right stock in his very first attempt. He was also very satisfied with the risk management method which he had implemented due to which he now had peace of mind. Feeling happy, he called up his broker in order to book profits.

The dealer picked up the call and Ramji told him to sell the stock and book profits. To this the dealer replied, "Sir, *aapka stop loss to trigger ho gayaa* (your stop loss has been triggered and now you do not hold a position in the stock)."

Unable to believe how such a thing could have happened, Ramji grew angry and shouted at the dealer. He accused the dealer of being jealous of his intelligence and stock picking skills which had helped him pick the right stock on the very first attempt. He added that most people were afraid of implementing stop losses and because he had done so, they (market professionals) did not want him to win, which is why they were playing mischief with him. After a long argument the dealer finally managed to convince Ramji by explaining how the price had first moved down triggering the stop loss, before moving back up. Finally, Ramji calmed down and thought it must have been his bad luck that such an event had happened where the price triggered the stop loss, but later moved in the right direction.

Thus, though he had made a loss in his first attempt there was one thing which made him extremely proud; his ability to pick the right stock since the one which he had traded moved up significantly on that day. With this confidence, he decided to trade another stock the next day.

When the market opened next morning, Ramji called his broker's office and placed an order to buy 500 shares of a stock. The dealer was cautious with Ramji as he had had a bad experience the previous day. He placed the order and again gave a confirmation on a recorded line as per compliance. The dealer said, "Sir, I bought 500 shares @ ₹255 per share." Continuing the conversation, he further asked, "Sir, *aaj apko stop loss lagana hain kya*? (Do you want to place a stop loss for the trade?)" Ramji replied in the affirmative, saying that his friends had told him that risk management was important and there must be a stop loss so that I don't end up losing all my money in very short time. He asked the dealer to place the stop loss ₹2 below his buying price for the current trade. He further said that he was placing a stop loss ₹2 below the buying price to avoid an issue like what had happened the previous day, and also in order to maintain a maximum risk of ₹1,000 per day, he had intelligently reduced the quantity to 500 shares. The dealer duly placed the stop loss and gave the confirmation.

Ramji then got busy in his work. In the afternoon he switched on a business channel and found that the stock which he had traded was locked in at 20% upper circuit. He was happy, in fact, he felt on top of the world; for the second time in a row the stock which he had traded had moved as per his view. To add to this, the current stock's move had managed to erase the loss made the previous day and bring his account back into profit. He began thinking that had he started trading some years back, by now he would be driving the best car and staying at the best of places. Controlling his emotions he made a call to his dealer and told the dealer to square off the trade and book profits. A bit scared, the dealer replied, "Sir, *aapka to stop loss trigger ho gaya* (The stop loss for your trade has been triggered)" and Ramji did not have an open position in that stock any more.

Hearing this, Ramji grew furious and started roundly cursing the dealer. The dealer patiently explained the series of events and the way the price first triggered the stop loss and only later moved in the direction predicted by Ramji. Ramji was truly angry this time because this event had shattered all his day dreams. After a while, the dealer managed to convince Ramji about the series of events. Another bad day had come to an end but Ramji was now more confident than ever about his stock picking skills. In his second attempt, too, the stock which he had picked had moved up — and this time it had even hit the upper circuit.

In his third attempt, Ramji again goes through the same series of events, placing an order, deciding a loss limit of ₹1,000, and accordingly placing a stop loss below his buying price so as to take care of the risk. But the stop loss again got triggered after which the price moved in the direction which he had predicted.

Now, considering that we all are governed by our experiences, based on Ramji's experience what do you think he would now do for his next attempt at making money?

Would he continue to use a stop loss to limit his losses?

Or, would his mind also say the same thing which circulates in the market — "*Operators ko stop loss dhikhte hain, wo stop loss trigger karte hain aur price ko chalate hain* (Market operators can see where you have placed your stop loss; first they trigger it, and then they manipulate the price)." Would you start believing this prevalent myth?

NSE and BSE are India's two premier exchanges. SEBI is the market regulator and keeps a strict vigil on any wrong doings in the markets, along with the exchanges which too continuously monitor transactions.

Can you see the stop loss levels of other traders or investors on the terminal? The answer is no.

A broker earns brokerage and tries to ensure that his client stays on the winning side so that he can keep generating additional brokerage. This requires that the relationship between a broker and a client, along with the service, technology and other things, be based on good advice. The broker's main objective is to ensure that his client flourishes.

Is it possible for somebody to hack into the computerised and secure systems of the stock exchanges? If at all that could happen it would mean that it is not the exchange but it is the country's economy which has been hacked.

Notwithstanding that, in my twenty-year career in the stock markets I have heard many people echo this myth. The only thing which changes as you move across India, to different states and cities from North to South and West to East, is the language. The myth remains the same everywhere, "*Mera stop loss operator ko dikhtaa hai, mera stop loss trigger kar ke wo stock ko baghaa le jata hai* — My stop loss is visible to the operator and first he triggers my stop loss and moves the price after that."

Now, who could this operator be about whom people complain? Every small wrong move in the market is monitored by the exchanges and SEBI. I don't deny the fact that there used to be operators who thought that stock markets were a gambler's den and they were the bosses of these dens. Those days are now long gone, and so have most of those people. Now the Indian markets are much more transparent and much better regulated than what they were before 2003.

What went wrong in Ramji's case can happen with anybody. And this makes many traders and investors apprehensive of using a stop loss. I believe the whole problem starts with the attitude.

Let me explain.

People have the wrong impression that every stock that they trade must work in their favour and generate a profit. They are not ready to accept that a trade can fail even after they have thoroughly studied or analysed a stock or a recommendation. So here one needs to change one's attitude and understanding of reality.

The second thing is that **a stop loss needs to be placed at the correct level**. What Ramji did is what most people do in the Indian stock markets. They decide a daily loss limit and then place stop losses which have no technical basis whatsoever. So when Ramji decided to place a stop loss ₹1 or ₹2 below his buying price, he was just thinking about his daily loss limit, rather than the right level for placing a stop loss — meaning a level which if broken would spell that the trader's view had failed. So the stop loss has to be at a level where the view was going to change. Implementing stop losses the way Ramji did is an invitation to making losses.

The logic for implementing a stop loss is simple — exit a trade when the reason for which you had entered it stands nullified.

Implementing Risk Management

Risk management is important because all trades carry risk. The risk is that your analysis can be wrong or your analysis can fail, and you can end up making a loss. Which is why it is important to limit your losses.

The basic rule for implementing risk management is that it should flag a price point which signals that your view, or strategy, has failed, and from there on the trend is expected to change. This is applicable to any stock which you may pick, whether based on fundamental analysis or technical analysis. The bottom line is that you are buying the price — and the transaction carries with it risks as well as returns.

Risk management can be implemented in different ways depending on your trading profile. Let's understand how.

Stop Loss for Intraday Traders

At times, intraday traders use the price as a trigger for entering a long or short trade; at other times they use indicators as triggers for entering the trade:

1. Traders who use the price as a trigger (*see* Figure 18.1), should implement a stop loss in case the price breakout fails.

2. Traders who enter trades using moving averages or indicators as a trigger, should implement a stop loss in case the average or the indicator gives the opposite signal.

In the chart in Figure 18.1, for example, the trader used the price breakout as the trigger for entering a trade. Being a downward breakout, the trade will be on the short side. Now because you are using a price breakout as a trigger, in this case risk management requires that the stop loss should trigger if the price breakout fails, which would also mean that the trade view has failed.

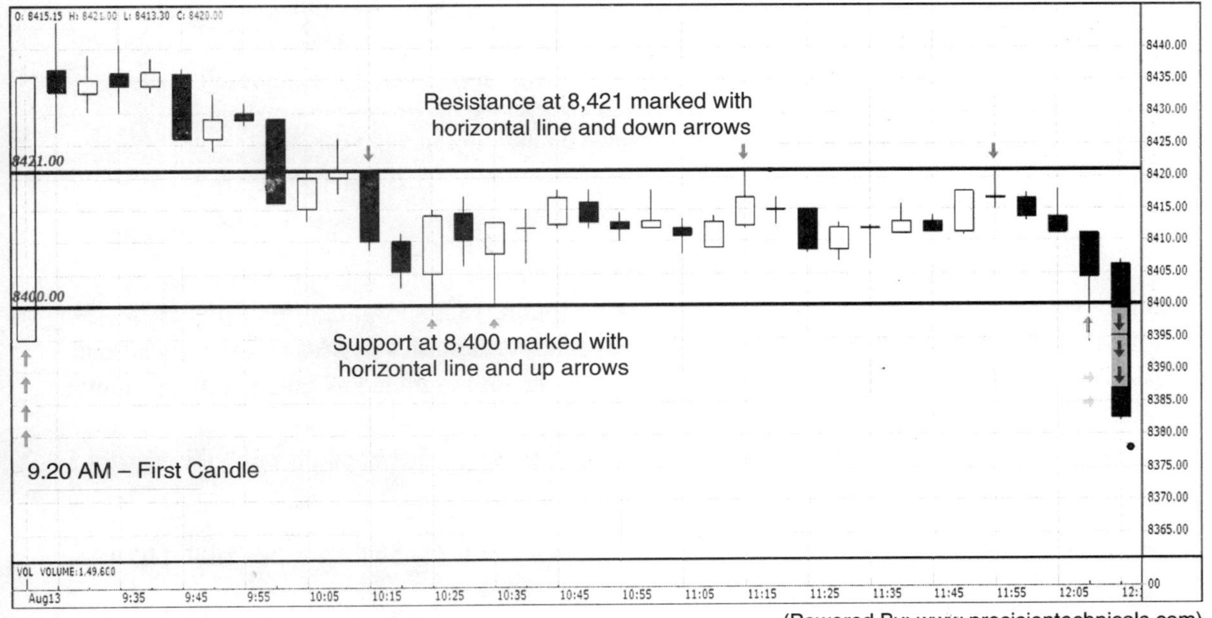

(Powered By: www.precisiontechnicals.com)

Figure 18.1: **Example of risk management: 5-minute candlestick chart of Nifty with a breakout below the support marked with down arrows on the extreme right candle.**

~

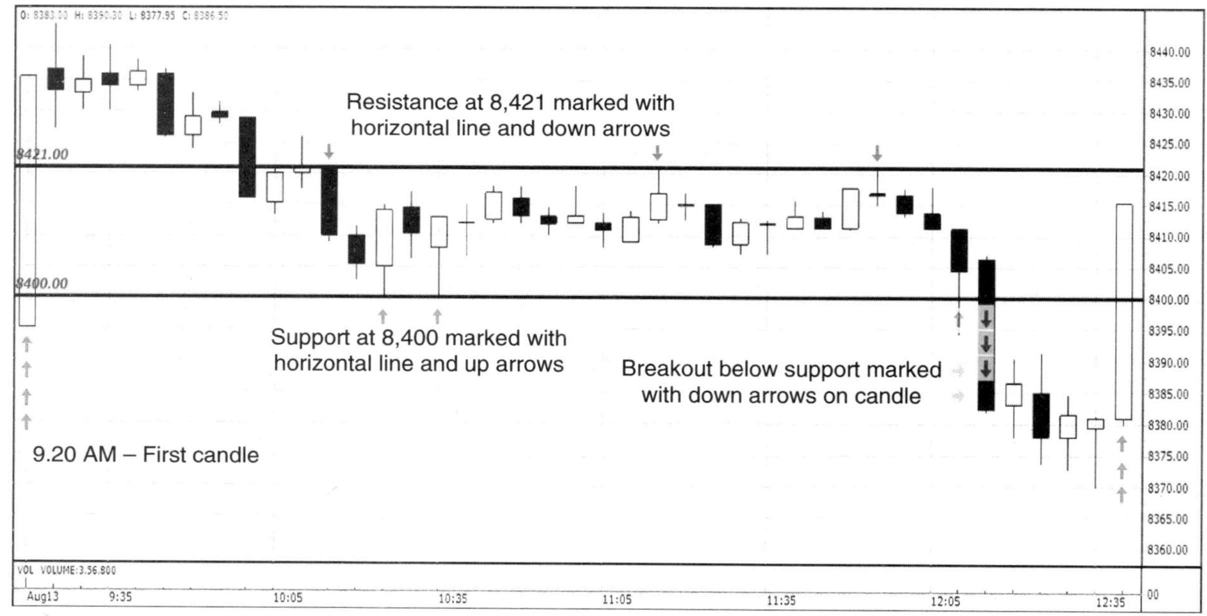

(Powered By: www.precisiontechnicals.com)

Figure 18.2: **Risk management example: 5-minute candlestick chart of Nifty showing a failure of the downward breakout as the price moves back above the downward breakout level as highlighted by up arrows marked on the extreme right candle.**

~

As you can see in the chart in Figure 18.2, the risk management (stop loss) is activated as the stock price again moves upward. The chart in Figure 18.2 shows that the fifth candle after the downward breakout moved up to close above the breakout level. This is a point where the stop loss needs to kick in because the original view about the trade has failed and one should, therefore, exit the trade.

So an intraday trader on a 5-minute chart who is trading price breakouts should place stop loss as follows:

- If the buy signal is an upward breakout, keep a stop loss 0.2% below the low of the breakout candle.
- If the sell signal is a downward breakout, keep a stop loss 0.2% above the high of the breakout candle.

Why 0.2% below or above?

You may trade differently priced stocks, say, a ₹20 stock, a ₹100 stock, ₹500 stock, ₹1,000 stock, or maybe trade Nifty which is priced at, say, 10,000. We can either decide a fixed amount as a difference for the stop loss level or decide a percentage. A percentage maintains uniformity for placing the stop loss level, irrespective of the price of the stock that you may trade.

0.2% for a ₹1,000 stock means the stop loss has to be either ₹2 above the high or ₹2 below the low of the breakout, based on the direction of the trade.

On the left half of the chart in Figure 18.3, you will be able to see the buy signal marked with up arrows when the moving average lines cross each other and move upwards. Then, a few candles later, you can see the sell signal where the down arrows are marked when the averages cross each other on the downward side. Basically, we are exiting a trade when the reason for which it was entered has failed. If you enter such a trade looking at a moving average crossover, then the stop loss should trigger when the averages cross in the opposite direction.

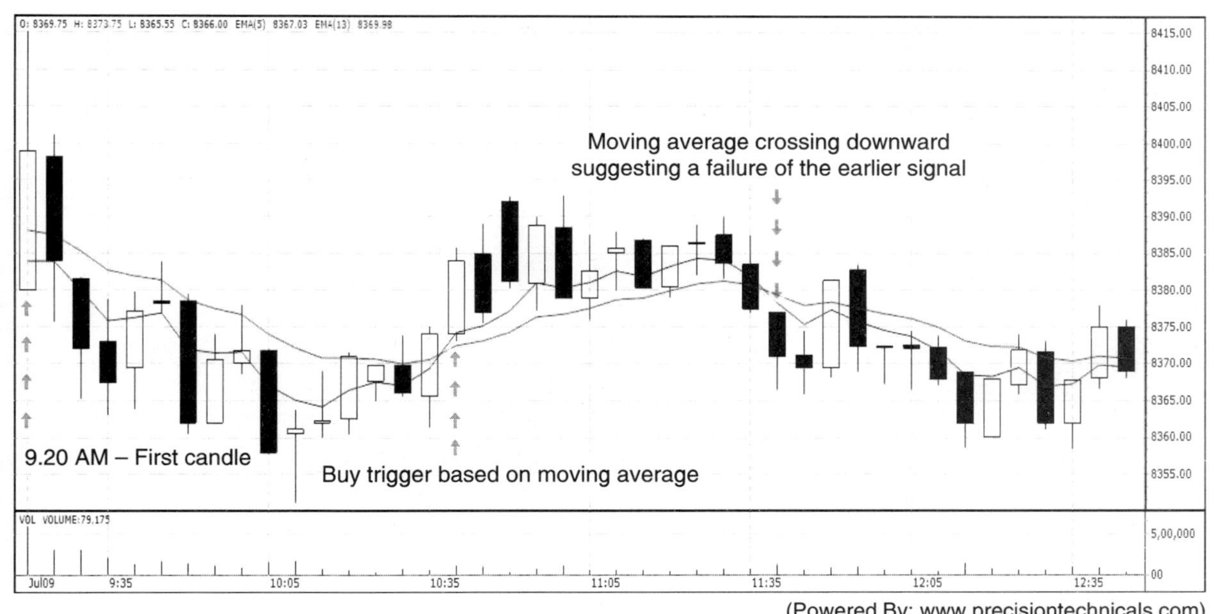

(Powered By: www.precisiontechnicals.com)

Figure 18.3: **Risk management example when using moving averages or indicators: 5-minute candlestick chart of Nifty with moving average crossovers as signals**

~

Stop Loss for Positional and Swing Traders, Short Term Investors or Long Term Investors

When it comes to risk management, the same logic applies for these categories of market players as for intraday traders. One important difference is the time period chart used to analyse and pick stocks.

Thus, for positional, swing, and short term trades one needs to be on the daily chart. The trades should be executed using price patterns as shown in Figure 18.4, because you will be trading the momentum in the price.

The chart in Figure 18.4 displays a trade which has been executed using a price pattern breakout on a daily chart. In such a case, the trader has a short term view and wants to trade the momentum in the stock price. Now, always remember that the risk increases when a trader has a short term view and seeks to catch the momentum.

In the example in Figure 18.4, we would be executing a long trade because the stock has given us an upward breakout from a consolidation of more than two months. We expect the price to now move fast towards its higher target. On Day-1, when you are buying into this stock, the chances of the stock hitting the stop loss and the chances of the stock reaching its

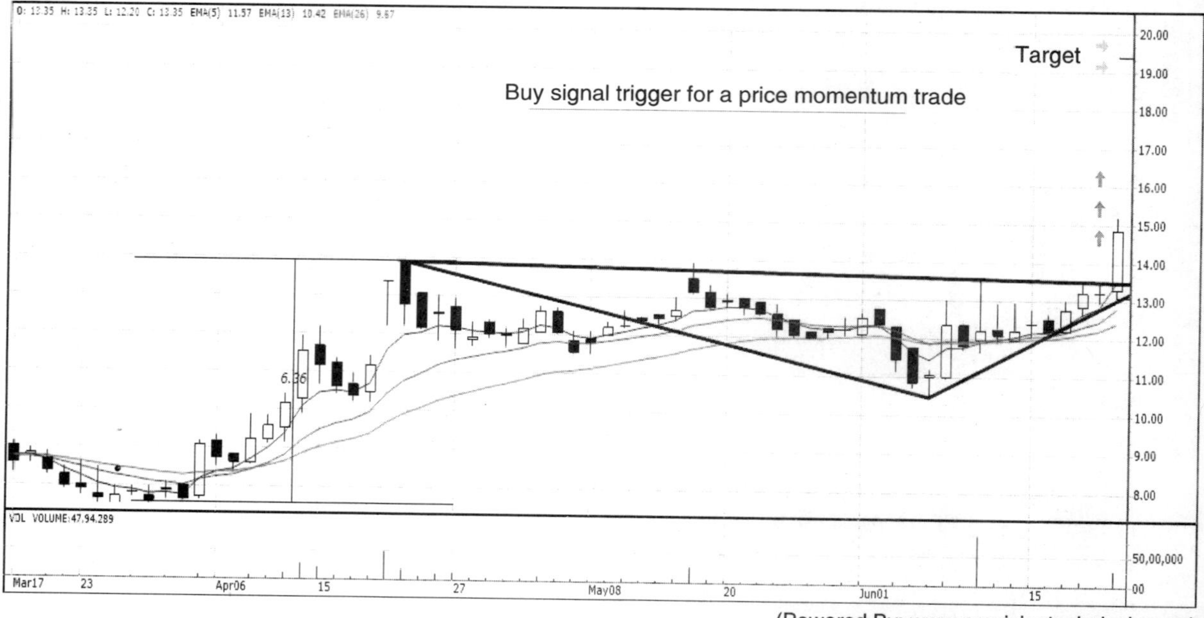

(Powered By: www.precisiontechnicals.com)

Figure 18.4: **Risk management example for positional, swing and short term traders: Daily chart of MIC Electronics with an up flag formation and an upward breakout on the extreme right**

target are 50:50. Therefore, once you are done with the analysis you should get into a trade only if the risk is acceptable to you. **Normally, people get into a trade looking at the possible profits but you must enter a trade only if the risk is acceptable to you.** That's because in case the analysis fails and the stock price moves down rather than up as expected and triggers your stop loss, you should be ready to exit the failed trade. If you don't do so, and if you don't prepare yourself for the risk before you enter a trade, then even when the trade fails you would try to find reasons to continue to hold on, which is not at all a good idea.

Therefore, enter a trade keeping the risk in mind, and enter it only if that risk is acceptable to you.

Coming back to the example in Figure 18.4, we have a nice breakout as can be seen on the chart. Such a breakout should normally not fail — but we cannot make the price move as per our expectations. We can do things which are in our control, such as deciding whether to trade the stock or not, deciding the quantity to trade, the timing, the price, and also limiting the risk by using a stop loss at the correct level. If such a nice breakout has to fail, then we should be the first ones to exit the trade.

An important thing for the trader to be clear about is the level where we can say that the trade seems to be failing.

To identify this risk management level you have to recall the topic, "Important Levels in a Candle" which we had discussed in Chapter 15. We discussed that every candle has four levels which act as support and resistance:

- In the case of a white (bullish) candle, there are three support levels, namely median, open, low — and one resistance level, the high of the candle.
- In the case of a black (bearish) candle, there are three resistance levels — median, open, high, and one support level, namely the low of the candle.

In the case of a positional trade or a short term investment trade, the stop loss has to be placed below the support in case of a long, namely a buy trade, and above the resistance in case of a short, i.e. a sell trade.

In the case of the example in Figure 18.4 it would be a good strategy to have the stop loss at a level 0.2% below the support, or the median, of the breakout candle. But, remember, this stop loss has to be on the basis of the end of the day closing price because intraday the stock price can even dip down below the median but by the end of the day the price could manually come back up above the median. You must therefore monitor the stop loss on closing basis and trigger it the next trading session if it gets violated on closing basis.

You also need to add a bit of discipline to your risk management strategy so as to minimize loss making trades as much possible. For this, check whether the current market condition is full of events or whether it is a normal market situation. By "full of events," I mean such periods when there are lots of external events which can make stock prices choppy; events like the budget, RBI policy review meetings, announcements of corporate earnings, global developments or meetings which can have impact on the Indian markets, etc.

In case there are such events coming up you should do two things; one, reduce the quantity traded and, two, implement stop loss below the third support level in the case of a buy trade, and above the third resistance level in the case of a sell trade.

This type of disciplined implementation will help minimize your risk in the event of trade failure and will also ensure that the stop loss does not get triggered due to the choppy price movement resulting from external events.

In normal market conditions, the stop loss can be implemented below the first support level in the case of a buy, and above the first resistance level in the case of a sell trade.

In the example we've been following, the momentum of the price can be clearly seen in the chart in Figure 18.5.

(Powered By: www.precisiontechnicals.com)

Figure 18.5: **Risk management example for positional / swing trader, short term and long term investor: Daily chart of MIC Electronics displays price momentum after the breakout from the up flag**

~

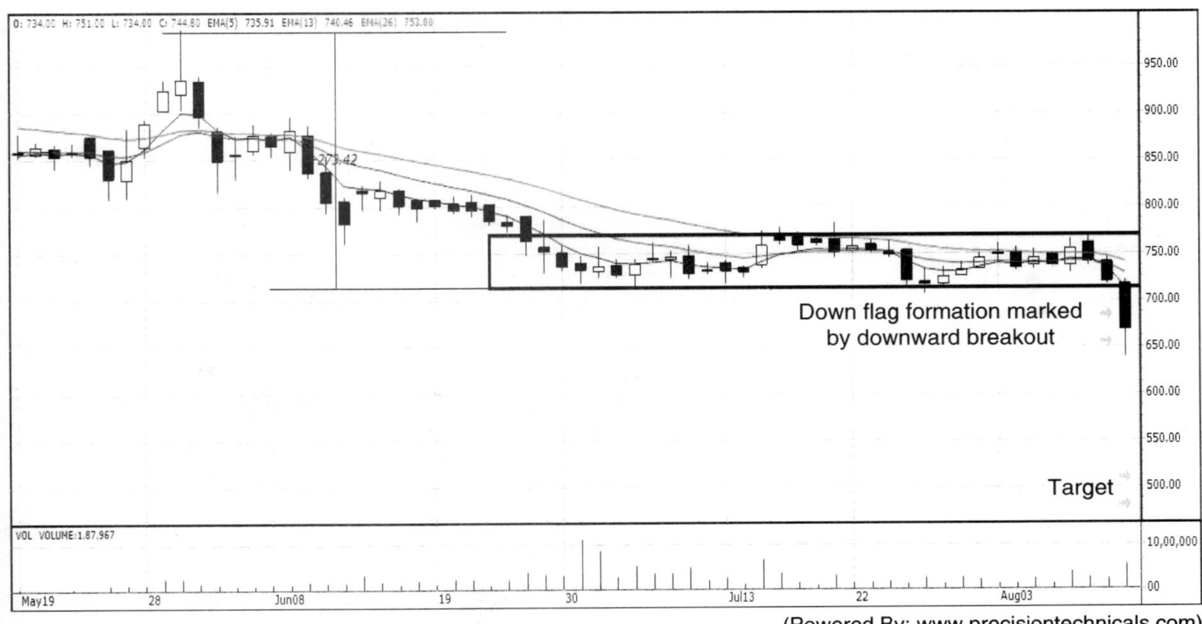

(Powered By: www.precisiontechnicals.com)

Figure 18.6: **Risk management example for positional / swing trader, short term and long term investor: Daily chart of Kaveri Seeds displays a sell signal because of a breakout from a down flag formation.**

~

Let's now look at a sell trade.

In the chart in Figure 18.6, the stop loss should be placed either above the median or above the first level resistance of the downward breakout candle as this is a sell signal. If this is a scenario during an event packed period, full of external events which can bring choppiness to the price, then the stop loss should be implemented above the third resistance level, i.e. the high of the black breakout candle so as to keep it at a safer level. And, always remember, **stop loss implementation in case of positional and investment trades must be on closing basis.**

You can see the momentum of the stock price in the chart in Figure 18.7.

Points to Remember

1. **Buy Trade:** Stop loss for a positional or swing trade, short or long term investment, has to be on closing basis, either below the median of the upward breakout candle, or below a good support. In eventful markets when price can be choppy, it should be placed below the third level of support to keep it safe. In addition, reducing the quantity traded at such times will further help in minimizing the risk inherent in choppy market conditions.

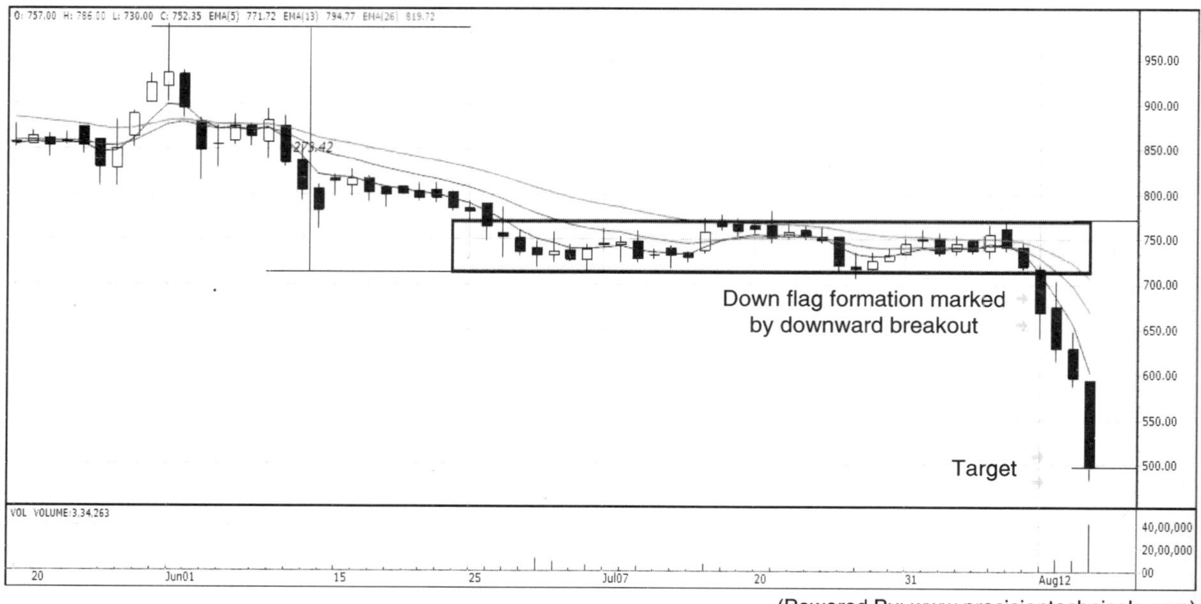

Figure 18.7: **Example of risk management for positional / swing trader, short term and long term investor — sell signal trigger for a price momentum trade. Daily chart of Kaveri Seeds displays price momentum after the down flag formation.**

~

2. **Sell Trade:** Stop loss for a positional or swing trade, short term or long term investment has to be on closing basis, either above the median of the downward breakout candle, or above a good resistance. During times of high news flow, when price can be choppy, the stop loss has to be above the third level of resistance to keep the trade safe. Plus, reducing the quantity traded at such times would add further help in minimizing risk in choppy market conditions.

Long Term Investor

People normally have a notion that a long term investor does not need risk management because in the long run everything tends to go up! This is the silliest of ideas that an investor can have. There are plenty of examples of stocks which don't see their previous high levels for years together. Also, it's most important to understand that there are many avenues for investment, and stock market is just one of them. All investment avenues have a benchmark based on the percentage and the time frame in which the returns are generated. Your stock market investments too need to be benchmarked in the same way. We invest in stocks for returns; if a stock which you have bought for the long term does not fetch you the required returns, nor outperform the other investing options available, then clearly your money is stuck in a non-performing stock.

Which is why risk management is very important even for a long term investor. The only difference in this case is that you need to implement the risk management strategy using weekly or monthly charts depending on the time period chart that you have analysed.

As a long term investor, you would normally initiate long investment trades and therefore the stop loss should be implemented below a major support on the weekly or monthly time frame chart.

Remember, the logic of risk management remains the same in all cases — exit a trade if the reason for which you entered it has failed.

Let us close this chapter with the example of Figure 18.8.

In this chapter we have tried to understand the importance of implementing risk management — and the different ways in which it can be implemented. We have also seen examples of trade failures wherein the implementation of risk management would have protected the investor or trader from needless losses.

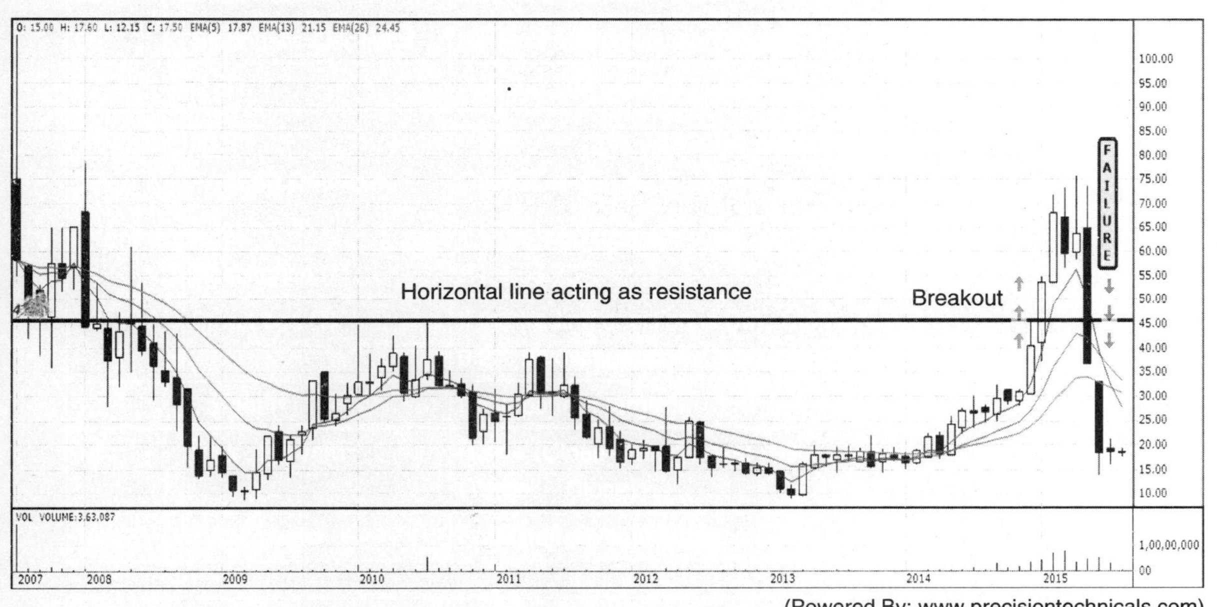

(Powered By: www.precisiontechnicals.com)

Figure 18.8: **Monthly chart of Celestial Bio displays the failure of a breakout above the horizontal resistance level and implementation of a stop loss. Breakout on monthly chart suggested a long term multiple-bagger stock but, eventually, the breakout failed with the price falling below the breakout level.**

~

Quiz: Risk Management

Questions

1. Risk management is a simple work but requires lot of courage for the implementation. (True / False?)
2. For positional and investment trades the stop loss has to be implemented in the terminal every day. (True / False?)
3. Intraday traders should implement the stop loss in the terminal? (True / False?)

Answers

1. True   2. False   3. True

RISK MANAGEMENT IS IMPORTANT BECAUSE WHILE WE CAN ANALYSE A STOCK WE CANNOT MAKE IT MOVE AS PER OUR WISH.

Chapter 19

~

Your Trading Plan

WHEN PEOPLE HEAR WORDS SUCH AS TRADING PLAN, money management, risk management, etc., they often believe that these must be complicated concepts, better suited for fund managers than individual investors and traders.

If you wish to survive and flourish in the stock market for a long period, however, you need to acquire knowledge of these matters. Whether you are a day trader, a swing trader, or an investor, you need to have knowledge of trade planning, money management and risk management.

It is somewhat like swimming; till the time you learn how to swim, you are scared of even getting into the water, but the moment you are able to swim, you start enjoying it.

For some people trading plan means first having a portfolio, and then managing it. This is a wrong idea. In fact, we need to plan and strategize an idea before getting into a business.

Your hard earned money is at stake in the stock market and you should therefore first have a trading plan and only then enter a trade.

Trading plan means working out a strategy based on your comfort, your expectations, your risk taking appetite, and your investment capital. Before you start investing, you should write down your strategy so that it becomes a blueprint or an investment road map as you move forward. Defining a strategy is nothing but defining your rules for investment and trading. And this is important because discipline is needed in all walks of life. A trading plan will help you survive and flourish in the market for a long period of time. The strategy, or plan, will be different for every individual because the reasons for trading, the expectations from it, the investment capital and the risk taking appetite is different in every case.

When writing down your trading plan, I suggest that you confine yourself to a room where no one can disturb you because you will now be laying down a set of rules which are going to help you limit the risk involved in the venture. I further suggest you switch off your mobile phone. Sit peacefully with a positive frame of mind and be optimistic and confident of the good things that you will now be achieving for yourself. When you enter a trade, it is important to tell yourself that the objective is to make money for yourself. Therefore if you are setting down rules for your trading and investment to be successful, then it is something good that you are doing for yourself. The trading plan that you will be putting down on paper is also going to help you stay calm and unflustered in the market. The day you lose your comfort level, you would start making mistakes and that is extremely harmful when it comes to the stock market.

So, now, you are sitting in a room with a notebook which will become the holy book for your stock market venture, phone switched off, no gadgets to disturb you in your mission.

The first thing that you need to do is select your profile by asking yourself "Who am I?" Then, decide your investment capital, then the allocation of that capital, risk that you can take, your expectations, and some other fine tuned rules.

Let's start.

1. Who am I? Select your market profile — intraday trader, positional trader, swing trader or investor:
   - For profile selection, use the criteria discussed in Chapter 3.
   - You may decide to select one, two, or all the three profiles.
   - You may decide to be a trader, a short term investor, and also an investor. But remember not to shift profiles during a trade. So your intraday trade should never change to short term investment or long term investment, etc., and *vice versa.*
2. Investment capital or trading capital.
3. Allocation of this capital among the profiles selected.
4. Number of stocks to be held open in the respective profiles.
5. Risk: the maximum loss amount to your portfolio which will trigger a review of your strategy.
6. Partial profit booking strategy: Deciding levels in percentage terms, to help in booking profits. The importance of partial profit booking is explained in Chapter 22.
7. Time: the period after which a review of your trading plan kicks in.

Once this set of rules, given in Table 19.1 is ready, you can start trading and investing in the stock market.

Table 19.1

Trading Plan Rules

Steps	*Parameter*	*Profile 1*	*Profile 2*	*Profile 3*
1	Profile			
2	Investment / Capital (₹)			
3	Investment Allocation			
4	Stocks to Hold			
5	Investment Per Stock (₹)			
6	Risk			
7	Partial Profit Booking			
8	Time			

This of rules, the profile selection, the investment amount, the fund allocation, risk, time of trade and the number of stocks to be held in the portfolio will vary from person to person. Some people would like to fit in all the three profiles whereas others may fit in one or may be two of the profiles. Examples of how the rules can be different are shown in Tables 19.2, 19.3 and 19.4.

Table 19.2

Trading Plan Rules — Sample 1

Steps	*Parameter*	*Profile 1*	*Profile 2*	*Profile 3*
1	Profile	Day Trader	Positional Trader	Investor
2	Investment Capital (₹)	2 lakh	3 lakh	5 lakh
3	Investment Allocation	20%	30%	50%
4	Stocks to Hold	2	2	10
5	Investment per Stock (₹)	1,00,000	1,50,000	50,000
6	Risk	20%	20%	20%
7	Partial Profit Booking	1%	5%	10%
8	Time	Max 1 hour	10 Days	12 Months

Table 19.3

Trading Plan Rules — Sample 2

Steps	*Parameter*	*Profile 1*	*Profile 2*	*Profile 3*
1	Profile		Positional Trader	Investor
2	Investment Capital (₹)		3 lakh	7 lakh
3	Investment Allocation		30%	70%
4	Stocks to Hold		6	10
5	Investment per Stock (₹)		50,000	70,000
6	Risk		10%	20%
7	Partial Profit Booking		5%	10%
8	Time		25 Days	12 to 24 Months

Table 19.4

Trading Plan Rules — Sample 3

Steps	*Parameter*	*Profile 1*	*Profile 2*	*Profile 3*
1	Profile			Investor
2	Investment Capital (₹)			10 lakhs
3	Investment Allocation			100%
4	Stocks to Hold			10
5	Investment per Stock (₹)			1,00,000
6	Risk			20%
7	Partial Profit Booking			10%
8	Time			12 to 24 Months

Quiz: Trading Plan

Questions

1. Trading plans are for fund managers and not for me. (True / False?)
2. Planning and deciding a strategy for investing or trading helps in implementing discipline. (True / False?)

Answers

1. False
2. True

PREPARE A TRADING PLAN BASED ON YOUR REQUIREMENT TO PROTECT AND GROW YOUR HARD EARNED MONEY!

Chapter 20

~

Risk to Reward Ratio

INVESTORS AND TRADERS ARE GRIPPED BY EMOTIONS OF FEAR AND GREED. When doing things such as reading this book you may not realize that you have an important organ in your body called the heart. Punch a trade in your trading terminal and the very next moment you will realize its pulsing existence. I am sure you have experienced this. Why does this happen? Why do you realize that you have a heart only after having entered a trade? The reason for this is the fear factor. Now tell me what is the objective behind the trade that you have entered? Did you enter the trade to make profits or to lose money? The answer will obviously be to make money; there is no reason for anybody to enter a trade to make a loss. Then why the fear? The answer is simple — often when a trade is entered the possible downside in that trade is not explicitly mapped. Instead, typically a trade is entered by only looking at the likely profits. The possibility of a loss is never thought off. This makes the fear factor overpower your mental process and makes your heart beat fast. When the price starts moving against the direction of the trade, the investor / trader is finally overpowered by fear and ends up taking wrong decisions.

In the same way, when a trade starts making profit, the trader / investor is gripped by greed for more profit. This is a never ending story. Discipline is therefore required to keep your emotions in check. The greed part will be taken care by the AIM strategy when we look at the monitoring part of trading. This is explained in the later chapters in detail.

Therefore calculating potential risk and reward before getting into a trade is very important. Your analysis is actually incomplete without this information.

Risk is the amount of money which you will end up losing if the stock price moves against your view and triggers your stop. A proper analysis will help you assess this risk before you get into a trade. After analysis, you should trade the stock only if you are comfortable with the risk; i.e. you are ready to accept the loss if the stop loss is hit. Your buying price less the stop loss price is the amount of money which you would end up losing when the stop loss is triggered.

In case of a positional and investment trade, you will be investing your funds. In such cases, therefore, one should follow a risk to reward ratio of 1:3, which means you should take a risk of ₹1 only when the analysis suggests that the stock presents a reward of at least ₹3. Low risk and high reward trades should be given preference.

Let's understand the reason behind having a risk to reward ratio of 1:3.

When we analyse and trade stocks, some of them will work and some of them will fail. Risk to reward ratio ensures that your cumulative end result does not turn negative. This ratio becomes important in ensuring that the overall end result remains positive.

Here is how:

Let us assume ten stocks are traded with an equal amount invested in each one and with a risk to reward ratio of say, 1:3. Now, say, 7 of the stocks do not work in our favour, namely they trigger the stop loss and we have to exit those trades, while the remaining 3 stocks manage to reach their target price levels. In such a case, we may end up losing 7 points and gaining 9 points, which means your end result will continue to remain positive (*see* Table 20.1).

Table 20.1

Risk Reward Ratio Explained

Stock No.	*Risk: Reward*		*Stock No.*	*Risk: Reward*
1	1: ~~3~~		6	1: ~~3~~
2	1: ~~3~~		7	1: ~~3~~
3	1: ~~3~~		8	~~1~~: 3
4	1: ~~3~~		9	~~1~~: 3
5	1: ~~3~~		10	~~1~~: 3

Risk to reward ratio is one of the parameters in our trading strategy, which is described in step by step detail in Part 2 of this book. It is a very important parameter for profitable trading. If at times, therefore, a promising trade fails to qualify in the risk to reward ratio of 1:3, then it is better to avoid that trade.

~

Quiz: Risk To Reward Ratio

Questions

1. I can take trades where the risk to reward ratio is less than 1:3. (True / False?)
2. Risk to reward ratio is only for the day trader and not for an investor. (True / False?)
3. Getting into trades where you are comfortable with the risk will always keep you in control. (True / False?)

Answers

1. False 2. False 3. True

RISK TO REWARD RATIO WILL ENSURE THAT YOUR PORTFOLIO REMAINS IN POSITIVE TERRITORY EVEN IF YOUR WINNING TRADES ARE FEW!

Chapter 21

~

Money Management

MONEY MANAGEMENT IS IMPORTANT FOR EVERY MARKET PARTICIPANT, irrespective of which profile you may fit into — day trader, short term investor, positional trader or investor. We all have limited amounts of money to put in the market. It could be ₹1 lakh for some, for others ₹5 lakh, ₹10 lakh, ₹1 crore or ₹10 crore, but we all finally have a limit. This is hard earned money and we intend to grow it further by investing it in the stock markets. Therefore, we need to respectfully take care of the money that we have with us.

Money management can be implemented in two ways:

- Maintaining a balance between risk and reward.
- Giving priority to managing risk.

Maintaining a Balance between Risk and Reward

Some stocks you trade or invest in might be trading at two digit prices, some at three, others at even more than three digit prices. **To maintain a balance between the risk and reward involved in trades of differently priced stocks, it is important to follow and implement money management.**

A simple rule for doing so is to decide your investment per stock or per trade. The trade quantity will then be decided by dividing the amount of investment per stock with the current market price of the stock. This will help in spreading and balancing risk and reward among the various stocks traded. Let's see how.

Normally when we trade a low-priced stock, the confidence with which we enter a trade and the quantity traded are both high. But when it comes to trading a higher priced stock, people become nervous. They are scared of the high price, often avoid such stocks, and if at all they decide to trade the quantity traded is so minimal that it hardly makes a difference to the portfolio.

Let us consider an example.

Suppose the two stocks you have decided to trade are Suzlon and TCS. Suzlon was then trading at ₹15 and TCS at ₹2,500. You are psychologically more confident when it comes to trading a lower priced stock due to an impression that a low priced stock may be less volatile and, eventually, give you a smaller loss in absolute terms if the trade were to go wrong. Conversely, many traders believe that while a high priced stock can display big moves, the volatility could also be high. This is nothing but a myth as a result of which people tend to buy smaller quantities of higher priced stocks.

So, for example, when it comes to entering a trade in Suzlon, I might buy 2,000 shares, but when it comes to trading TCS I may buy only 5 shares. Due to this fallacy, the value traded in both the stocks is different. Along with the investment there is also a difference in the risk and the return involved in both the trades.

Let's look at a case where we have entered a trade in both the stocks as shown in Table 21.1. TCS gives a profit and Suzlon gives a loss. The end result of the combined trade however remains negative though your overall strike rate in the two trades was 50%. The reason for this loss was the mismatch in investment in the two trades executed.

Table 21.1

Mismatched Trades

	Stock Name	*Price (₹)*	*Quantity*	*Investment (₹)*	*Risk of 2% (₹)*	*Reward of 2% (₹)*
1	Suzlon	15	2,000	30,000	600	600
2	TCS	2,500	5	12,500	250	250

To maintain a balance between the risk and reward involved in all the stocks traded in your portfolio, you must ensure that you maintain a balance in the investment amount in each. **So irrespective of the stock prices, the investment amount in each trade or investment must remain the same.**

This rule is applicable for all trades and for all the different profiles.

If you are a day trader, then you may have experienced the following. In the morning hours you enter a trade in one lot of Nifty and make a profit. With this profit your confidence is boosted and then in the afternoon the second trade that you enter is for two or more lots of Nifty. This second trade gives you a loss so your strike rate for the day is 50% — profit on the first trade, but loss on the second. But when you assess your absolute profit and loss you find that the end result is a loss. The earlier profit was eroded by the second trade, and as the lots traded in the second trade were more in number, you incurred a higher loss. So not only has the earlier profit gone, but extra money is lost.

This is also applicable to positional trading, and short term or long term investment.

The right way of maintaining a balance between the risk and rewards is by keeping the capital invested in all trades the same. This can be done as shown in the example in Table 21.2.

Table 21.2 **Risk Management by Uniform Investment in Each Trade**						
Sr. No.	*Stock Name*	*Investment (₹)*	*Price (₹)*	*Quantity*	*Risk of 2% (₹)*	*Reward of 2% (₹)*
1	Suzlon	30,000	15	2,000	600	600
2	TCS	30,000	2,500	12	600	600

As can be seen in Table 21.2, a balance can be maintained between the risk and the rewards when the total investment in each of the differently priced stocks is the same.

This is the strategy to use when trading normal markets.

Giving Priority to Managing Risk

The second way of implementing risk management is by focussing exclusively on risk when you decide the quantity to be traded, or the amount to be invested. **This is the strategy to follow when there are plenty of market events or external events which can cause choppiness in the stock price movements.** During periods which are filled with external events impacting stock prices, it is advisable to maintain low profile. Thus, giving emphasis to managing risk is always a good strategy during such periods. This means that quantity should be decided based on a pre-defined risk amount per trade.

By using this strategy you will be able to keep the risk in control during choppy periods.

For example, in Table 21.3, you can see that the risk has been balanced among the differently priced stocks that you trade. The stop loss remains at the correct level and what differs is the quantity based on the risk that is acceptable to you.

Table 21.3 **Risk Management by Balancing All Trades**							
Sr. No.	*Stock Name*	*Total Acceptable Risk (₹)*	*Price (₹)*	*Stop Loss (₹)*	*Risk*	*Quantity*	*Investment (₹)*
1	Suzlon	600	15	13.50	1.50	400	6,000.00
2	TCS	600	2,500	2,050	450	1	2,500.00

The figures in all the tables have been rounded off as the quantity cannot be traded in decimals, and also for simplifying the understanding.

Quantity will be decided by the risk involved in the trade if the stop loss is triggered divided by the total acceptable risk which a trader is ready to take in that trade.

Investment will be decided by multiplying the quantity with the price of the stock that you will be trading.

~

Quiz: Money Management

Questions

1. Money management helps in maintaining a balance between risk and rewards. (True / False?)
2. When entering a trade, should priority be given to managing risk or to expected returns?

Answers

1. True
2. Risk

MONEY MANAGEMENT HELPS IN DOING JUSTICE TO YOUR HARD EARNED MONEY BY MANAGING THE RISK.

Chapter 22

~

How to Stay Calm While Trading

SUCCESS IN THE STOCK MARKET is based only 20% on strategy and 80% on discipline. This chapter focuses on helping you with that 80% factor. The stock markets carry high risk and there are plenty of factors beyond your control that impact price movements. Staying disciplined, on the other hand, is entirely in your hands.

In the stock market you should endeavour to remain comfortable and calm at all times. This means you should have confidence in your analysis, and clarity about the risk and reward involved in each trade. Thus you should execute your trades with a positive frame of mind. This is something very important, because only with a calm mind can you take right decisions.

As your hard earned money is at risk at all times in the stock market, therefore a loss making transaction can disturb you or even make you panic, which, in turn, can lead you into taking wrong decisions. To ensure that this does not happen, I have always advocated that when entering a trade or a transaction, you should first assess the risk involved. Think first about the risk, think about the money that would be at stake, and get into a trade only if that risk amount is acceptable.

With a comfort level about the amount at risk, you can enter a trade with a positive mind which will help you withstand the volatility in that stock or in your portfolio. By doing so, you will ensure that you remain calm at all times. When you remain calm, you improve your chances of taking the correct decisions.

Staying calm will always help you follow your strategy with discipline. You will follow the rules you've set down for yourself.

Staying calm is important not only when entering a trade and dealing with the risk; it is equally important during the period you are in the trade, or when it comes to booking profits.

Staying calm is nothing but being able to keep a check on your emotions. Fear and greed are the two roller coaster emotions which every trader needs to keep a check on. You may not be able to completely avoid or master these emotions as they are a part of every human being but you can control them. It's difficult but not impossible.

Fear and greed can be kept at bay when you are in control of your trade. When I say being in control I mean that you must be aware of the risk before you initiate a trade — in other words, you must have clarity on how much money you could lose in the trade. Once you have set down an acceptable limit, you would feel relatively calm and comfortable. Then, once you are in the trade, the price will rise and fall every day, increasing the level of your heartbeat.

Many a time the volatility will even make you uncomfortable. As a result, and you may also have experienced this, people often exit a trade hastily only to later find the stock moving in the desired direction.

All this can be avoided if you are in control of the trade at all times:

- Fear makes one uncomfortable; it's the fear of losing money if the stock moves in a direction contrary to your expectation.
- Greed also makes one uncomfortable; while waiting for profit a sharp reaction in the stock price may get you worried about losing all your paper profit. This often makes for poor trade exits.

As analysts, investors or traders, we can only act on things which are in our control. Thus, we can analyse a stock, decide upon a strategy and risk management, implement the right money management, but we will not be able to make the price move in the direction we desire. In order to remain at ease at all times, you should focus on all that which can help you be comfortable.

Our AIM strategy will help you keep yourself comfortable at all times. I have discussed this strategy in detail in Part 2.

Now, Let's consider what can keep us calm and comfortable in a trade.

Analyze a Stock in Detail

Do all the required homework before entering a trade rather than trying to justify a trade after entry.

Enter a Trade Only If the Risk is Acceptable

Before entering a trade you should know the maximum amount that you can lose if your view of the trade fails. The risk can be reduced further by reducing the quantity to be traded.

Follow Your Trading Plan

Hold positions in only as many number of stocks as you have decided in your trading plan and stick to the plan.

Follow Money Management

Invest an equal amount in all the stocks you are trading during normal market conditions.

To further reduce risk during uncertain and choppy times, determine the quantity to be traded with a pre-defined risk value.

Monitor Trades on Appropriate Time Frames

If a stock is traded after analysing it on a daily time frame chart, then the monitoring should also be on the daily chart. If a stock is traded after analysing it on a weekly time period chart, then the monitoring too should be on its weekly chart, using end of the week prices. If a stock is traded after analysing it on the monthly time period chart, then the monitoring should be on the monthly chart, using end of the month price.

Don't Worry About Catching the Exact Tops and Bottoms

The reality is that nobody can catch the very tops and the very bottoms. This is not just difficult, it's impossible to do so consistently. Once you understand this, you won't waste time trying to do something which is not possible.

Partial Profit Booking

When the stock moves in our desired direction, we can get gripped by the fear of losing the available paper profits because of the apprehension that the price could react against your desired direction. This fear can at times tempt you to book profits prematurely.

At other times, when a trade is in a loss, fear can keep you in the trade for too long in the hope that the price may turn around. These are signs of indiscipline and not good for a trade. To avoid this you can do something that is in your control — book partial profits. As the trade starts moving in your direction, you can reduce your fear of a sudden fall by booking partial profits. This will help you in reducing the quantity at risk while also putting some profits in your pocket. You can do this at intervals by way of pre-defined percentages. This can also be done multiple times in small quantities or as often as you want till you feel comfortable in the ongoing successful trade.

Follow Moving Averages to Stay in the Trend

Once the stock is analysed, a trade entered, avoid looking at the colours of the candles while monitoring the trade — white candles will make you happy and black candles will needlessly worry you. To prevent the candlestick colours, shapes and sizes having an impact on your emotions, it is better to stay with the trend by following the moving averages.

~

Quiz: Stay Calm While Trading

Questions

1. A comfortable mind helps in taking good decision. (True / False?)
2. Knowing the risk involved in a trade before taking the trade can help you stay calm during the trade? (True / False?)

Answers

1. True
2. True

A CALM MIND TAKES CORRECT DECISIONS.

Part II

Technical Trading Course

Chapter 23

~

Trade Selection Ready-Reckoner

How to Select the Stocks to Trade

THIS CHAPTER INTRODUCES OUR INNOVATIVE TRADE SELECTION READY-RECKONER, a powerful trading tool for identifying and managing high reward trades.

When analysing potential stocks to trade, a structured and well-defined approach helps eliminate subjectivity and emotion to a large extent. Further, the approach should be simple and consistent for all the potential stocks and trades that you analyse. This is achieved by systematically analysing the various technical parameters that we studied in the earlier chapters and recording their verdicts in the Trade Selection Ready-Reckoner in order to arrive at a clear go / no-go decision with respect to every trading opportunity.

The Trade Selection Ready-Reckoner thus enforces discipline in the way you analyse and pick stocks and how you trade them. In short:

- The Trade Selection Ready-Reckoner leads to disciplined trading decisions, based on systematic technical analysis of charts and not on your whims and fancies of the moment.
- The Trade Selection Ready-Reckoner helps you remain calm and comfortable during a trade because you would have assessed the risk, the reward, and the time and price targets in advance.
- The Trade Selection Ready-Reckoner preserves your analysis for future reference and post-mortem. At all times, the analysis will be readily available with the reasons why you picked or rejected a particular trade.

Table 23.1 shows you how to compile the Trade Selection Ready-Reckoner for any trade under consideration.

Table 23.1

Rules for Filling in the Trade Selection Ready-Reckoner

Sr. No.	*Parameter*	*Observation*	*Verdict*
1	Candlestick	White candle	Buy
		Black candle	Sell
2	Volume	White candle with increased volume	Buy
		Black candle with increased volume	Sell
3	Moving Average (Crossover within the latest 5 candles)	5 MA crosses 13 MA or 26 MA on the upside	Buy
		5 MA crosses 13 MA or 26 MA on the downside	Sell
		Else	Indecision

(Contd . . .)

Table 23.1: **Rules for Filling in the Trade Selection Ready-Reckoner** *(. . . contd)*

Sr. No.	*Parameter*	*Observation*	*Verdict*
4	Candlestick Pattern	Bullish Piercing	Bullish — Buy
		Bullish Engulf	
		Hammer at Bottom	
		Morning Star	
		Bearish Piercing	Bearish — Sell
		Bearish Engulf	
		Inverted Hammer at Top	
		Evening Star	
		Hanging Man	
		Any Other	Indecision
5	Price Pattern	Inverted Head and Shoulder	Bullish — Buy
		Double Bottom	
		Rounding Bottom	
		Up Flag	
		Trend Change Upward	
		Listing Breakout	
		Head and Shoulder	Bearish — Sell
		Double Top	
		Down Flag	
		Trend Change Downward	
		Any Other	Indecision
	No Clear Price Pattern	Without a price pattern we will not have a price target, without which we will also neither have a risk to reward ratio nor a time target. Therefore, drop the stock if there is no clear price pattern	No Trade
6	Stochastic Oscillator (Crossover within the last 5 candles)	Uptrend and positive crossover	Buy
		Downtrend and negative crossover	Sell
		Any Other	Indecision
7	Relative Strength Index (RSI) (Crossover within the last 5 candles)	Uptrend and positive crossover	Buy
		Downtrend and negative crossover	Sell
		Any Other	Indecision
8	MACD (Crossover within the last 5 candles)	Positive crossover in positive zone	Buy
		Negative crossover in negative zone	Sell
		Any Other	Indecision
9	Trading Decision	If the parameter verdicts comprise only B and I	Buy
		If the parameters verdicts comprise only S and I	Sell
		If the parameter verdicts comprise either B, S, and I, or B and S	No Trade
10	Support	Always below the close of the analysis candle (In normal market = Median or Open) (In eventful market = Low)	

(Contd . . .)

Table 23.1: **Rules for Filling in the Trade Selection Ready-Reckoner** *(. . . contd)*

Sr. No.	*Parameter*	*Observation*	*Verdict*
11	Resistance	Always above the close of the analysis candle (In normal market = Median or Open) (In eventful market = High)	
12	Stop Loss	If the verdict is buy, place the stop loss 0.2% below support	
		If the verdict is sell, place the stop loss 0.2% above resistance	
13	Target Price	As per the price pattern target	
14	Risk : Reward	Should be at least 1:3	
15	Time Target — Based on the Price Pattern (*see* Chapter 16)	*Head and Shoulder:* Number of candles from the first neck point to the breakout candle, divided by 3	
		Double / Triple Top: Number of candles from the first top to the latest candle, divided by 3	
		Trend Change Downward Breakout: Number of candles from start of the up move before the consolidation to the breakout candle, divided by 3	
		Inverted Head and Shoulders: Number of candles from the first neck point to breakout candle, divided by 3	
		Double / Triple Bottom: Number of candles from the first bottom to the latest candle, divided by 3	
		Rounding Bottom: First target in 1 year and the final target in 3 years	
		Trend Change Upward Breakout: Number of candles from start of the down move before the consolidation to the breakout candle, divided by 3	
		Listing Breakout Pattern: 1 year	
		Up Flag: Number of candles from start of the pole to the breakout candle, divided by 3	
		Down Flag: Number of candles from start of the pole to the breakout candle, divided by 3	

Now, let's run through the rules for filling in the Trade Selection Ready-Reckoner:

- If there is any confusion or uncertainty in interpreting whether a parameter is generating a buy verdict or a sell verdict, then we consider the verdict to be indecision.
- A price pattern — see serial number 5 — exists only if it can be immediately and obviously seen on the chart. If you have to spend a lot of time to convince yourself that a pattern does indeed exist, then you must accept that it is not there.
- Without a price pattern, we can't have a price target. Without a price target we will also not have a risk to reward ratio, neither will we have a time target. **Therefore, we must drop the stock or trade from consideration if the verdict for the price pattern is indecision.**

~

Let us now see how to use the Trade Selection Ready-Reckoner with an example. Figure 23.1 is the daily chart of 8K Miles. From analysing the chart, we have recorded the analysis data in the Trade Selection Ready-Reckoner in Table 23.2.

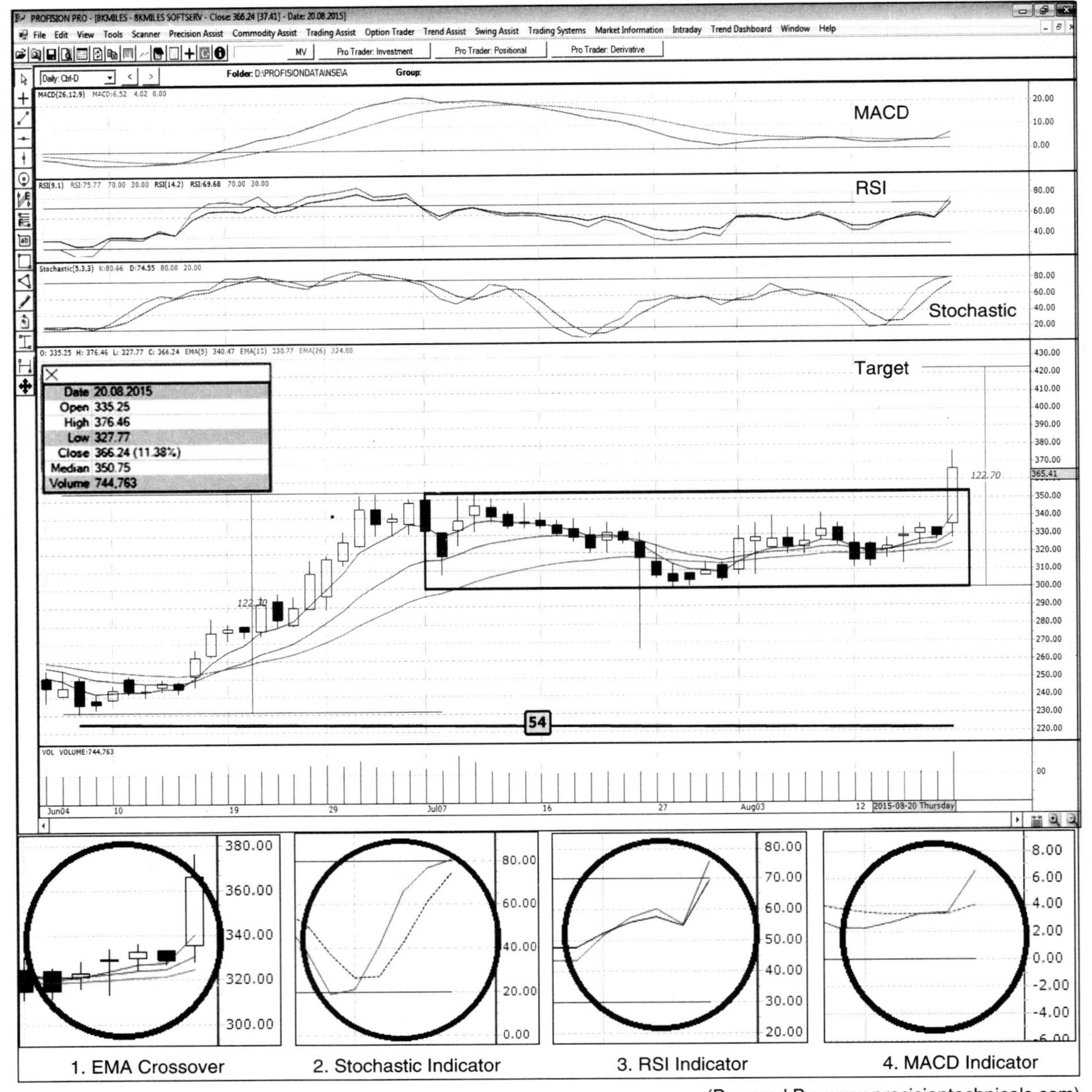

Figure 23.1: **Daily chart of 8K Miles**

~

Table 23.2

Trade Selection Ready-Reckoner for 8K Miles (*see* Figure 23.1)

Sr. No.	*Parameter*		
	Date >>>		20.08.2015
	Stock Symbol >>>		8K Miles
	Close (₹) >>>		₹366.24
	Time Period >>>		Daily
Sr. No.	*Parameter*	*Observation / Reason*	***Verdict***
01	Candlestick	White candlestick	Buy
02	Volume	White candle with increased volume	Buy
03	Moving Averages	5 MA crosses 13 MA on the upside	Buy
04	Candlestick Pattern	None	Indecision
05	Price Pattern	Up Flag	Up Flag – Buy
06	Stochastic Oscillator	Uptrend and positive crossover	Buy
07	R S I	Uptrend and positive crossover	Buy
08	MACD	Positive crossover in positive zone	Buy
09	**Trading Decision**	**Only B and I; no S**	**Buy**
10	Support (₹)	S1 = 350.75, S2 = 335.25, S3 = 327.77	350.75
11	Resistance (₹)	R1 = 376.46	376.46
12	Stop Loss (₹)	If verdict is buy, Stop Loss 0.2% below support	350
13	Target (₹)	Price pattern target (up flag formation)	423
14	Risk : Reward	Risk = (Close – Stop Loss) ÷ Reward = (Target – Close)	1:3.5
15	Time Target	Price pattern time target	18 days

Let us now review the Trade Selection Ready-Reckoner for 8K Miles given in Table 23.1 item by item.

Date: Date of analysis: 20 August 2015.
Name: Name of the stock analysed: 8K Miles.
Close: Closing price of the stock on that date: ₹366.24.
Time Period: Daily.

01. **Candlestick:** Since the colour of the last candle in Figure 23.1 is white, we record in Buy (B) as the verdict for this parameter.

02. **Volume:** We check the volume on the last candle and compare it with the volumes of the previous three candles. In this case, it is a white candle with an increase in volumes, therefore we fill Buy as the verdict for this parameter.

03. **Moving Averages:** We have to check whether there is a positive crossover between 5DEMA and either 13- or 26DEMA within the latest 5 candles as we are interested in the latest

trigger. In this case, there is indeed a positive crossover between 5DEMA and 26DEMA within the latest 5 days, and therefore this parameter suggests a Buy (B).

04. **Candlestick Pattern:** (*Hint* — If the latest candle is white, you need to look for a bullish candlestick pattern, while if the latest candle is black then you need to search for a bearish candlestick pattern.)

    Looking at the latest candle, the stock does not qualify in any of the candlestick patterns and we therefore put the verdict of this parameter as Indecision (I).

05. **Price Pattern:** (*Hint* — If the latest candle is white, search for a bullish price pattern; if the latest candle is black, search for a bearish price pattern.)

    In this case, the price pattern is an Up Flag — between 8 June and 2 July the price first moved up, it then went through a consolidation from 2 July to 19 August, and then on 20 August it finally gave an upward breakout. We therefore put a Buy (B).

06. **Stochastic Oscillator:** There is an uptrend in the stock price and the stochastic has given a positive crossover within the latest 5 candles, therefore this parameter signals a Buy (B).

07. **Relative Strength Index (RSI):** There is an uptrend in the stock price and the RSI has given a positive crossover within the latest 5 candles. Therefore, this parameter signals a Buy (B).

08. **MACD (Moving Average Convergence Divergence):** A positive crossover occurred in a positive zone within the latest 5 candles, therefore MACD is signalling a Buy (B).

09. **Trading Decision:** Since the 8 parameters are all either buys or indecisions, — and there is no sell verdict — therefore the final verdict is a buy.

    Remember, we are not counting the number of buy, sell or indecision verdicts. We are just checking whether the verdicts comprise B and I, or S and I, or B and S, or all three namely B, S and I. In this case we have only B and I verdicts, therefore the decision is Buy (B). The advantage of this format is that, even if you misinterpret one of the parameters, say for example you wrongly interpret a buy signal as a sell, the worst that can happen is that your final verdict will become an indecision as you would have both buy and sell verdicts featuring. Thus, the Trade Selection Ready Reckoner tool ensures that you do not enter poor trades.

10. **Support:** The latest candle being white, the three support levels will be, first, the median of the candle, then the open of the candle, and, finally the low of the candle.

11. **Resistance:** The latest candle channel being white, the resistance will be the high of that candle.

12. **Stop Loss:** In the case of a buy trade, the stop loss has to be below a good support.

    In normal market conditions your stop loss should be 0.2% below the median or the open, while during event filled markets, you must shift the stop loss below the low of the candle along with defining the risk value which will help reduce the quantity and the risk. Considering that we are in a normal market condition in this example, the stop loss will be placed 0.2% below the median (₹350.75), which would be at ₹350.05. You can round it down to ₹350.

13. **Price Target:** The price pattern helps us decide the price target. In this case it is an up flag formation, therefore the price pattern target is ₹423. **As a general rule, I recommend that if there is no price pattern it is better to avoid the trade altogether.** In case a price pattern exists, there is a sentimental shift happening — from bullish to bearish, bearish to bullish, neutral to bullish, or neutral to bearish. Due to such a sentiment shift, the chances of a build up of momentum in the stock price are high.

14. **Risk : Reward:** Not all the stocks that you trade will end up making a profit; some of them may trigger your stop loss. In other words, even the most meticulous analysis and trade selection do not guarantee profit. To ensure that you remain in profit for your overall portfolio, you should maintain a risk to reward ratio in each trade of at least 1:3 in normal market conditions. During event-filled markets, the minimum ratio could be 1:2. In this example of 8K Miles, the market conditions are normal so we have placed the stop loss below the median and therefore the risk reward ratio is 1:3.5. So for every ₹1 of risk, the reward in the trade if the target achieved is ₹3.5.

15. **Time Target:** For calculating the time target we have to count the number of candles from the start of the price pattern to the breakout candle, or the latest candle, and divide this number by 3. In this case, the time target is 18 candles. Being a daily chart this means 18 trading days. As discussed earlier in the book, the time target is helpful in understanding whether the stock fits the short term investment profile, positional trading profile or investment profile. If I call myself an investor, I may not be able to monitor my investments or positions on a daily basis and therefore I may not be interested in this stock. On the other hand, it could be of interest to a positional trader or a short term investor who is ready to take higher risk — and also has the time available for monitoring his short term positions.

Finally, always remember:

- Keep the analysis as simple as explained here.
- Do not discuss your conclusions with others as that can leave you confused.

~

THE INNOVATIVE TRADE SELECTION READY-RECKONER PROVIDES A DISCIPLINED APPROACH TO STOCK ANALYSIS AND TRADE MANAGEMENT. IT WILL ALSO HELP MAINTAIN A RECORD OF YOUR ANALYSIS AND WILL SERVE TO MAINTAIN CONSISTENCY IN YOUR TRADING.

Chapter 24

~

Step-by-Step Trading Guide

Select Your Profile

As we have discussed earlier, a person may fit into more than one trading and investing profile. You could be a day trader, a positional trader, a short term investor, or an investor. You could also be working with a broker or a financial institution as an analyst. The time needed to be spent on analysing charts and trades varies for the different profiles:

- **If you are a day trader**, the technical trading strategy which we are discussing in this book would require you to spend 30 minutes analysing charts every evening in order to identify stocks for the next day's trade.
- **As a positional trader or a short term investor**, you will need to spend 45 minutes every day in the evening — 30 minutes to pick and analyse potential new stocks to trade, and 15 minutes to monitor your existing trading positions.
- **As an investor**, you have to spend 15 minutes every day to monitor the stocks in your portfolio, and another 45 minutes on the weekend to hunt for, pick and analyse potential new stocks for fresh trades or investment. This time table is summarized in Table 24.1.

Table 24.1

Time Needed for Trade Analysis and Monitoring

Sr. No.	*Profile*	*Picking New Stocks*	*Time Needed for Monitoring Existing Portfolio*
1.	Day Trader	30 minutes every day	NA
2.	Positional Trader / Short Term Investor	30 minutes every day	15 minutes every day
3.	Investor	45 minutes on weekends, or when free	15 minutes every day

This is the minimum time you need to devote as per our strategy and methodology. The time could, of course, vary with each individual and with your computer's capability, the speed of your software and your own speed of analysing stocks. But it's important to keep in mind that more time spent on analysing a chart does not always mean that the end result would be better. I say this because if there is anything obvious or compelling in the chart, you should be able to see it immediately. When you have to spend a lot of time to spot an opportunity on the chart, it usually means that the chart does not present a clear or attractive opportunity, and you may be forcing yourself to identify some imaginary opportunity or the other. This may not result in a good trade.

A Word About Technical Analysis Software

It is important to understand that more than 2,000 stocks are traded everyday on NSE and more than 5,000 stocks on BSE. Obviously, you cannot analyse all these stocks. Even if you decide to stick to a particular group, the high stock count may consume far too much time. Therefore picking stocks out of such a big number of traded stocks manually is not an option. It is like trying to identify the names of the stars by looking at a star-filled night sky with your naked eye. This is a near impossible task. Identifying the constellations and the stars is made easier with the use of a telescope.

In the same way, you need a technical analysis software — with in-built scanners — in order to search for stocks that best meet your trading criteria. Such scanners help you identify suitable stocks out of the entire universe of listed stocks. These scanners should have the facility to pick stocks for the short, medium and long term. There are different ideas with which stocks can be filtered and selected. The most common parameters used by these scanners are price, volume and indicators. The technical analysis software that you use should have this basic facility to filter the best stocks for your analysis. You do not expect your doctor to generate medical reports simply by holding your hand. He needs diagnostic tests reports which help him analyse your medical condition. In the same way we need software for analysing the condition of a stock.

For example, Profision software has in-built scanners which help in picking stocks using the parameters listed in the Trade Selection Ready-Reckoner. A stock is picked when most of the criteria are fulfilled.

Step-by-Step Trading Guide

Let us now go through this step by step trading process with the help of some examples:*

If you are using Profision then you need to follow the process from Step 1, otherwise start following the process from Step 3.

Step 1. Update Data

First download data after 5.30 p.m. in the evening. This will update all the charts with open, high, low, close, and volume data for that day. In case of futures and options, it will also update open interest along with the rest of the data. This process takes approximately twenty

* In the examples we have used Profision software for our analysis purpose.

minutes as data for BSE, NSE, NSE F&O, NSE Currency, MCX, NCDEX are updated. While this data updation process is running in the background, you can continue with your work.

Step 2. Running the Scanner

Once the data is updated, you can then run the scanner on the updated data. You can see the list of in-built scanners in the Profision software displayed in Figure 24.1*.

In Figure 24.1, you can also see a drop down window which has opened under the "Scanner" tab. In this list you will be able to access the results generated by the following scanners:

- Short Term Picks (Bullish)
- Short Term Picks (Bearish)
- Medium Term Picks (Bullish)
- Medium Term Picks (Bearish)
- Turnaround Stocks.

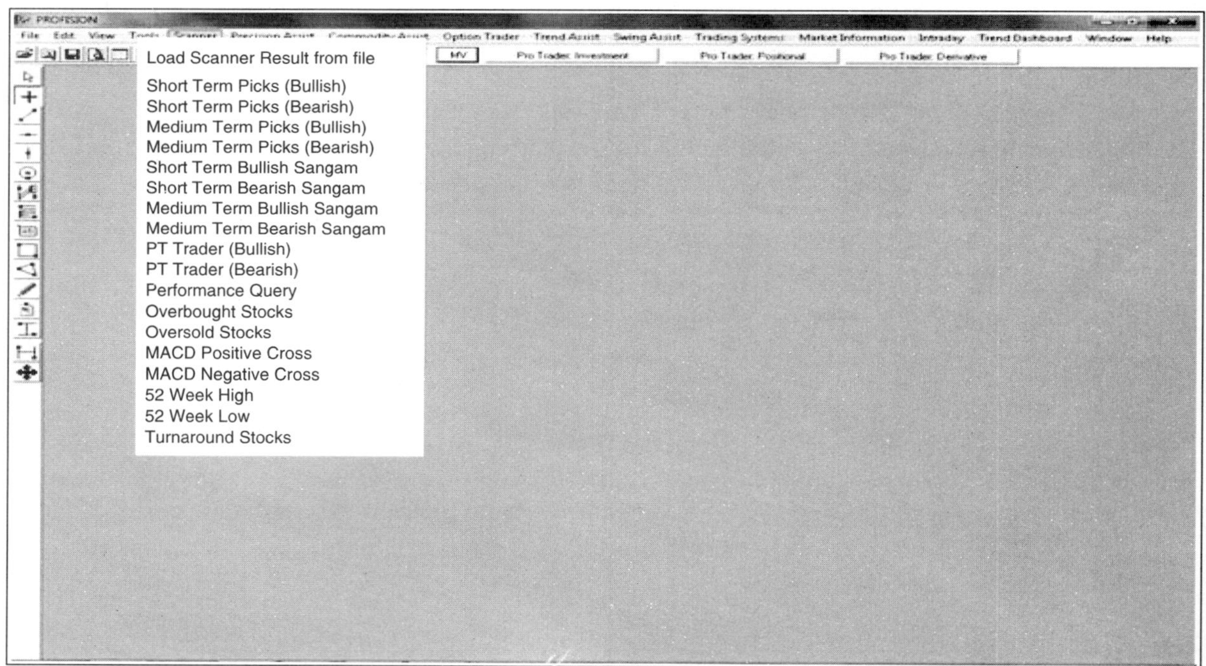

(Powered By: www.precisiontechnicals.com)

Figure 24.1: **Profision screen which displays the standard list of scanners to pick stocks**

~

* Other software would have similar scanners in-built or have the capability to create custom scans.

Short Term Picks (Bullish) and Short Term Picks (Bearish) scanners should be run on a daily basis as these run on a daily time period chart. These two scanners help a trader pick stocks on the bullish or the bearish side with a short term view, ranging from one week to one month. Readers are advised to use this scanner on a daily basis from Monday to Friday evening after the data is downloaded.

Medium Term Picks (Bullish) and Medium Term Picks (Bearish) scanners should be run only on the weekends because these two scanners run on weekly charts and this time period chart is completed only on Friday's closing.

These scanners help a trader pick stocks on the bullish or the bearish side with a medium term view ranging from one month to six months. Readers are advised to use this scanner only on weekends after the data is downloaded on Friday evenings for picking the winning stocks.

Turnaround Stocks scanner should be run only at the end of every month as it picks stocks which are showing signs of a turnaround happening in a business. The objective of this scanner is to search for stocks and companies where there is a probability of some fundamental change taking place. Whenever a fundamental change is taking place, it is always better to track it on long term charts. The reason for this is that short term charts — daily and weekly charts — can have a lot of noise, namely volatility. So, take care that you run this scanner at the end of every month. This scanner is useful for investors who have a long term view — a minimum of one year, and more.

There are several other in-built scanners in various software, including Profision. You can make use of those that suit your trading strategy. Let us suppose that you have decided to run the Short Term Picks (Bullish) scanner which scans all the stocks listed on the exchange or a particular group or those included in the NSE500 group. The output that you get will list stocks which fulfil the scanner's criteria. In order to further reduce risk and for you to pick the best choices we need to further filter the scanned list of stocks using the Trade Selection Ready-Reckoner as explained in Chapter 23.

The same process needs to be followed when running the second scanner, namely Short Term Picks (Bearish). And so on when it comes to running any scanner.

A sample output by the scanner in the case of Short Term Picks (Bullish) is shown in Figure 24.2.

Once the list, such as the one shown in Figure 24.2, is open, you need to click on the "Open All" tab which will open the charts of all the short-listed stocks one after the other so that you can start analysing them.

Stock scanner result 09.04.2018 13:37 - Short Term Picks (Bullish)

Name	Symbol	Close	Volume	Close: 06.04.2018	+/-	+/- %
ADLABS ENTERTAIN	ADLABS	55.55	184111	52.70	2.85	5.41
ALOK IND	ALOKTEXT	3.85	20702942	3.50	0.35	10.00
ASHAPURA MINES	ASHAPURMIN	76.55	563452	72.15	4.40	6.10
AUTOLINE IND	AUTOIND	80.90	73106	73.85	7.05	9.55
BALLARPUR IND	BALLARPUR	14.65	4454160	13.95	0.70	5.02
BINANI IND	BINANIIND	105.65	292629	100.95	4.70	4.66
BIRLA CABLE	BIRLACABLE	77.05	215147	70.40	6.65	9.45
BURNPUR CEMENT	BURNPUR	10.00	1058759	9.10	0.90	9.89
CANTABIL RETAIL	CANTABIL	141.30	495849	126.45	14.85	11.74
CENTURY ENKA	CENTENKA	364.20	142184	344.90	19.30	5.60
CMI LIMITED	CMICABLES	244.30	111088	229.50	14.80	6.45
CREATIVE PERI	CREATIVE	139.80	22400	134.30	5.50	4.10
DEEPAK FERT & PE	DEEPAKFERT	341.40	501155	323.50	17.90	5.53
DILIGENT MEDIA	DNAMEDIA	9.60	542320	8.00	1.60	20.00
EDELWEISSNIFTY50	NIFTYEES	10998.00	43	10100.00	898.00	8.89

Save Result | Open all | Open | Cancel

(Powered By: www.precisiontechnicals.com)

Figure 24.2: **Picks of Profision scanner of short term bullish stocks on 9 April 2018**

~

Pruning the Short List

It may well happen that the scanner suggests a greater number of stocks than you wish to trade. You may want to trade only one or, maybe, two stocks. For this final selection, you can use the following criteria:

1. **Price of the stock:** Some investors are comfortable trading stocks which quote at relatively lower prices, say less than ₹200; whereas others are comfortable trading higher priced stocks as well.
2. **Risk:** Stocks with lower risk should be given preference.
3. **Risk to reward ratio:** Higher this ratio, better the stock when compared with another.
4. **Time target:** This will help you decide whether the stock fits in your profile.

Let us now analyse the charts picked by the scanner. Since the scanner has picked stocks which have fulfilled the appropriate criteria, it means these stocks are worthy of further consideration.

Step 3. Trade Analysis

To pick the best stocks we will use the Trade Selection Ready-Reckoner tool described in Chapter 23.

The analysis consists of the following three phases in our AIM for profits strategies. These are:

Phase 1: Analysis — Stock analysis and selection using the Trade Selection Ready-Reckoner;

Phase 2: Implementation — Trade entry; and

Phase 3: Monitoring — Monitoring and managing the trade, so long as remains open.

Phase 1: Stock Analysis and Selection

The scanner will pick for us a list of stocks showing strength on the chart for that day. Now we open the chart and start analysing the stocks with the help of the Trade Selection Ready-Reckoner.

Phase 2: Implementation — Trade Entry

After completing the analysis, you then have to decide whether you want to enter the trade. It may sound odd to you but **it is in your long term interest to grasp the point that you should enter a trade based not so much on what profits you may make but based on the risk involved in the trade. In other words, enter a trade only if the risk is acceptable to you.** When you enter a trade with clarity about the risk involved, you are prepared for the worst. This helps in staying calm at all times during the trade, and helps in taking the right trading decisions.

Let's suppose you have decided to enter a trade. The next trading day when you check the price there are three possibilities *vis-a-vis* to the earlier close:

1. The stock can open flat.

2. The stock can open with a gap up.

3. The stock can open with a gap down.

Where the stock actually opens is beyond our control, but whether you get into a trade is surely in your control. Thus:

- If the stock opens flat, you can enter the trade.
- If the stock opens with a gap up, then you must immediately recalculate the risk to reward ratio based on the new price that is being traded in the market and enter the trade only if it still fulfils your acceptable risk to reward ratio. Wherever the price opens, your analysis would already have defined the stop loss level. This level will not change based on where

the price opens on the day of trade execution. If the stock opens with a gap up then the risk will increase compared to your earlier analysis done taking into consideration the closing price as the next day's execution price. Therefore, if the stock does not now fit your acceptable risk to reward ratio, then avoid the trade.

- If the selected stock opens with a gap down opening, then instead of feeling happy that you are getting the stock at a cheaper price you should be worried as to what went wrong with your analysis. This normally happens due to some external event. Check whether the stock price will be impacted due to the event for a relatively longer or shorter duration and only then decide whether you should trade the stock, or drop it.

Another important aspect which you need to understand when getting into a trade is that on the first day of the trade the chances of the stop loss getting triggered, or the target being achieved are 50:50. Which of the two outcomes comes to pass will be known only after a few days into the trade. It is the price movement which will tell you whether your analysis has worked or not — and this is what makes risk management important.

Phase 3: Monitoring and Managing Your Trade

This is the last and the most important step in the complete trade cycle.

Once you have entered a trade, there are three things which need to be regularly monitored:

1. Stop loss.
2. Price target.
3. Time target.

Whenever any of the three are reached, or triggered in the case of the stop loss, you have to act.

In case the stop loss is triggered, you need to square off, namely exit, the trade. But, remember, in the case of a positional trade, a short term investment, or a long term investment your stop loss should not be fed into the system. Instead, you need to monitor it at the end of each day, each week, or each month on closing basis, depending on the time period chart that you have analysed while picking the stock.

When the initial price target is reached traders normally square off trades when the price target is reached and put that money into a new stock, thus incurring new risk, new uncertainty, new taxes, new brokerage, etc., even though the earlier winning stock has confirmed your analysis to be correct. By booking profits what we did was to cut the good crop and started sowing again a new crop afresh.

Instead, you could consider the following alternate options when you see your stock moving successfully towards its target.

Option 1: As the stock price starts moving in the direction of the target, you may be concerned that the price may fall and erode your accrued paper profits. So, one option is that **you**

can book partial profits. It can be a quantity which helps you continue comfortably in the trade with the remaining quantity.

Option 2: For the first 5 days in the case of a stock analysed on a daily chart, first 5 weeks in the case of a stock analysed on a weekly chart, and first 5 months in the case of a stock analysed on a monthly time period chart, the stop loss will remain as per the value determined by the Trade Selection Ready-Reckoner tool. From the 6th day, or the 6th candle onwards, if the stock price keeps moving in the direction of your target, the gap between the stop loss and price will widen and you will therefore need to move your stop loss to a higher level. So the stop loss arrived at by the Trade Selection Ready-Reckoner should be monitored on closing basis for the first 5 candles, and after that the stop loss should be trailed using the moving average crossovers, specifically the 5EMA line crossing the 13EMA line on the downside in case of a buy trade. Such a negative crossover will generate an anticipatory sell as discussed in Chapter 14, while the 5EMA line crossing the 26EMA line on the downside will generate a confirmatory sell in which case we need to exit the entire quantity that we are holding.

In case of short positions, these would normally be entered in the futures segment. Therefore, it is advisable to square off on the first crossover itself, in this case it will be a positive crossover between 5EMA and 13EMA lines.

The logic behind this strategy is that you want to continue holding your position till such time as the price continues moving in the desired direction as per your analysis, and you will exit only when the price changes its trend. This change of trend is determined using the moving average crossovers.

Option 3. The stock price has started moving in the direction of your target. To allay apprehensions, you have booked partial profits in order to remain comfortable in the trade. As the stock reaches the price target, book 50% profits in the remaining quantity. This will ensure even greater comfort in riding the trend of the stock price.

Option 4. Check for moving average crossovers on a daily basis on the price chart. Do not check the colours and sizes of candles anymore; if you do, black candles will scare you and white candles will make you feel happy. They will work on your emotions and unsettle you. Also remember that you analysed the stock the day it was picked by the scanner. On that day there was an invitation for you on the price chart, but such invitations are not seen everyday. Therefore, there is no point in doing a fresh analysis till the time your earlier analysis is not brought to an end either by the stop loss, the price target or the time target being reached, or till the time the stock is picked by the scanner once again. If you try doing an analysis on any interim day, it will not get you any results.

~

Chapter 25

~

Practice Exercises

THE 32 PRACTICE EXERCISES IN THIS CHAPTER will enable you to grow proficient in using the Trade Selection Ready-Reckoner. In each of the exercises that follows, fill in the blank verdict column and then check your answer with the correct verdicts given below each table.

Practice Exercise 1: Gayatri Projects

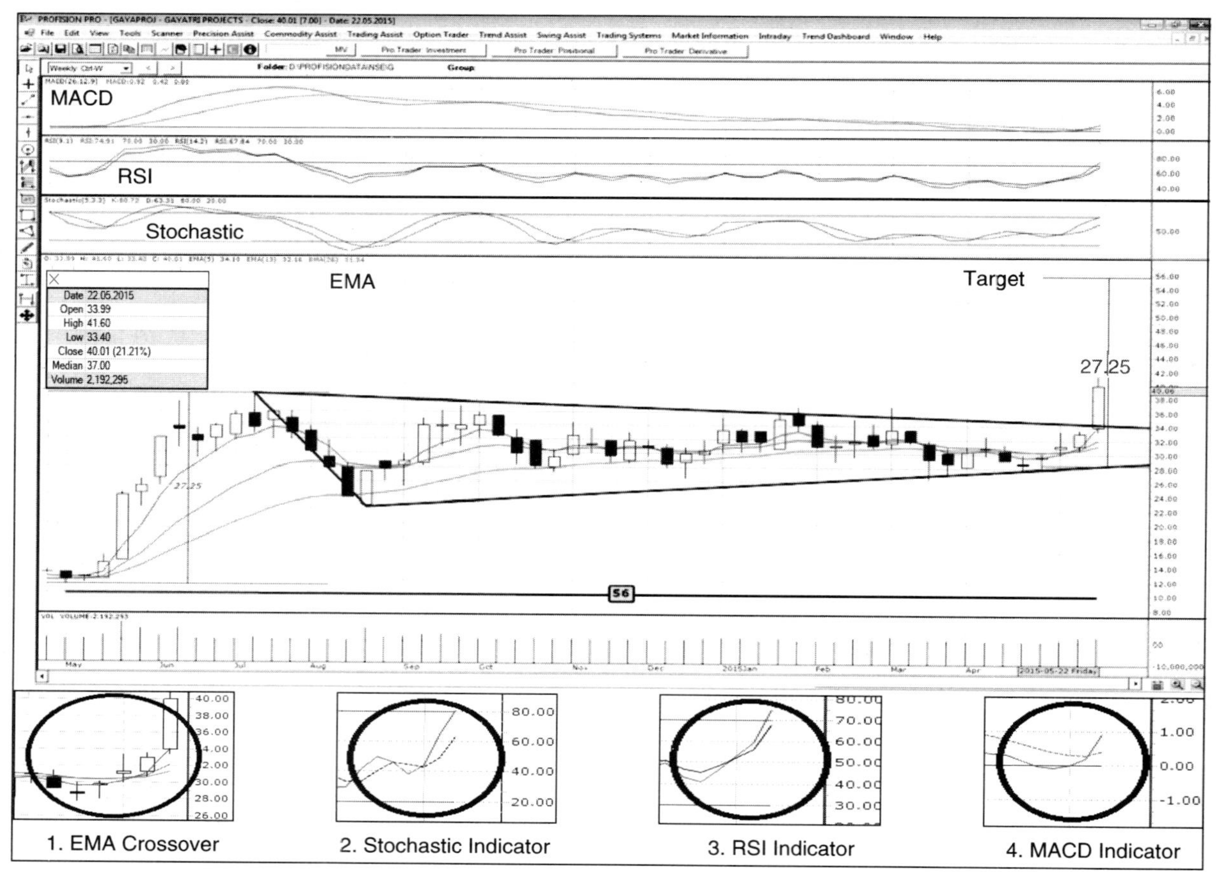

Figure 25.1: **Weekly chart of Gayatri Projects**

~

Table 25.1

Trade Selection Ready-Reckoner for Gayatri Projects

Sr. No.	*Parameter*		
	Date >>>		22.05.2015
	Stock Symbol >>>		GAYAPROJ
	Close (₹) >>>		40.01
	Time Period >>>		Weekly
Sr. No.	*Parameter*	*Observation / Reason*	***Verdict***
01	Candlestick	White candlestick	
02	Volume	White candle with increased volume	
03	Moving Averages	5 MA crosses 13 and 26 MA on the upside	
04	Candlestick Pattern	None	
05	Price Pattern	Up Flag	
06	Stochastic Oscillator	Uptrend and positive crossover	
07	R S I	Uptrend and positive crossover	
08	MACD	Positive crossover in positive zone	
09	**Trading Decision**	**Only B and I; no S**	
10	Support (₹)	S1 = 36.83, S2 = 33.60, S3 = 33.60	
11	Resistance (₹)	R1 = 41.60	
12	Stop Loss (₹)	If the trading decision is Buy, Stop Loss 0.2% below support	
13	Target (₹)	Price pattern target	
14	Risk : Reward	Risk = (Close – Stop Loss) ÷ Reward = (Target – Close)	
15	Time Target	Price pattern time target	

Correct Verdict				
01: Buy	04: Indecision	07: Buy	10: 36.83	13: 55.90
02: Buy	05: Buy	08: Buy	11: 41.60	14: 1:5.11
03: Buy	06: Buy	09: Buy	12: 36.90	15: 19 Weeks

Practice Exercise 2: Reliance Communication

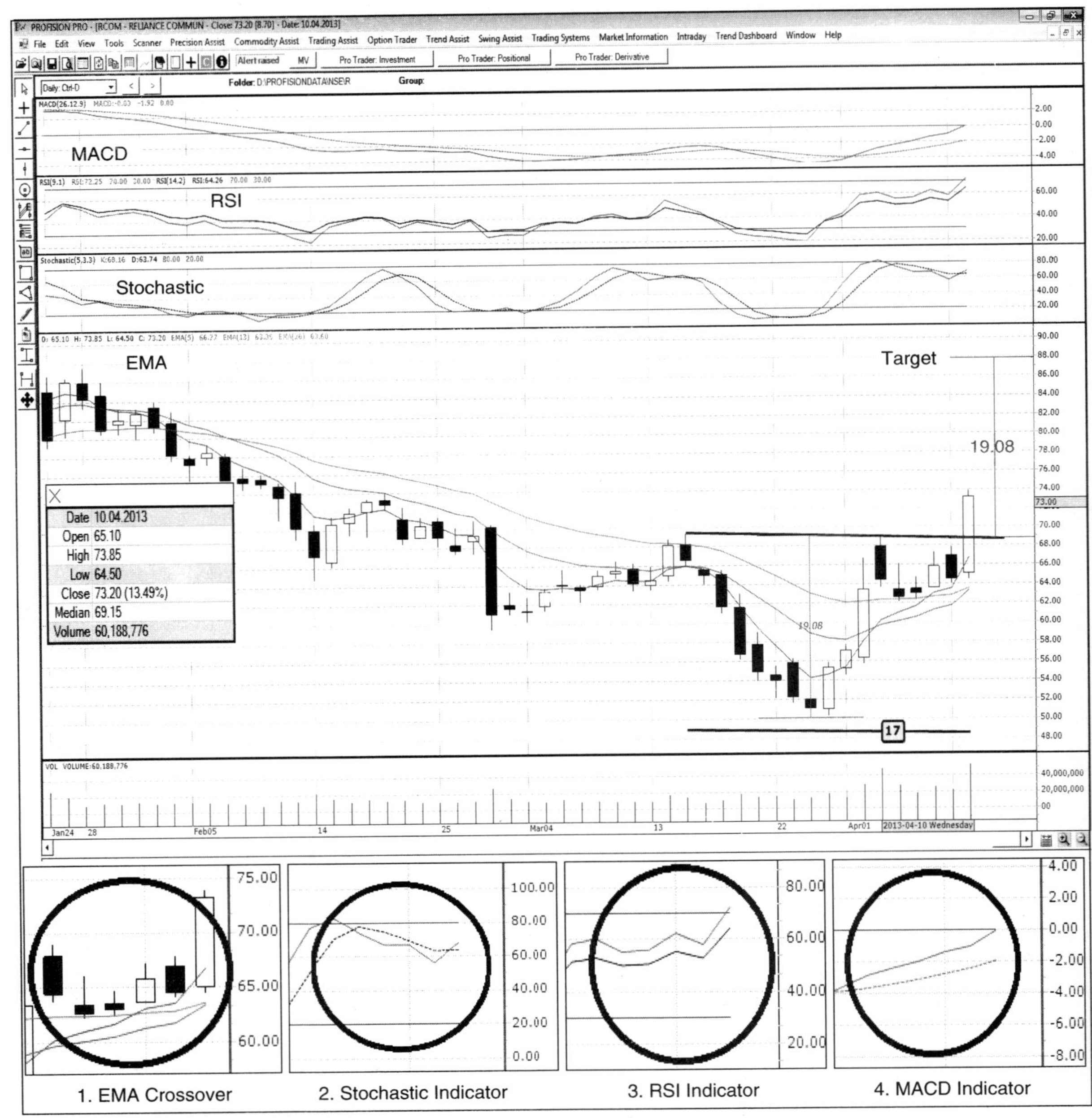

Figure 25.2: **Daily chart of Reliance Communication**

Table 25.2

Trade Selection Ready-Reckoner for Reliance Communication

Sr.	*Parameter*		
	Date >>>		10.04.2013
	Stock Symbol >>>		RCOM
	Close (₹) >>>		73.20
	Time Period >>>		Daily
Sr.	*Parameter*	*Observation / Reason*	***Verdict***
01	Candlestick	White candlestick	
02	Volume	White candle with increased volume	
03	Moving Averages	5 MA crosses 13 MA on the upside	
04	Candlestick Pattern	None	
05	Price Pattern	Inverted Head and Shoulder	
06	Stochastic Oscillator	Uptrend and positive crossover	
07	R S I	None	
08	MACD	None	
09	**Trading Decision**	**Only B and I; no S**	
10	Support (₹)	S1 = 69.15, S2 = 65.10, S3 = 64.50	
11	Resistance (₹)	R1 = 73.85	
12	Stop Loss (₹)	If the trading decision is Buy, Stop Loss 0.2% below support	
13	Target (₹)	Price pattern target	
14	Risk : Reward	Risk = (Close – Stop Loss) ÷ Reward = (Target – Close)	
15	Time Target	Price pattern time target	

Correct Verdict				
01: Buy	04: Indecision	07: Indecision	10: 69.15	13: 88
02: Buy	05: Buy	08: Indecision	11: 73.85	14: 1:3.52
03: Buy	06: Buy	09: Buy	12: 69	15: 6 days

Practice Exercise 3: JP Associates

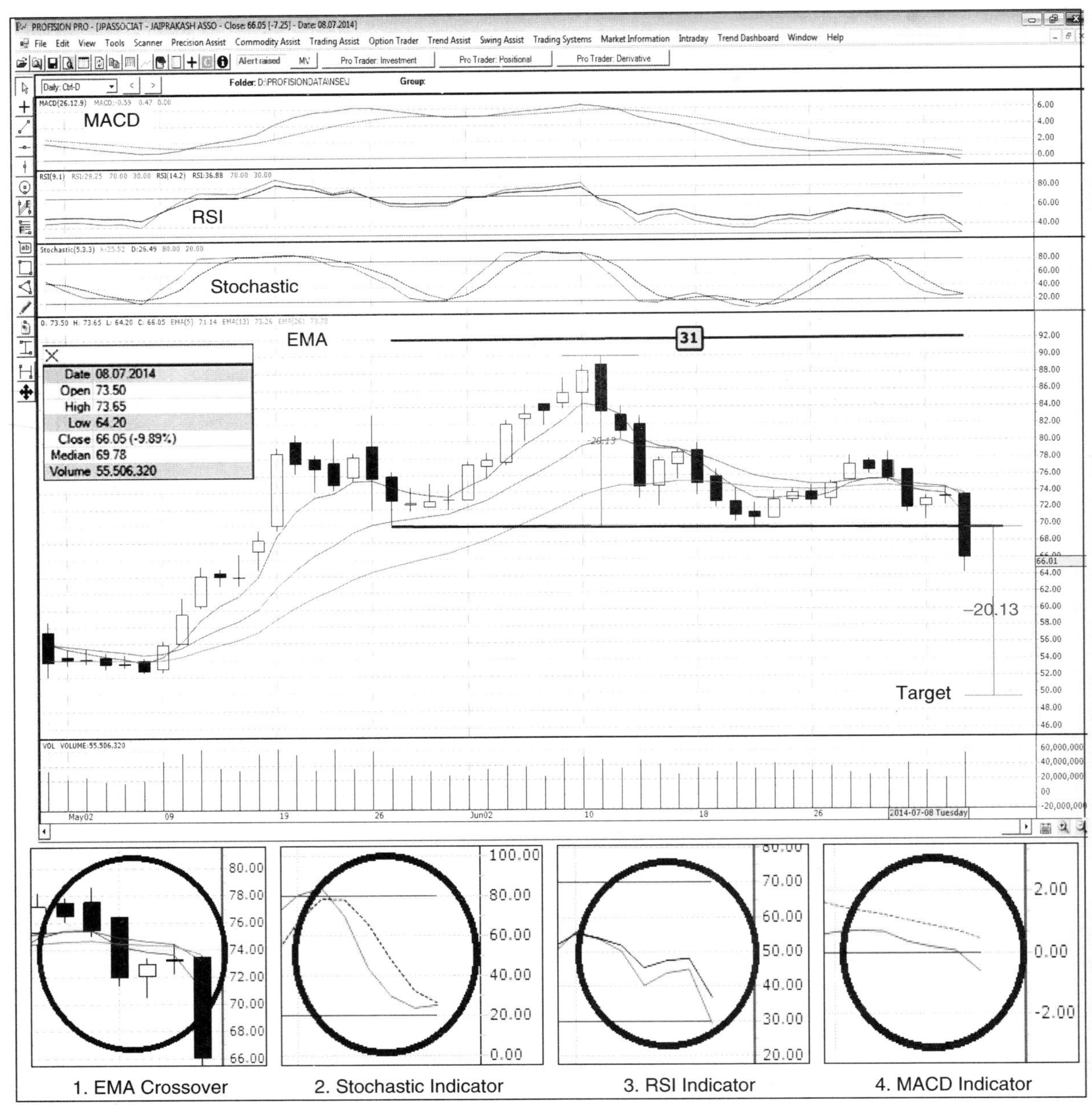

Figure 25.3: **Daily chart of JP Associates**

Table 25.3

Trade Selection Ready-Reckoner for JP Associates

Sr. No.	*Parameter*		
	Date >>>		08.07.2014
	Stock Symbol >>>		JPASSOCIAT
	Close (₹) >>>		66.05
	Time Period >>>		Daily
Sr. No.	*Parameter*	*Observation / Reason*	***Verdict***
01	Candlestick	Black candlestick	
02	Volume	Black candle with increased volume	
03	Moving Averages	5 MA crosses 26 MA on the downside	
04	Candlestick Pattern	Evening Star	
05	Price Pattern	Head and Shoulder	
06	Stochastic Oscillator	None	
07	R S I	None	
08	MACD	None	
09	**Trading Decision**	**Only S and I; no B**	
10	Support (₹)	S1 = 64.20	
11	Resistance (₹)	R1 = 69.78, R2 = 73.50, R3 = 73.65	
12	Stop Loss (₹)	If the trading decision is Sell, Stop Loss 0.2% above resistance	
13	Target (₹)	Price pattern target	
14	Risk : Reward	Risk = (Stop Loss – Close) ÷ Reward = (Close- Target)	
15	Time Target	Price pattern time target	

Correct Verdict				
01: Sell	04: Sell	07: Indecision	10: 64.20	13: 50
02: Sell	05: Sell	08: Indecision	11: 69.78	14: 1:4
03: Sell	06: Indecision	09: Sell	12: 70	15: 11 days

Practice Exercise 4: Whirlpool

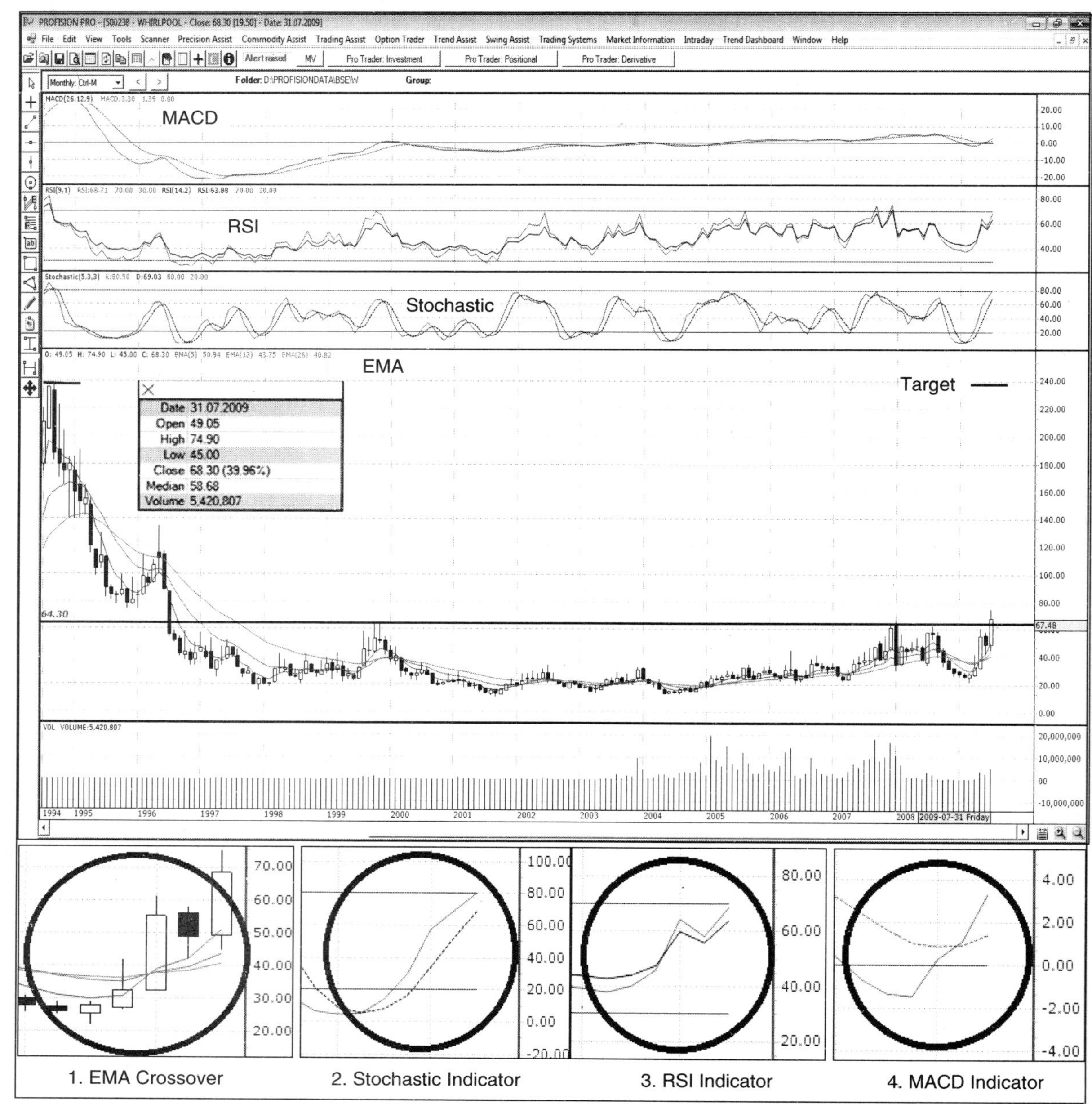

Figure 25.4: **Monthly chart of Whirlpool**

~

Table 25.4 **Trade Selection Ready-Reckoner for Whirlpool**			
Sr.	*Parameter*		
	Date >>>		31.07.2009
	Stock Symbol >>>		WHIRLPOOL
	Close (₹) >>>		68.30
	Time Period >>>		Monthly
Sr.	*Parameter*	*Observation / Reason*	***Verdict***
01	Candlestick	White candlestick	
02	Volume	White candle with increased volume	
03	Moving Averages	5 MA crosses 13 and 26 MA on the upside	
04	Candlestick Pattern	None	
05	Price Pattern	Rounding Bottom	
06	Stochastic Oscillator	None	
07	R S I	None	
08	MACD	None	
09	**Trading Decision**	**Only B and I; no S**	
10	Support (₹)	S1 = 58.68, S2 = 48.05, S3 = 45	
11	Resistance (₹)	R1 =74.90	
12	Stop Loss (₹)	If the trading decision is Buy, Stop Loss 0.2% below support	
13	Target (₹)	Price pattern target	
14	Risk : Reward	Risk = (Close – Stop Loss) ÷ Reward = (Target – Close)	
15	Time Target	Price pattern time target	

Correct Verdict				
01: Buy	04: Indecision	07: Indecision	10: 58.68	13: 237.50
02: Buy	05: Buy	08: Indecision	11: 74.90	14: 1:17.27
03: Buy	06: Indecision	09: Buy	12: 58.50	15: 1 to 3 years

Practice Exercise 5: Brigade Enterprises Ltd.

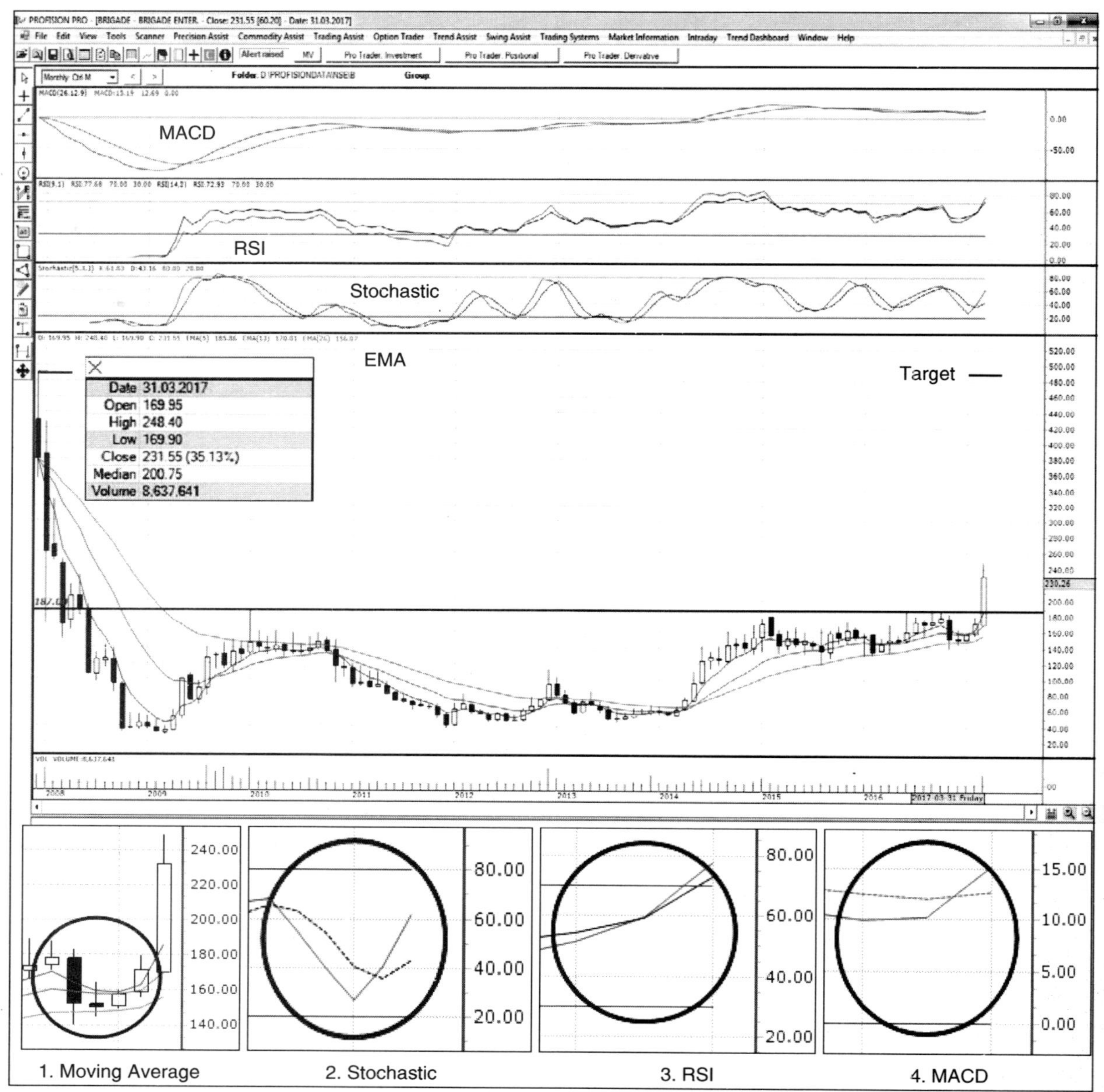

Figure 25.5: **Monthly chart of Brigade Enterprises Ltd.**

~

Table 25.5

Trade Selection Ready-Reckoner for Brigade Enterprises Ltd.

Sr. No.	*Parameter*		
	Date >>>		31.03.2017
	Stock Symbol >>>		BRIGADE
	Close (₹) >>>		231.55
	Time Period >>>		Monthly
Sr. No.	*Parameter*	*Observation / Reason*	***Verdict***
01	Candlestick	White candlestick	
02	Volume	White candle with increased volume	
03	Moving Averages	None	
04	Candlestick Pattern	None	
05	Price Pattern	Rounding Bottom	
06	Stochastic Oscillator	Uptrend and positive crossover	
07	R S I	Uptrend and positive crossover	
08	MACD	Positive crossover in positive zone	
09	**Trading Decision**	**Only B and I; no S**	
10	Support (₹)	S1 = 200.75, S2 = 169.95, S3 = 169.90	
11	Resistance (₹)	R1 = 248.40	
12	Stop Loss (₹)	If the trading decision is Buy, Stop Loss 0.2% below support	
13	Target (₹)	Price pattern target	
14	Risk : Reward	Risk = (Close – Stop Loss) ÷ Reward = (Target – Close)	
15	Time Target	Price pattern time target	

Correct Verdict				
01: Buy	04: Indecision	07: Buy	10: 200.75	13: 480
02: Buy	05: Buy	08: Buy	11: 248.40	14: 1:3.97
03: Indecision	06: Buy	09: Buy	12: 169	15: 1 to 3 years

Practice Exercise 6: Century Textiles & Industries Ltd

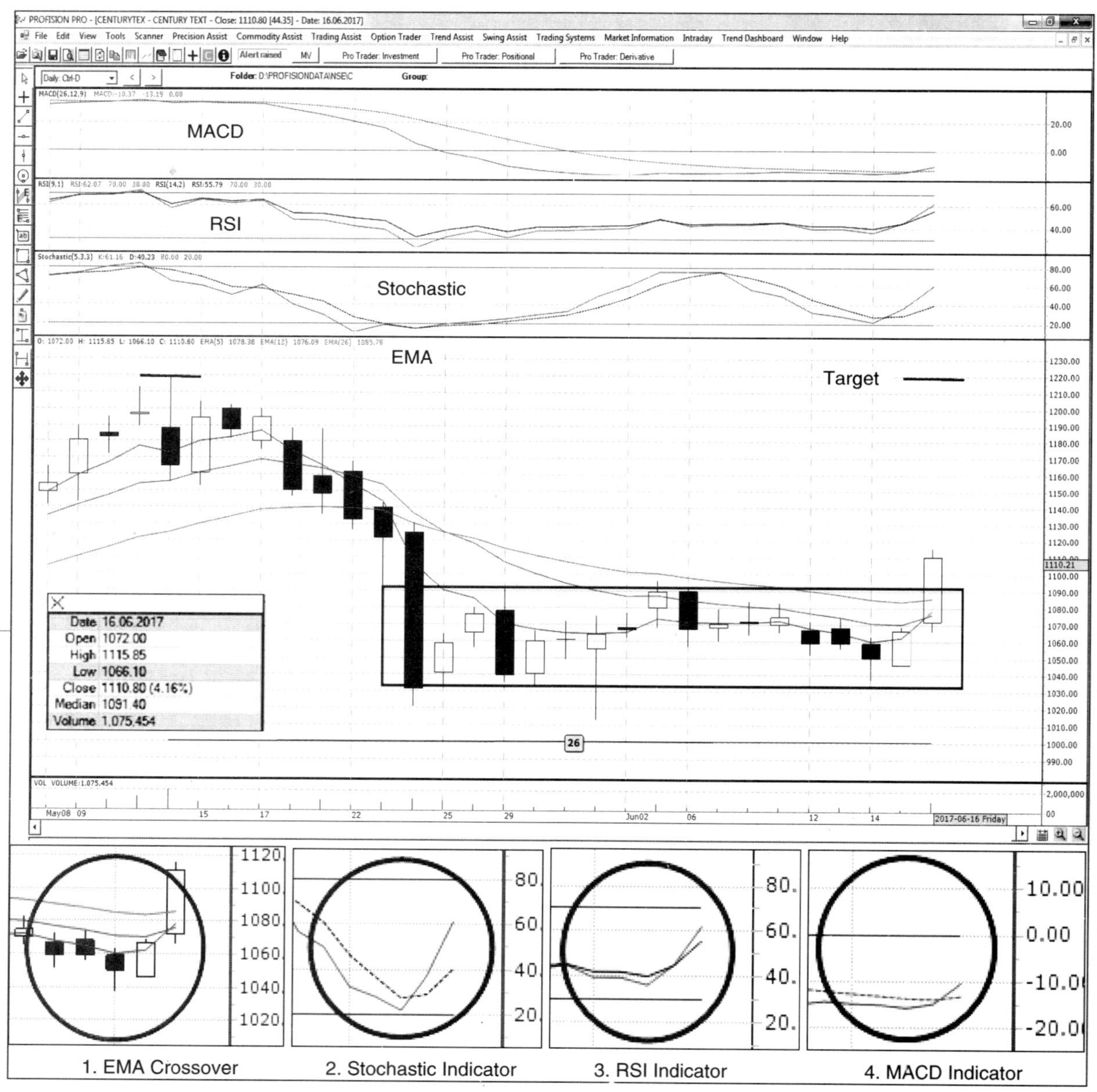

Figure 25.6: **Daily chart of Century Textiles & Industries Ltd**

Table 25.6

Trade Selection Ready-Reckoner for Century Textiles & Industries Ltd

Sr. No.	*Parameter*		
	Date >>>		16.06.2017
	Stock Symbol >>>		CENTURYTEX
	Close (₹) >>>		1110.80
	Time Period >>>		Daily
Sr. No.	*Parameter*	*Observation / Reason*	***Verdict***
01	Candlestick	White candlestick	
02	Volume	White candle with increased volume	
03	Moving Averages	5 MA crosses 13 MA on the upside	
04	Candlestick Pattern	None	
05	Price Pattern	Trend Change Upward Breakout	
06	Stochastic Oscillator	Uptrend and positive crossover	
07	R S I	Uptrend and positive crossover	
08	MACD	Positive crossover in positive zone	
09	**Trading Decision**	**Only B and I; no S**	
10	Support (₹)	S1 = 1091.40, S2 = 1072, S3 = 1066.10	
11	Resistance (₹)	R1 =1115.85	
12	Stop Loss (₹)	If the trading decision is Buy, Stop Loss 0.2% below support	
13	Target (₹)	Price pattern target	
14	Risk : Reward	Risk = (Close – Stop Loss) ÷ Reward = (Target – Close)	
15	Time Target	Price pattern time target	

Correct Verdict				
01: Buy	04: Indecision	07: Buy	10: 1091.40	13: 1218
02: Buy	05: Buy	08: Buy	11: 1115.85	14: 1:4.92
03: Buy	06: Buy	09: Buy	12: 1089	15: 9 days

Practice Exercise 7: Century Plyboards India Ltd.

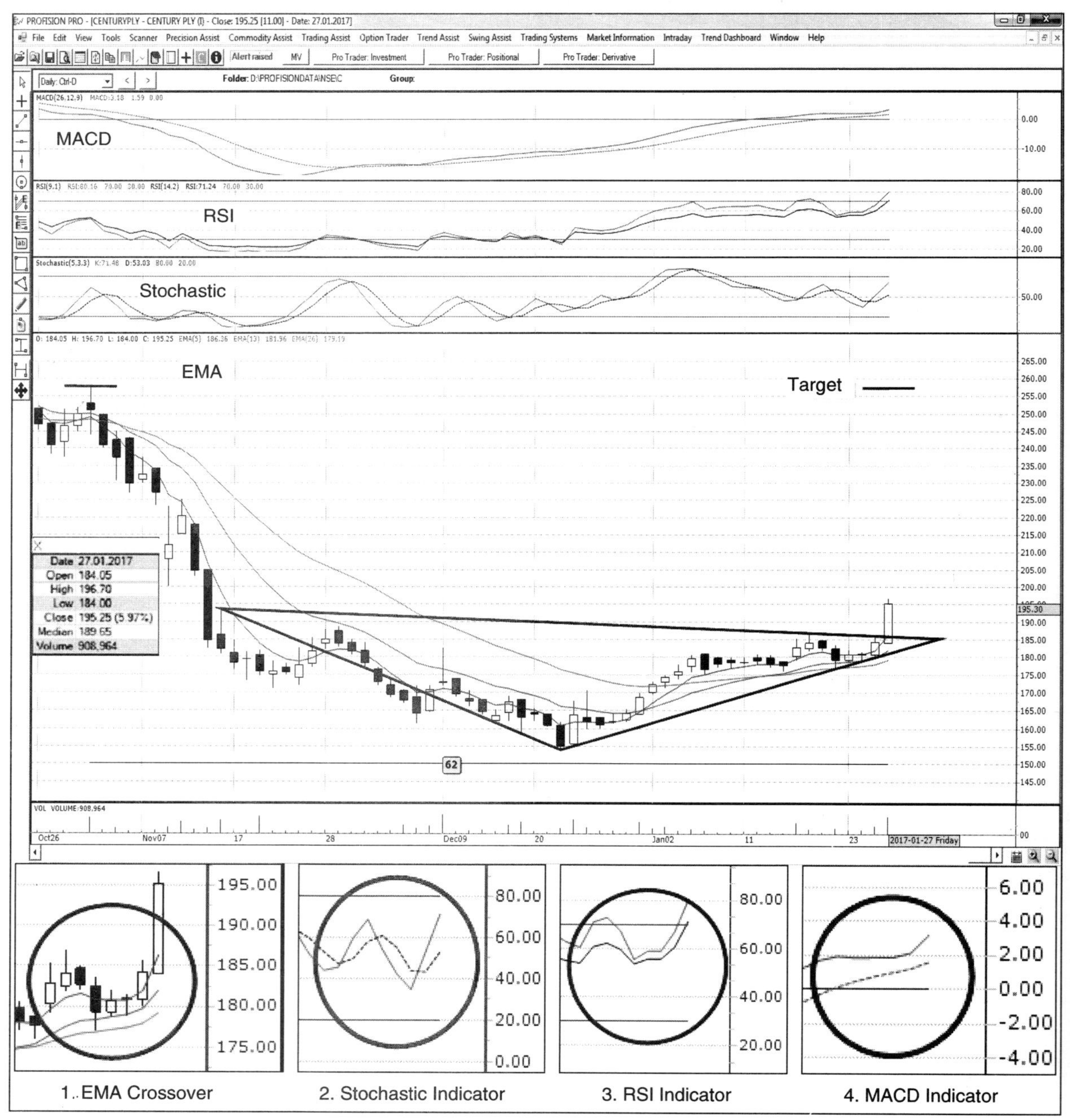

Figure 25.7: **Daily chart of Century Plyboards India Ltd.**

Table 25.7

Trade Selection Ready-Reckoner for Century Plyboards India Ltd.

Sr. No.	*Parameter*		
	Date >>>		27.01.2017
	Stock Symbol >>>		CENTURYPLY
	Close (₹) >>>		195.25
	Time Period >>>		Daily
Sr. No.	*Parameter*	*Observation / Reason*	***Verdict***
01	Candlestick	White candlestick	
02	Volume	White candle with increased volume	
03	Moving Averages	None	
04	Candlestick Pattern	None	
05	Price Pattern	Trend Change Upward Breakout	
06	Stochastic Oscillator	Uptrend and positive crossover	
07	R S I	Uptrend and positive crossover	
08	MACD	Positive crossover in positive zone	
09	**Trading Decision**	**Only B and I; no S**	
10	Support (₹)	S1 = 189.65, S2 = 184.05, S3 = 184	
11	Resistance (₹)	R1 = 196.70	
12	Stop Loss (₹)	If the trading decision is Buy, Stop Loss 0.2% below support	
13	Target (₹)	Price pattern target	
14	Risk : Reward	Risk = (Close – Stop Loss) ÷ Reward = (Target – Close)	
15	Time Target	Price pattern time target	

Correct Verdict				
01: Buy	04: Indecision	07: Buy	10: 189.65	13: 257
02: Buy	05: Buy	08: Buy	11: 196.70	14: 1:9.88
03: Indecision	06: Buy	09: Buy	12: 189	15: 21 days

Practice Exercise 8: Future Retail Ltd.

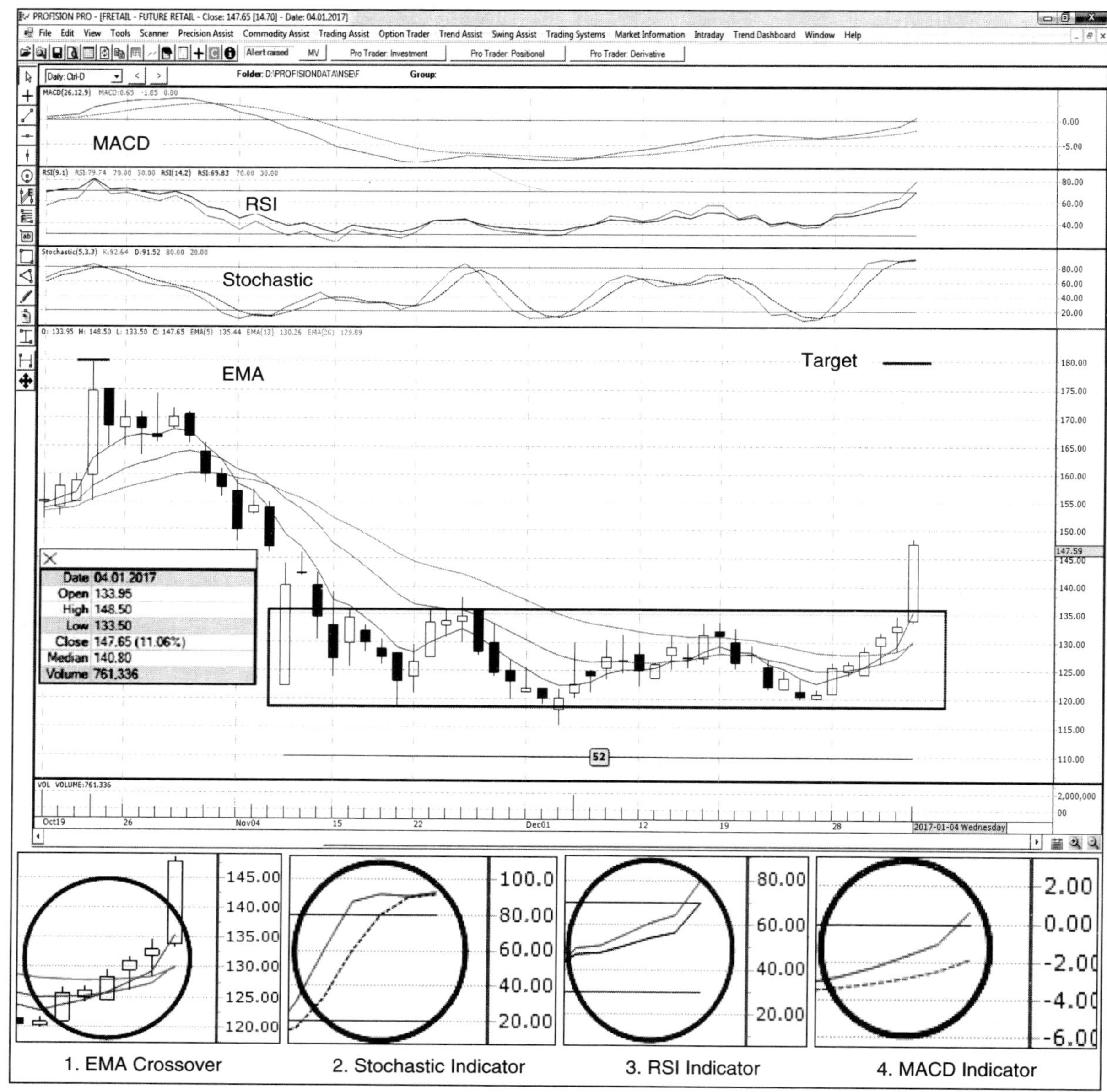

Figure 25.8: **Daily chart of Future Retail Ltd.**

~

Table 25.8

Trade Selection Ready-Reckoner for Future Retail Ltd.

Sr. No.	Parameter		
	Date >>>		04.01.2017
	Stock Symbol >>>		FRETAIL
	Close (₹) >>>		147.65
	Time Period >>>		Daily
Sr. No.	*Parameter*	*Observation / Reason*	***Verdict***
01	Candlestick	White Candlestick	
02	Volume	White candle with increased volume	
03	Moving Averages	5 MA crosses 13 MA and 26 MA on the upside	
04	Candlestick Pattern	None	
05	Price Patterns	Trend Change Upward Breakout	
06	Stochastic Oscillator	None	
07	R S I	None	
08	MACD	None	
09	**Trading Decision**	**Only B and I; no S**	
10	Support (₹)	S1 = 140.80, S2 = 133.95, S3 = 133.50	
11	Resistance (₹)	R1 =148.50	
12	Stop Loss (₹)	If the trading decision is Buy, Stop Loss 0.2% below support	
13	Target (₹)	Price pattern target	
14	Risk : Reward	Risk = (Close – Stop Loss) ÷ Reward = (Target – Close)	
15	Time Target	Price pattern time target	

Correct Verdict				
01: Buy	04: Indecision	07: Indecision	10: 140.80	13: 180
02: Buy	05: Buy	08: Indecision	11: 148.50	14: 1:4
03: Buy	06: Indecision	09: Buy	12: 140	15: 17 days

Practice Exercise 9: India Glycols Ltd.

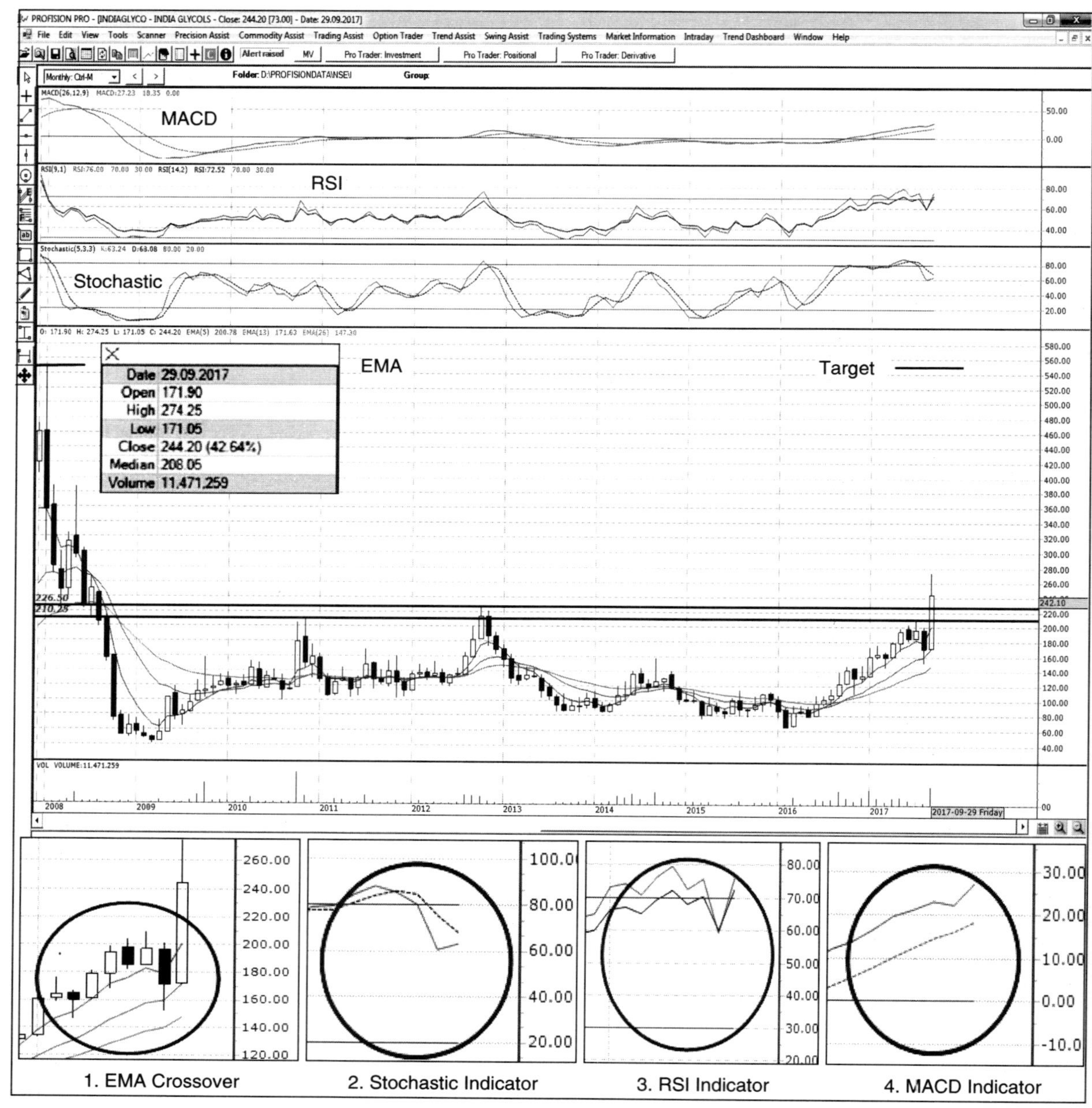

Figure 25.9: **Monthly chart of India Glycols Ltd.**

Table 25.9

Trade Selection Ready-Reckoner for India Glycols Ltd.

Sr. No.	*Parameter*		
	Date >>>		29.09.2017
	Stock Symbol >>>		INDIAGLYCO
	Close (₹) >>>		244.20
	Time Period >>>		Monthly
Sr. No.	*Parameter*	*Observation / Reason*	***Verdict***
01	Candlestick	White candlestick	
02	Volume	White candle with increased volume	
03	Moving Averages	None	
04	Candlestick Pattern	Bullish Engulf	
05	Price Pattern	Rounding Bottom	
06	Stochastic Oscillator	None	
07	R S I	Uptrend and positive crossover	
08	MACD	None	
09	**Trading Decision**	**Only B and I; no S**	
10	Support (₹)	S = 208.05, S2 = 171.90, S3 = 171.05	
11	Resistance (₹)	R1 =274.25	
12	Stop Loss (₹)	If the trading decision is buy, Stop Loss 0.2% below support	
13	Target (₹)	Price pattern target	
14	Risk : Reward	Risk = (Close – Stop Loss) ÷ Reward = (Target – Close)	
15	Time Target	Price pattern time target	

Correct Verdict				
01: Buy	04: Buy	07: Buy	10: 208.05	13: 550
02: Buy	05: Buy	08: Indecision	11: 274.25	14: 1:6.22
03: Indecision	06: Indecision	09: Buy	12: 195	15: 1 to 3 years

Practice Exercise 10: Man Infraconstruction Ltd.

Figure 25.10: **Daily chart of Man Infraconstruction Ltd.**

Table 25.10 **Trade Selection Ready-Reckoner for Man Infraconstruction Ltd.**			
Sr. No.	*Parameter*		
	Date >>>		30.03.2017
	Stock Symbol >>>		MANINFRA
	Close (₹) >>>		45.20
	Time Period >>>		Daily
Sr. No.	*Parameter*	*Observation / Reason*	***Verdict***
01	Candlestick	White candlestick	
02	Volume	White candle with increased volume	
03	Moving Averages	None	
04	Candlestick Pattern	None	
05	Price Pattern	Trend Change Upward Breakout	
06	Stochastic Oscillator	None	
07	R S I	None	
08	MACD	None	
09	**Trading Decision**	**Only B and I; no S**	
10	Support (₹)	S1 = 44.23, S2 = 43.25, S3 = 42.75	
11	Resistance (₹)	R1 = 46	
12	Stop Loss (₹)	If the trading decision is Buy, Stop Loss 0.2% below support	
13	Target (₹)	Price pattern target	
14	Risk : Reward	Risk = (Close – Stop Loss) ÷ Reward = (Target – Close)	
15	Time Target	Price pattern time target	

Correct Verdict				
01: Buy	04: Indecision	07: Indecision	10: 44.23	13: 54.50
02: Buy	05: Buy	08: Indecision	11: 46	14: 1:7.75
03: Indecision	06: Indecision	09: Buy	12: 44	15: 37 days

Practice Exercise 11: Oriental Bank of Commerce

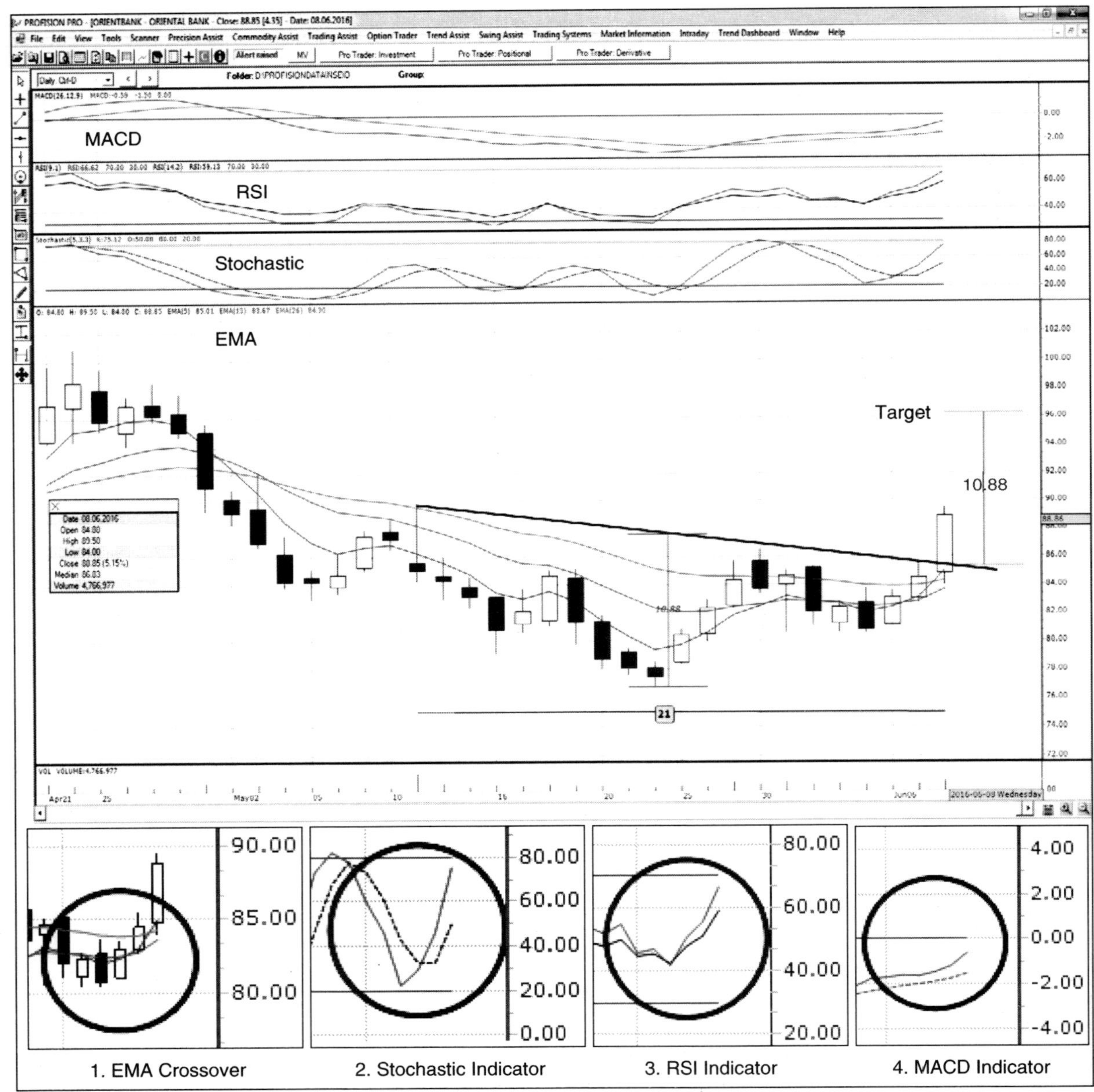

Figure 25.11: **Daily chart of Oriental Bank of Commerce**

Table 25.11

Trade Selection Ready-Reckoner for Oriental Bank of Commerce

Sr. No.	*Parameter*		
	Date >>>		08.06.2016
	Stock Symbol >>>		ORIENTBANK
	Close (₹) >>>		88.85
	Time Period >>>		Daily
Sr. No.	*Parameter*	*Observation / Reason*	***Verdict***
01	Candlestick	White candlestick	
02	Volume	White candle with increased volume	
03	Moving Averages	5 MA crosses 13 MA & 26 MA on the upside	
04	Candlestick Pattern	None	
05	Price Pattern	Inverted Head and Shoulder	
06	Stochastic Oscillator	Uptrend and positive crossover	
07	R S I	Uptrend and positive crossover	
08	MACD	None	
09	**Trading Decision**	**Only B and I; no S**	
10	Support (₹)	S1 = 86.83, S2 = 84.80, S3 = 84	
11	Resistance (₹)	R1 = 89.50	
12	Stop Loss (₹)	If the trading decision is Buy, Stop Loss 0.2% below support	
13	Target (₹)	Price pattern target	
14	Risk : Reward	Risk = (Close – Stop Loss) ÷ Reward = (Target – Close)	
15	Time Target	Price pattern time target	

Correct Verdict				
01: Buy	04: Indecision	07: Buy	10: 86.83	13: 96.10
02: Buy	05: Buy	08: Indecision	11: 89.50	14: 1:3.22
03: Buy	06: Buy	09: Buy	12: 86.60	15: 7 days

Practice Exercise 12: Tata Motors Ltd.

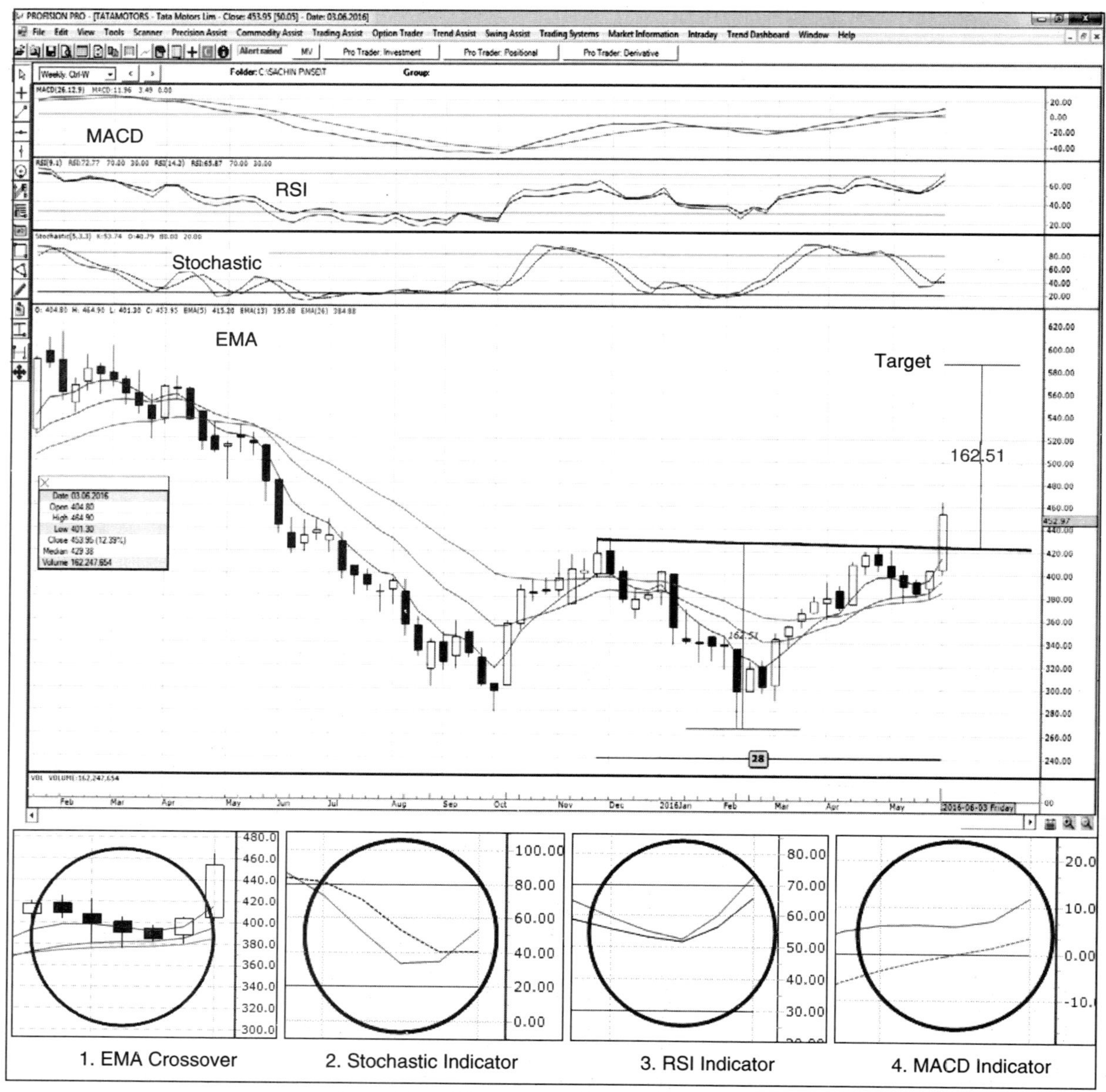

Figure 25.12: **Weekly chart of Tata Motors Ltd.**

~

Table 25.12

Trade Selection Ready-Reckoner for Tata Motors Ltd.

Sr. No.	*Parameter*		
	Date >>>		03.06.2016
	Stock Symbol >>>		TATAMOTORS
	Close (₹) >>>		453.95
	Time Period >>>		Weekly
Sr. No.	*Parameter*	*Observation / Reason*	***Verdict***
01	Candlestick	White candlestick	
02	Volume	White candle with increased volume	
03	Moving Averages	None	
04	Candlestick Pattern	None	
05	Price Pattern	Inverted Head and Shoulder	
06	Stochastic Oscillator	Uptrend and positive crossover	
07	R S I	None	
08	MACD	None	
09	**Trading Decision**	**Only B and I; no S**	
10	Support (₹)	S1 = 429.38, S2 = 404.80, S3 = 401.30	
11	Resistance (₹)	R1 =464.90	
12	Stop Loss (₹)	If the trading decision is Buy, Stop Loss 0.2% below support	
13	Target (₹)	Price pattern target	
14	Risk : Reward	Risk = (Close – Stop Loss) ÷ Reward = (Target – Close)	
15	Time Target	Price pattern time target	

Correct Verdict				
01: Buy	04: Indecision	07: Indecision	10: 429.38	13: 583
02: Buy	05: Buy	08: Indecision	11: 464.90	14: 1:4.97
03: Indecision	06: Buy	09: Buy	12: 428	15: 9 weeks

Practice Exercise 13: Majesco Inc.

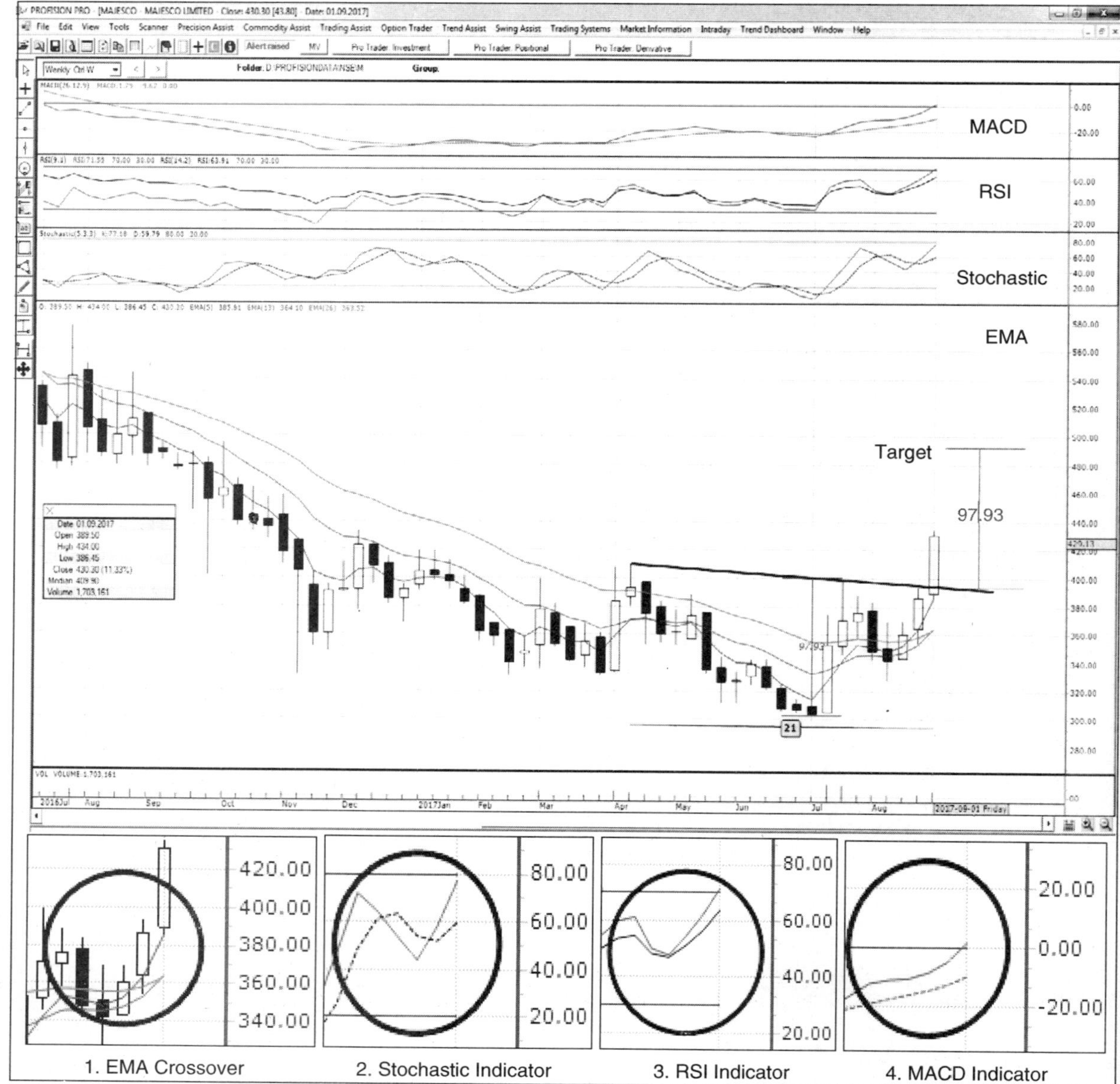

Figure 25.13: **Weekly chart of Majesco Inc.**

Table 25.13

Trade Selection Ready-Reckoner for Majesco Inc.

Sr. No.	*Parameter*		
	Date >>>		01.09.2017
	Stock Symbol >>>		MJCO
	Close (₹) >>>		430.30
	Time Period >>>		Weekly
Sr. No.	*Parameter*	*Observation / Reason*	***Verdict***
01	Candlestick	White candlestick	
02	Volume	White candle with increased volume	
03	Moving Averages	5 MA crosses 26 MA on the upside	
04	Candlestick Pattern	None	
05	Price Pattern	Inverted Head and Shoulder	
06	Stochastic Oscillator	Uptrend and positive crossover	
07	R S I	None	
08	MACD	None	
09	**Trading Decision**	**Only B and I; no S**	
10	Support (₹)	S1 = 409.90, S2 = 389.50, S3 = 386.45	
11	Resistance (₹)	R1 =434	
12	Stop Loss (₹)	If the trading decision is buy, Stop Loss 0.2% below support	
13	Target (₹)	Price pattern target	
14	Risk : Reward	Risk = (Close – Stop Loss) ÷ Reward = (Target – Close)	
15	Time Target	Price pattern time target	

Correct Verdict				
01: Buy	04: Indecision	07: Indecision	10: 409.90	13: 492
02: Buy	05: Buy	08: Indecision	11: 434	14: 1:2.90
03: Buy	06: Buy	09: Buy	12: 409	15: 7 weeks

Practice Exercise 14: Arvind Ltd.

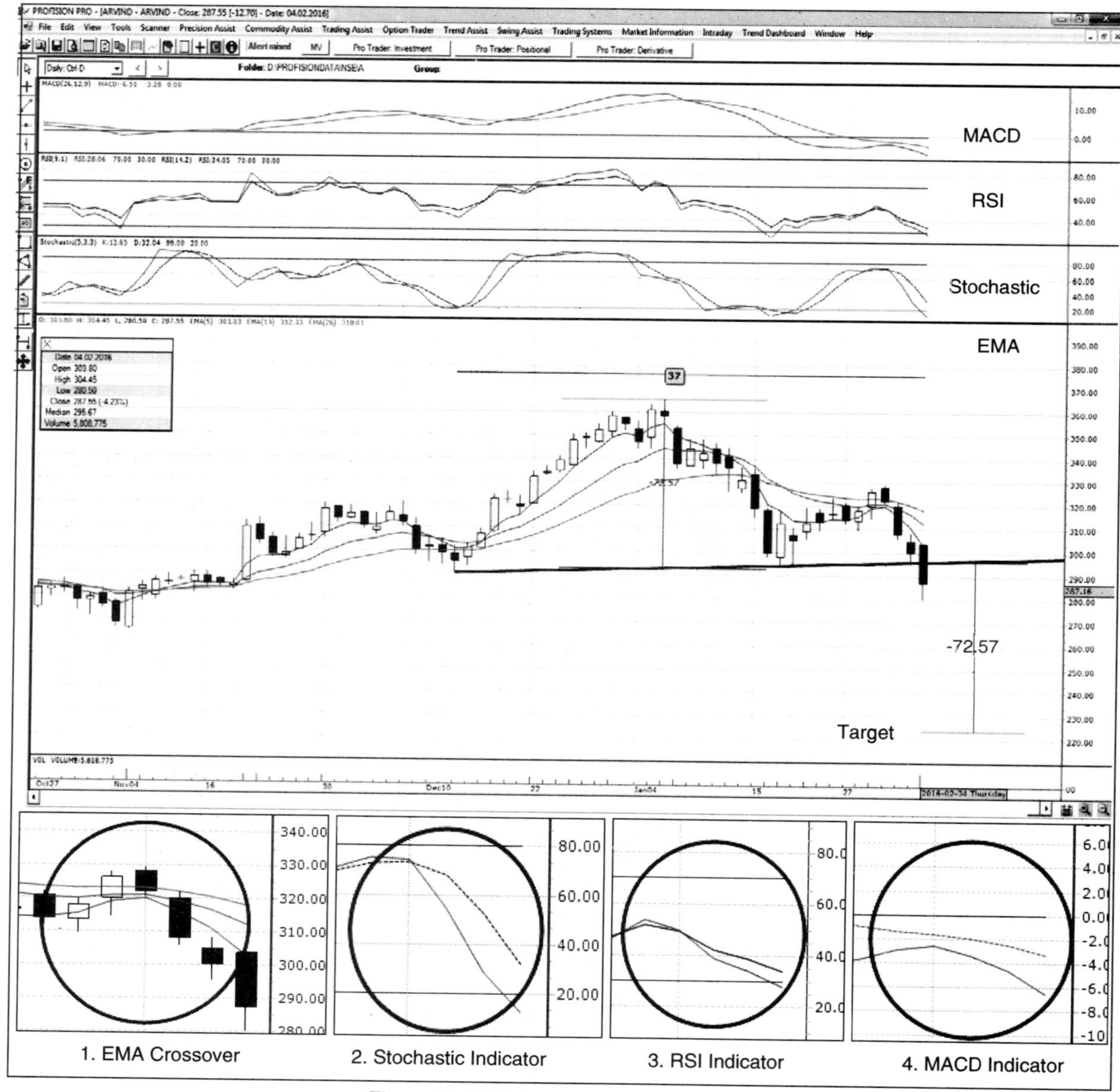

Figure 25.14: **Daily chart of Arvind Ltd.**

~

Table 25.14

Trade Selection Ready-Reckoner for Arvind Ltd.

Sr. No.	*Parameter*		
	Date >>>		04.02.2016
	Stock Symbol >>>		ARVIND
	Close (₹) >>>		287.55
	Time Period >>>		Daily
Sr. No.	*Parameter*	*Observation / Reason*	***Verdict***
01	Candlestick	Black candlestick	
02	Volume	Black candle with increased volume	
03	Moving Averages	None	
04	Candlestick Pattern	None	
05	Price Pattern	Head and Shoulder	
06	Stochastic Oscillator	Downtrend and negative crossover	
07	R S I	Downtrend and negative crossover	
08	MACD	None	
09	**Trading Decision**	**Only S and I; no B**	
10	Support (₹)	S1 = 280.50	
11	Resistance (₹)	R1 = 295.67, R2 = 303.80, R3 = 304.45	
12	Stop Loss (₹)	If the trading decision is Sell, Stop Loss 0.2% above resistance	
13	Target (₹)	Price pattern target	
14	Risk : Reward	Risk = (Stop Loss – Close) ÷ Reward = (Close-Target)	
15	Time Target	Price pattern time target	

Correct Verdict				
01: Sell	04: Indecision	07: Sell	10: 280.50	13: 223
02: Sell	05: Sell	08: Indecision	11: 295.67	14: 1:7.38
03: Indecision	06: Sell	09: Sell	12: 296.30	15: 12 days

Practice Exercise 15: JSW Steel Ltd.

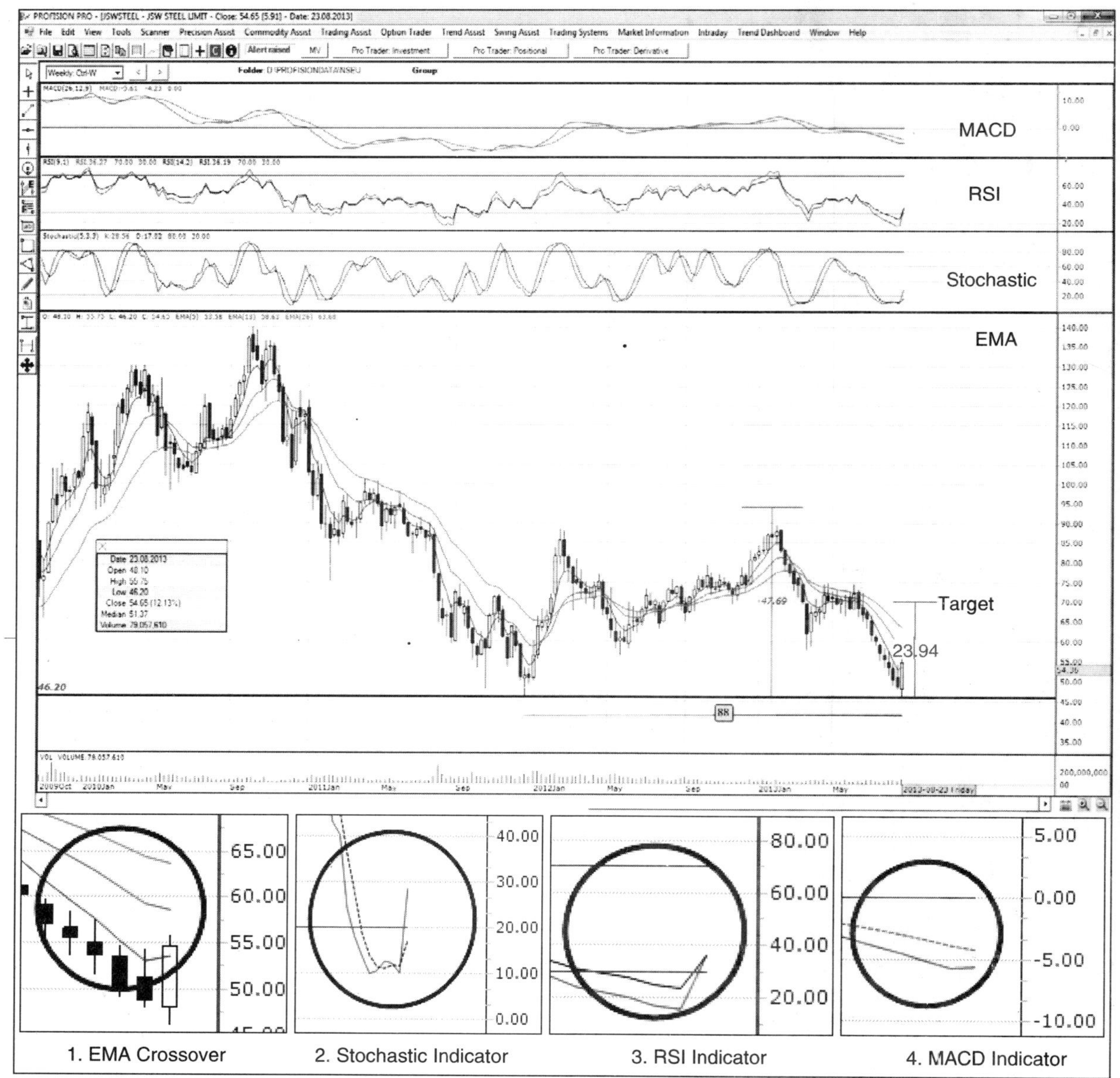

Figure 25.15: **Weekly chart of JSW Steel Ltd.**

Table 25.15

Trade Selection Ready-Reckoner for JSW Steel Ltd.

Sr. No.	*Parameter*		
	Date >>>		23.08.2013
	Stock Symbol >>>		JSWSTEEL
	Close (₹) >>>		54.65
	Time Period >>>		Weekly
Sr. No.	*Parameter*	*Observation / Reason*	***Verdict***
01	Candlestick	White candlestick	
02	Volume	White candle with increased volume	
03	Moving Averages	None	
04	Candlestick Pattern	Bullish Engulf	
05	Price Pattern	Double Bottom	
06	Stochastic Oscillator	Uptrend and positive crossover	
07	R S I	Uptrend and positive crossover	
08	MACD	None	
09	**Trading Decision**	**Only B and I; no S**	
10	Support (₹)	S1 = 51.37, S2 = 48.10, S3 = 46.20	
11	Resistance (₹)	R1 = 55.75	
12	Stop Loss (₹)	If the trading decision is Buy, Stop Loss 0.2% below support	
13	Target (₹)	Price pattern target	
14	Risk : Reward	Risk = (Close – Stop Loss) ÷ Reward = (Target – Close)	
15	Time Target	Price pattern time target	

Correct Verdict				
01: Buy	04: Buy	07: Buy	10: 51.37	13: 70
02: Buy	05: Buy	08: Indecision	11: 55.75	14: 1:4.45
03: Indecision	06: Buy	09: Buy	12: 51.20	15: 30 Weeks

Practice Exercise 16: Himachal Futuristic Communication Ltd.

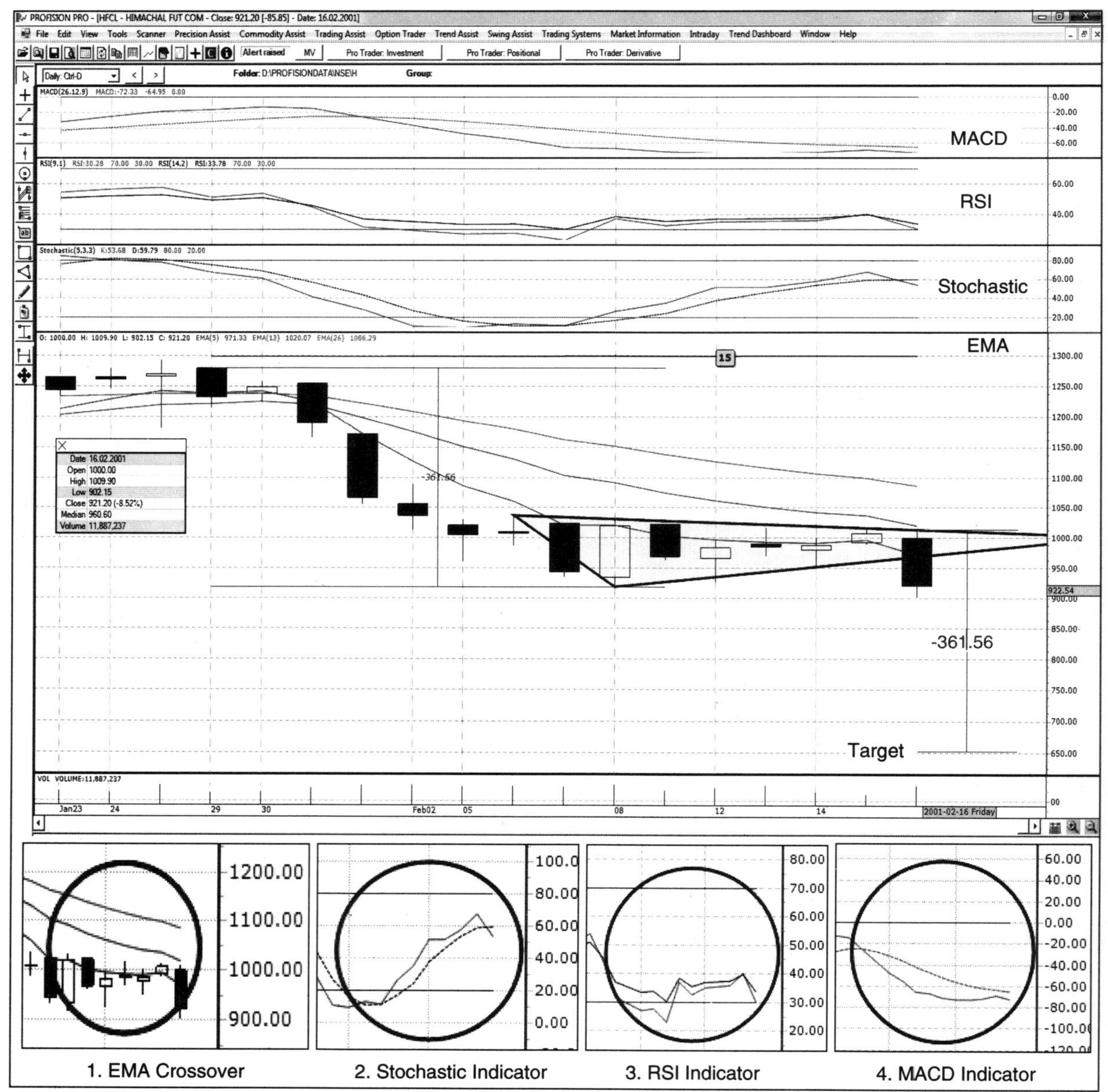

Figure 25.16: **Daily chart of Himachal Futuristic Communication Ltd.**

~

Table 25.16

Trade Selection Ready-Reckoner for Himachal Futuristic Communication Ltd.

Sr. No.	*Parameter*		
	Date >>>		16.02.2001
	Stock Symbol >>>		HFCL
	Close (₹) >>>		921.20
	Time Period >>>		Daily
Sr. No.	*Parameter*	*Observation / Reason*	***Verdict***
01	Candlestick	Black candlestick	
02	Volume	Black candle with increased volume	
03	Moving Averages	None	
04	Candlestick Pattern	None	
05	Price Pattern	Down Flag	
06	Stochastic Oscillator	Downtrend and negative crossover	
07	R S I	Downtrend and negative crossover	
08	MACD	None	
09	**Trading Decision**	**Only S, I, no B**	
10	Support (₹)	S1 = 902.15	
11	Resistance (₹)	R1 = 960.60, R2 = 1000, R3 = 1009.90	
12	Stop Loss (₹)	If the trading decision is Sell, Stop Loss 0.2% above resistance	
13	Target (₹)	Price pattern target	
14	Risk : Reward	Risk = (Stop Loss – Close) ÷ Reward = (Close – Target)	
15	Time Target	Price pattern time target	

Correct Verdict				
01: Sell	04: Indecision	07: Sell	10: 902.15	13: 650
02: Sell	05: Sell	08: Indecision	11: 960.60	14: 1:6.65
03: Indecision	06: Sell	09: Sell	12: 962	15: 6 days

Practice Exercise 17: Punjab National Bank

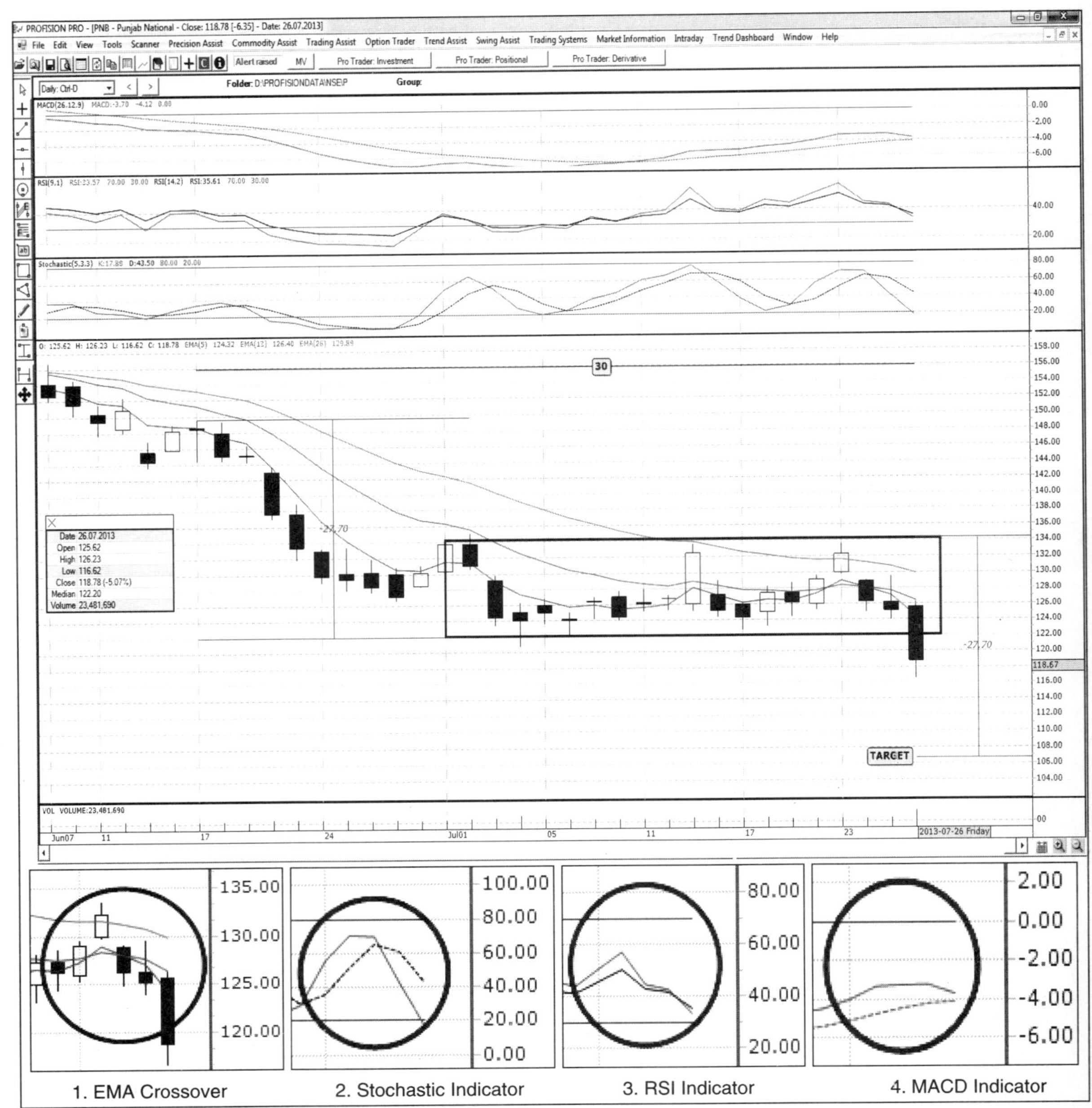

Figure 25.17: **Daily chart of Punjab National Bank**

Table 25.17

Trade Selection Ready-Reckoner for Punjab National Bank

Sr. No.	*Parameter*		
	Date >>>		26.07.2013
	Stock Symbol >>>		PNB
	Close (₹) >>>		118.78
	Time Period >>>		Daily
Sr. No.	*Parameter*	*Observation / Reason*	***Verdict***
01	Candlestick	Black candlestick	
02	Volume	Black candle with increased volume	
03	Moving Averages	5 MA crosses 13 MA on the downside	
04	Candlestick Pattern	None	
05	Price Pattern	Down Flag	
06	Stochastic Oscillator	Downtrend and negative crossover	
07	R S I	Downtrend and negative crossover	
08	MACD	None	
09	**Trading Decision**	**Only S and I; no B**	
10	Support (₹)	S1 = 116.62	
11	Resistance (₹)	R1 =122.20, R2 = 125.62, R3 = 126.23	
12	Stop Loss (₹)	If the trading decision is Sell, Stop Loss 0.2% above resistance	
13	Target (₹)	Price pattern target	
14	Risk : Reward	Risk = (Stop Loss – Close) ÷ Reward = (Close-Target)	
15	Time Target	Price pattern time target	

Correct Verdict				
01: Sell	04: Indecision	07: Sell	10: 116.62	13: 106.10
02: Sell	05: Sell	08: Indecision	11: 122.20	14: 1:3.41
03: Sell	06: Sell	09: Sell	12: 122.50	15: 10 days

Practice Exercise 18: IDBI Bank

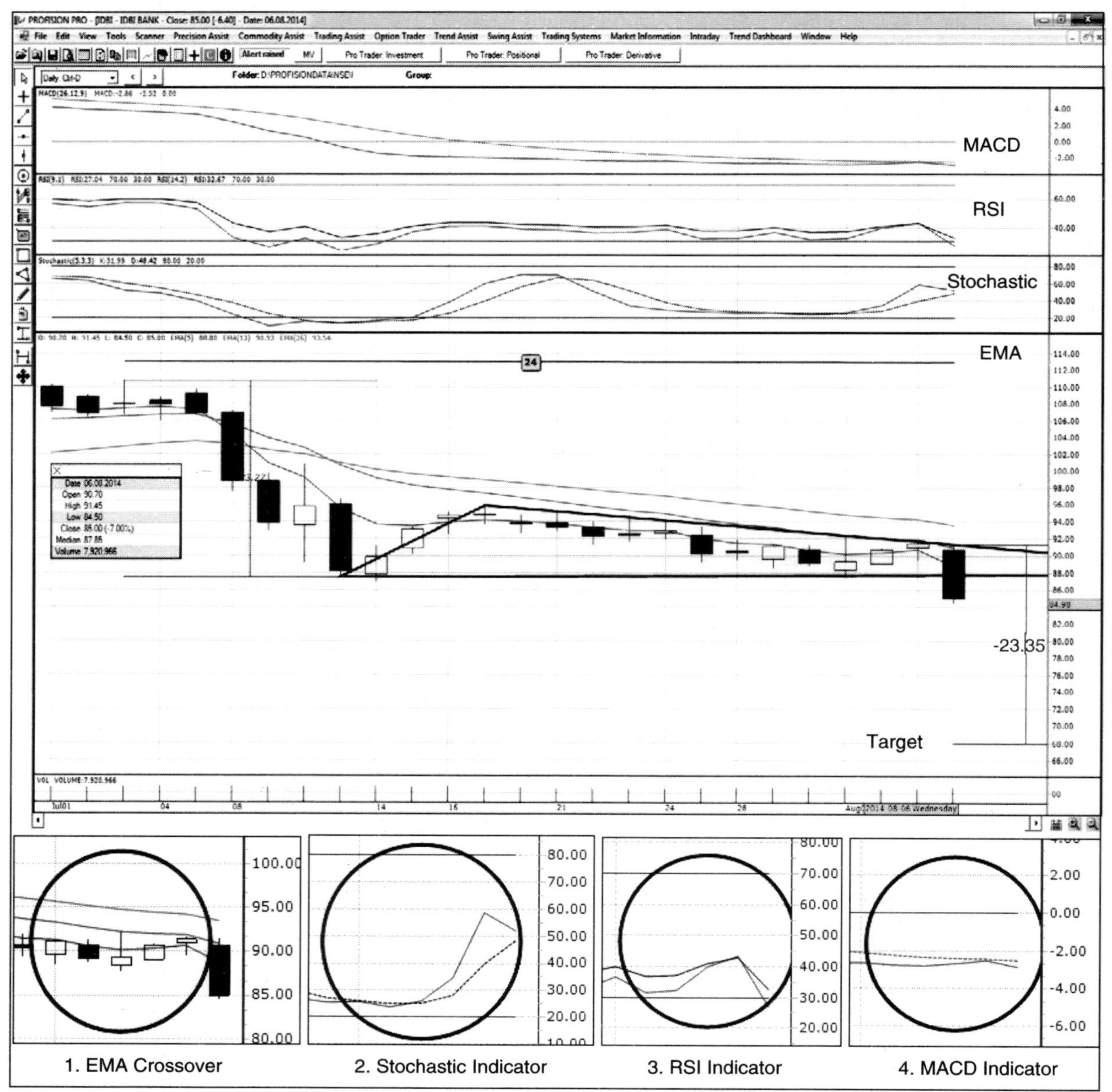

Figure 25.18: **Daily chart of IDBI Bank**

~

Table 25.18

Trade Selection Ready-Reckoner for IDBI Bank

Sr. No.	*Parameter*		
	Date >>>		06.08.2014
	Stock Symbol >>>		IDBI
	Close (₹) >>>		85
	Time Period >>>		Daily
Sr. No.	*Parameter*	*Observation / Reason*	***Verdict***
01	Candlestick	Black candlestick	
02	Volume	Black candle with increased volume	
03	Moving Averages	None	
04	Candlestick Pattern	Evening Star	
05	Price Pattern	Down Flag	
06	Stochastic Oscillator	None	
07	R S I	Downtrend and negative crossover	
08	MACD	None	
09	**Trading Decision**	**Only S and I; no B**	
10	Support (₹)	S1 = 84.50	
11	Resistance (₹)	R1 = 87.85, R2 = 90.70, R3 = 91.45	
12	Stop Loss (₹)	If the trading decision is sell, Stop Loss 0.2% above resistance	
13	Target (₹)	Price pattern target	
14	Risk : Reward	Risk = (Stop Loss – Close) ÷ Reward = (Close – Target)	
15	Time Target	Price pattern time target	

Correct Verdict				
01: Sell	04: Sell	07: Sell	10: 84.50	13: 68
02: Sell	05: Sell	08: Indecision	11: 87.85	14: 1:5.31
03: Indecision	06: Indecision	09: Sell	12: 88.20	15: 8 days

Practice Exercise 19: Adani Enterprises Ltd.

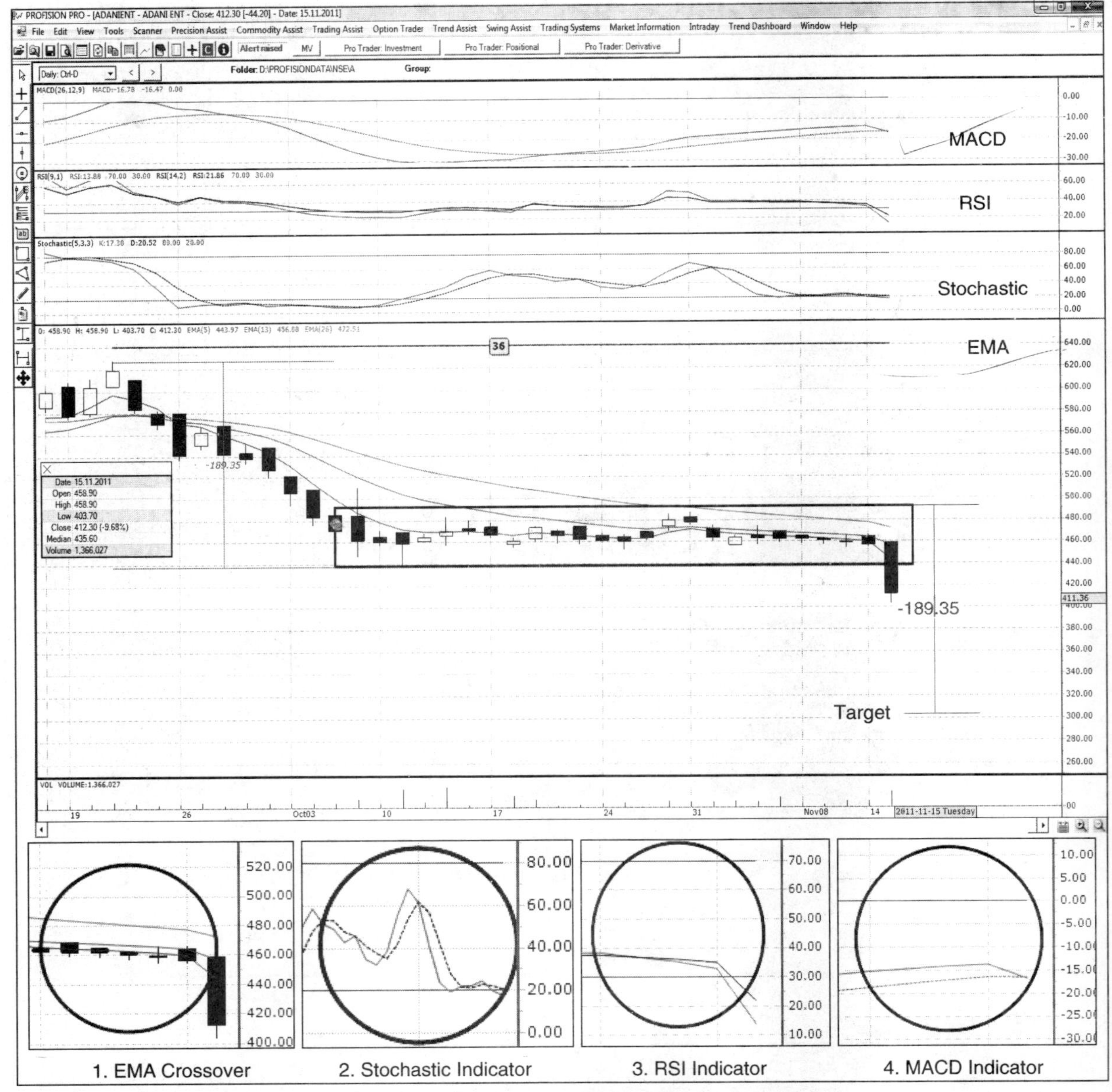

Figure 25.19: **Daily chart of Adani Enterprises Ltd.**

Table 25.19 **Trade Selection Ready-Reckoner for Adani Enterprises Ltd.**			
Sr. No.	*Parameter*		
	Date >>>		15.11.2011
	Stock Symbol >>>		ADANIENT
	Close (₹) >>>		412.30
	Time Period >>>		Daily
Sr. No.	*Parameter*	*Observation / Reason*	***Verdict***
01	Candlestick	Black candlestick	
02	Volume	Black candle with increased volume	
03	Moving Averages	None	
04	Candlestick Pattern	None	
05	Price Pattern	Down Flag	
06	Stochastic Oscillator	Downtrend and negative crossover	
07	R S I	Downtrend and negative crossover	
08	MACD	Negative crossover in negative zone	
09	**Trading Decision**	**Only S and I; no B**	
10	Support (₹)	S1 = 403.70	
11	Resistance (₹)	R1 = 435.60, R2 = 458.90, R3 =458.90	
12	Stop Loss (₹)	If the trading decision is Sell, Stop Loss 0.2% above resistance	
13	Target (₹)	Price pattern target	
14	Risk : Reward	Risk = (Stop Loss – Close) ÷ Reward = (Close-Target)	
15	Time Target	Price pattern time target	

Correct Verdict				
01: Sell	04: Indecision	07: Sell	10: 403.70	13: 301
02: Sell	05: Sell	08: Sell	11: 435.60	14: 1:4.48
03: Indecision	06: Sell	09: Sell	12: 436.60	15: 12 days

Practice Exercise 20: TVS Electronics

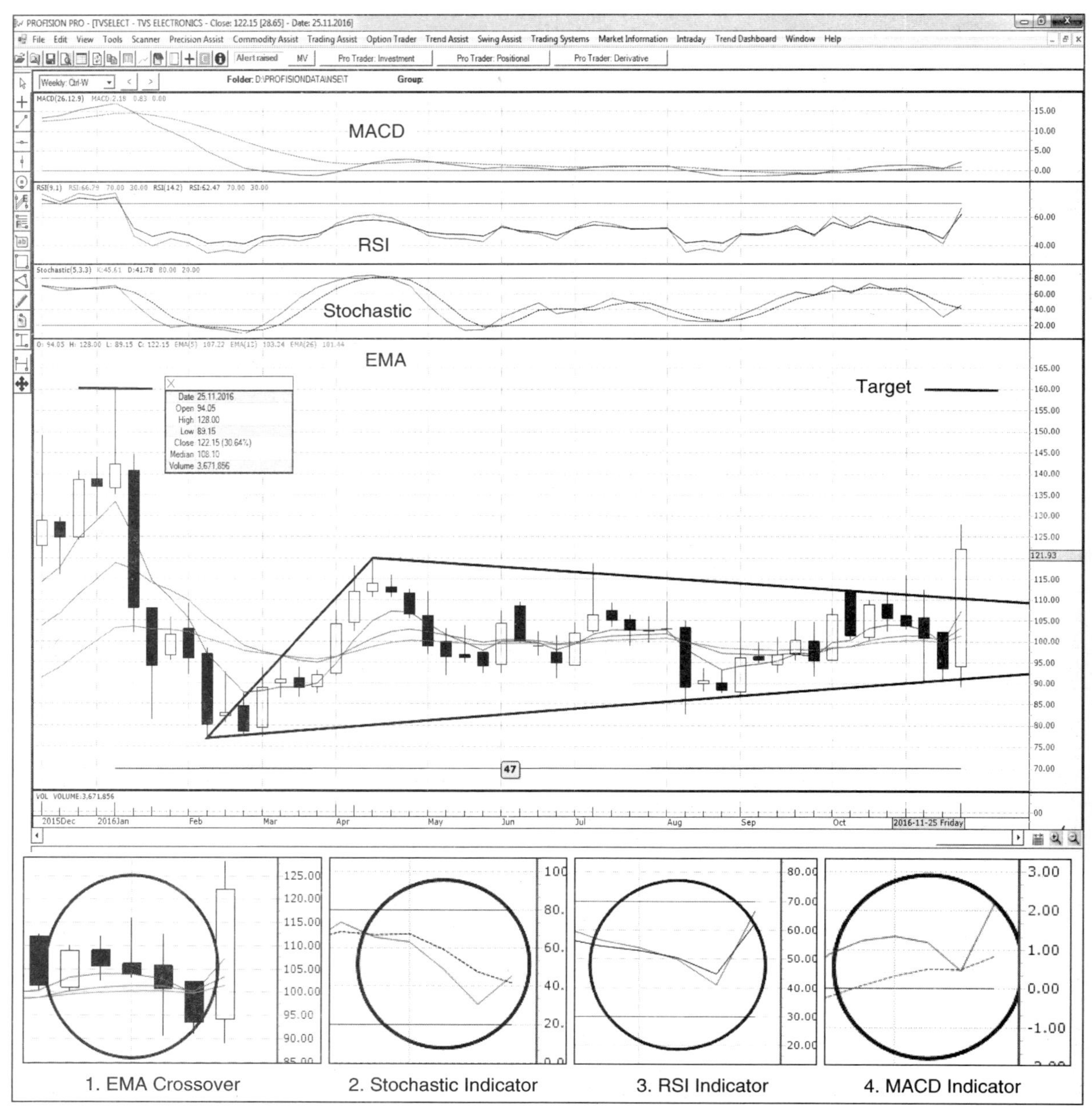

Figure 25.20: **Weekly chart of TVS Electronics**

~

Table 25.20

Trade Selection Ready-Reckoner for TVS Electronics

Sr. No.	*Parameter*		
	Date >>>		25.11.2016
	Stock Symbol >>>		TVSELECT
	Close (₹) >>>		122.15
	Time Period >>>		Weekly
Sr. No.	*Parameter*	*Observation / Reason*	***Verdict***
01	Candlestick	White candlestick	
02	Volume	White candle with increased volume	
03	Moving Averages	5 MA crosses 13 MA on the upside	
04	Candlestick Pattern	None	
05	Price Pattern	Trend Change Upward Breakout	
06	Stochastic Oscillator	Uptrend and positive crossover	
07	R S I	Uptrend and positive crossover	
08	MACD	Positive crossover in positive zone	
09	**Trading Decision**	**Only B and I; no S**	
10	Support (₹)	S1 = 108.10, S2=94.05, S3 = 89.15	
11	Resistance (₹)	R1 =128	
12	Stop Loss (₹)	If the trading decision is Buy, Stop Loss 0.2% below support	
13	Target (₹)	Price pattern target	
14	Risk : Reward	Risk = (Close – Stop Loss) ÷ Reward = (Target – Close)	
15	Time Target	Price pattern time target	

Correct Verdict				
01: Buy	04: Indecision	07: Buy	10: 108.10	13: 160
02: Buy	05: Buy	08: Buy	11: 128	14: 1:2.64
03: Buy	06: Buy	09: Buy	12: 107.80	15: 16 weeks

Practice Exercise 21: Bombay Burmah Trading Corporation Ltd.

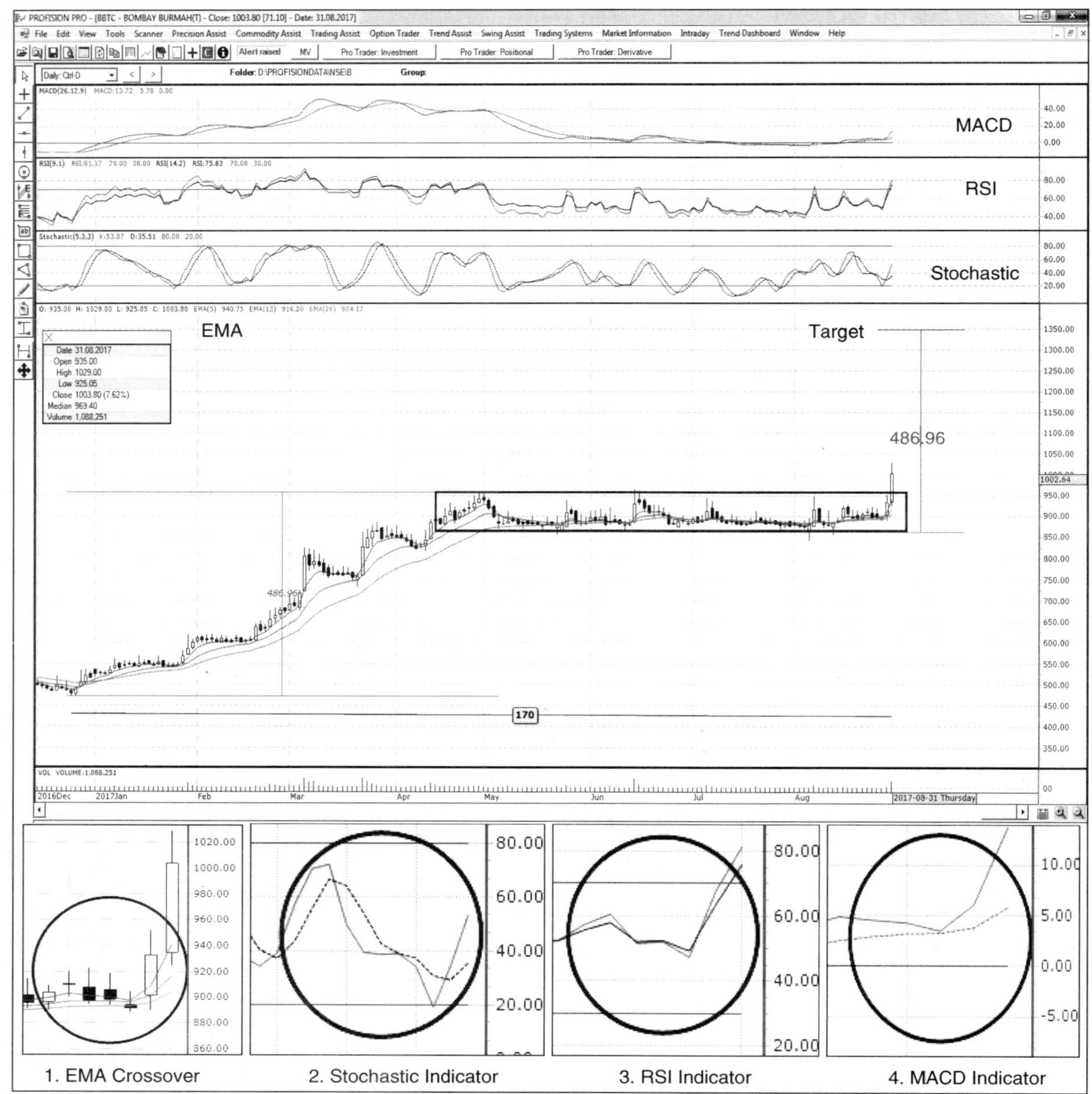

Figure 25.21: **Daily chart of Bombay Burmah Trading Corporation Ltd.**

~

Table 25.21

Trade Selection Ready-Reckoner for Bombay Burmah Trading Corporation Ltd.

Sr. No.	*Parameter*		
	Date >>>		31.08.2017
	Stock Symbol >>>		BBTC
	Close (₹) >>>		1003.80
	Time Period >>>		Daily
Sr. No.	*Parameter*	*Observation / Reason*	***Verdict***
01	Candlestick	White candlestick	
02	Volume	White candle with increased volume	
03	Moving Averages	None	
04	Candlestick Pattern	None	
05	Price Pattern	Up Flag	
06	Stochastic Oscillator	Uptrend and positive crossover	
07	R S I	Uptrend and positive crossover	
08	MACD	None	
09	**Trading Decision**	**Only B and I; no S**	
10	Support (₹)	S1 = 969.40, S2 = 935, S3 = 925.05	
11	Resistance (₹)	R1 = 1,029	
12	Stop Loss (₹)	If the trading decision is Buy, Stop Loss 0.2% below support	
13	Target (₹)	Price pattern target	
14	Risk : Reward	Risk = (Close – Stop Loss) ÷ Reward = (Target – Close)	
15	Time Target	Price pattern time target	

Correct Verdict				
01: Buy	04: Indecision	07: Buy	10: 969.40	13: 1350
02: Buy	05: Buy	08: Indecision	11: 1029	14: 1:9.51
03: Indecision	06: Buy	09: Buy	12: 967.40	15: 56 days

Practice Exercise 22: Kiri Industries Ltd.

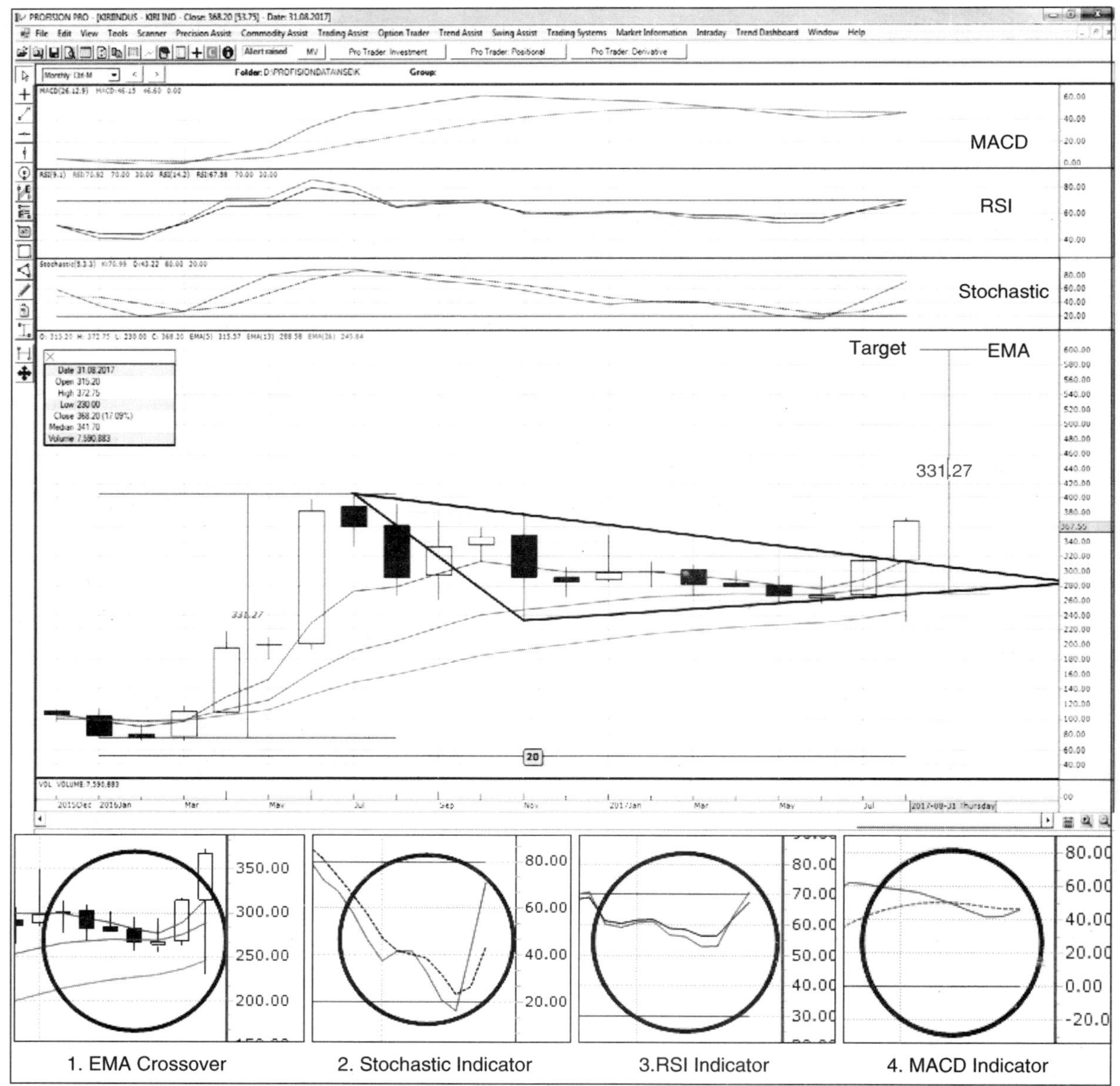

Figure 25.22: **Monthly chart of Kiri Industries Ltd.**

Table 25.22

Trade Selection Ready-Reckoner for Kiri Industries Ltd.

Sr. No.	*Parameter*		
	Date >>>		31.08.2017
	Stock Symbol >>>		KIRIINDUS
	Close (₹) >>>		368.20
	Time Period >>>		Monthly
Sr. No.	*Parameter*	*Observation / Reason*	***Verdict***
01	Candlestick	White candlestick	
02	Volume	White candle with increased volume	
03	Moving Averages	None	
04	Candlestick Pattern	None	
05	Price Pattern	Up Flag	
06	Stochastic Oscillator	Uptrend and positive crossover	
07	R S I	Uptrend and positive crossover	
08	MACD	None	
09	**Trading Decision**	**Only B and I; no S**	
10	Support (₹)	S1 = 343.60, S2 = 319, S3 = 314.50	
11	Resistance (₹)	R1 = 372.75	
12	Stop Loss (₹)	If the trading decision is Buy, Stop Loss 0.2% below support	
13	Target (₹)	Price pattern target	
14	Risk : Reward	Risk = (Close – Stop Loss) ÷ Reward = (Target – Close)	
15	Time Target	Price pattern time target	

Correct Verdict				
01: Buy	04: Indecision	07: Buy	10: 343.60	13: 600
02: Buy	05: Buy	08: Indecision	11: 372.75	14: 1:8.85
03: Indecision	06: Buy	09: Buy	12: 342	15: 7 months

Practice Exercise 23: Sree Rayalaseema Hi-Strength Hypo Limited

Figure 25.23: **Weekly chart of Sree Rayalaseema Hi-Strength Hypo Limited**

~

Table 25.23

Trade Selection Ready-Reckoner for Sree Rayalaseema Hi-Strength Hypo Limited

Sr. No.	*Parameter*		
	Date >>>		06.10.2017
	Stock Symbol >>>		SRHHYPOLTD
	Close (₹) >>>		172.15
	Time Period >>>		Weekly
Sr. No.	*Parameter*	*Observation / Reason*	***Verdict***
01	Candlestick	White candlestick	
02	Volume	White candle with increased volume	
03	Moving Averages	None	
04	Candlestick Pattern	Bullish Engulf	
05	Price Pattern	Up Flag	
06	Stochastic Oscillator	Uptrend and positive crossover	
07	R S I	Buy	
08	MACD	None	
09	**Trading Decision**	**Only B and I; no S**	
10	Support (₹)	S1 = 157.65, S2=143.15, S3 =143.15	
11	Resistance (₹)	R1 = 176.60	
12	Stop Loss (₹)	If the trading decision is Buy, Stop Loss 0.2% below support	
13	Target (₹)	Price pattern target	
14	Risk : Reward	Risk = (Close – Stop Loss) ÷ Reward = (Target – Close)	
15	Time Target	Price pattern time target	

Correct Verdict				
01: Buy	04: Buy	07: Buy	10: 157.65	13: 252
02: Buy	05: Buy	08: Indecision	11: 176.60	14: 1:5.27
03: Indecision	06: Buy	09: Buy	12: 157	15: 28 Weeks

Practice Exercise 24: Bhansali Engineering Polymers Ltd.

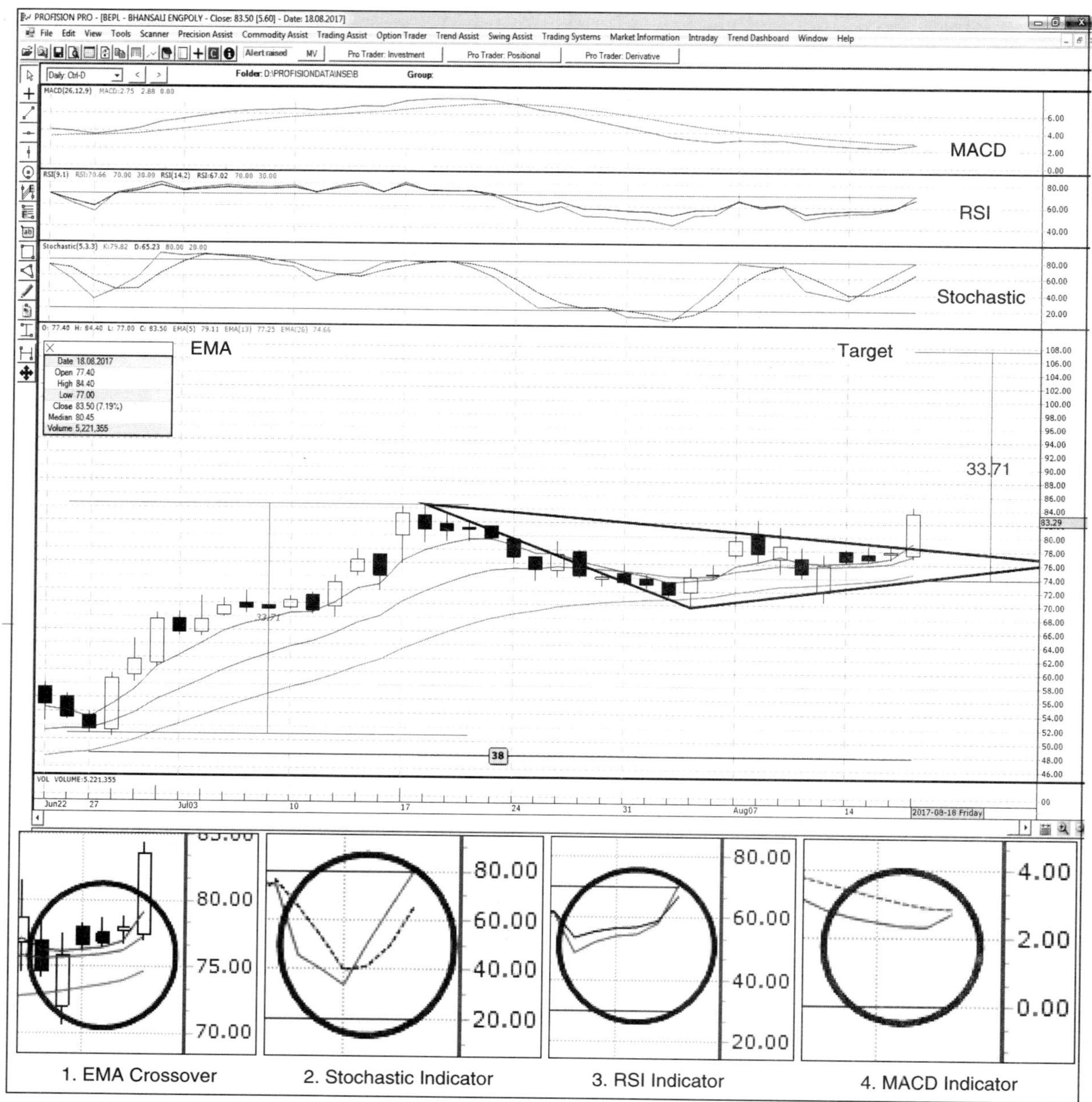

Figure 25.24: **Daily chart of Bhansali Engineering Polymers Ltd.**

Table 25.24

Trade Selection Ready-Reckoner for Bhansali Engineering Polymers Ltd.

Sr. No.	*Parameter*		
	Date >>>		18.08.2017
	Stock Symbol >>>		BEPL
	Close (₹) >>>		83.50
	Time Period >>>		Daily
Sr. No.	*Parameter*	*Observation / Reason*	***Verdict***
01	Candlestick	White candlestick	
02	Volume	White candle with increased volume	
03	Moving Averages	None	
04	Candlestick Pattern	None	
05	Price Pattern	Up Flag	
06	Stochastic Oscillator	Uptrend and positive crossover	
07	R S I	Uptrend and positive crossover	
08	MACD	None	
09	**Trading Decision**	**Only B and I; no S**	
10	Support (₹)	S1 = 80.45, S2 = 77.40, S3 = 77	
11	Resistance (₹)	R1 = 84.40	
12	Stop Loss (₹)	If the trading decision is Buy, Stop Loss 0.2% below support	
13	Target (₹)	Price pattern target	
14	Risk : Reward	Risk = (Close – Stop Loss) ÷ Reward = (Target – Close)	
15	Time Target	Price pattern time target	

Correct Verdict				
01: Buy	04: Indecision	07: Buy	10: 80.45	13: 108
02: Buy	05: Buy	08: Indecision	11: 84.40	14: 1:7
03: Indecision	06: Buy	09: Buy	12: 80	15: 13 days

Practice Exercise 25: HEG Limited

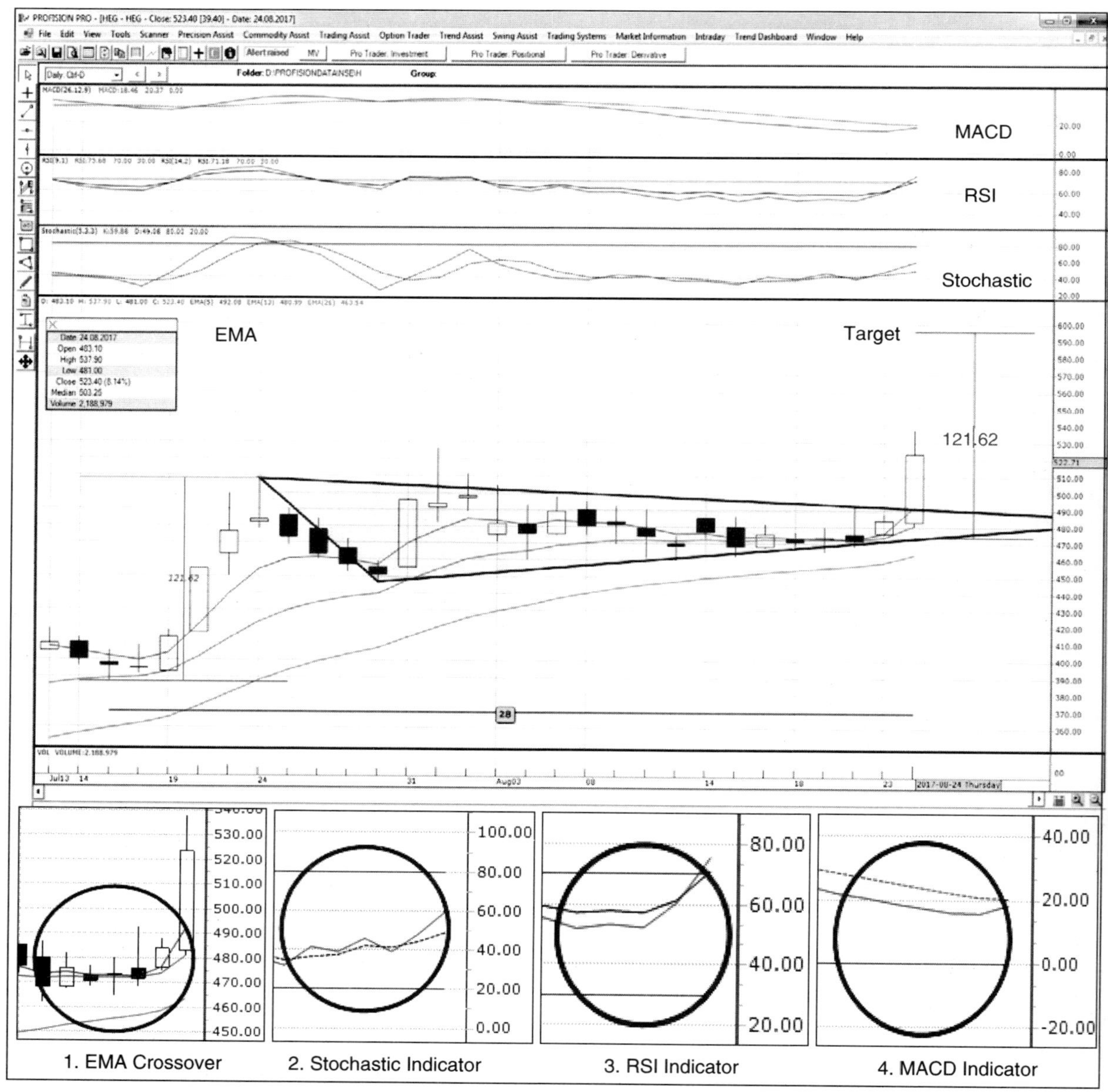

Figure 25.25: **Daily chart of HEG Limited**

Table 25.25

Trade Selection Ready-Reckoner for HEG Limited

Sr. No.	Parameter		
	Date >>>		24.08.2017
	Stock Symbol >>>		HEG
	Close (₹) >>>		523.40
	Time Period >>>		Daily
Sr. No.	*Parameter*	*Observation / Reason*	***Verdict***
01	Candlestick	White candlestick	
02	Volume	White candle with increased volume	
03	Moving Averages	None	
04	Candlestick Pattern	None	
05	Price Pattern	Up Flag	
06	Stochastic Oscillator	Uptrend and positive crossover	
07	R S I	Uptrend and positive crossover	
08	MACD	None	
09	**Trading Decision**	**Only B and I; no S**	
10	Support (₹)	S1 = 503.25, S2 = 483.10, S3 = 481	
11	Resistance (₹)	R1 = 537.90	
12	Stop Loss (₹)	If the trading decision is Buy, Stop Loss 0.2% below support	
13	Target (₹)	Price pattern target	
14	Risk : Reward	Risk = (Close – Stop Loss) ÷ Reward = (Target – Close)	
15	Time Target	Price pattern time target	

Correct Verdict				
01: Buy	04: Indecision	07: Buy	10: 503.25	13: 595
02: Buy	05: Buy	08: Indecision	11: 537.90	14: 1:3.35
03: Indecision	06: Buy	09: Buy	12: 502	15: 10 days

Practice Exercise 26: MEP Infrastructure Developers Ltd.

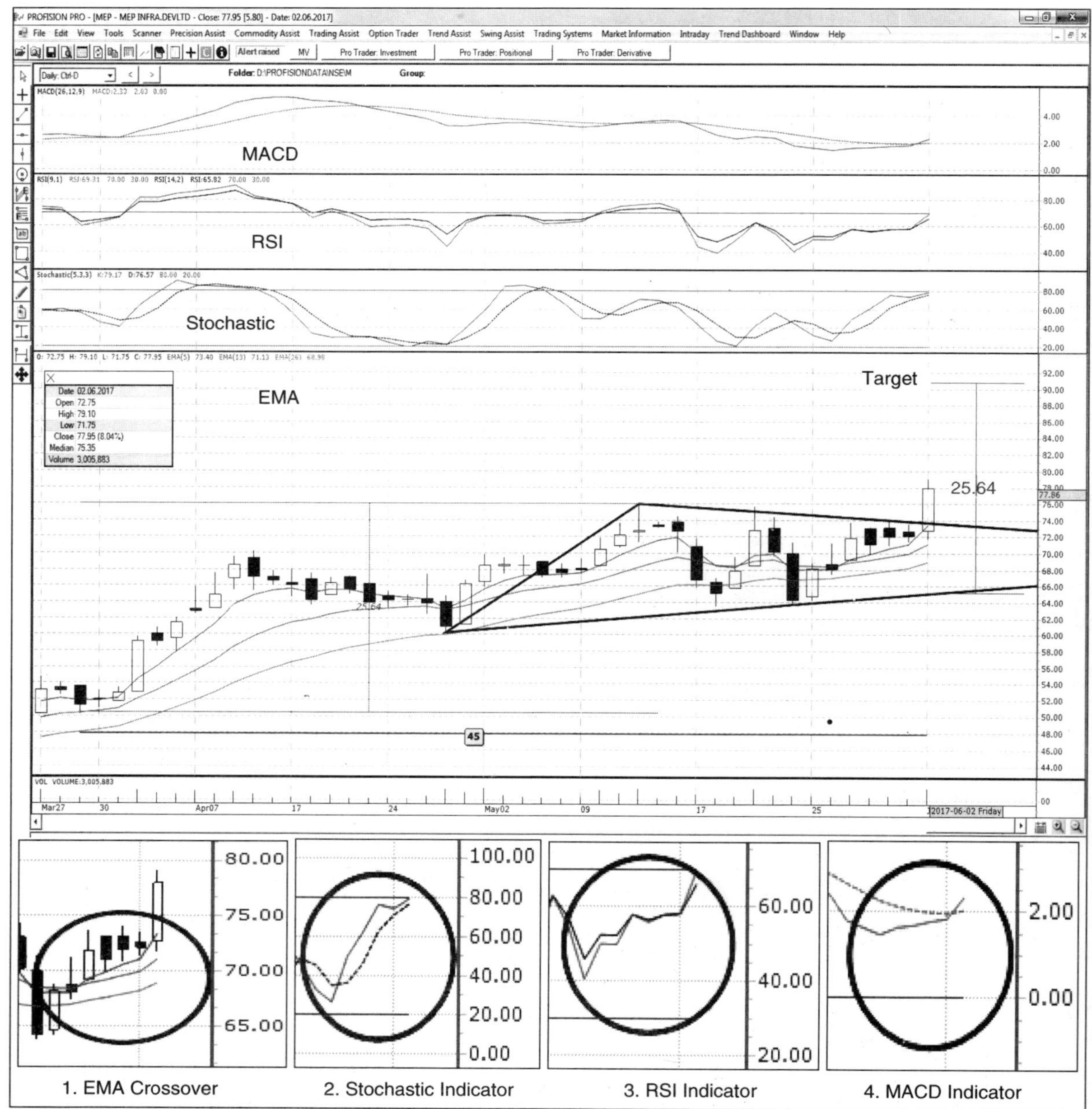

Figure 25.26: **Daily chart of MEP Infrastructure Developers Ltd.**

Table 25.26

Trade Selection Ready-Reckoner for MEP Infrastructure Developers Ltd.

Sr. No.	*Parameter*		
	Date >>>		02.06.2017
	Stock Symbol >>>		MEP
	Close (₹) >>>		77.95
	Time Period >>>		Daily
Sr. No.	*Parameter*	*Observation / Reason*	***Verdict***
01	Candlestick	White candlestick	
02	Volume	White candle with increased volume	
03	Moving Averages	None	
04	Candlestick Pattern	None	
05	Price Pattern	Up Flag	
06	Stochastic Oscillator	Uptrend and positive crossover	
07	R S I	Uptrend and positive crossover	
08	MACD	Positive crossover in positive zone	
09	**Trading Decision**	**Only B and I; no S**	
10	Support (₹)	S1 = 75.35, S2 = 72.75, S3 = 71.75	
11	Resistance (₹)	R1 = 79.10	
12	Stop Loss (₹)	If the trading decision is Buy, Stop Loss 0.2% below support	
13	Target (₹)	Price pattern target	
14	Risk : Reward	Risk = (Close – Stop Loss) ÷ Reward = (Target – Close)	
15	Time Target	Price pattern time target	

Correct Verdict				
01: Buy	04: Indecision	07: Buy	10: 75.35	13: 91
02: Buy	05: Buy	08: Buy	11: 79.10	14: 1:4.42
03: Indecision	06: Buy	09: Buy	12: 75	15: 15 days

Practice Exercise 27: Everest Industries Limited

Figure 25.27: **Daily chart of Everest Industries Limited**

Table 25.27

Trade Selection Ready-Reckoner for Everest Industries Limited

Sr. No.	*Parameter*		
	Date >>>		06.10.2017
	Stock Symbol >>>		EVERESTIND
	Close (₹) >>>		390.80
	Time Period >>>		Daily
Sr. No.	*Parameter*	*Observation / Reason*	***Verdict***
01	Candlestick	White candlestick	
02	Volume	White candle with increased volume	
03	Moving Averages	5 MA crosses 13 MA & 26 MA on the upside	
04	Candlestick Pattern	None	
05	Price Pattern	Up Flag	
06	Stochastic Oscillator	None	
07	R S I	Uptrend and positive crossover	
08	MACD	None	
09	**Trading Decision**	**Only B and I; no S**	
10	Support (₹)	S1 = 381.35, S2 = 371.90, S3 = 365.10	
11	Resistance (₹)	R1 = 399.20	
12	Stop Loss (₹)	If the trading decision is buy, Stop Loss 0.2% below support	
13	Target (₹)	Price pattern target	
14	Risk : Reward	Risk = (Close – Stop Loss) ÷ Reward = (Target – Close)	
15	Time Target	Price pattern time target	

Correct Verdict				
01: Buy	04: Indecision	07: Buy	10: 381.35	13: 479
02: Buy	05: Buy	08: Indecision	11: 399.20	14: 1:9.33
03: Buy	06: Indecision	09: Buy	12: 380	15: 32 days

Practice Exercise 28: Bata India Ltd.

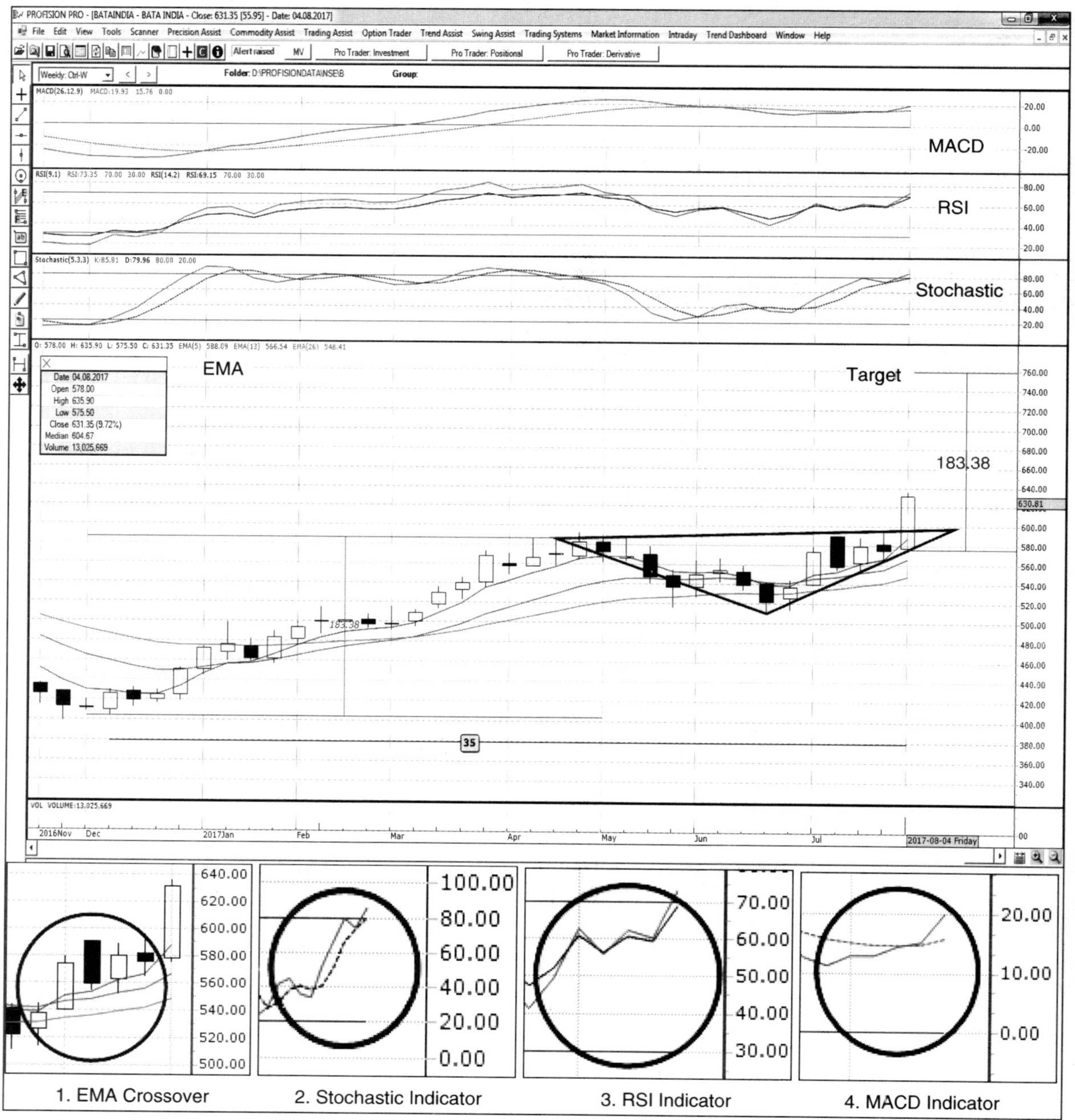

Figure 25.28: **Weekly chart of Bata India Ltd.**

~

Table 25.28

Trade Selection Ready-Reckoner for Bata India Ltd.

Sr. No.	*Parameter*		
	Date >>>		04.08.2017
	Stock Symbol >>>		BATAINDIA
	Close (₹) >>>		631.35
	Time Period >>>		Weekly
Sr. No.	*Parameter*	*Observation / Reason*	***Verdict***
01	Candlestick	White candlestick	
02	Volume	White candle with increased volume	
03	Moving Averages	5 MA crosses 13 MA on the upside	
04	Candlestick Pattern	None	
05	Price Pattern	Up Flag	
06	Stochastic Oscillator	Buy	
07	R S I	Uptrend and positive crossover	
08	MACD	Buy	
09	**Trading Decision**	**Only B and I; no S**	
10	Support (₹)	S1 = 604.67, S2 = 578, S3 = 575.50	
11	Resistance (₹)	R1 = 635.90	
12	Stop Loss (₹)	If the trading decision is Buy, Stop Loss 0.2% below support	
13	Target (₹)	Price pattern target	
14	Risk : Reward	Risk = (Close – Stop Loss) ÷ Reward = (Target – Close)	
15	Time Target	Price pattern time target	

Correct Verdict				
01: Buy	04: Indecision	07: Buy	10: 604.67	13: 760
02: Buy	05: Buy	08: Buy	11: 635.90	14: 1:4.54
03: Buy	06: Buy	09: Buy	12: 603	15: 12 weeks

Practice Exercise 29: Venky's (India) Ltd

Figure 25.29: **Daily chart of Venky's (India) Ltd**

Table 25.29

Trade Selection Ready-Reckoner for Venky's (India) Ltd

Sr. No.	*Parameter*		
	Date >>>		07.06.2017
	Stock Symbol >>>		VENKEYS
	Close (₹) >>>		1403.65
	Time Period >>>		Daily
Sr. No.	*Parameter*	*Observation / Reason*	***Verdict***
01	Candlestick	White candlestick	
02	Volume	White candle with increased volume	
03	Moving Averages	None	
04	Candlestick Pattern	None	
05	Price Pattern	Up Flag	
06	Stochastic Oscillator	Uptrend and positive crossover	
07	R S I	Uptrend and positive crossover	
08	MACD	Positive crossover in positive zone	
09	**Trading Decision**	**Only B and I; no S**	
10	Support (₹)	S1 = 1,339.83, S2 = 1,276, S3 = 1,275.60	
11	Resistance (₹)	R1 =1,444.95	
12	Stop Loss (₹)	If the trading decision is buy, Stop Loss 0.2% below support	
13	Target (₹)	Price pattern target	
14	Risk : Reward	Risk = (Close – Stop Loss) ÷ Reward = (Target – Close)	
15	Time Target	Price pattern time target	

Correct Verdict				
01: Buy	04: Indecision	07: Buy	10: 1,339.83	13: 1,762
02: Buy	05: Buy	08: Buy	11: 1,444.95	14: 1:5.38
03: Indecision	06: Buy	09: Buy	12: 1,337	15: 18 days

Practice Exercise 30: V2 Retail Ltd

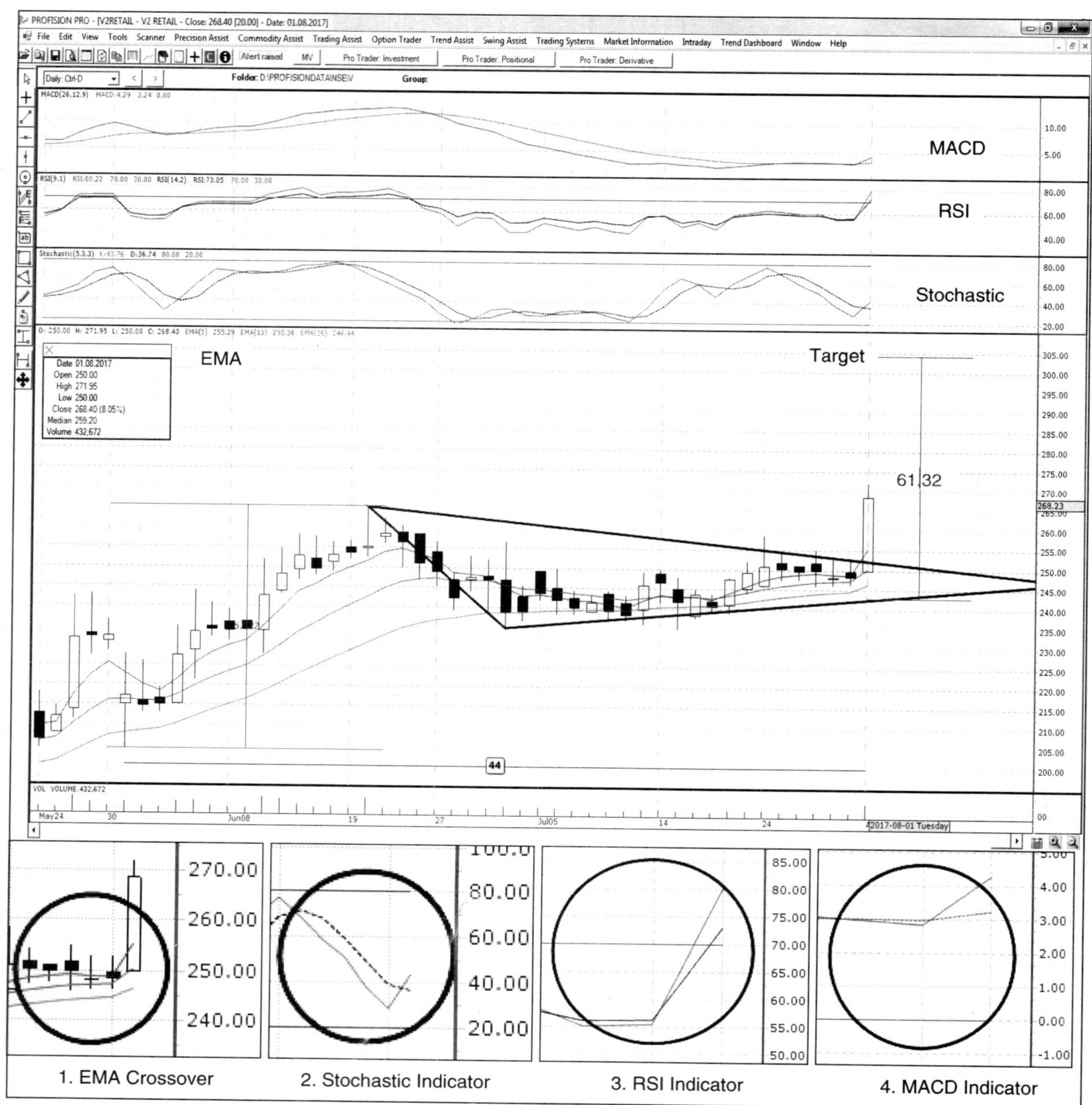

Figure 25.30: **Daily chart of V2 Retail Ltd.**

Table 25.30

Trade Selection Ready-Reckoner for V2 Retail Ltd

Sr. No.	*Parameter*		
	Date >>>		01.08.2017
	Stock Symbol >>>		V2RETAIL
	Close (₹) >>>		268.40
	Time Period >>>		Daily
Sr. No.	*Parameter*	*Observation / Reason*	***Verdict***
01	Candlestick	White candlestick	
02	Volume	White candle with increased volume	
03	Moving Averages	None	
04	Candlestick Pattern	None	
05	Price Pattern	Up Flag	
06	Stochastic Oscillator	Uptrend and positive crossover	
07	R S I	Uptrend and positive crossover	
08	MACD	Positive crossover in positive zone	
09	**Trading Decision**	**Only B and I; no S**	
10	Support (₹)	S1 = 259.20, S2 = 250, S3 = 250	
11	Resistance (₹)	R1 = 271.95	
12	Stop Loss (₹)	If the trading decision is buy, Stop Loss 0.2% below support	
13	Target (₹)	Price pattern target	
14	Risk : Reward	Risk = (Close – Stop Loss) ÷ Reward = (Target – Close)	
15	Time Target	Price pattern time target	

Correct Verdict				
01: Buy	04: Indecision	07: Buy	10: 259.20	13: 305
02: Buy	05: Buy	08: Buy	11: 271.95	14: 1:3.83
03: Indecision	06: Buy	09: Buy	12: 258.85	15: 15 days

Practice Exercise 31: TVS Electronics

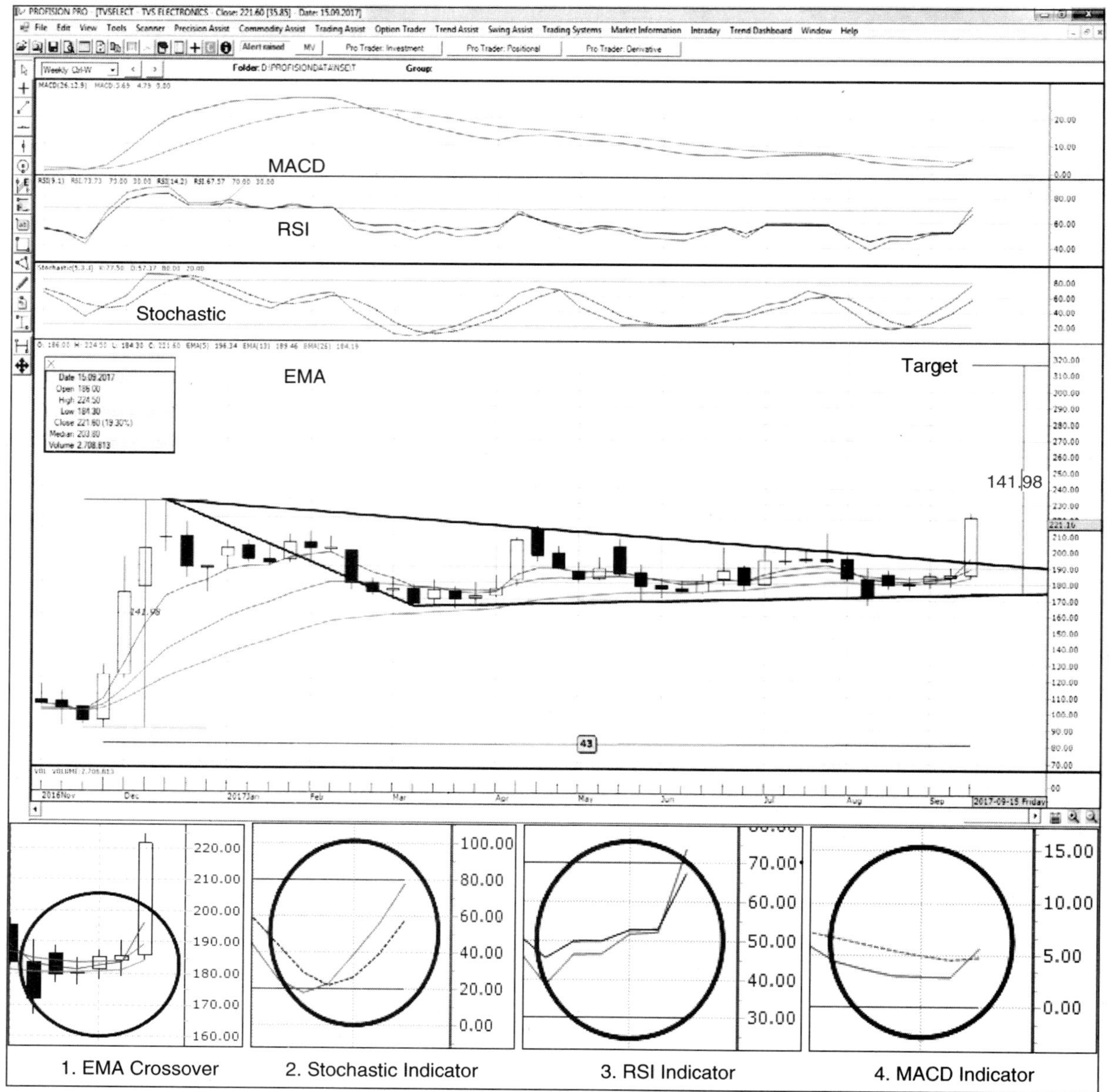

Figure 25.31: **Weekly chart of TVS Electronics**

~

Table 25.31

Trade Selection Ready-Reckoner for TVS Electronics

Sr. No.	*Parameter*		
	Date >>>		15.09.2017
	Stock Symbol >>>		TVSELECT
	Close (₹) >>>		221.60
	Time Period >>>		Weekly
Sr. No.	*Parameter*	*Observation / Reason*	***Verdict***
01	Candlestick	White candlestick	
02	Volume	White candle with increased volume	
03	Moving Averages	5 MA crosses 13 MA on the upside	
04	Candlestick Pattern	None	
05	Price Pattern	Up Flag	
06	Stochastic Oscillator	Uptrend and positive crossover	
07	R S I	Uptrend and positive crossover	
08	MACD	Positive crossover in positive zone	
09	**Trading Decision**	**Only B and I; no S**	
10	Support (₹)	S1 = 203.80, S2 = 186, S3 = 184.30	
11	Resistance (₹)	R1 = 224.50	
12	Stop Loss (₹)	If the trading decision is Buy, Stop Loss 0.2% below support	
13	Target (₹)	Price pattern target	
14	Risk : Reward	Risk = (Close – Stop Loss) ÷ Reward = (Target – Close)	
15	Time Target	Price pattern time target	

Correct Verdict				
01: Buy	04: Indecision	07: Buy	10: 203.80	13: 318
02: Buy	05: Buy	08: Buy	11: 224.50	14: 1:5.30
03: Buy	06: Buy	09: Buy	12: 203.40	15: 15 weeks

Practice Exercise 32: Persistent Systems Limited

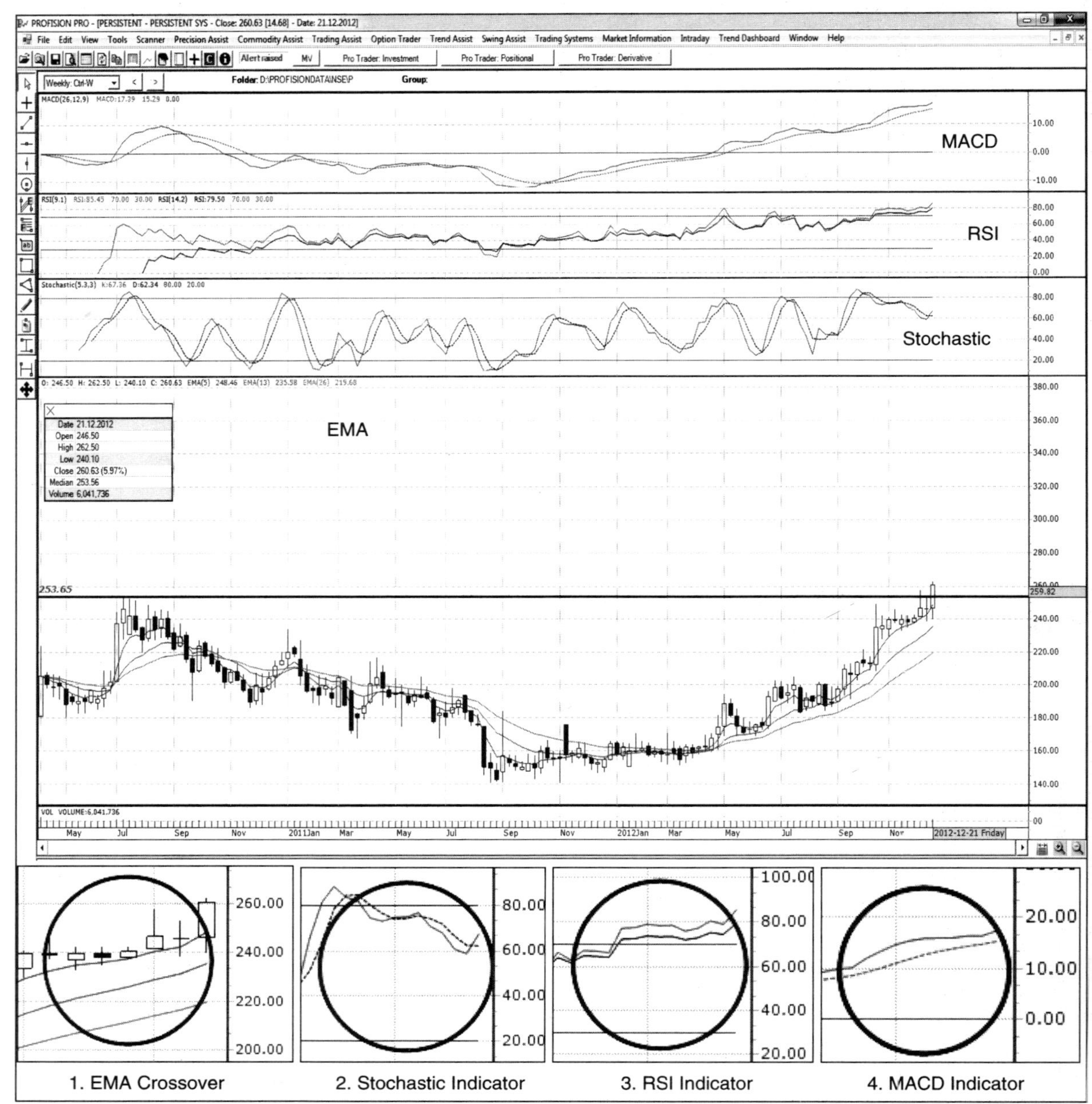

Figure 25.32: **Weekly chart of Persistent Systems Limited**

~

Table 25.32

Trade Selection Ready-Reckoner for Persistent Systems Limited

Sr. No.	*Parameter*		
	Date >>>		21.12.2012
	Stock Symbol >>>		PERSISTENT
	Close (₹) >>>		260.63
	Time Period >>>		Weekly
Sr. No.	*Parameter*	*Observation / Reason*	***Verdict***
01	Candlestick	White candlestick	
02	Volume	White candle with increased volume	
03	Moving Averages	None	
04	Candlestick Pattern	None	
05	Price Pattern	Listing Breakout Pattern	
06	Stochastic Oscillator	Uptrend and positive crossover	
07	R S I	None	
08	MACD	None	
09	**Trading Decision**	**Only B and I; no S**	
10	Support (₹)	S1 = 253.56, S2 = 246.50, S3 = 240.10	
11	Resistance (₹)	R1 = 262.50	
12	Stop Loss (₹)	If the trading decision is Buy, Stop Loss 0.2% below support	
13	Target (₹)	Price pattern target	
14	Risk : Reward	Risk = (Close – Stop Loss) ÷ Reward = (Target – Close)	
15	Time Target	Price pattern time target	

Correct Verdict				
01: Buy	04: Indecision	07: Indecision	10: 253.56	13: 500
02: Buy	05: Buy	08: Indecision	11: 262.50	14: 1:11.37
03: Indecision	06: Buy	09: Buy	12: 239	15: 1 year

Conclusion: Salient Features of Profitable Technical Trading

- Technical trading using chart analysis provides you great clarity about trade entry, stop loss and trade management. It helps you take informed decisions which, in turn, ensures that you remain comfortable in the trade.
- Every trade entry must be based on a reason. It is not something to be decided subjectively but as a result of an objective analysis summarised in writing in the Trade Selection Ready-Reckoner tool. You may have a subjective preference towards a stock but such emotions must be shunned.
- There is no compulsion to enter a trade after having done the analysis.
- A systematic analysis makes you aware of the risk involved in a trade. Normally, people enter a trade keeping profits uppermost in mind. But you should enter a trade only if the risk, namely the amount of money you may lose in case the trade fails, is acceptable to you.
- With a proper pre-trade analysis, you can further manage the trade risk by reducing the quantity that you trade.
- A proper pre-trade analysis not only gives you the stop loss and the target price, but also provides you a tentative time frame within which the target is expected to be achieved. The advantage of this is that at times you may come across stocks in your portfolio which may neither trigger your stop loss nor reach the price target. During this time a new stock may get thrown up by the scanner. In such a case, it is the time target parameter that can help you judge whether you need to get out of the earlier stock, which has crossed the time target without reaching the price target, and add the new one instead.
- If by mistake you interpret a parameter wrongly, say a parameter is actually a buy but you wrongly interpret it as a sell, your final verdict will become indecision. The Trade Selection Ready-Reckoner tool thus ensures that you won't enter a trade when some parameter is wrongly interpreted.
- With a thorough pre-trade analysis, you would be able to keep your emotions in check. Though you may not be able to fully control your emotions at all times, but the rigorous analysis will ensure that you don't panic.
- After entering a trade based on a disciplined pre-trade analysis, you then just need to monitor the trend of the stock. You remain in the trade so long as the stop loss is not triggered, or till the price reaches its target, or till the time target gets fulfilled without either of the first two being achieved.
- You don't need to analyse the stock again and again. You just need to track the stop loss, price target and the time target parameters. Trailing stop loss strategy has to be followed by using the moving average crossovers.

- If your interest lies primarily in day trading, then you would profit by also studying my book, *How to Make Money in Day Trading — Trade on an Invitation.*[*] There are important variations in the strategies used for day trading and positional trading on the one hand, and investment on the other. Stock picking, implementing of the stop loss, trailing of the stop loss, booking profit or squaring off the trade are a few concepts which differ.

~

PRACTICE WILL MAKE YOU PERFECT. KEEP PRACTISING!

---

[*] *How to Make Money in Day Trading — Trading on an Invitation* by Mandar Jamsandekar, published by Vision Books. (www.visionbooksindia.com)

Chapter 26

~

Safe Trading Procedure

NOW THAT YOU ARE A PROFICIENT TECHNICAL ANALYST, you are equipped with the right knowledge to make your own informed trading decisions and stick to them. Here we re-iterate in a summary form the important considerations you must always keep in mind for safe trading.

Have Clarity About Your Profile

You should be clear about your profile, namely whether you are an intraday trader, a positional trader, a short term investor, or a long term investor.

Always Remember that Reality and Perception Can be Different

Figure 26.1

Reality and perception can be different, as depicted in the illustrations in Figure 25.1. Don't go by perception when trading; go by the chart because it better reveals the unfolding reality.

Control Your Emotions

The market is driven by sentiment and the powerful emotions of fear and greed which can overwhelm you. To prevent this, enter a trade only if the risk is acceptable to you.

Make Sure You Have Control on Your Investments at All Times

We live in a democracy — everybody has a right to voice his or her opinion, whether right or wrong. Unregulated media are risky and can be misleading. Stay away from the social media, blogs, WhatsApp, Facebook and all other such media while investing your hard earned money in the stock market.

Neither Fundamental Nor Technical Analysis is Foolproof

Right knowledge and analysis are the only assets which can help you make money in trading. Predictions can go wrong. Success will come in due course. Have realistic expectations from the stock market. You can analyse but it is the market which will decide your profits or losses, which is why a stop loss is vital. Before you start trading, you need to accept that every trade will not be a winning trade.

The Market Demands a Positive Attitude

Analyse and enter trades with a positive attitude. When you analyse you are aware of the risk, rewards and the time horizon of a trade. Enter a trade only if the analysis leads to an acceptable trade. Don't get herded into entering any trade simply because others are doing so.

Mandar's 80:20 Rule of the Stock Markets

Success in the stock market is based 80% on discipline and only 20% on strategy. Follow this rule and you will stay on the winning side in the stock market.

Measure Returns on a 1-Year Basis

Fixed deposits generate fixed returns over a 1-year period, gold and real estate generate returns in the long term. Benchmarking your stock market returns on a 1-year period will make you comfortable and stop judging your trading and analysis in short term periods.

Technical Analysis Works Only in Liquid Markets

You must always keep in mind that technical analysis works only on liquid stocks. Therefore do not try and analyse stocks or instruments which trade low volumes.

Stock Market Trading is a Business Which Involves Risk

You must learn to place the stop loss at the correct level. If triggered, learn to execute it to ensure that you do not take an avalanche of losses.

Hold a Low Trading Profile During Periods of External Events

Quarterly results (four times in a year), F&O expiry, RBI policy review meets, FOMC meets, Budget, elections etc., are events external to the market, the outcomes of which are unknown and the volatility may not always give you the real picture. It is useful, therefore, to maintain low market exposure at such times.

Keep it Simple

A complicated action may not necessarily be an intelligent one. Your experience will tell you that people first try to do things in a simple way and when that is not possible only then complicated ways of doing things are attempted, usually with indifferent results. Simple strategies have greater chances of success.

Mantra for Trading Success

1. Discipline.
2. Patience.
3. Perseverance.
4. Positive attitude.
5. Attitude of accepting a mistake and moving forward.

~